Reading STREET

Program Authors

Peter Afflerbach

Camille Blachowicz

Candy Dawson Boyd

Elena Izquierdo

Connie Juel

Edward Kame'enui

Donald Leu

Jeanne R. Paratore

P. David Pearson

Sam Sebesta

Deborah Simmons

Alfred Tatum

Sharon Vaughn

Susan Watts Taffe

Karen Kring Wixson

PEARSON

Glenview, Illinois • Boston, Massachusetts
Chandler, Arizona • Upper Saddle River, New Jersey

We dedicate Reading Street to
Peter Jovanovich.

His wisdom, courage,
and passion for education
are an inspiration to us all.

ISBN-13: 978-0-328-47029-7
ISBN-10: 0-328-47029-5
2 3 4 5 6 7 8 9 10 V064 14 13 12 11 10
CC1

Any Path, Any Pace

Reading STREET

CALLE de la Lectura

"Welcome to Reading Street! Bienvenidos too."

PEARSON

PEARSON SCOTT FORESMAN

Find Your Place on Reading Street!

Who said so?

The Leading Researchers,

Program Authors

Peter Afflerbach, Ph.D.
Professor
Department of Curriculum
and Instruction
University of Maryland
at College Park

Camille L. Z. Blachowicz, Ph.D.
Professor of Education
National-Louis University

Candy Dawson Boyd, Ph.D.
Professor
School of Education
Saint Mary's College of California

Elena Izquierdo, Ph.D.
Associate Professor
University of Texas at El Paso

Connie Juel, Ph.D.
Professor of Education
School of Education
Stanford University

Edward J. Kame'enui, Ph.D.
Dean-Knight Professor of Education and Director
Institute for the Development of Educational Achievement and the Center on Teaching and Learning
College of Education
University of Oregon

Donald J. Leu, Ph.D.
John and Maria Neag Endowed Chair in Literacy and Technology Director, The New Literacies Research Lab
University of Connecticut

Jeanne R. Paratore, Ed.D.
Associate Professor of Education
Department of Literacy and
Language Development
Boston University

P. David Pearson, Ph.D.
Professor and Dean
Graduate School of Education
University of California, Berkeley

Sam L. Sebesta, Ed.D.
Professor Emeritus
College of Education
University of Washington, Seattle

Deborah Simmons, Ph.D.
Professor
College of Education and
Human Development
Texas A&M University

Alfred W. Tatum, Ph.D.
Associate Professor and Director of the UIC Reading Clinic
University of Illinois at Chicago

Sharon Vaughn, Ph.D.
H. E. Hartfelder/Southland Corporation Regents Professor Director, Meadows Center for Preventing Educational Risk
University of Texas

Susan Watts Taffe, Ph.D.
Associate Professor in Literacy
Division of Teacher Education
University of Cincinnati

Karen Kring Wixson, Ph.D.
Professor of Education
University of Michigan

Consulting Authors

Jeff Anderson, M.Ed.
Author and Consultant
San Antonio, Texas

Jim Cummins, Ph.D.
Professor
Department of Curriculum,
Teaching and Learning
University of Toronto

Lily Wong Fillmore, Ph.D.
Professor Emerita
Graduate School of Education
University of California, Berkeley

Georgia Earnest García, Ph.D.
Professor
Language and Literacy Division
Department of Curriculum
and Instruction
University of Illinois at
Urbana-Champaign

George A. González, Ph.D.
Professor (Retired)
School of Education
University of Texas-Pan American,
Edinburg

Valerie Ooka Pang, Ph.D.
Professor
School of Teacher Education
San Diego State University

Sally M. Reis, Ph.D.
Board of Trustees Distinguished Professor
Department of Educational
Psychology
University of Connecticut

Jon Scieszka, M.F.A.
Children's Book Author Founder of GUYS READ Named First National Ambassador for Young People's Literature 2008

Grant Wiggins, Ed.D.
Educational Consultant
Authentic Education
Concept Development

Lee Wright, M.Ed.
Pearland, Texas

iv

Practitioners, and Authors.

Consultant

Sharroky Hollie, Ph.D.
Assistant Professor
California State University
Dominguez Hills, CA

Teacher Reviewers

Dr. Bettyann Brugger
Educational Support Coordinator—Reading Office
Milwaukee Public Schools
Milwaukee, WI

Kathleen Burke
K–12 Reading Coordinator
Peoria Public Schools, Peoria, IL

Darci Burns, M.S.Ed.
University of Oregon

Bridget Cantrell
District Intervention Specialist
Blackburn Elementary School
Independence, MO

Tahira DuPree Chase, M.A., M.S.Ed.
Administrator of Elementary English Language Arts
Mount Vernon City School District
Mount Vernon, NY

Michele Conner
Director, Elementary Education
Aiken County School District
Aiken SC

Georgia Coulombe
K–6 Regional Trainer/Literacy Specialist
Regional Center for Training and Learning (RCTL), Reno, NV

Kelly Dalmas
Third Grade Teacher
Avery's Creek Elementary, Arden, NC

Seely Dillard
First Grade Teacher
Laurel Hill Primary School
Mt. Pleasant, SC

Jodi Dodds-Kinner
Director of Elementary Reading
Chicago Public Schools, Chicago, IL

Dr. Ann Wild Evenson
District Instructional Coach
Osseo Area Schools, Maple Grove, MN

Stephanie Fascitelli
Principal
Apache Elementary, Albuquerque
Public Schools, Albuquerque, NM

Alice Franklin
Elementary Coordinator, Language Arts & Reading
Spokane Public Schools, Spokane, WA

Laureen Fromberg
Assistant Principal
PS 100 Queens, NY

Kimberly Gibson
First Grade Teacher
Edgar B. Davis Community School
Brockton, MA

Kristen Gray
Lead Teacher
A.T. Allen Elementary School
Concord, NC

Mary Ellen Hazen
State Pre-K Teacher
Rockford Public Schools #205
Rockford, IL

Patrick M. Johnson
Elementary Instructional Director
Seattle Public Schools, Seattle, WA

Theresa Jaramillo Jones
Principal
Highland Elementary School
Las Cruces, NM

Sophie Kowzun
Program Supervisor, Reading/Language Arts, PreK–5
Montgomery County Public Schools
Rockville, MD

David W. Matthews
Sixth Grade Teacher
Easton Area Middle School
Easton, PA

Ana Nuncio
Editor and Independent Publisher
Salem, MA

Joseph Peila
Principal
Chappell Elementary School
Chicago, IL

Ivana Reimer
Literacy Coordinator
PS 100 Queens, NY

Sally Riley
Curriculum Coordinator
Rochester Public Schools
Rochester, NH

Dyan M. Smiley
Independent Educational Consultant

Michael J. Swiatowiec
Lead Literacy Teacher
Graham Elementary School
Chicago, IL

Dr. Helen Taylor
Director of English Education
Portsmouth City Public Schools
Portsmouth, VA

Carol Thompson
Teaching and Learning Coach
Independence School District
Independence, MO

Erinn Zeitlin
Kindergarten Teacher
Carderock Springs Elementary School
Bethesda, MD

Any Path, Any Pace

UNIT 6

Freedom

Key
SI Strategic Intervention
OL On-Level
A Advanced
ELL ELL

In the **First Stop** on Reading Street

- **Dear Third Grade Teacher**

- **Research into Practice on Reading Street**

- **Guide to Reading Street**

- **Assessment on Reading Street**

- **Customize Writing on Reading Street**

- **Differentiated Instruction on Reading Street**

- **ELL on Reading Street**

- **Customize Literacy on Reading Street**

- **Digital Products on Reading Street**

- **Teacher Resources for Grade 3**

- **Index**

GO Digital!

See It!

- **Big Question Video**
- **Concept Talk Video**
- **Interactive Sound-Spelling Cards**
- **Envision It! Animations**

Hear It!

- **eSelections**
- **eReaders**
- **Grammar Jammer**
- **Leveled Reader Database**

Do It!

- **Vocabulary Activities**
- **Story Sort**
- **21st Century Skills Activities**
- **Online Assessment**
- **Letter Tile Drag and Drop**

Living and Learning

Volume 1

WEEK 1 • When Charlie McButton Lost Power
Narrative Poem...20a–55q
How a Kite Changed the World Narrative Nonfiction

Differentiated Instruction **SI** **OL** **A** **ELL** .... DI•1–DI•25

WEEK 2 • What About Me? Fable 56a–89q
How the Desert Tortoise Got Its Shell Porquoi Tale

Differentiated Instruction **SI** **OL** **A** **ELL** .... DI•26–DI•50

WEEK 3 • Kumak's Fish Tall Tale 90a–121q
How to Catch a Fish Newspaper Article

Differentiated Instruction **SI** **OL** **A** **ELL** .... DI•51–DI•75

Volume 2

WEEK 4 • Supermarket Expository Text .,.....................122a–159q
Money from Long Ago Picture Encyclopedia

Differentiated Instruction **SI** **OL** **A** **ELL** .... DI•76–DI•100

WEEK 5 • My Rows and Piles of Coins
Realistic Fiction...160a–193q
Learning About Money Web Sites

Differentiated Instruction **SI** **OL** **A** **ELL** .... DI•101–DI•125

WEEK 6 • Interactive Review.............................IR•1–IR•60
Which skills help us make our way in the world?
Unit 1 Reading Poetry.............................194–197a

Customize Writing .... CW•1–CW•20
Customize Literacy .... CL•1–CL•47
Let's Learn Amazing Words .... OV•1–OV•3

Smart Solutions

UNIT 2

Volume 1

Volume 2

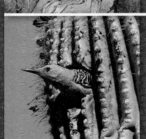

UNIT 3

People and Nature

Volume 1

WEEK 1 • How Do You Raise a Raisin?
Expository Text 370a–403q
Worms at Work Procedural Text

Differentiated Instruction SI OL A ELL .... DI•1–DI•25

WEEK 2 • Pushing Up the Sky Drama 404a–437q
Catch It and Run! Myth

Differentiated Instruction SI OL A ELL .... DI•26–DI•50

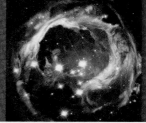

WEEK 3 • Seeing Stars Expository Text 438a–467q
Scien-Trickery: Riddles in Science Poetry

Differentiated Instruction SI OL A ELL .... DI•51–DI•75

Volume 2

WEEK 4 • A Symphony of Whales Fiction.......468a–501q
He Listens to Whales Magazine Article

Differentiated Instruction SI OL A ELL .... DI•76–DI•100

WEEK 5 • Around One Cactus
Narrative Nonfiction 502a–537q
The Water Cycle Search Engines

Differentiated Instruction SI OL A ELL .... DI•101–DI•125

WEEK 6 • Interactive Review .... IR•1–IR•60
How are people and nature connected?
Unit 3 Reading Poetry 538–541a

One of a Kind

Key
- SI Strategic Intervention
- OL On-Level
- A Advanced
- ELL ELL

Volume 1

Volume 2

UNIT 5

Cultures

Volume 1

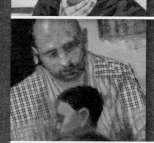

Volume 2

Freedom

Volume 1

Volume 2

UNIT 6

Skills Overview

	WEEK 1	WEEK 2
	The Story of the Statue of Liberty Narrative Nonfiction, pp. 374–385 **A Nation of Immigrants** Textbook, pp. 390–391	**Happy Birthday Mr. Kang** Realistic Fiction, pp. 402–419 **Once Upon a Constitution** Expository Text, pp. 424–427
Question of the Week	Why do we have symbols that represent freedom?	What does it mean to grant freedom?
Amazing Words	*impressive, recognizable, enlighten, tribute, competition, staggering, contribution, disgrace, fund, dedication*	*release, territory, deserve, loyal, affectionate, retrieve, companion, manage, nag, wandering*
Phonics/Word Analysis	T 🔄 Vowel Sounds for /ü/ and / u̇ /	T 🔄 Schwa
Literary Terms	Word Choice	Metaphor
Story Structure/ Text Features	Chronological/Sequence	Climax
Comprehension	T 🔄 **Skill** Fact and Opinion 🔄 **Strategy** Questioning Review **Skill** Author's Purpose	T 🔄 **Skill** Cause and Effect 🔄 **Strategy** Inferring Review **Skill** Theme
Vocabulary	T 🔄 **Skill** Prefix *un-*	T 🔄 **Skill** Antonyms
Fluency	Rate	Appropriate Phrasing
Writing	Notes Trait: Focus/Ideas	Poetry Trait: Organization
Conventions	Capital Letters	Abbreviations
Spelling	Vowel Sounds in *moon* and *foot*	Schwa
Speaking/Listening	Announcement	Express an Opinion
Research Skills	Time Line	Maps

Get Ready to Read

Read and Comprehend

Language Arts

The Big Question

What does freedom mean?

WEEK 3 	WEEK 4 	WEEK 5 	WEEK 6 
Talking Walls: Art for the People Photo Essay, pp. 438–451 **The History of Palindromes** Palindromes, pp. 456–457	**Two Bad Ants** Animal Fantasy, pp. 468–485 **Hiking Safety Tips** Evaluating Online Sources, pp. 490–491	**Atlantis: The Legend of a Lost City** Legend, pp. 502–519 **The Monster in the Maze** Drama, pp. 524–529	**Interactive Review**
Why is freedom of expression important?	Why are rules and laws important to freedom?	What is the best way to keep your freedom?	Connect the Question of the Week to the Big Question
emotion, artistic, creative, expressive, exquisite, lecture, significant, pause, view, lyrics	*obey, responsibility, consequence, permission, citizen, encounter, guilt, eerie, fascinate, forbid*	*equality, justice, witty, perish, blight, demonstration, wept, mourn, violence*	**Review** Amazing Words for Unit 6
T ⏱ Final Syllables	T ⏱ Prefixes	T ⏱ Related Words	
Personification	Imagery	Foreshadowing	
Conflict	Conflict	Climax	
T ⏱ **Skill** Graphic Sources ⏱ **Strategy** Important Ideas **Review** **Skill** Fact and Opinion	T ⏱ **Skill** Plot and Theme ⏱ **Strategy** Story Structure **Review** **Skill** Cause and Effect	T ⏱ **Skill** Generalize ⏱ **Strategy** Inferring **Review** **Skill** Plot and Theme	**Review** Unit 6 Target Comprehension Skills
T ⏱ **Skill** Unknown Words	T ⏱ **Skill** Prefixes and Suffixes	T ⏱ **Skill** Homographs	**Review** Unit 6 Target Vocabulary Skills
Accuracy	Rate	Expression	**Review** Unit 6 Fluency Skills
Description Trait: Word Choice	Comic Book Trait: Conventions	Writing for Tests: Historical Fiction Trait: Word Choice	Quick Write for Fluency
Combining Sentences	Commas	Quotations and Parentheses	**Review** Conventions
Final Syllables	Prefixes, Suffixes, and Endings	Related Words	**Review** Spelling patterns
Media Literacy: Talk Show	Description	Song	
Alphabetical Order	Electronic Text	Quote Source/Paraphrase Source	

UNIT 6 Monitor Progress

Don't Wait Until Friday!

SUCCESS PREDICTOR	WEEK 1	WEEK 2	WEEK 3	WEEK 4
Word Reading — **Phonics**	T Vowel Sounds for /ü/ and /ú/	T Schwa	T Final Syllables	T Prefixes
WCPM — **Fluency**	Rate 110–120 WCPM	Appropriate Phrasing 110–120 WCPM	Accuracy 110–120 WCPM	Rate 110–120 WCPM
Vocabulary — **Oral Vocabulary/ Concept Development** (assessed informally)	impressive recognizable enlighten tribute competition staggering contribution disgrace fund dedication	release territory deserve loyal affectionate retrieve companion manage nag wandering	emotion artistic creative expressive exquisite lecture significant pause view lyrics	obey responsibility consequence permission citizen encounter guilt eerie fascinate forbid
Lesson Vocabulary	T liberty T unveiled T crown T torch T tablet T models T symbol T unforgettable	T narrow T foolish T perches T bows T recipe T chilly T foreign	T encourages T native T settled T social T local T expression T support	T discovery T scoop T crystal T journey T joyful T disappeared T unaware T goal
Retelling — **Text Comprehension**	T **Skill** Fact and Opinion **Strategy** Questioning	T **Skill** Cause and Effect **Strategy** Inferring	T **Skill** Graphic Sources **Strategy** Important Ideas	T **Skill** Plot and Theme **Strategy** Story Structure

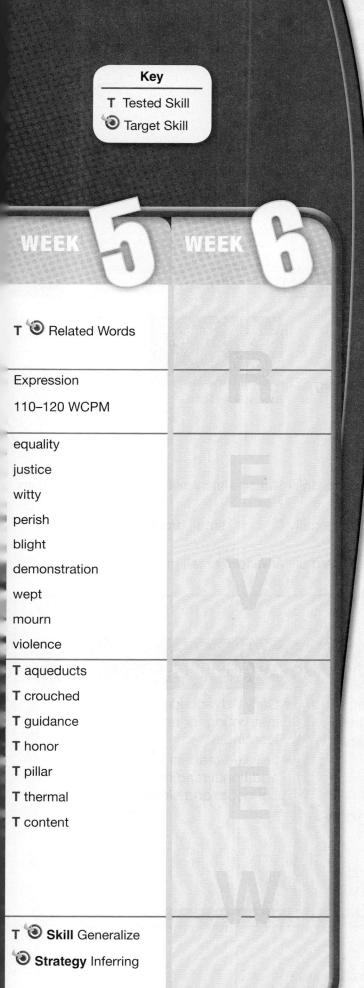

Key

T Tested Skill

⊙ Target Skill

WEEK 5 / WEEK 6

T ⊙ Related Words

Expression 110–120 WCPM
equality
justice
witty
perish
blight
demonstration
wept
mourn
violence
T aqueducts
T crouched
T guidance
T honor
T pillar
T thermal
T content

T ⊙ **Skill** Generalize

⊙ **Strategy** Inferring

Online ASSESSMENT
ReadingStreet.com

Online Classroom

Manage Data

- Assign the Unit 6 Benchmark Test for students to take online.

- Online Assessment records results and generates reports by school, grade, classroom, or student.

- Use reports to disaggregate and aggregate Unit 6 skills and standards data to monitor progress.

- Based on class lists created to support the categories important for AYP (gender, ethnicity, migrant education, English proficiency, disabilities, economic status), reports let you track adequate yearly progress every six weeks.

Group

- Use results from Unit 6 Benchmark Tests taken online through Online Assessment to measure whether students have mastered the English-Language Arts Content Standards taught in this unit.

- Reports in Online Assessment suggest whether students need Extra Support or Intervention.

Individualized Instruction

- Tests are correlated to Unit 6 tested skills and standards so that prescriptions for individual teaching and learning plans can be created.

- Individualized prescriptions target instruction and accelerate student progress toward learning outcome goals.

- Prescriptions include remediation activities and resources to reteach Unit 6 skills and standards.

UNIT 6

Assessment and Grouping
for Data-Driven Instruction

4-Step Plan for Assessment
1 Diagnose and Differentiate
2 Monitor Progress
3 Assess and Regroup
4 Summative Assessment

STEP 1 Diagnose and Differentiate

Baseline Group Tests

Diagnose

To make initial grouping decisions, use the Baseline Group Test, the *Texas Primary Reading Inventory (TPRI),* or another initial placement test. Depending on student's ability levels, you may shave more than one of each group.

Differentiate

If... student performance is **then...** use the regular instruction and the daily Strategic Intervention small group lessons.

If... student performance is **then...** use the regular instruction and the daily On-Level small group lessons.

If... student performance is **then...** use the regular instruction and the daily Advanced small group lessons.

Small Group Time

SI Strategic Intervention

- Daily small group lessons provide more intensive instruction, more scaffolding, more practice, and more opportunities to respond.
- Reteach lessons in the *First Stop on Reading Street* provide more instruction with target skills.
- Leveled readers build background and provide practice for target skills and vocabulary.

OL On-Level

- Explicit instructional routines teach core skills and strategies.
- Daily On-Level lessons provide more practice and more opportunities to respond.
- Independent activities provide practice for core skills and extension and enrichment options.
- Leveled readers provide additional reading and practice for core skills and vocabulary.

A Advanced

- Daily Advanced lessons provide instruction for accelerated learning.
- Leveled readers provide additional reading tied to lesson concepts and skills.

Additional Differentiated Learning Options

Reading Street Response to Intervention Kit
- Focused intervention lessons on the five critical areas of reading: phonemic awareness, phonics, vocabulary, comprehension, and fluency

My Sidewalks on Reading Street
- Intensive intervention for struggling readers

STEP 2 Monitor Progress

Use these tools during lesson teaching to **monitor student progress.**

- **Skill and Strategy** instruction during reading
- **Don't Wait Until Friday** boxes to check word reading, retelling, fluency, and oral vocabulary
- **Weekly Assessment** on Day 5 checks comprehension and fluency
- **Reader's and Writer's Notebook** pages at point of use
- **Weekly Tests** assess target skills for the week
- **Fresh Reads** for Fluency and Comprehension

Weekly Tests

Fresh Reads for Fluency and Comprehension

STEP 3 Assess and Regroup

Use these tools during lesson teaching to **assess and regroup.**

- **Weekly Assessments** Record results of weekly assessments in retelling, comprehension, and fluency to track student progress.
- **Unit Benchmark Tests** Administer this assessment to check mastery of unit skills.
- **Regroup** We recommend the first regrouping to be at the end of Unit 2. Use weekly assessment information and Unit Benchmark Test performance to inform regrouping decisions. Then regroup at the end of each subsequent unit.

Unit Assessment Charts in First Stop

Group

Baseline Group Test → Regroup Units 1 and 2 → Regroup Unit 3 → Regroup Unit 4 → Regroup Unit 5 → End of Year

| Weeks 1-6 | Weeks 7-12 | Weeks 13-18 | Weeks 19-24 | Weeks 25-30 | Weeks 31-36 |

Outside assessments, such as *TPRI, DRA,* and *DIBELS,* may recommend regrouping at other times during the year.

STEP 4 Summative Assessment

Use these tools after lesson teaching to **assess students.**

- **Unit Benchmark Tests** Use to measure a student's mastery of each unit's skills.
- **End-of-Year Benchmark Test** Use to measure a student's mastery of program skills covered in all six units.

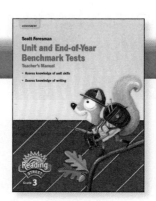

Unit and End-of-Year Benchmark Tests

Understanding By Design

Grant Wiggins, Ed. D.
Reading Street Author

"The best questions point to and highlight the big ideas. They serve as door-ways through which learners explore the key concepts, themes, theories, issues, and problems that reside within the content, perhaps as yet unseen: it is through the process of actively 'interrogating' the content through provocative questions that students deepen their understanding...."

Freedom

Reading Street Online

www.ReadingStreet.com
• Big Question Video
• eSelections
• Envision It! Animations
• Story Sort

THE BIG
?

What does freedom mean?

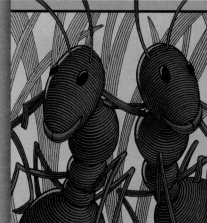

UNIT 6

Small Group Time

Flexible Pacing Plans

SI OL A

5 Day Plan

DAY 1
- Reinforce the Concept
- Read Leveled Readers Concept Literacy Below-Level

DAY 2
- Comprehension Skill
- Comprehension Strategy
- Revisit Main Selection

DAY 3
- Vocabulary Skill
- Revisit Main Selection

DAY 4
- Practice Retelling
- Read/Revisit Paired Selection

DAY 5
- Reread for Fluency
- Reread Leveled Readers

4 Day Plan

DAY 1
- Reinforce the Concept
- Read Leveled Readers Concept Literacy Below-Level

DAY 2
- Comprehension Skill
- Comprehension Strategy
- Revisit Main Selection

DAY 3
- Vocabulary Skill
- Revisit Main Selection

DAY 4
- Practice Retelling
- Read/Revisit Paired Selection
- Reread for Fluency
- Reread Leveled Readers

3 Day Plan

DAY 1
- Reinforce the Concept
- Read Leveled Readers Concept Literacy Below-Level

DAY 2
- Comprehension Skill
- Comprehension Strategy
- Revisit Main Selection

DAY 3
- Practice Retelling
- Read/Revisit Paired Selection
- Reread for Fluency
- Reread Leveled Readers

ELL

5 Day Plan

DAY 1
- Frontload Concept
- Preteach Skills
- Conventions/Writing

DAY 2
- Review Concept/Skills
- Frontload and Read Main Selection
- Conventions/Writing

DAY 3
- Review Concept/Skills
- Reread Main Selection
- Conventions/Writing

DAY 4
- Review Concept/Skills
- Read ELL or ELD Reader
- Conventions/Writing

DAY 5
- Review Concept/Skills
- Reread ELL or ELD Reader
- Conventions/Writing

4 Day Plan

DAY 1
- Frontload Concept
- Preteach Skills
- Conventions/Writing

DAY 2
- Review Concept/Skills
- Frontload and Read Main Selection
- Conventions/Writing

DAY 3
- Review Concept/Skills
- Reread Main Selection
- Conventions/Writing

DAY 4
- Review Concept/Skills
- Read ELL or ELD Reader
- Conventions/Writing

3 Day Plan

DAY 1
- Frontload Concept
- Preteach Skills
- Conventions/Writing

DAY 2
- Review Concept/Skills
- Frontload and Read Main Selection
- Conventions/Writing

DAY 3
- Review Concept/Skills
- Read ELL or ELD Reader
- Conventions/Writing

This Week's ELL Overview

ELL Handbook

- Maximize Literacy and Cognitive Engagement
- Research Into Practice
- Full Weekly Support for Every Selection

The Story of the Statue of Liberty

- Multi-Lingual Summaries in Five Languages
- Selection-Specific Vocabulary Word Cards
- Frontloading/Reteaching for Comprehension Skill Lessons
- ELD and ELL Reader Study Guides

- Transfer Activities
- Professional Development

Daily Leveled ELL Notes

ELL notes appear throughout this week's instruction and ELL Support is on the DI pages of your Teacher's Edition. The following is a sample of an ELL note from this week.

English Language Learners

Beginning Write several words with the vowel sound /ü/ from the Decodable Reader on the board, such as *zoo, true, fruit,* and *chew.* Point to each word as you say it aloud. Then underline the letters that spell the sound /ü/ in each word. Repeat for the sound /u̇/, using words such as *bush, shook,* and *put.*

Intermediate After reading, have students find pairs of words with the vowel sound /ü/ or /u̇/ that are spelled the same. For example: *zoo* and *raccoon; Sue* and *true; bush* and *put; Cook* and *shook.*

Advanced Have students find sentences from the story that contain words with /ü/ or /u̇/. Then have students restate the sentence in their own words.

Advanced High After reading the story, have students choose four or five words with the vowel sounds /ü/ or /u̇/ and write a sentence for each word.

ELL by Strand

The ELL lessons on this week's Support for English Language Learners pages are organized by strand. They offer additional scaffolding for the core curriculum. Leveled support notes on these pages address the different proficiency levels in your class. See pages DI•16–DI•25.

ELL Guy
Dr. Jim Cummins

The Three Pillars of ELL Instruction

ELL Strands	Activate Prior Knowledge	Access Content	Extend Language
Vocabulary pp. DI•17–DI•18	Preteach	Reteach	Leveled Writing Activities
Reading Comprehension p. DI•22	Frontloading	Sheltered Reading	Fluency: Rate
Phonics, Spelling, and Word Analysis p. DI•20	Preteach and Model	Practice	Leveled Practice Activities
Listening Comprehension p. DI•19	Prepare for the Read Aloud	First Listening	Second Listening
Conventions and Writing pp. DI•24–DI•25	Preteach/Introduce	Practice	Leveled Practice Activities/ Leveled Writing Activities
Concept Development p. DI•16	Prior Knowledge	Discuss Concept	Daily Concept and Vocabulary Development

This Week's Practice Stations Overview

Six Weekly Practice Stations with Leveled Activities can be found at the beginning of each week of instruction. For this week's Practice Stations, see pp. 366h–366i.

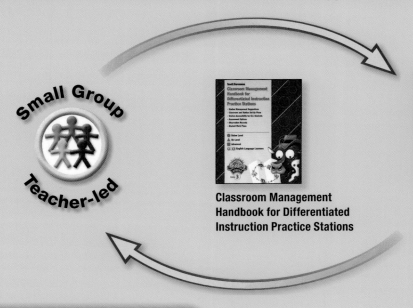

Small Group Teacher-led

Classroom Management Handbook for Differentiated Instruction Practice Stations

Practice Stations

Daily Leveled Center Activities

◯ Below   ▢ Advanced

△ On-Level   **ELL**

Practice Stations Flip Charts

	Word Wise	Word Work	Words to Know	Let's Write	Read For Meaning	Get Fluent
Objectives	• Spell words with suffixes *-y, -ish, -hood, -ment.*	• Identify and pronounce words with suffixes *-y, -ish, -hood, -ment.*	• Identify and define homonyms.	• Write a book review.	• Identify author's purpose.	• Read aloud with appropriate phrasing.
Materials	• *Word Wise* Flip Chart Activity 26 • Teacher-made word cards • paper • pencils	• *Word Work* Flip Chart Activity 26 • Teacher-made word cards • paper • pencils	• *Words to Know* Flip Chart Activity 26 • Teacher-made word cards • paper • pencils	• *Let's Write* Flip Chart Activity 26 • paper • pencils	• *Read for Meaning* Flip Chart Activity 26 • Leveled Readers • paper • pencils	• *Get Fluent* Flip Chart Activity 26 • Leveled Readers

This Week on Reading Street!

Question of the Week

Why do we have symbols that represent freedom?

Freedom

Daily Plan

Don't Wait Until Friday

Whole Group

- Fact and Opinion
- Prefixes
- Fluency/Rate
- Writing/Conventions
- Research and Inquiry

MONITOR PROGRESS | **Success Predictor**

Day 1	Day 2	Day 3	Day 4	Day 5
Check Oral Vocabulary	Check Word Reading	Check Retelling	Check Fluency	Check Oral Vocabulary

Small Group

Teacher Led

- Reading Support
- Skill Support
- Fluency Practice

Practice Stations

Independent Activities

Customize Literacy More support for a balanced literacy approach, see pp. CL•1–CL•47.

Customize Writing More support for a customized writing approach, see pp. CW•1–CW•10.

Whole Group

- Writing: Notes
- Conventions Capital Letters
- Spelling: Vowel Sounds

Assessment

- Weekly Tests
- Day 5 Assessment
- Fresh Reads

You Are Here! Unit 6 Week 1

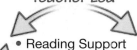

This Week's Reading Selections

Main Selection
Genre: **Narrative Nonfiction**

Paired Selection
Genre: **Textbook**

Decodable Readers

Leveled Readers

ELL and ELD Readers

Resources on Reading Street!

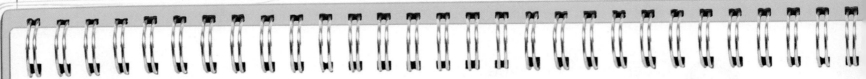

	Build Concepts	Phonics	Comprehension
Whole Group	 Let's Talk About pp. 366–367	 Phonics Skill Lesson pp. 368–369 Decodable Readers Sound-Spelling Cards	 Envision It! Skills/ Strategies  Comprehension Skill Lesson pp. 370–371
Go Digital	• Concept Talk Video	• Interactive Sound-Spelling Cards • Decodable eReaders	• Envision It! Animations • eSelections
Small Group and Independent Practice	 The Story of the Statue of Liberty pp. 374–385 ELL and ELD Readers Leveled Readers Decodable Readers	 Decodable Readers Practice Station Flip Chart	The Story of the Statue of Liberty pp. 374–385 ELL and ELD Readers Leveled Readers  Envision It! Skills/Strategies Reader's and Writer's Notebook Practice Station Flip Chart
Go Digital	• eReaders • eSelections • Decodable eReaders	• Letter Tile Drag and Drop • Decodable eReaders	• Envision It! Animations • eSelection • eReaders
Customize Literacy	• Leveled Readers • Decodable Readers	• Decodable Readers	• Envision It! Skills/Strategies Handbook • Leveled Readers
Go Digital	• Concept Talk Video • Decodable eReaders • eReaders	• Decodable eReaders	• Envision It! Animations • eReaders • Decodable eReaders

Question of the Week
Why do we have symbols that represent freedom?

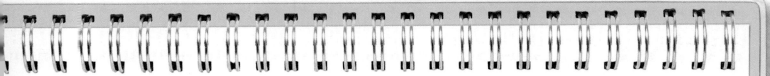

Vocabulary	Fluency	Conventions and Writing
 **Envision It! Vocabulary Cards** — **Vocabulary Skill Lesson** pp. 372–373	 **Let's Learn It!** pp. 392–393 — **Decodable and Leveled Readers**	 **Let's Write It!** pp. 388–389 — **Decodable Readers**
• Envision It! Vocabulary Cards • Vocabulary Activities	• eSelection • Decodable eReaders • eReaders	• Grammar Jammer
  **Envision It! Vocabulary Cards** — **The Story of the Statue of Liberty** pp. 374–385 — **Practice Station Flip Chart** **Words!** — **Reader's and Writer's Notebook**	 **The Story of the Statue of Liberty** pp. 374–385 — **Practice Station Flip Chart** **Leveled Readers** — **ELL and ELD Readers**	**Reader's and Writer's Notebook** — **The Story of the Statue of Liberty** pp. 374–385 **Practice Station Flip Chart**
• Envision It! Vocabulary Cards • Vocabulary Activities • eSelection	• eSelection • eReaders	• Grammar Jammer
• Envision It! Vocabulary Cards	• Leveled Readers • Decodable Readers	• Reader's and Writer's Notebook
• Vocabulary Activities	• eReaders • Decodable eReaders	• Grammar Jammer

You Are Here!
Unit 6
Week 1

Week 1

The Story of the Statue of Liberty **366c**

My 5-Day Planner for Reading Street!

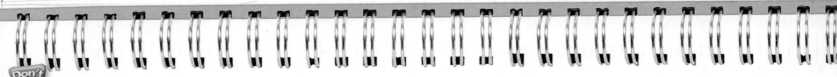

	Check Oral Vocabulary **Day 1** pages 366j–371f	**Check Word Reading** **Day 2** pages 372a–381e

Get Ready to Read	**Concept Talk,** 366j–367
	Oral Vocabulary, 367a
	    impressive, tribute, enlighten, contribution
	Listening Comprehension, Read Aloud, 367b
	Phonics/Word Analysis, 368a–369b
	    ⊚ Vowel Sounds /ü/ and /u̇/
	READ Decodable Practice Reader, 369a–369b
		Concept Talk, 372a
		Oral Vocabulary, 372b
		    dedication, competition
		Phonics/Word Analysis, 372c
		    ⊚ Vowel Sounds /ü/ and /u̇/
		Literary Terms, 372d
		    Word Choice
		Text Structure, 372d
		    Chronological/Sequence

Read and Comprehend	**Comprehension Skill,**
	    ⊚ Fact and Opinion, 370a
	Comprehension Strategy,
	    ⊚ Questioning, 370a
	READ Comprehension 370–371
	Model Fluency, Rate, 370–371
	Introduce Lesson Vocabulary, 371a
	    liberty, unveiled, crown, torch, tablet, models,
	    symbol, unforgettable
		Vocabulary Skills, ⊚ Prefix *un-*, 372e
		Vocabulary Strategy, Word Structure, 372e
		Lesson Vocabulary, 372–373
		    liberty, unveiled, crown, torch, tablet, models,
		    symbol, unforgettable
		READ Vocabulary, 372–373
		Reread for Fluency, Rate, 372–373
		READ Main Selection
		    The Story of the Statue of Liberty, 374–381a

Language Arts	**Research and Inquiry,** Identify Questions, 371b **Spelling,** Vowel Sounds in *moon* and *foot,* 371c **Conventions,** Capital Letters, 371d **Handwriting,** Cursive Letters *T, F,* 371d **Writing,** Notes, Introduce, 371e–371f	**Research and Inquiry,** Navigate/Search, 381b **Conventions,** Capital Letters, 381c **Spelling,** Vowel Sounds in *moon* and *foot,* 381c **Writing,** Notes, Focus/Ideas, 381d–381e

You Are Here! Unit 6 Week 1

Question of the Week
Why do we have symbols that represent freedom?

Check Retelling	Check Fluency	Check Oral Vocabulary
Day 3 pages 382a–389c	**Day 4** pages 390a–393e	**Day 5** pages 393f–393q

Concept Talk, 382a
Oral Vocabulary, 382b
  recognizable, disgrace
Phonics/Word Analysis, 382c–382d
◉ Vowel Sounds /ü/ and /ů/
Decodable Story, 382d
Comprehension Check, 382e
Check Retelling, 382f
	Concept Talk, 390a
	Oral Vocabulary, 390b
	  staggering, fund
	Phonics/Word Analysis, 390c–390f
	Review Suffixes
	Decodable Story, 390f
	Genre: Textbook, 390g
		Concept Wrap Up, 393f
		Check Oral Vocabulary, 393g
		  impressive, tribute, enlighten, contribution, dedication, competition, recognizable, disgrace, staggering, fund
		Amazing Ideas, 393g
		Review ◉ Fact and Opinion, 393h
		Review ◉ Prefix *un-*, 393h
		Review ◉ Vowel Sounds /ü/ and /ů /, 393i
		Review Literary Terms, 393i

READ Main Selection,
The Story of the Statue of Liberty,
382–385a
Retelling, 386–387
Think Critically, 387a
Model Fluency, Rate, 387b
Research and Study Skills, Time Line, 387c
	READ Paired Selection,
	"A Nation of Immigrants,"
	390–391a
	Let's Learn It! 392–393a
	Fluency: Rate
	Vocabulary: ◉ Prefix *un-*
	Listening and Speaking:
	Announcement
		Fluency Assessment,
		  WCPM, 393j–393k
		Comprehension Assessment,
		  ◉ Fact and Opinion, 393l–393m

Research and Inquiry, Analyze, 387d **Conventions,** Capital Letters, 387e **Spelling,** Vowel Sounds in *moon* and *foot,* 387e **Let's Write It!** Notes, 388–389 **Writing,** Notes, Paraphrase, 389a–389c	**Research and Inquiry,** Synthesize, 393b **Conventions,** Capital Letters, 393c **Spelling,** Vowel Sounds in *moon* and *foot,* 393c **Writing,** Notes, Revising, 393d–393e	**Research and Inquiry,** Communicate, 393n **Conventions,** Capital Letters, 393o **Spelling Test,** Vowel Sounds in *moon* and *foot,* 393o **Writing,** Notes, Capital Letters, 393p–393q **Quick Write for Fluency,** 393q

Week 1

Grouping Options for Differentiated Instruction
Turn the page for the small group time lesson plan.

Planning Small Group Time on Reading Street!

SMALL GROUP TIME RESOURCES

Look for this Small Group Time box each day to help meet the individual needs of all your children. Differentiated Instruction lessons appear on the DI pages at the end of each week.

DAY 1

Teacher Led

SI Strategic Intervention	**OL** On-Level	**A** Advanced
Teacher Led • Reinforce the Concept • **Read** *Concept Literacy Reader* or *Below-Level Reader*	**Teacher Led** • Expand the Concept • **Read** *On-Level Reader*	**Teacher Led** • Extend the Concept • **Read** *Advanced Reader*

ELL Place English language learners in the groups that correspond to their reading abilities in English.

Practice Stations	**Independent Activities**
• Read for Meaning • Get Fluent • Word Work	• Concept Talk Video • *Reader's and Writer's Notebook* • Research and Inquiry

ELL

ELL Reader
Advanced
Advanced High

ELD Reader
Beginning
Intermediate

ELL Poster

Day 1

SI Strategic Intervention	**Reinforce the Concept,** DI•1– DI•2 **Read Decodable Reader** and **Concept Literacy Reader** or **Below-Level Reader**
OL On-Level	**Expand the Concept,** DI•7 **Read On-Level Reader**
A Advanced	**Extend the Concept,** DI•12 **Read Advanced Reader**
ELL English Language Learners	DI•16–DI•25 **Frontload Concept Preteach Skills Writing**

You Are Here! Unit 6 Week 1

Reading Street
Response to
Intervention Kit

Reading Street
Practice Stations Kit

SI Strategic Intervention

OL On-Level

A Advanced

Decodable
Practice Readers
Units 4–6
• Practice phonics skills
• Blending practice
• Reread for fluency

The Statue of
Liberty
By Michele Spirn

Concept Literacy Reader

Symbols, Signs, and Songs of America
by Alma Ransford

The French Connection
by Sharon Franklin

Decodable
Reader

Below-Level
Reader

On-Level
Reader

Advanced
Reader

The Story of the Statue of Liberty pp. 374–385

A Nation of Immigrants pp. 390–391

Small Group Weekly Plan

Day 2	Day 3	Day 4	Day 5
Reinforce Comprehension, DI•3 **Revisit Main Selection**	**Reinforce Vocabulary,** DI•4 **Read/Revisit Main Selection**	**Reinforce Comprehension,** Practice Retelling, DI•5 Genre Focus **Read/Revsit Paired Selection**	**Practice Fluency,** DI•6 **Reread Concept Literacy Reader** or **Below-Level Reader**
Expand Comprehension, DI•8 **Revisit Main Selection**	**Expand Vocabulary,** DI•9 **Read/Revisit Main Selection**	**Expand Comprehension,** Practice Retelling, DI•10 **Read/Revisit Paired Selection**	**Practice Fluency,** DI•11 **Reread On-Level Reader**
Extend Comprehension, DI•13 **Revisit Main Selection**	**Extend Vocabulary,** DI•14 **Read/Revisit Main Selection**	**Extend Comprehension,** Genre Focus DI•15 **Read/Revisit Paired Selection**	**Practice Fluency,** DI•15 **Reread Advanced Reader**
DI•16–DI•25 **Review Concepts/Skills** **Frontload Main Selection** **Practice**	DI•16–DI•25 **Review Concepts/Skills** **Reread Main Selection** **Practice**	DI•16–DI•25 **Review Concept** **Read ELL/ELD Readers** **Practice**	DI•16–DI•25 **Review Concepts/Skills** **Read ELL/ELD Reader** **Writing**

Week 1

Practice Stations for Everyone on Reading Street!

Word Wise
Suffixes -y, -ish, -hood, -ment

Objectives
• Spell words with suffixes -y, -ish, -hood, -ment.

Materials
• *Word Wise* Flip Chart Activity 26
• Teacher-made word cards
• paper   • pencils

Differentiated Activities

⬤ Write a pair of homonyms. Draw pictures to illustrate the meaning of each word. Think of other words with suffixes -y, -ish, -hood, and -ment. Make a list.

▲ Choose seven word cards, and write them in a list. Write sentences using each word. Add other words with suffixes -y, -ish, -hood, and -ment to the list.

■ Choose nine word cards, and list the words. Write sentences using each word. Think of other words with suffixes -y, -ish, -hood, and -ment. Add them to the list.

Technology
• Online Dictionary

Word Work
Suffixes -y, -ish, -hood, -ment

Objectives
• Identify and pronounce words with suffixes -y, -ish, -hood, -ment.

Materials
• *Word Work* Flip Chart Activity 26
• Teacher-made word cards
• paper   • pencils

Differentiated Activities

⬤ Choose eight word cards. List the words. Say each word. Circle the suffix in each word.

▲ Choose ten word cards, and write the words in a list. Say each word, and circle the suffix in each word.

■ Choose twelve word cards, and say each word. List the words. Circle the suffix in each word.

Technology
• Modeled Pronunciation Audio CD

Words to Know
Homonyms

Objectives
• Identify and define homonyms.

Materials
• *Words to Know* Flip Chart Activity 26
• Teacher-made word cards
• paper   • pencils

Differentiated Activities

⬤ Choose three pairs of homonyms from the word cards. Write your words in a list. Write a sentence for each word to show the different meanings homonyms have.

▲ Choose five pairs of homonyms from the word cards. List each pair of homonyms on paper. Write sentences for each pair to show their different meanings.

■ Write ten homonym pairs on word cards. Turn them upside down. Play a matching game with a partner.

Technology
• Online Dictionary

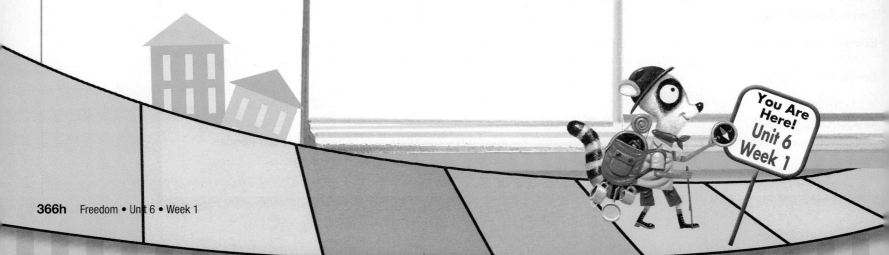

You Are Here! Unit 6 Week 1

Use this week's materials from the
*Reading Street Leveled Practice Stations
Kit* to organize this week's stations.

Key
● Below-Level Activities
▲ On-Level Activities
■ Advanced Activities

Practice Station
Flip Chart

Let's Write!
Book review

Objectives
• Write a book review.

Materials
• *Let's Write!* Flip Chart Activity 26
• paper • pencils

Differentiated Activities
● Think about a book you have read. Write a book review that tells your opinion of the book. Write at least three sentences. Include details that would be helpful to readers. Underline the book's title.

▲ Write a review of a book you have read. Tell who wrote the book, and underline the title. Give your opinion of the book, and include details that would be helpful to readers.

■ Write the title and the author of a book you've read. Think about what happened in the book. Think of an interesting way to begin your review, and then write a summary of the book. Tell readers why or why not they should read it.

Technology
• Online Graphic Organizers

Read for Meaning
Author's purpose

Objectives
• Identify author's purpose.

Materials
• *Read for Meaning* Flip Chart Activity 26
• Leveled Readers • paper • pencils

Differentiated Activities
● Choose a book from those your teacher provided. Did the author write to entertain, inform, or persuade you? Write one sentence that tells the author's purpose. Write one sentence with a story detail that supports your thinking.

▲ Read one of the books your teacher provided. Think about the author's reason for writing. Write a sentence that tells the purpose. Add two sentences with details to support your thinking.

■ Choose and read a leveled reader. As you read, think about the author's purpose for writing. Write a paragraph telling the purpose. Include details to support your reasoning.

Technology
• Leveled Reader Database

Get Fluent
Practice fluent reading

Objectives
• Read aloud with appropriate phrasing.

Materials
• *Get Fluent* Flip Chart Activity 26
• Leveled Readers

Differentiated Activities
● Work with a partner. Choose a Concept Literacy Reader or Below-Level Reader. Take turns reading a page from the book. Use the readers to practice reading with appropriate phrasing. Provide feedback as needed.

▲ Work with a partner. Choose an On-Level Reader. Take turns reading a page from the book. Use the reader to practice reading with appropriate phrasing. Provide feedback as needed.

■ Work with a partner. Choose an Advanced Reader. Take turns reading a page from the book. Use the reader to practice reading with appropriate phrasing. Provide feedback as needed.

Technology
• Leveled Reader Database
• Reading Street Readers CD-ROM

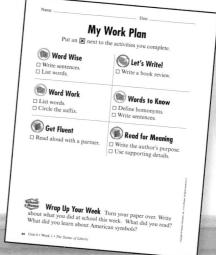

My Weekly Work Plan

week 1

Objectives
- Introduce the weekly concept.
- Develop oral vocabulary.

Today at a Glance

Oral Vocabulary
impressive, tribute, enlighten, contribution

Phonics/Word Analysis
◉ Vowel sounds /ü/ and /u̇/

Comprehension
◉ Fact and opinion
◉ Questioning

Reading
"Coming to America"

Fluency
Rate

Lesson Vocabulary
Tested Vocabulary

Research and Inquiry
Identify questions

Spelling
Vowel sounds in *moon* and *foot*

Conventions
Capital letters

Handwriting
Cursive letters *T, F*

Writing
Notes

Concept Talk

Question of the Week

Why do we have symbols that represent freedom?

Introduce the concept

To explore the unit concept of Freedom, this week students will read, write, and talk about symbols that represent freedom. Write the Question of the Week on the board.

ROUTINE **Activate Prior Knowledge** **Team Talk**

(1) **Think** Have students think about symbols that represent freedom.

(2) **Pair** Have pairs of students discuss the Question of the Week.

(3) **Share** Call on a few students to share their ideas with the group. Guide the discussion and encourage elaboration with prompts such as:

- What is a symbol? What are some examples of symbols?
- What are some symbols of freedom you have seen? Where?

Routines Flip Chart

Anchored Talk

Develop oral vocabulary

Have students turn to pp. 366–367 in their Student Editions. Look at each of the photos. Then, use the prompts to guide discussion and create the *Why we have symbols that represent freedom* concept map. Remind students to ask and answer questions with appropriate details.

- Why is an *impressive* monument like the Alamo a good symbol for freedom? (People fought and died for freedom at the Alamo.) Symbols often have important characteristics, such as *impressive* history. Let's add *Characteristics* and *impressive* to our concept map.

- What important *contributions* does the American flag symbolize? (It can be a symbol of the sacrifices soldiers and others have made for country.) Let's add *Contributions* to the concept map.

Oral Vocabulary

Let's Talk About

Symbols of Freedom

- Comment about symbols of freedom.
- Pose and answer questions about symbols of freedom and unity.
- Offer suggestions for what it means to be free.

READING STREET ONLINE
CONCEPT TALK VIDEO
www.ReadingStreet.com

Objectives
- Work together with other students. Take part in discussions led by teachers and other students; ask and answer questions, and offer ideas that build on the ideas of others.

You've learned **2 4 6**
Amazing Words
so far this year!

Student Edition pp. 366–367

Amazing Words

You've learned **2 4 6** words so far.

You'll learn **0 1 0** words this week!

impressive	competition
tribute	recognizable
enlighten	disgrace
contribution	staggering
dedication	fund

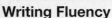

Writing on Demand

Writing Fluency
Ask students to respond to the photos on pp. 366–367 by writing as well as they can and as much as they can about why we have symbols that represent freedom.

- How is the Liberty Bell a *tribute* to our nation? (It was made to ring out for freedom on July 4, 1776.) Let's add *Documents* and *Declaration of Independence* to the map.

- After discussing the photos, ask: Why do we have symbols that represent freedom?

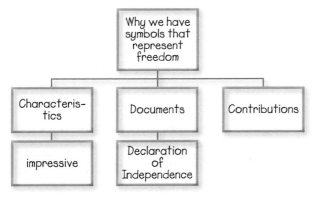

Connect to reading

Tell students that this week they will be reading about how and why an important symbol of freedom was created. Encourage students to add concept-related words to this week's concept map.

ELL Preteach Concepts Use the Day 1 instruction on ELL Poster 26 to assess and build background knowledge, develop concepts, and build oral vocabulary.

ELL

English Language Learners
ELL support Additional ELL support and modified instruction is provided in the *ELL Handbook* and in the ELL Support lessons on pp. DI•16–DI•25.

Listening comprehension
English learners will benefit from additional visual support to understand the key terms in the concept map. Use the pictures on pp. 366–367 to scaffold understanding.

Frontload for read aloud Use the modified Read Aloud on p. DI•19 of the ELL Support lessons to prepare students to listen to "Let Freedom Ring" (p. 367b).

ELL Poster 26

The Story of the Statue of Liberty **366–367**

Objectives
- Develop listening comprehension.
- Develop oral vocabulary.

Check Oral Vocabulary
SUCCESS PREDICTOR

Oral Vocabulary
Amazing Words

Introduce Amazing Words

"Let Freedom Ring" on p. 367b is about the Liberty Bell. Tell students to listen for this week's Amazing Words—*impressive, tribute, enlighten,* and *contribution*—as you read.

Model fluency

As you read "Let Freedom Ring," model appropriate rate by reading at a speed appropriate to the text that will improve listener's comprehension.

Amazing Words Oral Vocabulary Routine

impressive
tribute
enlighten
contribution

Teach Amazing Words

1 **Introduce** Write the word *impressive* on the board. Have students say the word aloud with you. In "Let Freedom Ring," we learn that the Liberty Bell is an *impressive* symbol of America even though it is cracked. Supply a student-friendly definition.

2 **Demonstrate** Have students answer questions to demonstrate understanding. Is coming to school on a bus *impressive*? Is winning a national spelling contest *impressive*?

3 **Apply** Ask students to name actions that would be *impressive*.

See p. OV•1 to teach *tribute, enlighten,* and *contribution*.

Routines Flip Chart

Apply Amazing Words

To build oral language, lead the class in a discussion about the meanings of the Amazing Words. Remind students to listen attentively to speakers and to build on the ideas of others in a discussion.

MONITOR PROGRESS **Check Oral Vocabulary**

During discussion, listen for students' use of Amazing Words.

If... students are unable to use the Amazing Words to discuss the concept,

then... use Oral Vocabulary Routine in the Routines Flip Chart to demonstrate words in different contexts.

Day 1	Day 2	Day 3	Day 4	Day 5
Check Oral Vocabulary	Check Word Reading	Check Retelling	Check Fluency	Check Oral Vocabulary

Let Freedom Ring

The most famous bell in the world has a big crack in it. The Liberty Bell tells the story of freedom, the freedom that was found in America. The crack destroyed the bell's sound, but its message still rings clear. The Liberty Bell makes Americans proud of the country they live in. It helps them remember that we live in a free land.

The Liberty Bell now rests in Philadelphia, Pennsylvania. That is where the Declaration of Independence was signed. That is where America became a free country. For many years, however, the bell traveled around the country. It took seven train trips and stopped at 400 cities! The Liberty Bell even traveled to seven of America's World's Fairs.

People read about the bell's travels in their city newspapers. When it would arrive on their streets, they would have big parades. Bands would play a tribute to the country, and people would sing songs to spread the bell's message of freedom. The songs were meant to enlighten America's children about our great nation's strength.

The Liberty Bell in Philadelphia is the third bell that was made. The first bell cracked the first time it was struck. Then someone made a new bell, using metal from the first one. But that bell had a problem, too. So two more men made yet another bell. The third one was their contribution to our country. The bell weighs 13,000 pounds—1,000 pounds for each of the first 13 states.

This Liberty Bell has a big crack in it too. No one knows for sure when the crack happened. At first the crack was small and the bell still rung clearly. But the crack got bigger and bigger and the sound got worse and worse. Soon the bell fell silent. However, it was no less impressive. For years it hung in a building called Independence Hall. People from all over the world came to visit it every single day.

Several years ago, the Liberty Bell was moved from Independence Hall to a new building in Philadelphia. The bell now hangs in Liberty Bell Center. The building is open all year so people can see the bell and learn about it. The story of the bell's travels is told in 12 different languages.

The Liberty Bell is only one of our country's symbols of freedom. These symbols are important because they make people think. They make people remember when and why Americans built a new nation. They make people feel proud that they can vote and govern themselves.

Until the Liberty Bell cracked, it rang every year—each July 4th on the birthday of our nation. It rang through the streets of Philadelphia for 61 years. But freedom still rings in the United States of America, and the Liberty Bell sends a message that is heard throughout the country.

Oral Vocabulary

Success Predictor

Objectives

⊚ Associate the sounds /ü/ and /ů/ with the spellings *oo, ew, ue, ui, oo,* and *u.*

⊚ Blend, read, and spell with /ü/ and /ů/ spelled *oo, ew, ue, ui, oo,* and *u.*

Skills Trace

⊚ **Vowel Sounds /ü/ and /ů/**
Introduce U6W1D1
Practice U6W1D3; U6W1D4
Reteach/Review U6W1D5; U6W2D4
Assess/Test Weekly Test U6W1
Benchmark Test U6
Key: U = Unit, W = Week, D = Day

Sound-Spelling
Cards 90, 68

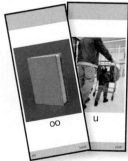

Sound-Spelling
Cards 102, 103

Sound-Spelling
Cards 89, 101

Phonics
🔊 Vowel Sounds /ü/ and /ů/

ROUTINE **Blending Strategy**

① **Connect** Write the words *rain* and *meat.* Ask students what they know about the vowel sounds in these words. (Two letters stand for one vowel sound.) Today you will learn how to spell and read words with the sound /ü/ as in the word *moon,* spelled *oo, ew, ue, ui,* and /ů/ as in the word *foot,* spelled *oo* and *u.*

② **Use Sound-Spelling Cards** Display Card 90. Point to *oo.* The sound /ü/ can be spelled *oo.* Repeat with Cards 68, 102, and 103 to show other spellings for /ü/: *ew, ue,* and *ui.* Have students say /ü/ several times as you point to *oo, ew, ue,* or *ui.* Follow the same procedure with Cards 89 and 101, the sound /ů/, which can be spelled either *oo* or *u.*

③ **Model** Write *blew.* In this word, the letters *e* and *w* stand for the sound /ü/. Point to each spelling as you say its sound. Then blend the word: /b//l//ü/. Follow the same procedure to model blending the sounds in *cook,* /k//ů//k/.

④ **Guide Practice** Continue the process in step 3. This time have students blend with you.

took	book	flew	suit	tool	hook
fruit	grew	look	blue	fool	put

⑤ **Review** What do you know about reading these words? The letters *oo, ew, ue,* and *ui* stand for /ü/. The letters *oo* and *u* stand for /ů/.

Routines Flip Chart

Model

Have students turn to p. 368 in their Student Editions. Each word on this page has the vowel sound /ü/ or /ů/. The first word is *raccoon.* I hear /ü/ in the second syllable. In *raccoon,* /ü/ is spelled *oo.* When I say *threw,* I hear /ü/. In *threw,* /ü/ is spelled *ew.*

Guide practice

For each word in Words I Can Blend, ask for the sound of each letter or group of letters. Make sure that students identify the correct sounds for the vowel combinations *oo, ew, ue, ui,* and *u.* Then have them blend the words.

Corrective feedback

If... students have difficulty blending a word,
then... model blending the word, and then ask students to blend it with you.

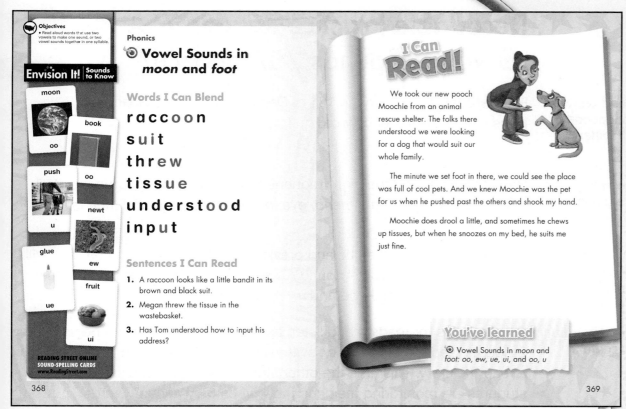

Student Edition pp. 368–369

SI Strategic Intervention

Blend words If students have difficulty blending words with vowel sounds in *tooth* and *cook*, then use Blending Strategy: Whole Word routine card in the Routines Flip Chart.

Blend and Read

Read words independent of context

After students can successfully segment and blend the words on p. 368 in their Student Editions, point to words in random order and ask students to read them naturally.

Read words in context

Have students read each of the sentences on p. 368. Have them identify words in the sentences that have the vowel sounds /ü/ and /ù/.

Team Talk Pair students and have them take turns reading each of the sentences aloud.

Chorally read the I Can Read! passage on p. 369 with the students. Then have them read the passage aloud to themselves.

On their own

For additional practice, use *Reader's and Writer's Notebook* p. 385.

Reader's and Writer's Notebook p. 385

ELL

English Language Learners
Support phonics Speakers of Chinese, French, Italian, Korean, Spanish, and Urdu may have difficulty distinguishing the sounds in *book* and *moon*. Help them practice saying and writing word pairs like *cook/cool, took/tool, shook/shoot*.

Objectives

- Apply knowledge of sound-spellings to decode unknown multisyllabic words when reading.
- Decode and read words in context and independent of context.
- Practice fluency with oral rereading.

Decodable Practice Reader 26A
Vowel Sounds /ü/ and /u̇/

Read words independent of context

Have students turn to page 121 of *Decodable Practice Readers 3.2*. Have students read each word.

Read high-frequency words

Have students read the high-frequency words *was, to, a, some, wanted, could, said, do, you, the, friend, eye, of, live, they, only,* and *their* on the first page.

Preview Decodable Practice Reader

Have students read the title and preview the story. Tell them that they will read words with the vowel sound /ü/ spelled *oo, ew, ue,* and *ui* and the vowel sound /u̇/ spelled *oo* and *u.*

Read words in context

Pair students for reading and listen as they read. One student begins. Students read the entire story, switching readers after each page. Partners reread the story. This time the other student begins. Make sure that students are monitoring their accuracy when they decode words.

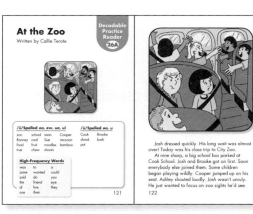

Decodable Practice Reader 26A

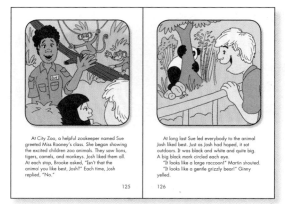

Corrective feedback

If... students have difficulty decoding a word, **then...** refer them to the Sound-Spelling Cards to identify the sounds in the word. Then prompt them to blend the word.

- What is the new word?
- Is the new word a word you know?
- Does it make sense in the story?

Check decoding and comprehension

Have students retell the story to include characters, setting, and events. Then have students find words in the story that have the vowel sounds /ü/ and /ù/ spelled *oo, ew, ue, ui, oo,* and *u.* Students should supply *zoo, Cooper, Sue, fruit, true, school, Rooney, raccoon, noodles, chew, soon, cool, food, bamboo, shoots, Cook, bush, Brooke, put,* and *shook.*

Reread for Fluency

Have students reread Decodable Reader 26A to develop automaticity decoding words with vowel sounds /ü/ and /ù/.

ROUTINE **Oral Rereading**

1. **Read** Have students read the entire book orally.

2. **Reread** To achieve optimal fluency, students should reread the text three or four times.

3. **Corrective Feedback** Listen as students read. Provide corrective feedback regarding their fluency and decoding.

Routines Flip Chart

ELL

English Language Learners

Beginning Write several words with the vowel sound /ü/ from the Decodable Reader on the board, such as *zoo, true, fruit,* and *chew.* Point to each word as you say it aloud. Then underline the letters that spell the sound /ü/ in each word. Repeat for the sound /ù/, using words such as *bush, shook,* and *put.*

Intermediate After reading, have students find pairs of words with the vowel sound /ü/ or /ù/ that are spelled the same. For example: *zoo* and *raccoon; Sue* and *true; bush* and *put, Cook* and *shook.*

Advanced/Advanced High After reading the story, have students choose four or five words with the vowel sounds /ü/ or /ù/ and write a sentence for each word.

Objectives
- ◎ Identify facts and opinions to aid comprehension.
- ◎ Use the questioning strategy to aid comprehension.
- • Read grade-level text at an appropriate rate.

Skills Trace
◎ **Fact and Opinion**
Introduce U4W3D1; U4W4D1; U6W1D1
Practice U1W4D2; U1W4D3; U4W3D2; U4W3D3; U4W4D2; U4W4D3; U6W1D2; U6W1D3; U6W3D3
Reteach/Review U4W3D5; U4W4D5; U6W1D5
Assess/Test Weekly Tests U4W3; U4W4; U6W1
Benchmark Tests U4
Key: U = Unit, W = Week, D = Day

Reader's and Writer's
Notebook p. 386

Skill ↔ Strategy
🔄 Fact and Opinion
🔄 Questioning

Introduce fact and opinion

Envision It!

A statement of fact tells something that can be proved true or false. How can I prove that something is true? (reading a reference book or asking an expert) The second bullet says that a statement of opinion tells someone's ideas or feelings. How can I identify a statement of opinion when I'm reading? (Look for words that tell feelings. Words such as *should* or *best* are clues to opinions.) Have students turn to p. EI•7 in the Student Edition to review fact and opinion. Then read "Coming to America" with students.

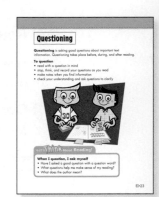

Student Edition p. EI•7

Model the skill

Think Aloud

Today we're going to read about immigrants to America. Have students follow along as you read the first paragraph of "Coming to America." The first paragraph of "Coming to America" has three statements of fact: your homeland is where you were born, immigrants are people who leave their homeland to come to another country, and America has been called a "Nation of Immigrants." I can check in a reference book to verify that these statements are true.

Guide practice

Have students finish reading "Coming to America" on their own. After they read, have them use a graphic organizer like the one on p. 370 and identify statements of fact and opinion from the passage.

Questioning Remind students that if they have difficulty understanding "Coming to America," they can use the strategy of questioning. Model how to stop, think, and record questions as you read.

Strategy check

Model the strategy

Envision It!

Think Aloud

When I first read, I didn't understand the nickname for America, "Nation of Immigrants." I noted my question and read the passage with that question in mind. The second paragraph answered my question: Everyone who lives in America now once came, or has ancestors who came, from somewhere else. Have students review the strategy of questioning on p. EI•23 of the Student Edition.

Student Edition p. EI•23

On their own

Use p. 386 in the *Reader's and Writer's Notebook* for additional practice with statements of fact and opinion.

Objectives
- Ask questions, clean up anything you don't understand, and look for facts and details. Support your answers with details from the text.

Envision It | Skill Strategy

Skill

Fact and Opinion

Strategy

Questioning

READING STREET ONLINE
ENVISION IT! ANIMATIONS
www.ReadingStreet.com

370

Comprehension Skill

Fact and Opinion

- A statement of fact tells something that can be proven true or false. You can prove it by reading a reference source.
- A statement of opinion tells someone's ideas or feelings. Words that tell feelings, such as *should* or *best*, are clue words.
- Use what you learned about fact and opinion and a chart like the one below as you read "Coming to America." Then use the facts to draw a conclusion about immigrants in America.

Fact	How to Prove

Opinion	Clue Words

Comprehension Strategy

Questioning

Active readers use questions to help them understand what they read. While you read, ask literal questions to make sure you understand. You can also ask yourself questions using what you already know or have read to interpret, connect to, or evaluate what you are reading.

Coming to America

The country where you were born is called your *homeland*. People who leave their homeland and come to another country—such as America—are called *immigrants*. America has been called a "nation of immigrants." Why?

Everyone who lives in America now (except for Native Americans) once came from somewhere else. This may have happened a very long time ago in your family. Or maybe you and your family arrived here recently.

Immigrants leave their homeland for different reasons. Some came to America looking for religious freedom. Others came to escape war or hunger. But mostly, people came looking for a better life.

People came to America from all over the world, but together we are one nation!

Skill What are the facts in the paragraph? How could you prove whether they are true or false?

Strategy Ask questions to make sure you understand the text, such as *What are the different reasons people immigrate?*

Your Turn!

Need a Review? See the *Envision It! Handbook* for more information about fact and opinion and questioning.

Let's Think About...

Ready to Try It? As you read *The Story of the Statue of Liberty*, use what you've learned about fact and opinion and asking questions to understand the text.

371

Student Edition pp. 370–371

Skill Facts are the definitions of *homeland* and *immigrants*. I could look them up in a dictionary or glossary to prove if they were true or false. Another fact is that America has been called a "Nation of Immigrants." I could look that up in reference books.
Strategy You can ask questions such as *When did people immigrate to the United States?*

Model Fluency
Rate

Model fluent reading

Have students listen as you read paragraph 3 of "Coming to America" at an appropriate rate. Explain that when you are reading an expository text for comprehension, you slow down the rate of your reading so that all the points in the text are clear.

ROUTINE **Oral Rereading**

1. **Read** For "Coming to America," use paragraph 1 on p. 371.

2. **Model** Have students listen as you read the paragraph at an appropriate rate.

3. **Guide practice** Have students read along with you.

4. **On their own** For optimal fluency, students should reread three or four times at an appropriate rate.

Routines Flip Chart

ELL

English Language Learners
Fact and Opinion Provide oral practice by having students state facts and opinions about the city or town where they live.

Objectives
- Activate prior knowledge of words.
- Identify questions for research.

Vocabulary
Tested Vocabulary

Lesson vocabulary

Use the following Question and Answer activity to help students acquire word knowledge that improves reading, speaking, listening, and writing vocabularies.

Activate prior knowledge

Display the lesson words. Ask volunteers to tell what they already know about the words. Then ask oral questions like those below. Students should respond *yes* or *no* and give reasons for their choice.

- Do people who are in jail have *liberty*?
- Can something that is covered be *unveiled*?
- Does a *crown* rest on top of someone's head?
- Would you hold a *torch* away from your body?
- Can you write on a *tablet*?
- Are *models* small versions of larger structures?
- Is the American flag a *symbol* of our country?
- Would you forget an *unforgettable* day?

Homophones

Ask students if they know a musical instrument that is pronounced the same as *symbol.* Explain that *cymbal* and *symbol* are homophones because they are pronounced the same but have different spellings and meanings.

By the end of the week, students should know the lesson words. Students can use lesson words to write *yes* and *no* questions for classmates to answer.

Preteach Academic Vocabulary

 Academic Vocabulary Write the following terms on the board:

capitalization	focus
proper noun	announcement
chronological order	textbook

Have students share what they know about this week's Academic Vocabulary. Use the students' responses to assess their prior knowledge. Preteach the Academic Vocabulary by providing a student-friendly description, explanation, or example that clarifies the meaning of each term. Then ask students to restate the meaning of the Academic Vocabulary term in their own words.

Research and Inquiry
Identify Questions

Teach

Discuss the Question of the Week: *Why do we have symbols that represent freedom?* Tell students that they will each research one national symbol and why it represents freedom. They will present their findings to the class on Day 5 as an informational article.

Model

Think Aloud I need to choose one national symbol to research. To help me decide, I'll brainstorm a list of questions about symbols that represent freedom. *What are some symbols of freedom? Which symbols are national symbols that represent freedom? What is the history and meaning of the symbols?*

Guide practice

After students have formulated open-ended inquiry questions about the research topic, explain that tomorrow they will collect information from multiple sources of oral and written information, including reference texts, such as textbooks, and on-site inspections. To generate a research plan, help students identify key words that will guide their search for relevant information.

On their own

Have students work individually, in pairs, or in small groups to write an inquiry question.

INTERNET GUY
Don Leu

21st Century Skills

Weekly Inquiry Project
Day 1 Identify Questions
Day 2 Navigate/Search
Day 3 Analyze
Day 4 Synthesize
Day 5 Communicate

Academic Vocabulary

textbook a source of informational text, usually written about a specific topic

---

Small Group Time

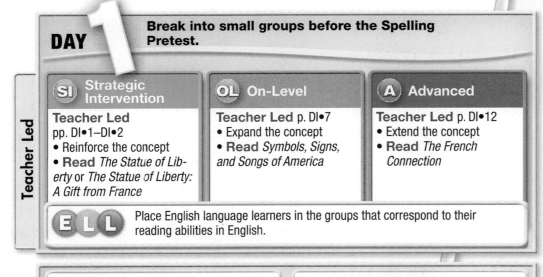

DAY 1

Break into small groups before the Spelling Pretest.

Teacher Led

SI Strategic Intervention	**OL On-Level**	**A Advanced**
Teacher Led pp. DI•1–DI•2 • Reinforce the concept • **Read** *The Statue of Liberty* or *The Statue of Liberty: A Gift from France*	**Teacher Led** p. DI•7 • Expand the concept • **Read** *Symbols, Signs, and Songs of America*	**Teacher Led** p. DI•12 • Extend the concept • **Read** *The French Connection*

ELL Place English language learners in the groups that correspond to their reading abilities in English.

Practice Stations	**Independent Activities**
• Read for Meaning • Get Fluent • Word Work	• Concept Talk Video • *Reader's and Writer's Notebook* • Vocabulary Activities

---

English Language Learners
Multilingual vocabulary
Students can apply knowledge of their home languages to acquire new English vocabulary by using the Multilingual Vocabulary Lists (*ELL Handbook* pp. 433–444).

Objectives

- Spell words with the vowel sounds in *moon* and *foot.*
- Correctly use capital letters.
- Write uppercase cursive letters *T* and *F.*

Spelling Pretest
Vowel Sounds in *moon* and *foot*

Introduce   Tell students to think of words with the vowel sounds they hear in the words *moon* and *foot.* This week we will spell words with the same vowel sounds you hear in *moon* and *foot.*

Pretest   Use these sentences to administer the spelling pretest. Say each word, read the sentence, and repeat the word.

1. **few**	I brought a **few** apples.
2. **school**	I forgot my backpack at **school.**
3. **true**	Is the answer **true** or false?
4. **goose**	The **goose** is on the pond.
5. **fruit**	I eat **fruit** as my snack.
6. **cookie**	Would you like a **cookie?**
7. **cushion**	The **cushion** is tied to the chair.
8. **noodle**	The **noodle** is long and skinny.
9. **bookmark**	Put the **bookmark** in the book.
10. **balloon**	I got a **balloon** at the party.
11. **suit**	Did Dad wear a **suit** to work?
12. **chew**	It is hard to **chew** taffy.
13. **glue**	Just a drop of **glue** is enough.
14. **Tuesday**	I was sick on **Tuesday.**
15. **bushel**	We need a **bushel** of apples.

Challenge words

16. **bamboo**	Pandas like to eat **bamboo.**
17. **mildew**	The basement smelled of **mildew.**
18. **soothe**	She tried to **soothe** the crying baby.
19. **barefoot**	I like to go **barefoot** in the summer.
20. **renewal**	Spring is a time of **renewal.**

Self-correct   After the pretest, you can either display the correctly spelled words or spell them orally. Have students self-correct their pretests by rewriting misspelled words correctly.

On their own   For additional practice, use *Let's Practice It!* page 361 on the *Teacher Resources DVD-ROM.*

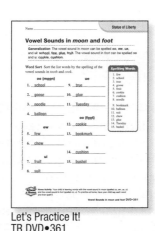

Let's Practice It!
TR DVD•361

Conventions
Capital Letters

Teach

Display Grammar Transparency 26, and read aloud the explanation and examples in the box. Remind students proper nouns and proper adjectives that should be capitalized include names, official titles of people, days of the week, months of the year, holidays, most words in book titles, and names of famous periods in history.

Model

Model writing correctly the words that should have capital letters for items 1 and 2. Apply the rules for capital letters to show how you determined which words should be capitalized.

Guide practice

Guide students to complete items 3–5. Record the correct responses on the transparency.

Daily Fix-It

Use Daily Fix-It numbers 1 and 2 in the right margin.

Connect to oral language

Have students read sentences 6 and 7 on the transparency and write them using capital letters correctly.

Grammar Transparency 26, TR DVD

Handwriting
Cursive Letters *T, F*

 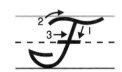

Model etter formation

Display capital cursive letters *T* and *F.* Follow the stroke instructions pictured to model letter formation.

Model letter slant

Explain that writing legibly means letters are the correct size, form, and slant. When you write in cursive, make sure all of the letters slant the same way. They may slant to the right, to the left, or straight up and down, but all letters should slant in the same direction. Model writing this sentence with proper letter slant: *Three students from Fairbanks won awards.* Make sure the letters aren't too light, dark, or jagged.

Guide practice

Have students write these sentences: *Fred and Tom went to school. Frieda lives in Toledo.* Circulate around the room, guiding students.

Academic Vocabulary

Capitalization is when you use capital letters to begin a word.

A **proper noun** is the name of a specific person, place, or thing, which is capitalized.

Daily Fix-It

1. The classes visits the Washington Monument on tuesday. *(visit; Tuesday)*

2. is the Statue of Liberty or the Washington Monument biggest? *(Is; bigger)*

ELL

English Language Learners

Identifying vowel sounds Have students write the words *moon* and *foot* on index cards. Have them practice saying each word correctly. Then read the following list of words aloud: *good, shoot, boot, stood, hook, blue, new, should, boo,* and *wood.* Have students hold up either *moon* or *foot,* indicating which vowel sound they hear.

Handwriting: Place names To give students more practice writing capital cursive letters *T* and *F,* have them use an atlas to find names of countries, states, cities, or rivers that begin with *T* and *F.* Have them list these names in cursive.

MINI-LESSON

5-Day Planner
Guide to Mini-Lessons

DAY 1	Read Like a Writer
DAY 2	Main Ideas and Supporting Details
DAY 3	In Your Own Words
DAY 4	Revising Strategy: Adding
DAY 5	Proofread for Capitalization

Writing—Notes
Introduce

MINI-LESSON

Read Like a Writer

■ **Introduce** This week you will learn to take **notes.** Taking notes helps you keep track of and remember the most important information from an article or story. When you take notes, you write down in your own words the information that you want to remember.

Prompt	Think about the most important ideas in the selection. Now take notes on one part of the selection.
Trait	Focus/Ideas
Mode	Expository

Reader's and Writer's Notebook p. 387

■ **Examine Model Text** Let's read an example of notes taken on the selection "The Story of the Statue of Liberty." Have students read p. 387 of their *Reader's and Writer's Notebook.*

■ **Key Features** Notes focus on the most important facts and ideas in a selection. Have student volunteers read aloud each bullet point in the model and tell why it is important.

Notes often help you with a future writing task. Ask students to list the kinds of writing tasks in which notes would be helpful (i.e., research papers or tests).

Notes do not have to follow all the rules of writing. They may include abbreviations, short sentences, and sentence fragments. They may include key words. But it is still important that you spell and capitalize correctly. Remember, you may want to use your notes for a future writing task. Have students identify the proper nouns that must be spelled and capitalized correctly.

Review
Key features

Review the key features of notes with students. You may want to post the key features in the classroom or have students write them on note cards. As students take notes, they can refer to these key features.

Key Features of Notes

- used to capture the most important facts and ideas
- often help with a future writing task

- may include abbreviations, short sentences, and sentence fragments
- includes proper spelling and capitalization of proper nouns

ROUTINE **Quick Write for Fluency** **Team Talk**

1. **Talk** Have pairs take a few minutes to discuss the features of notes.
2. **Write** Each person writes one reason good notes are important.
3. **Share** Partners share their reasons with each other.

Routines Flip Chart

Wrap Up Your Day

✔ **Build Concepts** Have students discuss why we have symbols to represent freedom.

✔ **Oral Vocabulary** Have students use the Amazing Words they learned in context sentences.

✔ **Homework** Send home this week's Family Times Newsletter, *Let's Practice It!* pages 362–363 on the *Teacher Resources DVD-ROM.*

Let's Practice It!
TR DVD•362–363

Write Guy
Jeff Anderson

Trait-by-Trait: Organization

Organization is a trait of good writing, but let's not be so concerned with form that we forget about meaning. A student may develop a good way to communicate ideas that does not precisely follow the format we expect. There isn't only one way to reach the goal. And there isn't just one way to organize your writing. Reward creativity and help students see what other writers do in mentor texts.

English Language Learners
Read like a writer Remind students that notes help them keep track of important information. Select and reread aloud a paragraph from *The Story of the Statue of Liberty,* and guide students' note-taking by emphasizing important facts and ideas.

Preview DAY 2

Tell students that tomorrow they will read about the man who designed the Statue of Liberty.

Objectives
- Expand the weekly concept.
- Develop oral vocabulary.

Today at a Glance

Oral Vocabulary
dedication, competition

Phonics/Word Analysis
Ⓢ Vowel sounds /ü/ and /ů/

Literary Terms
Word choice

Text Structure
Chronological/sequence

Lesson Vocabulary
Ⓢ Prefix *un-*

Reading
"Emma and Liberty"
The Story of the Statue of Liberty

Fluency
Rate

Research and Inquiry
Navigate/Search

Conventions
Capital letters

Spelling
Vowel sounds in *moon* and *foot*

Writing
Notes

Concept Talk

Question of the Week

? **Why do we have symbols that represent freedom?**

Expand the concept

Remind students of the weekly concept question. Tell students that today they will begin reading *The Story of the Statue of Liberty.* As they read, encourage students to think about symbols of freedom.

Anchored Talk

Develop oral vocabulary

Use the photos on pp. 366–367 and the Read Aloud, "Let Freedom Ring," to talk about the Amazing Words: *impressive, tribute, enlighten,* and *contribution.* Add the words to the concept map to develop students' knowledge of the topic. Discuss the following questions. Remind students to listen attentively to other students and to answer with appropriate detail. Encourage students to build on others' ideas when they answer.

- What kinds of *contributions* might a symbol of freedom recognize?
- What types of *tributes* can citizens participate in to celebrate their freedom? Why is it important to participate in these events?
- How can the idea of freedom *enlighten* people? How does that help explain why there are many symbols that represent freedom?
- What might be *impressive* about a symbol of freedom?

Oral Vocabulary
Amazing Words

Amazing Words

Amazing Words

impressive	competition
tribute	recognizable
enlighten	disgrace
contribution	staggering
dedication	fund

Amazing Words   **Oral Vocabulary Routine**

Teach Amazing Words

① Introduce Write the Amazing Word *dedication* on the board. Have students say it aloud with you. Relate *dedication* to the photographs on pp. 366–367 and "Let Freedom Ring." Why might the Liberty Bell or the other items in the photographs have a *dedication* ceremony? Have students determine the definition of the word. (At a *dedication* ceremony, something or someone is named or honored.)

② Demonstrate Have students answer questions to demonstrate understanding. Why might there be a *dedication* for a historical building? Why might there be a *dedication* for a new road or bridge? Why might a person give a speech at a *dedication* ceremony?

③ Apply Have students apply their understanding. Do you think a dedication ceremony was held when our school first opened? (Possible response: Yes, because people would want to dedicate the school to education.)

See p. OV•1 to teach *competition.*

Routines Flip Chart

Apply Amazing Words

As students read "Emma and Liberty" on p. 373, have them think about why a *competition* to create a *dedication* for the Statue of Liberty would be popular.

Connect to reading

Explain that today students will read about how the Statue of Liberty was designed and built. As they read, they should think about how the Question of the Week and the Amazing Words *dedication* and *competition* apply to the Statue of Liberty.

ELL Reinforce Vocabulary Use the Day 2 instruction on ELL Poster 26 to teach lesson vocabulary and discuss the lesson concept.

ELL Poster 26

ELL

English Language Learners
Cognates Point out that the Amazing Words *dedication* and *competition* have Spanish cognates *dedicación* and *competición.*

Objectives

- Apply knowledge of letter-sound correspondences and syllable patterns to decode words in context and independent of context.

Check Word Reading

SUCCESS PREDICTOR

Phonics

 Vowel Sounds /ü/ and /ů/

Review — Review the vowel sounds /ü/ and /ů/ using Sound-Spelling Cards 68, 89, 90, 101, 102, and 103.

Read words independent of context — Display these words. Have the class blend the words. Then point to the words in random order and ask students to read them quickly.

clues	mood	igloo	pudding
juice	due	crook	wood

Corrective feedback — Model blending decodable words and then ask students to blend them with you.

Read words in context — Display these sentences. Have the class read the sentences.

Team Talk Have pairs take turns reading the sentences naturally.

> I read a **good book** today.
> A shingle on the **roof** came **loose**.
> I tested the water by **putting** my **foot** in the **pool**.

Don't Wait Until Friday

MONITOR PROGRESS **Check Word Reading**

Words with Vowel Sounds in *moon* and *foot*

Write the following words and have the class read them. Notice which words students miss during the group reading. Call on individuals to read some of the words.

cook	put	loon	glue	suit
tulip	relax	rapid	music	pupil
understood	bamboo	unhook	trooper	scooter

Spiral Review
Row 2 reviews words with V/CV and VC/V.

Row 3 contrasts words with /ü/ and *oo* /ů/.

If... students cannot read words with vowel sounds /ü/ and /ů/ at this point,

then... use the Day 1 Blending Strategy routine on p. 368a to reteach the vowel sounds /ü/ and /ů/. Use words from the Decodable Practice Passages (or Reader). Continue to monitor students' progress using other instructional opportunities during the week. See the Skills Trace on p. 368a.

Day 1	Day 2	Day 3	Day 4	Day 5
Check Oral Vocabulary	Check Word Reading	Check Retelling	Check Fluency	Check Oral Vocabulary

Success Predictor

Literary Terms
Word Choice

Teach word choice

Tell students that word choice refers to the specific words and phrases that authors choose to use in their writing. A writer's choice of words should be appropriate to the purpose of the text and for the audience. Writers can make their writing more interesting by choosing strong verbs, using memorable words and phrases, and including adjectives and adverbs that make ideas more specific.

Model word choice

Think Aloud Let's look at "Emma and Liberty" on page 373. The first sentence in the second paragraph uses good word choice to tell us a lot about what is happening in the story. Specific locations and adjectives tell us where Emma is. The phrase "breathless view" is a memorable phrase—only two words tell us what Emma is doing *and* what she is feeling at the same time.

Guide practice

Find an example of good word choice in "Coming to America."

On their own

Have students look for examples of word choice in other selections of their Student Edition.

Text Structure
Chronological/Sequence

Teach chronological/ sequence

Remind students that text structure refers to the way information or events in a story are organized. Stories follow a logical sequence but many historical selections are written in chronological order to show exactly when the real events occurred. Dates mentioned in the text help the reader understand chronological order.

Model the strategy

Think Aloud To discover the chronological order of *The Story of the Statue of Liberty,* let's look at the text. Page 376 introduces the Statue of Liberty and tells the sculptor's ideas for building it. It mentions that he came to America in 1871 and saw Bedloe's Island. On page 379, it says the arm was sent to Philadelphia in 1876. That tells the reader that the sculptor began work after 1871 and had completed the arm five years later.

Guide practice

Find other dates in *The Story of the Statue of Liberty.*

On their own

Have students list facts from *The Story of the Statue of Liberty* in chronological order.

Academic Vocabulary

chronological order events that are related in the order of their happening; also called **time order**

Word Reading

Success
Predictor

Objectives
- Use knowledge of word structure to find meanings of words with prefixes.
- Read grade-level text at an appropriate rate.

Vocabulary Strategy for
Prefix *un-*

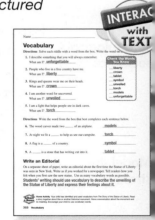

Student Edition p. W•5

Teach prefix *un-*

Tell students that prefixes can give clues to the meanings of unfamiliar words. Explain that they can use what they know about prefixes to determine the meaning of a word they don't know. When the prefix *un-* is added to the beginning of an adverb or adjective, it usually means "not _____." When it is added to a verb, it means the opposite of the verb. Refer students to *Words!* on p. W•5 in the Student Edition for additional practice. Then read "Emma and Liberty" on p. 373 with students.

Model the strategy

 Think Aloud Write on the board: *They pulled the cloth off, and as the statue was unveiled, we clapped.* I can use my understanding of word structure to determine the meaning of *unveiled.* I see the prefix *un-* in the word *unveiled.* I know that a prefix is added to the beginning of a word and changes the meaning of the root word. When I cover *un-,* I see the root word is *veiled,* which means "covered." When *un-* is added to a verb, such as *veiled,* it usually means the reverse of the verb. So the word *unveiled* means "removed the cover."

Guide practice

Write this sentence on the board: *The spectacular fireworks that lit up the sky were an unforgettable sight.* Have students determine the meaning of *unforgettable* using what they know about the prefix *un-* and root words. For additional support, use *Envision It! Pictured Vocabulary Cards* or *Tested Vocabulary Cards.*

On their own

Reread "Emma and Liberty" on p. 373. Have students look at the words *remarkable, seen,* and *like* and consider what their meanings would be if they added the prefix *un-.* For additional practice use *Reader's and Writer's Notebook* p. 388.

Reader's and Writer's Notebook p. 388

Objectives
• Understand the meaning of common prefixes and common suffixes, and understand how they affect the root word.

Envision It! | Words to Know

crown

liberty

torch

models
symbol
tablet
unforgettable
unveiled

READING STREET ONLINE
VOCABULARY ACTIVITIES
www.ReadingStreet.com

372

Vocabulary Strategy for

Prefix *un-*

Word Structure Prefixes can give you clues to the meanings of unfamiliar words. The prefix *un-* at the beginning of a word means "not ____." For example, *unpleasant* means "not pleasant." When *un-* is added to a verb, it usually means the reverse of the verb. For instance, *uncover* means "to remove a cover."

1. When you see an unfamiliar word with a prefix, cover up the prefix.

2. What does the base word mean without the prefix?

3. Add "not" in front of the word. Does this meaning make sense in the sentence?

Read "Emma and Liberty" on page 373. Look for words that have prefixes. Use your knowledge of prefixes to find the meanings of these words.

Words to Write Reread "Emma and Liberty." What symbols of freedom have you seen or heard about? Write about symbols of freedom. Use as many words from the Words to Know list as you can.

Emma and Liberty

Emma is visiting New York City. What she wants to see more than anything else is the remarkable Statue of Liberty. Emma knows everything about Liberty. She knows why the statue was made, who made it, and when it was unveiled. She knows how tall it is from its base to its crown, what its torch is made of, and what is written on the tablet. Emma has collected pictures of the statue and reproduced models of it. However, she has never seen the real Liberty.

From Battery Park in Lower Manhattan, Emma has a breathless view of the Statue of Liberty in the distance. She waits in line for the boat that will safely take her to the island. As the boat gets nearer, Emma imagines what it was like for the immigrants who sailed past Liberty as they arrived in America.

At last Emma is standing at Liberty's feet. She tilts her head back to look up at this symbol of freedom. It is an unforgettable moment.

Your Turn!

 Need a Review? For additional help with prefixes, see *Words!*

Ready to Try It? Read *The Story of the Statue of Liberty* on pp. 374–385.

373

Student Edition pp. 372–373

Reread for Fluency
Rate

Model fluent reading

Read paragraph 1 of "Emma and Liberty" aloud with appropriate rate and expression. Tell students that you are reading the passage at a comfortable rate and with expression by varying your tone and volume. You read the passage just the way you speak.

ROUTINE **Oral Rereading**

1 **Read** For "Emma and Liberty," use paragraph 2 on p. 373.

2 **Model** Have students listen as you read the paragraph with appropriate rate and expression.

3 **Guide practice** Have students read along with you.

4 **On their own** For optimal fluency, students should reread three or four times at an appropriate rate.

Routines Flip Chart

Differentiated Instruction

SI Strategic Intervention

Prefix *un-* Provide additional practice with using the prefix *un-* to figure out the meaning of a word: *unhappy, uncertain,* and *uncomfortable.*

ELL

English Language Learners

Word structure Provide extra support to develop students' understanding of the *un-*. Write *unforgettable* and *unbelievable* on the board and point out the prefix, root, and suffix. Have volunteers draw lines between the word parts. Then have them define each word and use it in a sentence.

Build Academic Vocabulary
Use the lesson vocabulary pictured on p. 372 to teach the meanings of *crown, liberty,* and *torch.* Call on pairs to write the words on sticky notes and use them to label images of the words on the ELL Poster.

Objectives

- Understand key features of narrative nonfiction.
- Use the title and illustrations to preview and predict.
- Set a purpose for reading.

The Story of the Statue of Liberty

by Betsy & Giulio Maestro

Genre **Narrative nonfiction** gives information about real people and events in the form of a story. What special event does this selection tell about?

374

Question of the Week
Why do we have symbols that represent freedom?

Let's **Think About Reading!**

Student Edition pp. 374–375

Build Background

Discuss symbols of freedom

Team Talk Have students turn to a partner and discuss the Question of the Week and these questions about symbols of freedom. Remind students to ask and answer questions with appropriate detail and to give suggestions that build on the ideas of others.

- What does freedom mean to you? When do you feel free?
- What are some freedoms that people have in the United States?
- What is an example of a symbol?

Connect to selection

Have students discuss their answers with the class. Remind students to listen attentively to speakers, to ask relevant questions, and to make pertinent comments. Possible responses: Freedom is when you are allowed to do what you want or say what you think. I feel free when my friends and I ride our bikes. In the United States people are free to say what they think. There are many symbols of freedom, including the eagle and the American flag. For additional opportunities to build background, use the Background Building Audio.

Prereading Strategies

Genre

Tell students that **narrative nonfiction** is writing that shares true information with the reader in the form of a story. Narrative nonfiction tells about real people, places, and events. It often follows chronological order—the order in which events occurred. It sometimes has a beginning, middle, and end.

Preview and predict

Have students preview the title and illustrations in *The Story of the Statue of Liberty*. Be sure they notice the poem on the last page. Have students predict what they will find out as they read.

Set purpose

Prior to reading, have students set their own purpose for reading this selection. To help students set a purpose, ask them to think about symbols they know and why they are important.

Strategy Response Log

Have students use p. 32 in the *Reader's and Writer's Notebook* to review and use the strategy of questioning.

Small Group Time

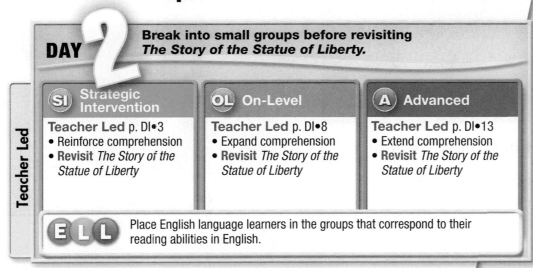

DAY 2

Break into small groups before revisiting *The Story of the Statue of Liberty*.

Teacher Led

SI Strategic Intervention

Teacher Led p. DI•3
• Reinforce comprehension
• **Revisit** *The Story of the Statue of Liberty*

OL On-Level

Teacher Led p. DI•8
• Expand comprehension
• **Revisit** *The Story of the Statue of Liberty*

A Advanced

Teacher Led p. DI•13
• Extend comprehension
• **Revisit** *The Story of the Statue of Liberty*

ELL Place English language learners in the groups that correspond to their reading abilities in English.

Practice Stations
• Words to Know
• Get Fluent
• Word Wise

Independent Activities
• Background Building Audio
• *Reader's and Writer's Notebook*
• Research and Inquiry

Differentiated Instruction

A **Advanced**

Symbols Have students create a bulletin board for posting symbols and descriptions of what they represent.

 **Multidraft Reading**

For **Whole Group** instruction, choose one of the reading options below. For each reading have students set the purpose indicated.

Option 1

Day 2 Read the selection. Use Guide Comprehension to monitor and clarify understanding.

Day 3 Reread the selection. Use Extend Thinking to develop higher-order thinking skills.

Option 2

Day 2 Read the first half of the selection, using both Guide Comprehension and Extend Thinking instruction.

Day 3 Read the second half of the selection, using both Guide Comprehension and Extend Thinking Instruction.

English Language Learners

Build background To build background, review the selection summary in English (*ELL Handbook* p. 181). Use the Retelling Cards to provide visual support for the summary.

Objectives

◎ Identify statements of fact and opinion to aid comprehension.

OPTION 1 Guide Comprehension Skills and Strategies

Teach Fact and Opinion

 Fact and Opinion Write the following sentences on the board and have students determine which is a statement of fact and which is a statement of opinion. *The Statue of Liberty stands on an island in New York Harbor.* (fact) *She is a beautiful sight to all who pass her by.* (opinion)

Corrective Feedback

If... students are unable to distinguish between statements of fact and statements of opinion,
then... use the model to guide students in identifying facts and opinions.

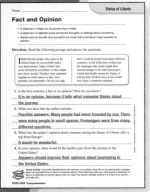

Let's Practice It!
TR DVD•364

Model the Skill

Think Aloud How could I check that the first sentence is a statement of fact? **(check a reference source)** So, the first sentence can be proved true or false.

Let's Think About...

Before you read, ask questions. Look at the pictures and scan the highlighted words. Then focus on what you want to find out.
◎ **Questioning**

1

Let's Think About...

As you read, keep asking yourself, "What does this mean?" and "Is this important? Why?"
◎ **Questioning**

2

The Statue of Liberty stands on an island in New York Harbor. She is a beautiful sight to all who pass by her. Each year, millions of visitors ride the ferry out to the island. They climb to the top of the statue and enjoy the lovely view.

A young French sculptor named Frédéric Auguste Bartholdi visited America in 1871. When he saw Bedloe's Island in New York Harbor, he knew it was just the right place for a statue he wanted to build.

Bartholdi had created many other statues and monuments, but this one was to be very special. It was to be a present from the people of France to the people of America, as a remembrance of the old friendship between the two countries.

376

Student Edition pp. 376–377

OPTION 2 Extend Thinking Think Critically

Higher-Order Thinking Skills

 Fact and Opinion • Evaluation What is another statement of fact on these pages? How do you know? What is another statement of opinion on these pages? How do you know? Possible responses: Another statement of fact is *A young French sculptor named Frédéric Auguste Bartholdi visited America in 1871.* This is a fact because the statement can be proved true or false. Another statement of opinion is *They climb up to the top of the statue to enjoy the lovely view.* It is someone's judgment or belief that the view from the top of the statue is lovely.

Let's Think About...

1 Examples might include: *What is the view like from the top of the statue? What other statues did Bartholdi create?*

2 Examples might include: What is Bedloe's Island? Why is the friendship between America and France important? It will help me understand what I am reading.

3 Examples might include: Why is the statue modeled after a woman? Who is Bartholdi? What did he create? Where is it located? How did he get picked to make the statue?

What word in the second sentence tells me that it might be a statement of opinion? *(beautiful)* A statement of opinion is someone's judgment, belief, or way of thinking. It cannot be proved true or false.

When Bartholdi got back to Paris, he made sketches and some small models. The statue would be a woman whom he would call Liberty. She would be a symbol of the freedom in the New World. She would hold a lamp in her raised hand to welcome people who came to America. She would be *Liberty Enlightening the World.*

Let's Think About...

Ask yourself, "Who, what, where, why, how?"

 Questioning

3

377

Compare and Contrast • Analysis How was creating the Statue of Liberty similar to other projects that Frédéric Auguste Bartholdi had done? How was it different? **Possible response:** Frédéric Auguste Bartholdi had created many other statues and monuments. The Statue of Liberty project was different because it was a gift from the people of France to the people of America.

On Their Own

Have students reread pp. 376–377 to find more statements of fact about the Statue of Liberty and its creator. Have them discuss opinions people might have about the statue. For additional practice, use *Let's Practice It!* page 364 on the *Teacher Resources DVD-ROM.*

Differentiated Instruction

 Strategic Intervention

Fact and opinion Give students additional examples of statements of fact and opinion. Have students work in pairs to identify facts and opinions.

Connect to Social Studies

Have students locate New York City and Paris, France, on a world map. Ask them to estimate the distance between them. Explain that New York City is a city in the state of New York in the United States of America on the continent of North America. Paris is in the country of France on the continent of Europe. Use a ruler and map scale to figure the approximate distance between the cities (3,635 miles).

ELL

English Language Learners
Activate prior knowledge Discuss with students how the Statue of Liberty was designed. Ask students to share what they know about how a *sketch* or a *model* might be used to design a statue or building. Provide an example of each design technique. Then have students sketch or make a clay model of a statue or building that they would like to build.

Objectives
• Identify author's purpose to aid comprehension.

OPTION 1 Skills and Strategies, continued

Teach Author's Purpose

Review **Author's Purpose** Remind students that an author's purpose is the reason or reasons that an author has for writing. Then ask students what the authors' purpose is on pp. 378–379.

Corrective Feedback

If... students are unable to explain the authors' purpose,

then... use the model to guide students in identifying the author's purpose.

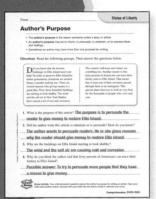

Let's Practice It!
TR DVD•365

Model the Skill

Think Aloud What details do the authors describe? (what the statue was like, who worked on it, where parts of the statue traveled) I can tell that the authors' purpose is to inform, to describe the statue and how it was built.

The statue would be very large and very strong. Bartholdi wanted people to be able to climb up inside the statue and look out over the harbor from the crown and torch.

Many well-known artists, engineers, and craftsmen gave him ideas about how to build the statue. First, a huge skeleton was constructed from strong steel.

Many people worked together in a large workshop. Some worked on Liberty's head and crown. Others worked on her right hand, which would hold the torch

In her left hand she would hold a tablet with the date July 4, 1776, written on it. This is when the Declaration of Independence was signed.

Let's **Think** About...

Why was the date July 4, 1776, included on the statue? Why is that important?
Important Ideas

4

378

Student Edition pp. 378–379

OPTION 2 Think Critically, continued

Higher-Order Thinking Skills

Review **Author's Purpose • Analysis** If the author's purpose was to entertain, how might the selection have been different? Possible response: There might have been dialogue and fewer facts. The authors probably would have given more information about what Bartholdi was like as a person and told some stories about his life.

Let's **Think** About...

4 July 4, 1776 is included on the statue because that is the date of the signing of the Declaration of Independence. It is important because it stands for the beginning of freedom and liberty for America.

5 Possible response: Exhibiting parts of the Statue of Liberty was a way for many people to see it and learn about its creation. It also encouraged people to donate money to help pay the expense.

The authors are also writing to persuade. They want to convince the reader that the Statue of Liberty is an impressive and important monument to freedom. For example, the authors say the statue was very large and strong, and that many well-known artists, engineers, and craftsmen worked on it.

The arm holding the torch was sent to Philadelphia for America's 100th birthday celebration in 1876. Afterward, it stood in Madison Square in New York City for a number of years.

Liberty's head was shown at the World's Fair in Paris during this time. Visitors were able to climb inside and look around. In this way, money was raised to pay for the statue.

Let's Think About...

Why might the makers of the Statue of Liberty exhibit it in different parts and places for a few years?
Inferring

5

379

Generalize • Evaluation What is a generalization you could make about how people felt about the Statue of Liberty? Provide text evidence to support it. **Possible response:** People were excited and anxious to see it. People paid money to go inside the head at the World's Fair.

Inferring • Synthesis Using information you know, why do you think well-known artists, engineers, and craftsmen helped Bartholdi build the statue? **Possible response:** The Statue of Liberty was a well-known project at the time, so talented builders probably wanted to take part. It was also a symbol of freedom, an idea that the builders probably believed in.

On Their Own

Have students reread pp. 378–379. Ask them to explain what details are included to persuade the reader that Americans value the Statue of Liberty as an impressive and important monument to freedom. For additional practice, use *Let's Practice It!* page 365 on the *Teacher Resources DVD-ROM*.

Differentiated Instruction

 Strategic Intervention

Generalize Remind students that you make a generalization after thinking about a number of facts and what they have in common. Provide additional examples of generalizations. Then guide students to use details from the text to make a generalization about how people in America and France felt about each other.

Connect to Social Studies

Read a copy of the Declaration of Independence and discuss its meaning as a class.

ELL

English Language Learners

Multisyllabic words Guide students through steps for reading multisyllabic words. First, look for word parts or chunks you recognize. Say the parts or chunks to yourself. Then read the whole word. Finally, ask yourself if the word makes sense in the sentence. Have students work in small groups to read *constructed, Independence,* and *celebration.*

Author's purpose Remind students that the authors used the adjectives *large* and *strong* to persuade readers that the Statue of Liberty is an important monument. Have pairs of students discuss words they might use to persuade a friend that something is important.

Objectives

◎ Ask relevant questions to aid comprehension.

OPTION 1 Skills and Strategies, continued

Teach Questioning

🔊 Questioning Explain that good readers check their understanding by asking literal, interpretive, and evaluative questions to clarify any confusion and identify statements of fact and opinion. Ask students what questions they have about how the Statue of Liberty was completed.

Corrective Feedback

If... students are unable to provide questions,

then... use the model to guide students to ask questions about the text.

Student Edition pp. 380–381

OPTION 2 Think Critically, continued

Higher-Order Thinking Skills

🔊 Questioning • Analysis How might you clarify the information in the text about how the Statue of Liberty was packed and shipped from France to the United States? Possible response: To clarify information, I can think of literal questions about how the statue was packed and shipped. For example, *How were the pieces packed? How were the pieces transported?* Then I can locate details in the text to answer my questions.

Model the Strategy

Think Aloud As I read, I stop, think, and record questions that I have about the text. For example, I'm not sure I understand how the copper on the outside of the statue was held in place. That is a literal question because I should be able to find the answer in the text.

Then, skin of gleaming copper was put onto the skeleton and held in place with iron straps. As the huge statue grew, all of Paris watched with great fascination.

380

Let's Think About...

6 It was much too big to ship in one piece so they had to take it apart and pack it into crates.

Check Predictions Have students look back at the predictions they made earlier and discuss whether they were accurate. Then have students preview the rest of the selection and either adjust their predictions accordingly or make new predictions.

Then I can go back and reread page 380 with that question in mind. What can you find in the text about how the copper was attached to the statue's skeleton? **(It was held in place with iron straps.)** Asking questions helps me monitor and clarify my understanding, making corrections and adjustments as I read.

On Their Own

Have students think of literal, interpretive, and evaluative questions they have about the information on pp. 380–381. Then have them reread the pages to answer the questions.

Differentiated Instruction

Strategic Intervention

Questioning Review with students that asking *relevant* questions means asking questions about the most important information in the text.

A **Advanced**

Questioning Have students write three questions (one literal, one interpretive, and one evaluative) for discussion about the text they have read so far. Then have them discuss their questions with partners.

Finally, in 1884, Liberty was completed. There was a big celebration in Paris. Many famous people came to see her. Only a few had the energy to climb all the way to the crown—168 steps!

Then began the hard work of taking Liberty apart for the long voyage across the Atlantic Ocean. Each piece was marked and packed into a crate. There were 214 crates in all. They were carried by train and then put on a ship to America.

Let's **Think** About...

Why did they take the statue apart after it was finally finished?
Inferring

6

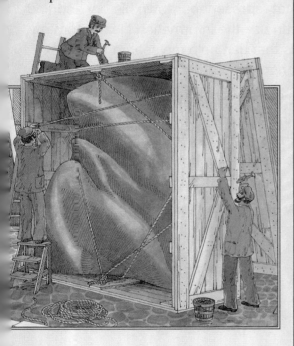

381

English Language Learners
Monitor comprehension Have students work in small groups to summarize the story events so far. Have them discuss questions they have about story events to clarify understanding. Use a graphic organizer to show the events.

Background Knowledge • Synthesis • Text to World On page 380, the authors describe people's fascination with the statue as it was completed in Paris. Can you think of something being built today that fascinates people? Possible responses: There are many impressive building projects today. Some examples include buildings over 100 stories high, bridges over a mile long, large ships and planes, sports arenas, and space shuttles.

Main Idea and Details • Analysis What is the main idea of the last paragraph on page 381? What details support it? Possible response: The statue was taken apart and shipped to America. Details include: Each piece was packed into a crate. There were 24 crates in all. They were carried by train to a ship.

If you want to teach this selection in two sessions, stop here.

Objectives

- Find pertinent information from multiple sources of oral and written information.
- Use capital letters for proper nouns.
- Capitalize beginnings of sentences and greetings.
- Practice correctly spelling words with the vowel sounds in *moon* and *foot*.

Research and Inquiry
Navigate/Search

Teach

Have students generate a research plan for gathering information about their topics. Suggest that students use multiple sources of written and oral information to gather facts for their informational article. Have students review their inquiry questions and decide on the best sources for answers to their questions: reference texts, online sources, or an on-site inspection. Have students search reference sources and the Internet using their questions and keywords. Remind them to skim and scan each source and use headings and other text features to locate information about their topic.

Model

Think Aloud When looking for information about symbols that represent freedom, I can go to our town hall and see the American flag that is raised outside. I can also interview town officials and historians about the flag and other symbols that represent our town history and find out why they stand for freedom. I can use the information I learn from my on-site inspection to form keywords that can help me search for more information in reference texts and on the Internet.

Guide practice

Have students review the reference texts they identified. Show them how to use an index to find information in a textbook or other reference text. Explain that indexes list keywords in alphabetical order and give the page number where the keyword or topic can be found. Using an index is an important way to locate information in a reference text quickly.

On their own

Have students continue their review of reference texts, taking notes as they find relevant information.

Conventions
Capital Letters

Teach

Remind students that names of particular people, places, and things, and the first letter in a sentence or greeting, begin with capital letters. Abbreviations, official titles, and initials in a person's name should also be capitalized.

Guide practice

Write these sentences: *every year, on the fourth of july, the united states of america celebrates its independence. It is officer michael jones' favorite holiday.* Then explain which letters should be capitalized. *Every* should be capitalized. It is the first word in the sentence. *Fourth* and *July* are capitalized. They are important words in the name of a holiday. *United, States,* and *America* are capitalized. They are words in the name of a country. *Officer Michael Jones* is also capitalized, because it is an official title that appears directly before a formal name.

Daily Fix-It

Use Daily Fix-It numbers 3 and 4 in the right margin.

Connect to oral language

Have students list proper nouns, titles, and abbreviations that are capitalized in the first part of *The Story of the Statue of Liberty.* Have students explain orally why capital letters were used.

On their own

For additional practice, use *Reader's and Writer's Notebook* p. 389.

Spelling
Vowel Sounds in *moon* and *foot*

Teach

Remind students that their spelling words for this week have the vowel sounds in *moon (oo, ew, ue, ui)* and *foot (oo, u).* Model how to spell words with these vowel sounds. Listen to the sounds in *school: /s/ /k/ /ü/ /l/.* I'll write the first two sounds, */s/ /k/.* Then I'll write the next sound, */ü/.* Then I'll write the final sound, */l/.* I spelled the sounds in *school, s-c-h-o-o-l.*

Guide practice

Have students write each spelling word and underline the vowels that make the vowel sound in *moon* or *foot.*

On their own

For additional practice, use *Reader's and Writer's Notebook* p. 390.

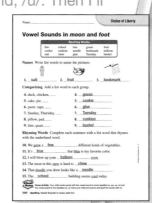
Reader's and Writer's Notebook p. 390

Daily Fix-It

3. Maria and her daugter came to the United States in november. *(daughter; November)*
4. The Statue of Liberty greated Maria and she. *(greeted; her)*

Reader's and Writer's Notebook p. 389

English Language Learners

Conventions To provide students with practice on capitalization, use the modified grammar lessons in the *ELL Handbook* and the Grammar Jammer online: www.ReadingStreet.com

Practice proper nouns Remind students that proper nouns name particular places. Use a map to point out some of the places mentioned in *The Story of the Statue of Liberty.* Translate, show pictures, or draw to show the meaning of unfamiliar words, such as *harbor, island,* and *fair.* Have students repeat the names after you.

DAY 2 Language Arts

Objectives
• Identify and record the main ideas and supporting details of a selection.

Writing—Notes
Writing Trait: Focus/Ideas

Introduce the prompt

Remind students that the selection they are reading this week, *The Story of the Statue of Liberty,* is an example of narrative nonfiction. It tells a story, so it is a narrative. It tells a true story, so it is nonfiction. Narrative nonfiction often includes many details about the topic. These details support—or give more information about—the main ideas.

> **Writing Prompt**
> Think about the most important ideas in the selection.
> Now take notes on one part of the selection.

Select main ideas

 Think Aloud

To help students practice taking simple notes, tell or display a short story about eating breakfast. Have students list only the important information. Remind students that they do not need to write complete sentences. Jane had a good breakfast. She had cereal and toast. She drank a glass of orange juice. Then she ate a banana and threw the peel in the trash. When she looked at the clock, it was time to leave for school. She grabbed her backpack and went to school.

Corrective feedback

Circulate around the room as students begin to list information from the story. Confer briefly with students who seem to be having trouble. Ask them what information in the story supports the main idea that Jane had a good breakfast.

MINI-LESSON

Main Idea and Details

▪ When you take notes, you only write down the most important information. A Main Idea and Details chart can help you identify the most important information. Display the graphic organizer and show students where to write the main idea of a section and where to write the supporting details.

▪ Read aloud the first two paragraphs on p. 378. Point out that "The statue would be very large and strong" is a main idea.

▪ Point out that the next sentence tells you why Bartholdi wanted the statue to be so large and strong, so this is a supporting detail. Ask students what other details the author gives that tell more about the main idea.

Have students use the Main Idea and Details chart on p. 391 of their *Reader's and Writer's Notebook* to continue adding details to their lists.

ROUTINE Quick Write for Fluency Team Talk

1. **Talk** Have pairs talk about why it is important to identify the main ideas and supporting details in an article or story.

2. **Write** Each student writes a sentence telling why he or she should include main ideas and supporting details in his or her notes.

3. **Share** Pairs read one another's writing and share what they wrote.

Routines Flip Chart

Wrap Up Your Day

✓ **Build Concepts** What did you learn about symbols of freedom?

✓ **Fact and Opinion** How did identifying facts and opinions in the text help you understand the text?

✓ **Questioning** What questions did you ask to help you find out what was important in the text?

Differentiated Instruction

 Strategic Intervention

Main idea and details Have students write each main idea on one side of an index card. The other side of the index card can be used for writing the supporting details.

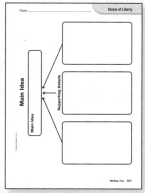

Reader's and Writer's Notebook p. 391

Teacher Tip

If students are having trouble differentiating between main ideas and supporting details, remind them that the main idea is the big idea or most important idea of a paragraph or section. The main idea answers the question "What is this section mainly about?"

Preview DAY 3

Tell students that tomorrow they will read about how the statue got to the United States.

Objectives
- Expand the weekly concept.
- Develop oral vocabulary.

Today at a Glance

Oral Vocabulary
recognizable, disgrace

Phonics/Word Analysis
Vowel sounds /ü/ and /u̇/

Comprehension Check/Retelling
Discuss questions

Reading
The Story of the Statue of Liberty

Think Critically
Retelling

Fluency
Rate

Research and Study Skills
Time line

Research and Inquiry
Analyze

Conventions
Capital letters

Spelling
Vowel sounds in *moon* and *foot*

Writing
Notes

Concept Talk

Question of the Week
Why do we have symbols that represent freedom?

Expand the concept

Remind students of the Question of the Week. Discuss how the question relates to symbols of freedom. Remind students to make pertinent comments in a discussion. Tell students that today they will read about how the Statue of Liberty was assembled on Bedloe's Island in New York Harbor and how Americans celebrated the new symbol of freedom. Encourage students to think about why a recognizable symbol of freedom like the Statue of Liberty is so powerful.

Anchored Talk

Develop oral vocabulary

Use text features—the title and illustrations—to review pp. 374–381 of *The Story of the Statue of Liberty.* Discuss the Amazing Words *dedication* and *competition.* Add these and other concept related words to the concept map. Use the following questions to develop students' understanding of the concept. Remind students to ask and answer questions with appropriate detail and to give suggestions based on the ideas of others.

- Why is a celebration of a symbol, such as a *dedication* ceremony, important?

- At times, the United States has held *competitions* for artists or architects to design a symbol or monument to represent an important person or event. Why do you think designers would want to enter a *competition* to design a symbol for our country?

Oral Vocabulary
Amazing Words

Amazing Words

impressive   competition
tribute   recognizable
enlighten   disgrace
contribution staggering
dedication   fund

Amazing Words **Oral Vocabulary Routine**

Teach Amazing Words

1 **Introduce** Write the Amazing Word *recognizable* on the board. Have students say it aloud with you. Yesterday we learned that the Statue of Liberty is one of the most *recognizable* symbols of freedom. Have students determine the definition of the word. (Something that you know and can identify is *recognizable*.)

2 **Demonstrate** Have students answer questions to demonstrate understanding. Can you think of other symbols of freedom that are *recognizable* to many people? (Possible responses: American flag, bald eagle, Liberty Bell) What are the most *recognizable* symbolic features of the Statue of Liberty? (Possible responses: the tablet with July 4, 1776 on it, the lamp, the crown)

3 **Apply** Have students apply their understanding. What is a synonym for *recognizable*? *(familiar)*

See p. OV•1 to teach *disgrace*.

Routines Flip Chart

Apply Amazing Words

As students read pp. 382–385 of *The Story of the Statue of Liberty,* have them consider how the Amazing Words *recognizable* and *disgrace* apply to the effort to erect the Statue of Liberty on Bedloe's Island.

Connect to reading

Explain that today students will read about how the Statue of Liberty was assembled in the United States and how Americans celebrate this important symbol. As they read, students should think about how the Question of the Week and the Amazing Words *recognizable* and *disgrace* apply to the story of the statue.

ELL **Expand Vocabulary** Use the Day 3 instruction on ELL Poster 26 to help students expand vocabulary.

ELL Poster 26

The Story of the Statue of Liberty **382b**

DAY 3 Get **Ready** to **Read**

Objectives

◎ Blend and read words with vowel sounds /ü/ and /u̇/.

• Apply knowledge of sound-spellings to decode unknown words when reading.

• Decode and read words in context and independent of context.

Phonics
Build Words

Model word building

Now we are going to build words with the vowel sounds /ü/ and /u̇/. Write *cook* and blend it. Watch me change *k* in *cook* to *l*. Model blending the new word, *cool*.

Guide practice

Write *book* and have the class blend it with you. Have students spell *book* with their letter tiles. Monitor students' work.

Corrective feedback

For corrective feedback, model the correct spelling and have students correct their tiles.

• Change the *k* in *book* to *m*. Say the new word together.

b o o m

• Change the *b* in *boom* to *l*. Say the new word together.

l o o m

• Change the *m* in *loom* to *k*. Say the new word together.

l o o k

• Change the *l* in *look* to *sh*. Say the new word together.

s h o o k

Fluent Word Reading

Model

Write *shoot*. I know the sounds for *sh, oo,* and *t.* Blend them and read the word *shoot.*

Guide practice

Write the words below. Say the sounds in your head for each spelling you see. When I point to the word, we'll read it together. Allow one second per sound previewing time for the first reading.

| bloom | push | foot | blue | newt | ruin |

On their own

Have students read the list above three or four times, until they can read one word per second.

Blend and Read

Read words independent of context

Have students turn to p. 129 in *Decodable Practice Readers 3.2* and find the first list of words. Each word in this list has the vowel sound /ü/, spelled *oo, ew, ue,* or *ui,* or the vowel sound /ů/, spelled *oo* or *u.* Let's blend and read these words. Be sure that students identify the correct vowel sound in each word.

Next, have students read the high-frequency words.

Preview Decodable Practice Passage

Have students read the title and preview the story. Tell them that they will read words with vowel sounds /ü/ and /ů/.

Read words in context

Chorally read the story along with the students. Have students identify words in the story that have the vowel sounds /ü/ and /ů/. Make sure that students are monitoring their accuracy when they decode words.

Team Talk Pair students and have them take turns reading the story aloud to each other. Monitor students as they read to check for proper pronunciation and appropriate pacing.

Decodable Practice
Passage 26B

Differentiated Instruction

 Advanced

Paragraph writing Have students work in pairs to choose 4 or 5 /ü/ and /ů/ words to use in writing a paragraph. Have pairs exchange and read each other's paragraphs.

Objectives

◎ Identify statements of fact and opinion to support comprehension.

◎ Use the questioning strategy to aid comprehension.

◎ Use prefixes to determine the meanings of words.

Comprehension Check

Have students discuss each question with a partner. Ask several pairs to share their responses.

☑ **Genre • Analysis**

Narrative nonfiction often uses time-order words such as *first, next, then, when,* and *finally* to signal the sequence of events. Find some time-order words on the pages you just read. How do they help tell the story? Possible responses: *When* (p. 377), *First* (p. 378), *Afterward* (p. 379), and *Finally* (p. 381). These words help the reader understand the order of the events.

☑ **Fact and Opinion • Evaluation**

Read the first sentence on page 379. Is the sentence a statement of fact or opinion? How do you know? Possible response: The sentence is a statement of fact, because it can be proved true or false. I could check an encyclopedia to find out whether the statue's torch was sent to Philadelphia for America's 100th birthday celebration.

☑ **Questioning • Analysis**

What details did Bartholdi include in the design of the Statue of Liberty to symbolize freedom? Possible response: Bartholdi designed the statue as a woman holding up a lamp. The lamp is a symbol of welcoming people to the United States. The lamp also represents the idea of freedom that enlightened the New World. Liberty also holds a tablet with the date July 4, 1776 to represent the Declaration of Independence.

☑ **Prefix *un-* • Synthesis**

A prefix is a group of letters added to the beginning of a word that changes the meaning of the word. You will see the word *unveiled* in the next part of the story. If the prefix *un-* means "not" or "do the opposite of," what does *unveiled* mean? Possible response: I know that *veiled* means "covered." If something is *unveiled* it means it is not covered, or that a cover is removed.

☑ **Connect text to world**

The Statue of Liberty represents liberty and friendship. What other things does it represent? Possible response: The statue represents freedom and a welcome to immigrants.

Strategy Response Log

Have students write questions about the events of *The Story of the Statue of Liberty* on p. 32 in the *Reader's and Writer's Notebook.*

Check Retelling

Have students retell pp. 376–381 of *The Story of the Statue of Liberty,* summarizing information in the text in logical order. Encourage students to use the illustrations in their retellings.

Corrective feedback

If... students leave out important details,
then... have students look back through the illustrations in the selection.

Small Group Time

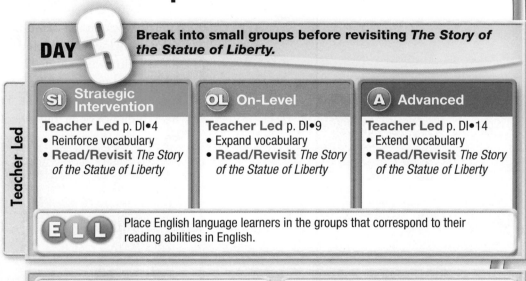

DAY 3

Break into small groups before revisiting *The Story of the Statue of Liberty.*

Teacher Led

SI Strategic Intervention	**OL On-Level**	**A Advanced**
Teacher Led p. DI•4 • Reinforce vocabulary • **Read/Revisit** *The Story of the Statue of Liberty*	Teacher Led p. DI•9 • Expand vocabulary • **Read/Revisit** *The Story of the Statue of Liberty*	Teacher Led p. DI•14 • Extend vocabulary • **Read/Revisit** *The Story of the Statue of Liberty*

ELL Place English language learners in the groups that correspond to their reading abilities in English.

Practice Stations
• Let's Write
• Get Fluent
• Word Work

Independent Activities
• AudioText: *The Story of the Statue of Liberty*
• *Reader's and Writer's Notebook*
• Research and Inquiry

English Language Learners
Check retelling To support retelling, review the multilingual summary for *The Story of the Statue of Liberty* with the appropriate Retelling Cards to scaffold understanding.

Objectives

◎ Evaluate facts and opinions to aid comprehension.

OPTION **1** Skills and Strategies, continued

Teach Fact and Opinion

🔊 **Fact and Opinion** Explain that good readers evaluate the statements of fact and opinion as they read. Ask students to evaluate statements of fact and opinion about why and how the people paid for and felt about the statue.

Corrective Feedback

If... students are unable to find statements of fact and opinion,
then... model examining the text for information.

🔵 Multidraft Reading
Double Day Read!

If you chose . . .

Option 1 Return to the Extend Thinking instruction starting on p. 376–377.

Option 2 Read pp. 382–385. Use the Guide Comprehension and Extend Thinking instruction.

Student Edition pp. 382–383

OPTION **2** Think Critically, continued

Higher-Order Thinking Skills

🎯 **Fact and Opinion • Synthesis** On page 383, the authors describe the celebration that took place when Liberty was unveiled. Why do you think they combined some statements of opinion with statements of fact? Possible response: Statements of fact are important because this is a true story but if the authors didn't include words like *wonderful* and *gleaming in all her glory,* it would not be as interesting.

Model the Skill

Think Aloud The newspaper got people to donate money. That's a statement of fact because I could look in other reference sources to see if it is true. It is an opinion that there was "new excitement." Statements about how people felt cannot be proven true or false.

Let's Think About...

What big structure have you seen being built, and how does that help you understand how Liberty was built? **Background Knowledge**

7

But in America people had lost interest in the Statue of Liberty. Money had run out and work on Bedloe's Island had stopped. The base for the statue was not finished. With the help of a large New York newspaper, the money was raised. People all over the country, including children, sent in whatever they could. By the time the ship reached New York in 1885, it was greeted with new excitement.

The work on the island went on, and soon the pedestal was completed. Piece by piece, the skeleton was raised. Then the copper skin was riveted in place. Liberty was put back together like a giant puzzle. The statue had been built not once, but twice!

382

Let's Think About...

7 Answers will vary, but should include the ideas that it takes a lot of work to build something so big and how many people are involved in such a project.

Sequence • Analysis What details on page 382 tell how Liberty was put back together? Possible response: First the pedestal was completed. Then the skeleton was raised. Last, the copper skin was riveted into place.

On Their Own

Have students discuss the last sentence on p. 382 to determine if it is a statement of fact or opinion.

Differentiated Instruction

 **SI Strategic Intervention**

Sequence Have students use a graphic organizer to map the sequence of events on p. 382.

A Advanced

Word choice Have students identify additional examples where the author's choice of a particular word enhances the meaning of the text. Then encourage them to point out examples where they could make a different word choice.

Connect to Social Studies

By the early 20th century, the Statue of Liberty was a well-known symbol to welcome visitors. Nearby Ellis Island was the entrance point for millions of immigrants to the United States. In 1924, the Statue of Liberty became a national monument. In 1965, Ellis Island was added to the Statue of Liberty National Monument.

At last, in 1886, Liberty was standing where she belonged. A wonderful celebration was held. Boats and ships filled the harbor. Speeches were read, songs were sung. Bartholdi himself unveiled Liberty's face and she stood, gleaming in all her glory, for everyone to see. There was a great cheer from the crowd. Then President Grover Cleveland gave a speech.

383

ELL

English Language Learners

Sequence Direct students' attention to the description of the unveiling of the Statue of Liberty on p. 383. Tell students that *sequence* is the order in which events occur. Have students act out the sequence of events at the celebration for the Statue of Liberty, using signal words, such as *first, next,* and *last* to announce each event.

Questioning • Evaluation What questions can you ask to evaluate the first statement on page 383? What do the answers tell you? Possible response: *What part of the statement is fact?* The date is a fact. *What part of the statement is opinion?* It is an opinion that Liberty was standing where she belonged.

Word Choice • Synthesis On page 382, the authors explain that Liberty was put back together like a giant puzzle. How does the word *puzzle* help the reader visualize how Liberty was assembled on Bedloe's Island? Possible response: I know that a puzzle has pieces that fit together in a certain way to make something complete. By using the word *puzzle,* the author tells me a lot about the process of reassembling Liberty. The word helps me understand that there were many pieces that fit together in a certain way to make the statue complete.

Objectives

◎ Identify the meaning of the prefix *un-* and know how it changes the meaning of a root word.

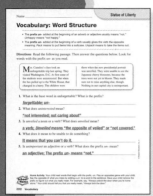

Reader's and Writer's Notebook p. 392

OPTION 1 Skills and Strategies, continued

Teach Prefix *un-*

Prefix *un-* Write the word *unlucky* on the board and underline the prefix *un-*. Explain that a prefix is letters added to the beginning of a word that change the meaning of the word. Tell students that the prefix *un-* means "not" or "do the opposite of." Then ask students to determine the meaning of the word *unlucky*.

Corrective Feedback

If… students are unable to determine the meaning of the word *unlucky*, **then…** model how to use a prefix to figure out the meaning of an unknown word.

Model the Skill

Think Aloud What is the prefix in *unlucky*? *(un-)* What does *un-* mean? ("not" or "do the opposite of") I can use my knowledge of the prefix to figure out the meaning of the word. I'll cover the prefix and read the root word.

Student Edition pp. 384–385

Let's **Think** About...

Do you understand what you've read? Can you summarize the text using information from the selection to support your answer? **Summarize**

⑧

Over the years, immigrants have arrived to begin new lives in America. To them, the Statue of Liberty is a symbol of all their hopes and dreams. She has welcomed millions of people arriving in New York by ship.

384

OPTION 2 Think Critically, continued

Higher-Order Thinking Skills

Prefix *un-* • Analysis Read the last sentence on page 385. What does the word *unforgettable* mean? Possible response: I know that forget means to "fail to remember." Something *forgettable* is easy to fail to remember. Since the prefix *un-* means "not" or "do the opposite of," I know that *unforgettable* means "not forgettable." Something *unforgettable* is difficult to forget.

Genre • Synthesis The title of this selection is *The Story of the Statue of Liberty*. Why do you think the authors used the word *story* if it is not fiction? Possible response: The selection has facts, but it is told like a story.

Let's **Think** About...

⑧ Possible response: Yes. A French sculptor made a statue to remember the friendship between France and America. Many people worked on the statue and parts of the statue were displayed to raise money. It was taken apart to be shipped and rebuilt in New York.

⑨ The poem invites the tired, the poor, the huddled masses yearning to breathe free, the wretched refuse, the homeless, and tempest-tost. The poem invites all those looking for a new life, signifying that America will open its doors to provide that opportunity.

I know that when people are *lucky,* good things come to them by chance. Since the prefix *un-* means "not" or "do the opposite of," *unlucky* means "not lucky." When people are *unlucky,* bad things come to them by chance.

Every year, on the Fourth of July, the United States of America celebrates its independence. Fireworks light up the sky above New York Harbor. The Statue of Liberty is a truly unforgettable sight—a symbol of all that is America.

"Give me your tired, your poor,
Your huddled masses yearning to breathe free,
The wretched refuse of your teeming shore.
Send these, the homeless, tempest-tost to me,
I lift my lamp beside the golden door!"

—from "The New Colossus" by Emma Lazarus, 1883, placed on a tablet on the pedestal of the Statue of Liberty in 1903

Let's Think About...

In the poem at the base of the Statue of Liberty, who are the people the Statue of Liberty invites? Why does she invite them?

Questioning

9

385

On Their Own

Have pairs of students list and define other words with the prefix *un-*. For additional practice, see *Reader's and Writer's Notebook* p. 392.

Differentiated Instruction

 Strategic Intervention

Prefix *un-* Provide additional practice with using the prefix *un-* to figure out the meaning of a word. Use the following words: *unsafe, untie, unstoppable, unkind, unlock.*

 Advanced

Critical thinking Have students think about why the Statue of Liberty became an important symbol of freedom. Have them answer the question: Do you think the Statue of Liberty would be as famous if it were standing somewhere other than New York harbor? Why do you think so?

English Language Learners

Monitor comprehension Focus students' attention on the poem on p. 385. Guide students through the poem line by line. Discuss the words they know and help define unfamiliar words. Encourage students to ask questions to clarify meaning. Then have partners create an illustration that represents the meaning of the poem to confirm understanding.

Comprehension Check

Spiral Review

Cause and Effect • Analysis Why had Americans lost interest in the Statue of Liberty? Possible response: Money had run out so the work had stopped.

Text Structure • Analysis What is the text structure of the selection? How do you know? Possible responses: The text structure of the story is chronological order. The authors tell

the story in the order that the events actually occurred. The story includes words such as *first, then,* and *at last* to signal sequence of events.

Check Predictions Have students return to the predictions they made earlier and confirm whether they were accurate.

DAY 3 Read and Comprehend

Objectives

⊙ Identify facts and opinions to aid comprehension.

⊙ Use questioning to check understanding.

Check Retelling

SUCCESS PREDICTOR

Plan to Assess Retelling

☑ **This week assess Strategic Intervention students.**

☐ **Week 2** Assess Advanced students.

☐ **Week 3** Assess Strategic Intervention students.

☐ **Week 4** Assess On-Level students.

☐ **Week 5** Assess any students you have not yet checked during this unit.

Envision It! | **Retell**

READING STREET ONLINE
STORY SORT
www.ReadingStreet.com

386

Objectives
• Identify the topic and find the author's purposes for writing. • Ask questions, clear up anything you don't understand, and look for facts and details. Support your answers with details from the text.

Think Critically

1. In the story, the author writes about celebrating the Fourth of July. What do you do with your family, friends, and community to show your feelings about freedom? **Text to Self**

2. Read "Meet the Authors" on page 387. What is the topic in this selection? Why did the author write this story? What questions would you ask the authors about why they write? **Think Like an Author**

3. Look back at the story. Find some statements of opinion. Do you agree or disagree with any of the opinions? Tell why or why not using evidence from the text to support your answer. **Fact and Opinion**

4. What questions does the story bring up for you? Ask a literal, an interpretive, and an evaluative question and see if you or your classmates can answer them. **Questioning**

5. **Look Back and Write** Look back through the story to find what is interesting or important about the Statue of Liberty. Write a paragraph using facts and details to support this idea.
TEST PRACTICE Extended Response

Meet the Authors

Betsy and Giulio Maestro

Betsy and Giulio Maestro are husband and wife. They have published more than 100 books together! "We work on so many interesting books about so many different topics that we're always learning new things," Ms. Maestro says.

Ms. Maestro wrote this story because she feels a special connection to the Statue of Liberty. Her grandmother saw the statue for the first time as she arrived at Ellis Island from Russia in 1918. Because Ms. Maestro grew up in New York City, she visited the Statue of Liberty many times. On a class field trip, she even climbed to the crown. Ms. Maestro feels the statue is "a symbol of human freedom and human rights throughout the world."

Read more books by Betsy and Giulio Maestro.

The New Americans:
Colonial Times: 1620–1689

The Story of Money

Use the Reader's and Writer's Notebook to record your independent reading.

387

Student Edition pp. 386–387

Retelling

Envision It! — Have students work in pairs to retell the selection, using the Envision It! Retelling Cards as prompts. Remind students that they should accurately describe the main topic and important ideas and use key vocabulary in their retellings. Monitor students' retellings.

Scoring rubric

Top-Score Response A top-score response makes connections beyond the text, describes the main topic and important ideas using accurate information, evaluates facts and opinions, and draws conclusions from the text.

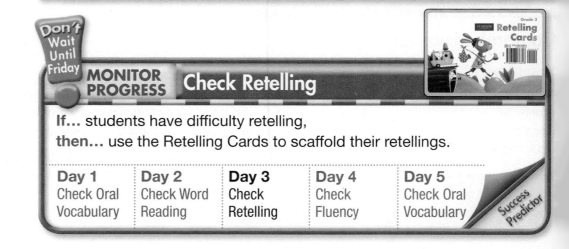

Don't Wait Until Friday

MONITOR PROGRESS **Check Retelling**

Retelling Cards

If... students have difficulty retelling,
then... use the Retelling Cards to scaffold their retellings.

Day 1	**Day 2**	**Day 3**	**Day 4**	**Day 5**
Check Oral Vocabulary	Check Word Reading	Check Retelling	Check Fluency	Check Oral Vocabulary

Success Predictor

Think Critically

Text to self

1. Possible response: To celebrate the Fourth of July, my family goes to a parade that honors soldiers. We wear red, white, and blue and wave American flags. We watch fireworks and think about how lucky we are to be American.

Think like an author

2. The authors wanted us to know that the Statue of Liberty is "a symbol of human freedom." Ms. Maestro was inspired by remembering that her grandmother saw the statue for the first time when she arrived at Ellis Island from Russia. I would like to ask the authors: *How do you decide what you will write about? Why do you write for children instead of adults?*

Fact and opinion

3. Some statements of opinion in the text are that the statue is an "unforgettable" sight and that people watched "in fascination" as it grew in Paris. I agree with these opinions because the text says that the statue is very large and the design includes many symbolic details. I think that a statue like that would be hard to forget and it would be fascinating to watch it being assembled.

Questioning

4. The story brings up these questions: literal: *Who made the statue and why did he make it?* interpretive: *Why is the Statue of Liberty an important symbol of freedom?* evaluative: *Is it a successful symbol of freedom?*

Writing on Demand

5. **Look Back and Write** To build writing fluency, assign a 10–15 minute time limit.

Suggest that students use a prewriting strategy, such as brainstorming or using a graphic organizer, to organize their ideas. Remind them to establish a topic sentence and support it with facts, details, or explanations. As students finish, encourage them to reread their responses, revise for organization and support, and proofread for errors in grammar and conventions.

Scoring rubric

> **Top-Score Response** A top-score response uses details from the selection to tell what the Statue of Liberty holds in her hands and why she is on Bedloe's Island.
>
> **A top-score response should include:**
>
> • The Statue of Liberty is on Bedloe's Island because the island is in New York Harbor.
>
> • Liberty holds a lamp that welcomes people to America.
>
> • The statue is called *Liberty Enlightening the World.*

Differentiated Instruction

 Strategic Intervention
Have students who are unable to respond independently to the Look Back and Write question respond as a group. Guide the groups to identify details in the story that give clues to why the Statue of Liberty stands on Bedloe's Island.

Meet the Authors

Have students read about the authors Betsy and Giulio Maestro on p. 387. Ask them why they like writing together.

Independent Reading

After students enter their independent reading information into their Reading Logs, have them paraphrase a portion of the text they have just read. Remind students that when we paraphrase, we express the meaning of a passage using other words and maintaining logical order.

English Language Learners
Retelling Use the Retelling Cards to discuss the selection with students. Place the cards in an incorrect order and have volunteers correct the mistake. Then have students explain where each card should go as they describe the sequence of the selection.

387a

Retelling

Success Predictor

Objectives

• Read aloud grade-level text with appropriate rate.
• Reread for fluency.
• Understand information displayed in a time line.

Model Fluency
Rate

Model fluent reading

Have students turn to p. 376 of *The Story of the Statue of Liberty*. Have students follow along as you read this page. Tell them that you will try to read about the Statue of Liberty just the way you speak. Vary your tone and volume, and don't read too fast or too slow.

Guide practice

Have the students follow along as you read the page again. Then have them reread the page as a group without you until they read the page at the correct rate. Ask questions to be sure students comprehend the text. Continue in the same way on p. 377.

Reread for Fluency

Corrective feedback

If... students are having difficulty reading at the correct rate,

then... prompt:

• Do you think you need to slow down or read more quickly?

• Read the sentence more quickly. Now read it more slowly. Which helps you understand what you are reading?

• Tell me the sentence. Read it at the rate that would help me understand it.

ROUTINE **Oral Rereading**

1) **Read** For *The Story of the Statue of Liberty,* use p. 379.

2) **Model** Have students listen as you read the page at an appropriate rate.

3) **Guide practice** Have students read along with you.

4) **On their own** For optimal fluency, students should reread three or four times at an appropriate rate.

Routines Flip Chart

Research and Study Skills
Time Line

Teach

Tell students that time lines provide information about events in correct time order. A time line is a line with dates on it. An important event is usually described for each date. Display a time line and review that it presents information in time order. Then review information about time lines:

- The dates on a time line are in order from the earliest date to the latest date.

- Each date has information that goes along with it.

- Time lines are read from left-to-right or top-to-bottom.

Have students review the events in *The Story of the Statue of Liberty.* Have them look for dates in the text to make a time line. Work together as a class to make a time line that shows the dates and events in the story of how the statue was designed and built.

Guide practice

Discuss these questions:

Why would someone want to make a time line? (Time lines can make information in a text easier to understand.)

How can you decide what time periods to use to divide your time line? (Think about the whole period you want to show and then add important events and dates that occurred during that period.)

Have students look at different time lines and discuss the information that each shows.

On their own

Have students review the instructions and complete p. 393 of the *Reader's and Writer's Notebook.*

Reader's and Writer's Notebook p. 393

English Language Learners
Professional Development: What ELL experts say about accessing content "We can *scaffold* students' learning by modifying the input itself. [There] are a variety of ways of modifying the presentation of academic content to students so that they can more effectively gain access to the meaning…. Visuals enable students to 'see' the basic concepts we are trying to teach much more effectively than if we rely only on words."
—Dr. Jim Cummins

Time lines Point out that creating a time line may help students better understand events in stories or other texts. Encourage them to make time lines of their lives. Have them compare their time lines with partners to see how they are the same and where they differ.

Objectives
- Analyze data for usefulness.
- Use proper capitalization.
- Spell frequently misspelled words.

Research and Inquiry
Analyze

Teach

Tell students that today they will analyze their research findings. Suggest that students record historical information about a symbol that they are collecting into a time line. Then explain that students may have to improve the focus of their research by returning to their on-site inspections to gather more information.

Model

Think Aloud Originally I thought that the American flag was the only flag that our town has that represents freedom. During my on-site inspection I learned that our town has other flags that represent other important historical events in our town. For example, there is a flag that shows the date that the town was incorporated. The flags represent our town's freedom and accomplishments. I will refocus my inquiry question to include this information from my on-site inspection. Now my inquiry question is *How do flags, including the American flag, represent the history and freedom of our town and our country?*

Guide practice

Have students analyze their findings. They may need to refocus their inquiry question to better fit the information they found. Remind students that if they have difficulty improving their focus they can do another on-site inspection and ask local experts for guidance.

Have students continue to take notes and to record the historical information they gather in a time line.

On their own

Have small groups of students share their inquiry questions and time lines and evaluate the information they have gathered. Students should discuss whether they need to collect additional information to answer the inquiry question. Students can brainstorm additional ideas for locations for on-site inspections.

Conventions
Capital Letters

Review

Remind students that this week they learned about capitalization: days of the week, months of the year, titles and abbreviations of people, and the first word in a sentence or greeting are all capitalized.

Daily Fix-It

Use Daily Fix-It numbers 5 and 6 in the right margin.

Connect to oral language

Write the letter on the board, omitting capital letters. Have students tell which words should begin with capital letters, and why.

> **sat., dec. 5, 2011**
>
> **dear principal martinez,**
>
> **our family decided that we would visit national landmarks this summer. we visited the statue of liberty in new york. the statue is a symbol of freedom. the tablet in her hand is a symbol of the declaration of independence.**
>
> **your student,**
>
> **frederico**

On their own

For additional support, use *Let's Practice It!* page 366 on the *Teacher Resources DVD-ROM.*

Spelling
Vowel Sounds in *moon* and *foot*

Frequently misspelled words

The words *through, took, would,* and *could* are words that students often misspell. Think carefully before you write these words. Have students practice these words by writing the following sentences.

1. **I want to walk through the woods.**
2. **She took two cookies.**
3. **Would you please come in?**
4. **I could go for a bike ride, or I could go swimming.**

On their own

For additional practice, use *Reader's and Writer's Notebook* p. 394.

Differentiated Instruction

SI Strategic Intervention

List proper nouns Have students keep track of proper nouns they hear, read, or say during the day. At the end of the day, have them write one sentence using each of the proper nouns, being careful to capitalize each one.

Daily Fix-It

5. Didnt you climb to the top of the statue on Toosday? *(Didn't; Tuesday)*
6. You cant go to the top anymore but you can go inside the base. *(can't; anymore, but)*

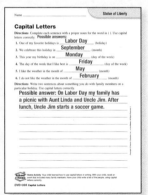

Let's Practice It!
TR DVD•366

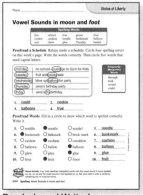

Reader's and Writer's
Notebook p. 394

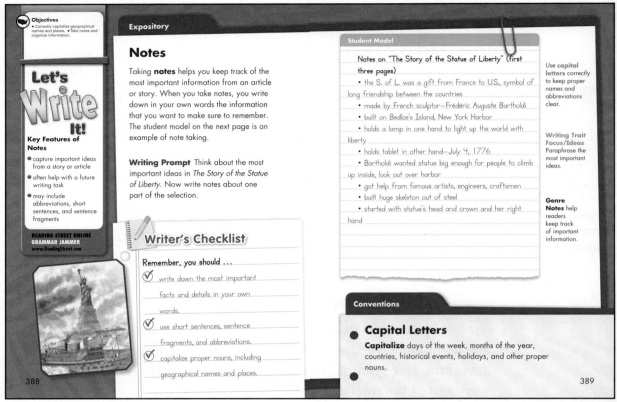

Student Edition pp. 388–389

Let's Write It!
Notes

Teach

Use pp. 388–389 in the Student Edition. Direct students to read the key features of notes, which appear on p. 388. Remind students that they can refer to the information in the Writer's Checklist as they write their own notes.

Read the student model on p. 389. Point out the key features of notes in the model.

Connect to conventions

Remind students that the names of people, official places (e.g., *the White House*), days, months, official historical events, holidays, and other proper nouns are always capitalized, even when taking notes.

Writing—Notes
Writer's Craft: Paraphrase

Display rubric

Display Scoring Rubric 26 from the *Teacher Resources DVD-ROM* and go over the criteria for each trait under each score. Then, using the model in the Student Edition, have student volunteers explain why the model should score a 4 for one of the traits. If a student says that the model should score below 4 for a particular trait, the student should offer support for that response. Remind students that this is the rubric that will be used to evaluate the notes they write.

Scoring Rubric: Notes

	4	3	2	1
Focus/Ideas	Includes most important information from selection	Includes some important information from selection	Includes irrelevant information from selection	Does not include any important information from selection
Organization	Information is clear and orderly	Information is mostly clear and orderly	Information is somewhat clear and orderly	Information is neither clear nor orderly
Voice	Objective; no personal bias or opinions	Mostly objective; a little personal bias or opinions	Somewhat objective; some personal bias or opinions	Not objective; too much bias or personal information
Word Choice	Avoids unnecessary words and information	Uses some unnecessary words and information	Uses many unnecessary words; vague information	Notes are wordy and irrelevant
Sentences	Uses clear, short sentences and sentence fragments	Uses mostly clear, short sentences and sentence fragments	Uses somewhat clear, short sentences and fragments	Sentences are unclear or too long
Conventions	All proper nouns are capitalized	Most proper nouns are capitalized	Some proper nouns are capitalized	Few or no proper nouns are capitalized

Main idea and details charts

Have students get out the Main Idea and Details charts they created yesterday. If their charts are not complete, allow additional time for them to finish. Have students work in pairs if they are struggling to complete their charts.

Write

You will use your Main Idea and Details charts to write the draft of your notes on the selection, *The Story of the Statue of Liberty*. When you are drafting, make sure to get the most important information down on paper. You will have time to revise tomorrow.

Objectives
- Paraphrase the selection text.
- Recognize that notes should be in the reader's own words.
- Take notes on a selection.

Writing, continued
Writer's Craft: Paraphrase

MINI-LESSON

In Your Own Words

■ **Introduce** Explain to students that when you take notes about a topic, you should paraphrase in your own words rather than using the author's words. Paraphrasing means putting an idea in your own words. This way, if you use your notes for a future writing project, you won't accidentally copy the author's words. Display Writing Transparency 26A.

Notes on *The Story of the Statue of Liberty*
(pages 380–381)

- To finish the statue, the skeleton was covered in copper
- The statue was put together in paris
- Liberty was finished in 1884
- Famous people celebrated
- Liberty has 168 steps up to her crown
- Pieces were packed for the trip across the Atlantic Ochen
- 214 crates were shipped to america

Unit 6 The Story of the Statue of Liberty   Writing Model **26A**

Writing Transparency 26A, TR DVD

Note-Taking Tips

✔ To get started, read one or two paragraphs of the selection. Think about what the most important information is. The important information can be main ideas or details.

✔ Use short sentences or sentence fragments in your notes.

✔ Remember to spell and capitalize all proper nouns correctly.

Think Aloud I'm going to take notes on pp. 380–381 of the main selection. This part of the selection is about how the Statue of Liberty was finished in Paris. I think that how and where the statue was made is important information. I'll write this information in my own words in my notes.

Guide students through the next page of the selection, showing students where the information appears in the text and in the notes. Then have students take notes on the remainder of the selection. Have students use the note-taking tips as a guide as they draft their notes. Remind them that their notes must include the most important information paraphrased in their own words.

ROUTINE **Quick Write for Fluency** **Team Talk**

1. **Talk** Pairs talk about what it means to put something in their own words.

2. **Write** Students write one or two sentences about what they like to do in the summer, using proper capitalization for people and place names.

3. **Share** Pairs trade papers and try to restate their partner's sentences in their own words, retaining proper capitalization.

Routines Flip Chart

 Strategic Intervention

Read aloud If students are having difficulty, have them work with a partner. One partner reads aloud a paragraph, then pauses while both students list important information in their notes. Then the other partner takes a turn reading aloud.

Wrap Up Your Day

✔ **Build Concepts** Have students discuss the importance of symbols of freedom like the Stature of Liberty.

✔ **Fact and Opinion** Why is important to know which statements are fact and which are opinion?

✔ **Questioning** Why is it helpful to stop and ask questions as you read?

Preview DAY 4

Tell students that tomorrow they will read about people who have immigrated to the United States.

Concept Talk

Question of the Week

? **Why do we have symbols that represent freedom?**

Expand the concept

Remind students that this week they have read about how the Statue of Liberty, a symbol of freedom, was designed and built. Tell students that today they will read about why, how, and when immigrants came to the United States.

Anchored Talk

Develop oral language

Use the title and illustrations to review pp. 382–385 of *The Story of the Statue of Liberty*. Discuss the Amazing Words *recognizable* and *disgrace*. Add these words to the concept map. Use the following questions to develop students' understanding of the concept. Remind students to ask and answer questions with appropriate detail and to build on other students' answers.

• What are some *recognizable* symbols of freedom?

• Why do people consider it a *disgrace* to damage or destroy a symbol?

Strategy Response Log

Have students complete p. 32 in *Reader's and Writer's Notebook.* Then have students work with a partner to answer their questions.

INTERACT with TEXT

Oral Vocabulary
Amazing Words

Amazing Words

impressive	competition
tribute	recognizable
enlighten	disgrace
contribution	staggering
dedication	fund

Teach Amazing Words

Amazing Words Oral Vocabulary Routine

1 **Introduce** Write the word *staggering* on the board. Have students say it aloud with you. Yesterday we read about how the Statue of Liberty was assembled on Bedloe's Island in New York. Why was building the Statue of Liberty a *staggering* accomplishment during that time? (Possible response: It was a big accomplishment because the builders did not have the transportation options or the building tools that exist today.) Have students provide a definition of the word. (Something that is *staggering* is very surprising or huge.)

2 **Demonstrate** Have students answer questions to demonstrate understanding. Is collecting 50 pennies in a jar a *staggering* number of pennies? The White House has a table that can seat 140 guests. Is that a *staggering* number of guests for one table?

3 **Apply** Have students apply their understanding. When have you seen a *staggering* number of people?

See p. OV•1 to teach *fund.*

Routines Flip Chart

Apply Amazing Words

As students read "A Nation of Immigrants" on pp. 390–391, have them think about the *staggering* number of immigrants that came to the United States and how immigrants might have *funded* their journey to the United States.

Connect to reading

As students read today's selection about where immigrants to the United States came from and why they came, have them think about how the Question of the Week and the Amazing Words *staggering* and *fund* apply to immigrants to the United States.

ELL Produce Oral Vocabulary Use the Day 4 instruction on ELL Poster 26 to extend and enrich language.

ELL Poster 26

The Story of the Statue of Liberty **390b**

Objectives
- Review words with suffixes -y, -ish, -hood, and -ment.
- Read words fluently independent of context.

Phonics Review
Suffixes

Review suffixes

To review last week's word analysis skill, write *fluffy, babyish, motherhood,* and *statement.* You studied words like these last week. What do you know about reading words with suffixes? (Read the base word first. Then read the suffix. Put the parts together to read the word.) What is the base word in the first word? *(fluff)* What is the suffix? *(-y)* Let's read the whole word: *fluffy.* Remember, the suffix *-y* means "like or having the quality of." Continue in the same way for the other words. Remind students that the suffix *-ish* means "like"; *-hood* means "a state or condition"; and *-ment* means "act of."

Corrective feedback

If students are unable to answer the questions about suffixes, refer them to Sound-Spelling Cards 168, 170, 174, and 177.

Guide practice

Draw a three-column chart. I'll write a word in the first column. (Write *chilly.*) Then I will read the base word and write that word in the second column. (Write *chill.*) I will write the suffix in the third column. (Write *y.*) Let's put the parts together to read the word. *(chilly)* Continue writing words and having students read the base word, suffix, and then the word.

Word	Base	Suffix
chilly	chill	y
sisterhood	sister	hood
selfish	self	ish
government	govern	ment
speedy	speed	y
amusement	amuse	ment

On their own

For additional practice, use *Let's Practice It!* page 367 on the *Teacher Resources DVD-ROM.*

Let's Practice It! DVD
TR DVD•367

Fluent Word Reading
Spiral Review

Read words independent of context

Display these words. Tell students that they can decode some words on this list. Explain that other words they should know because they appear often in reading.

Have students read the list three or four times until they can read at the rate of two to three seconds per word.

Word Reading

two	eight	reins	reindeer	people
neighbor's	height	receipt	full	were
many	sleigh	thought	bought	ought
all	have	caused	seized	caught

Corrective feedback

If... students have difficulty reading whole words,
then... have them use sound-by-sound blending for decodable words or chunking for words that have word parts, or have them say and spell high-frequency words.

If... students cannot read fluently at a rate of two to three seconds per word,
then... have pairs practice the list until they can read it fluently.

Differentiated Instruction

 Strategic Intervention

Vowel sounds To assist students having difficulty decoding words with long *a* spelled *ei* or *eigh,* focus on one spelling at a time. Write words with long *a* spelled *ei,* such as *rein, vein,* and *veil.* Have students read the words with you and identify the letters that spell the vowel sound. Repeat with long *a* spelled *eigh* (*eight, weight, neighbor, sleigh*).

Spiral Review

These activities review:

- previously taught high-frequency words *full, have, many, people, two, were.*
- words with long *a, e,* or *i* spelled *ei* or *eigh;* words with /ò/ spelled *a, au, aw, al, augh, ough.*

English Language Learners

Fluent word reading Have students listen to a more fluent reader say the words. Then have them repeat the words.

Objectives
- Read words fluently in context.
- Apply knowledge of sound-spellings to decode unknown words when reading.
- Practice fluency with oral rereading.

Read words in context

Display these sentences. Call on individuals to read a sentence. Then randomly point to review words and have students read them. To help you monitor word reading, high-frequency words are underlined and decodable words are italicized.

MONITOR PROGRESS | **Sentence Reading**

We *all ought* to find what our *height* is.
Do you <u>have</u> a *receipt* for the <u>two</u> things you *bought*?
We <u>were</u> excited to see *eight reindeer* pulling a *sleigh* <u>full</u> of toys.
Dad *seized* the *reins* and *caught* our *neighbor's* horse.
She *thought* the ice *caused* <u>many</u> <u>people</u> to slip.

If... students are unable to read an underlined high-frequency word,

then... read the word for them and spell it, having them echo you.

If... students have difficulty reading an italicized decodable word,

then... guide them in using sound-by-sound blending or chunking.

Reread for Fluency

Have students reread the sentences to develop automaticity decoding words.

ROUTINE | **Oral Rereading**

 Read Have students read all the sentences orally.

 Reread To achieve optimal fluency, students should reread the sentences three or four times.

 Corrective Feedback Listen as students read. Provide corrective feedback regarding their fluency and decoding.

Routines Flip Chart

Blend and Read

Read words independent of context

Have students turn to p. 131 in *Decodable Practice Readers 3.2* and find the first list of words. Each word in this list has the vowel sound /ü/, spelled *oo, ew, ue, ui,* and /ů/, spelled *oo* and *u.* Let's blend and read these words. Be sure that students identify the correct vowel sound in each word.

Next, have students read the high-frequency words.

Preview Decodable Practice Passage

Have students read the title and preview the story. Tell them that they will read words with vowel sounds /ü/ and /ů/.

Read words in context

Chorally read the story along with students. Have students identify words in the story that have the vowel sounds /ü/ and /ů/. Make sure that students are monitoring their accuracy when they decode words.

Team Talk Pair students and have them take turns reading the story aloud to each other. Monitor students as they read to check for proper pronunciation and appropriate pacing.

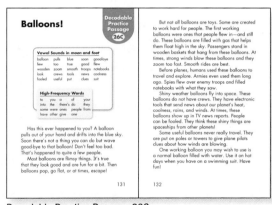

Decodable Practice Passage 26C

Differentiated Instruction

 Advanced

Decodable words Have students write their own sentences using some of the decodable words found in the sentences on p. 390e.

Let's Think About Genre
Textbook

Introduce the genre

Explain to students that what we read is structured differently depending on the author's reasons for writing and what kind of information he/she wishes to convey. Different types of texts are called genres. Tell them that a textbook is one type of genre.

Discuss the genre

Remind students that a textbook is a type of reference source, and a reference source is a type of expository text. Remind students that a textbook can be about any subject taught in school.

On the board, draw a T-chart like the one shown below. Label the columns *Graphic Source or Text Feature* and *Purpose.* Ask the following questions:

- What text features are in most textbooks? (tables of contents, chapters heads, subheads)

- Why does a textbook have a table of contents? (Possible response: It helps the reader find information.)

- Why do many textbooks include graphic sources, such as charts? (Possible response: Graphic sources can make information easier for readers to understand.)

- How can graphic sources help when you preview a textbook? (Possible response: They let you know what kind of information you will find in the book before you begin reading.)

Graphic Source or Text Feature	Purpose
table of contents	help find information
chart	make information clear

Guide practice

Have students work in pairs to list the parts of a textbook and their purposes. Ask them to share their lists with the class.

Connect to reading

Tell students that they will now read about why, how, and when immigrants came to the United States. Have students think about why their ancestors may have come to the United States.

Small Group Time

DAY 4

Break into small groups before reading or revisiting "A Nation of Immigrants."

Teacher Led

SI Strategic Intervention

Teacher Led p. DI•5
- Practice retelling
- Genre focus
- **Read/Revisit** "A Nation of Immigrants"

OL On-Level

Teacher Led p. DI•10
- Practice retelling
- Genre focus
- **Read/Revisit** "A Nation of Immigrants"

A Advanced

Teacher Led p. DI•15
- Genre focus
- **Read/Revisit** "A Nation of Immigrants"

ELL Place English language learners in the groups that correspond to their reading abilities in English.

Practice Stations
- Read for Meaning
- Get Fluent
- Words to Know

Independent Activities
- AudioText: "A Nation of Immigrants"
- *Reader's and Writer's Notebook*
- Research and Inquiry

Academic Vocabulary

textbook a reference source, usually written about a specific topic

English Language Learners

Graphic organizer Provide support to students when creating a T-chart. Help them choose two heads for their T-charts, and then work together to add the names of textbook elements and purposes in each column. Show them different textbooks so they can understand the different elements.

Objectives
• Discuss text features in a textbook.

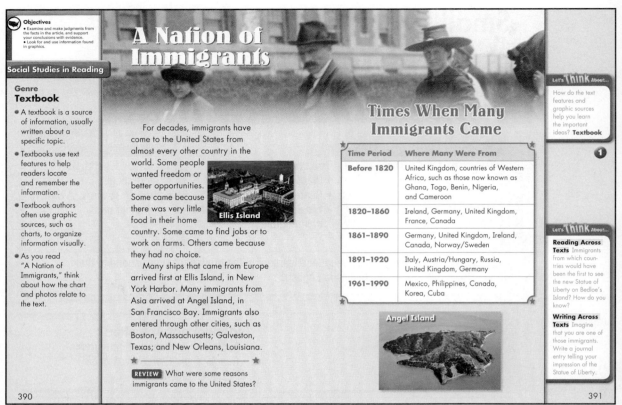

Student Edition pp. 390–391

The student edition pages shown:

Objectives
• Examine and make judgments from the facts in the article, and support your conclusions with evidence.
• Look for and use information found in graphics.

Social Studies in Reading

Genre
Textbook
• A textbook is a source of information, usually written about a specific topic.
• Textbooks use text features to help readers locate and remember the information.
• Textbook authors often use graphic sources, such as charts, to organize information visually.
• As you read "A Nation of Immigrants," think about how the chart and photos relate to the text.

A Nation of Immigrants

For decades, immigrants have come to the United States from almost every other country in the world. Some people wanted freedom or better opportunities. Some came because there was very little food in their home country. Some came to find jobs or to work on farms. Others came because they had no choice.

Ellis Island

Many ships that came from Europe arrived first at Ellis Island, in New York Harbor. Many immigrants from Asia arrived at Angel Island, in San Francisco Bay. Immigrants also entered through other cities, such as Boston, Massachusetts; Galveston, Texas; and New Orleans, Louisiana.

REVIEW What were some reasons immigrants came to the United States?

Times When Many Immigrants Came

Time Period	Where Many Were From
Before 1820	United Kingdom, countries of Western Africa, such as those now known as Ghana, Togo, Benin, Nigeria, and Cameroon
1820–1860	Ireland, Germany, United Kingdom, France, Canada
1861–1890	Germany, United Kingdom, Ireland, Canada, Norway/Sweden
1891–1920	Italy, Austria/Hungary, Russia, United Kingdom, Germany
1961–1990	Mexico, Philippines, Canada, Korea, Cuba

Angel Island

Let's Think About...
How do the text features and graphic sources help you learn the important ideas? **Textbook**

1

Let's Think About...
Reading Across Texts Immigrants from which countries would have been the first to see the new Statue of Liberty on Bedloe's Island? How do you know?

Writing Across Texts Imagine that you are one of those immigrants. Write a journal entry telling your impression of the Statue of Liberty.

390   391

Guide Comprehension

Teach the genre

Genre: Textbook Have students preview "A Nation of Immigrants" on pp. 390–391. Have them identify and discuss the text features and graphics in the text. Ask students: What does the chart on page 391 tell you? How does the chart organize the information?

Corrective feedback

If... students are unable to identify the topic of the chart and how information is organized,
then... model how to interpret information in a chart.

Model the genre

Think Aloud The title tells me that the chart gives information about when immigrants came to the United States. The chart organizes information in rows and columns. What is the heading of the first column? **(Time Period)** That column shows the periods of time when immigrants came. What is the heading of the other column? **(Where Many Were From)** The other column shows the countries that immigrants came from during each time period.

On their own

Have students work in pairs to continue previewing text features and graphics. Have pairs tell about the features that they identify.

Extend Thinking
Think Critically

Higher-order thinking skills

Cause and Effect • Analysis Immigrants coming to the United States is an effect. What were some causes? Possible response: lack of jobs, opportunities, or food where they lived, lack of freedom

 Fact and Opinion • Evaluation Is this sentence a statement of fact or opinion? *Many immigrants from Asia arrived at Angel Island in San Francisco Bay.* How do you know? Possible response: The sentence is a statement of fact because it can be proved true or false.

 Questioning • Analysis What literal, interpretative, and evaluative questions can you ask to help you better understand the text? Possible response: Where did many immigrants from Asia go first? Why did some people have "no choice" about coming? Why did many people from Western Africa come before 1820?

Let's **Think** About...

1 Possible responses: The photos and captions show what Ellis Island and Angel Island look like. The chart gives additional information about when immigrants came to the United States and where they came from.

Reading Across Texts

Have students review p. 383 to locate the date that the Statue of Liberty was completed on Bedloe's Island. (1886) Then have them look at the chart to find the time period that includes the date.

Writing Across Texts

Before writing, have students review *The Story of the Statue of Liberty* for details about the statue's design, and have students think about what they've learned about why immigrants came.

Connect to Social Studies

For many years, Ellis Island was the chief immigration station for the United States. From 1892 to 1954, over twelve million immigrants entered the United States via the Ellis Island station.

Differentiated Instruction

 **SI** Strategic Intervention

Cause and effect Review the concept of cause and effect. Give students additional examples of cause and effect. Then have pairs write a cause and effect statement.

A Advanced

Genealogy Tell students that genealogy is the study of family ancestors. Have students talk to family members about their ancestors, and use the information to create a genealogical chart (family tree).

ELL

English Language Learners
Visual learning: graphic sources Provide extra practice with interpreting textbook graphics. Call on volunteers to tell what they know about different graphics in their textbooks. Point out the key features of each type of graphic. Then focus students' attention on the chart on p. 391 and say, A chart has rows and columns. There is information in each space. The rows and columns are often labeled with headings. What are the headings on this chart? What do the headings tell you?

Objectives

- Read aloud grade-level appropriate text with fluency.
- Use word structure to determine the meanings of words with the prefix *un-*.
- Present an announcement.

Check Fluency WCPM
SUCCESS PREDICTOR

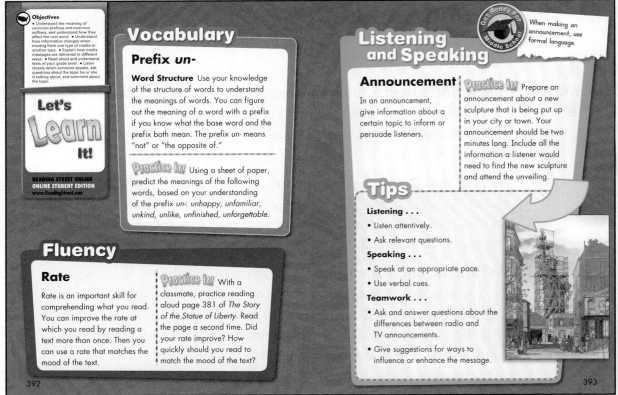

Student Edition pp. 392–393

Fluency
Rate

Guide practice

Use the Student Edition activity as an assessment tool. Make sure the reading passage is at least 200 words in length. As students read aloud with partners, walk around to make sure their reading rate is appropriate and that they are timing each other correctly.

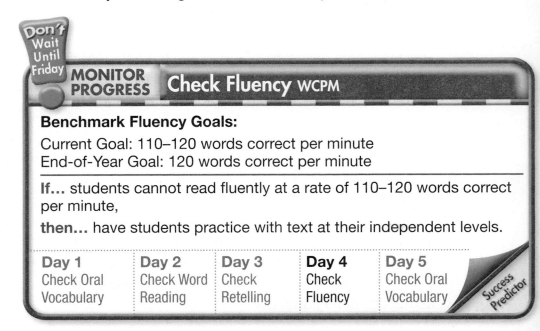

Don't Wait Until Friday

MONITOR PROGRESS Check Fluency WCPM

Benchmark Fluency Goals:

Current Goal: 110–120 words correct per minute
End-of-Year Goal: 120 words correct per minute

If... students cannot read fluently at a rate of 110–120 words correct per minute,

then... have students practice with text at their independent levels.

Day 1	Day 2	Day 3	Day 4	Day 5
Check Oral Vocabulary	Check Word Reading	Check Retelling	Check Fluency	Check Oral Vocabulary

Success Predictor

Vocabulary
 Prefix *un-*

Teach prefix *un-*

Word Structure Tell students that they can use their knowledge of word structure to understand the meanings of words. If they know the meaning of the base word and of the prefix or suffix, they can figure out the word's meaning. Write *unknown* on the board. Cover *un-* and ask students to tell the meaning of *known.* Explain that the prefix *un-* means "not" or "the opposite of." Write *not known* on the board.

Guide practice

Have students work in pairs to write the base words for *unhappy, unfamiliar, unkind, unlike, unfinished,* and *unforgettable.* Have them discuss the meaning of each base word and how *un-* changes the meaning of the base word.

On their own

Walk around the room as partners discuss what the prefix *un-* adds to the base word. Check to make sure that partners correctly predict the meaning of each word.

Listening and Speaking
Announcement

Teach

Tell students that they will make an announcement as they pretend to unveil a new sculpture. Explain that their announcement should name the sculpture and the artist who created it, and explain why it was created. Encourage students to use descriptive words and offer complimentary opinions about the sculpture. Suggest that students conclude their announcements by asking the audience to applaud the work of the artist.

Guide practice

Remind students to be aware of the nonverbal cues they use when they are speaking, including facial expressions and body language. Encourage them to speak coherently, employing eye contact, speaking rate, volume, enunciation, and conventions of language to communicate their ideas effectively. Remind students to listen attentively when others are speaking.

On their own

Have students write their announcements. Have them time themselves when they practice reading them to be sure they are about two minutes long.

Announcement

Tell students that they should deliver oral presentations that employ conventions of language to communicate ideas effectively. Their presentation should use standard English, appropriate grade-level vocabulary, and grammatically correct sentences. Speakers should also use parts of speech correctly and observe usage rules.

Academic Vocabulary

announcement a public or formal notice of something

English Language Learners
Root words Review word parts such as roots, prefixes, and suffixes. Write words on the board and help students identify the roots. Then have volunteers circle the prefixes and underline the suffixes in the word. Then have them use the words in sentences that show they understand the words' meanings.

Success Predictor

Research and Inquiry
Synthesize

Teach

Have students synthesize their research findings and results. Explain that when they synthesize, they combine relevant ideas from multiple sources of oral and written information to create an answer to their inquiry questions. Remind students that they can record historical information about symbols that they gather in a time line. Review how to choose relevant information from a number of sources and organize it logically. After students have reviewed their material, have them synthesize information by combining the most important pieces of information from reference texts and on-site inspections into a short paragraph.

Guide practice

Have students use a word processing program or poster board to prepare for their presentations on Day 5. If students are using a time line, check to see that students are recording information in chronological order. Students' time lines should include the most important information from multiple sources, including reference texts and their on-site inspections.

On their own

Have students write a brief informational article about their research findings. Then have them organize and combine information for their presentations.

Conventions
Capital Letters

Test practice

Remind students that grammar skills, such as capitalization, are often assessed on important tests. Remind students that proper nouns such as days of the week, months of the year, holidays, titles before names, historical periods, geographical places and names, abbreviations, and the first word in a sentence or greeting are the kinds of words that are capitalized.

Daily Fix-It

Use Daily Fix-It numbers 7 and 8 in the right margin.

On their own

For additional practice, use *Reader's and Writer's Notebook* p. 395.

Reader's and Writer's Notebook p. 395

Daily Fix-It

7. Fue people had saw the Statue of Liberty until 1886. *(Few; seen)*

8. The statues torch shines over every one. *(statue's; everyone)*

Spelling
Vowel Sounds in *moon* and *foot*

Practice spelling strategy

Supply pairs of students with index cards on which the spelling words have been written. Have one student read a word while the other writes it. Then have students switch roles. Have them use the cards to check their spelling and correct any misspelled words.

On their own

For additional practice, use *Let's Practice It!* page 368 on the *Teacher Resources DVD-ROM.*

Let's Practice It!
TR DVD•368

Objectives
- Review notes for accuracy.
- Reread and add information.
- Apply revising strategy of adding.

Writing—Notes
Revising Strategy

MINI-LESSON

Revising Strategy: Adding

Yesterday we took notes on the selection, *The Story of the Statue of Liberty.* Today we will reread the selection and add any information to our notes we may have missed the first time. The goal is to make your notes clearer, more complete, and more informative and accurate.

Writing Transparency 26B, TR DVD

Display Writing Transparency 26B. Remind students that revising does not include corrections of grammar and mechanics. Tell them that this will be done during the lesson as they proofread their work. Then introduce the revising strategy of adding.

As I reread pages 380 and 381, I can see that it wasn't just famous people who celebrated. I'll change that note so it just says "People celebrated." I can also see that I left out how the statue was taken apart to be shipped. That is important, so I'll add another bullet point with this information.

Revising Tips

✔ Make sure that all the important information is included in your notes.

✔ Check to make sure that all of your original notes are correct, especially dates.

✔ Check the spellings of proper nouns.

Peer conferencing

Peer Revision Have students work with a partner to review their notes. Partners should read each others' notes and suggest information that should be added or correct information that is inaccurate.

Have students finish checking their notes for accuracy and adding information. They should use the suggestions their partner wrote during Peer Revision as well as the key features of notes to guide their revision. Be sure that students are using the revising strategy adding.

Corrective feedback

Circulate around the room to monitor and confer with students as they revise. Remind any students correcting errors that they will have time to edit tomorrow. They should be working on content today.

Write Guy
Jeff Anderson

Experiment and Use What You Know!

Encourage students to experiment or stretch themselves to try new things with spelling, punctuation, and grammar. Though they shouldn't "worry" about it when drafting, they can make an attempt to use all that they know. Reward students when they reach to spell a word.

ROUTINE — Quick Write for Fluency — Team Talk

1. **Talk** Pairs talk about what they learned about the Statue of Liberty.

2. **Write** Students write a paragraph telling three things they learned about the statue from the selection.

3. **Share** Pairs read their paragraphs to each other and then check each other's paragraphs for important ideas and correct information, such as dates.

Routines Flip Chart

Wrap Up Your Day

✔ **Build Concepts** Have students discuss how people feel when they see symbols of freedom.

✔ **Oral Vocabulary** Monitor students' use of oral vocabulary as they respond: Why is Ellis Island recognizable as a tribute to immigrants?

✔ **Text Features** Discuss how the time line helps students understand the chronology of the immigration to the United States.

English Language Learners
Identifying important information Help students identify important information that they may have missed in their notes. Read aloud the text on which students have taken notes. Ask students to call out important people, places, objects, or events. Then have them include short sentences or phrases containing these words.

Preview DAY 5

Remind students to think about why we have symbols to represent freedom.

Today at a Glance

Oral Vocabulary

Comprehension
◉ Fact and opinion

Lesson Vocabulary
◉ Prefix *un-*

Phonics
◉ Vowel sounds /ü/ and /ù/

Literary Terms
Word choice

Assessment
Fluency
Comprehension

Research and Inquiry
Communicate

Spelling
Vowel sounds in *moon* and *foot*

Conventions
Capital letters

Writing
Notes

Check Oral Vocabulary
! SUCCESS PREDICTOR

Concept Wrap Up

Question of the Week

Why do we have symbols that represent freedom?

Review the concept

Have students look back at the reading selections to find examples that demonstrate why we have symbols that represent freedom.

Review Amazing Words

Display and review this week's concept map. Remind students that this week they have learned ten Amazing Words related to symbols of freedom. Have students use the Amazing Words and the concept map to answer the question of the week, *Why do we have symbols that represent freedom?*

Why we have symbols that represent freedom

Tributes	Characteristics	Documents	Contributions	Recognizable symbols
dedication	impressive	Declaration of Independence	military service	American flag
national monument	symbolic detail	Constitution	elected office	bald eagle
show respect	large or staggering size	Magna Carta	community service	Liberty Bell
competitions	enlightening message	poems	donations or other funds	Statue of Liberty

ELL Check Concepts and Language Use the Day 5 instruction on ELL Poster 26 to monitor students' understanding of the lesson concept.

ELL Poster 26

Amazing Ideas

Connect to the Big Question

Have pairs of students discuss how the Question of the Week connects to the Big Question: *What does freedom mean?* Tell students to use the concept map and what they have learned from this week's Anchored Talks and reading selections to form an Amazing Idea—a realization or "big idea" about Freedom. Remind partners to give suggestions that build on each other's ideas. Then ask each pair to share its Amazing Idea with the class.

Amazing Ideas might include these key concepts:

- Freedom allows people to do, say, and think what they want.
- Symbols that represent freedom remind us of the contributions and sacrifices people have made to protect this idea.

Write about it

Have students write a few sentences about their Amazing Idea beginning with "This week I learned…"

 It's Friday

MONITOR PROGRESS | Check Oral Vocabulary

Have individuals use this week's Amazing Words to describe symbols that represent freedom. Monitor students' abilities to use the Amazing Words and note which words you need to reteach.

If… students have difficulty using the Amazing Words,

then… reteach using the Oral Vocabulary Routine, pp. 367a, 372b, 382b, 390b, OV•1.

Day 1	**Day 2**	**Day 3**	**Day 4**	**Day 5**
Check Oral Vocabulary	Check Word Reading	Check Retelling	Check Fluency	Check Oral Vocabulary

Success Predictor

Amazing Words

impressive	competition
tribute	recognizable
enlighten	disgrace
contribution	staggering
dedication	fund

ELL

English Language Learners
Concept Map Work with students to add new words to the concept map.

Check Oral Vocabulary **Success Predictor**

Objectives
◎ Review fact and opinion.
◎ Review the prefix *un-*.
◎ Review vowel sounds /ü/ and /ů/.
• Review word choice.

Comprehension Review
 Fact and Opinion

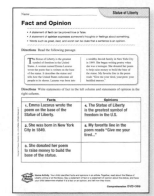

Student Edition p. EI•7

Teach fact and opinion

Envision It!

Review the definition of fact and opinion on p. 370. Remind students that a statement of fact tells something that can be proved true or false and a statement of opinion tells someone's ideas or feelings. For additional support have students review p. EI•7 on fact and opinion.

Guide practice

Have student pairs find an example of a statement of fact and an example of a statement of opinion in *The Story of the Statue of Liberty.* Have students tell why the statement of fact can be proved true or false, and how the statement of opinion tells an idea or feeling.

On their own

For additional practice with fact and opinion, use *Let's Practice It!* page 369 on the *Teacher Resources DVD-ROM.*

Let's Practice It!
TR DVD•369

Vocabulary Review
Prefix *un-*

Teach prefix un-

Remind students that they can use what they know about word structure and the prefix *un-* to figure out the meaning of a word. Review that the prefix *un-* added to the beginning of an adverb or adjective usually means "not." When *un-* is added to a verb, it usually means the reverse of the verb.

Guide practice

Review with students how to use the word structure strategy to determine the meaning of *unhappiness.* Guide students to identify the root, prefix, and suffix in the word.

On their own

Have students use the word structure strategy to determine the meaning of *unveiled.* Then have them use the word correctly in a sentence. Have volunteers share their sentences.

Phonics Review
↻ Vowel Sounds /ü/ and /ủ/

Review
Vowel sounds /ü/ and /ủ/

Write the following sentences on the board. Have students read each one, first quietly to themselves and then aloud as you track the print.

1. **Mom gave us fruit for our snack after school.**

2. **I spilled a few noodles on the book.**

3. **A goose flew south on a chilly Tuesday morning.**

4. **Drew put blueberries on his cereal.**

5. **Sue told us the good news.**

(**Team Talk**) Have students discuss with a partner which words have the vowel sound /ü/ and which words have the vowel sound /ủ/, and ask them to identify the letters that spell each sound. Then call on individuals to share with the class.

Literary Terms Review
Word Choice

Teach word choice

Have students reread "Emma and Liberty" on p. 373. Remind students that word choice refers to the specific words and phrases that authors choose to use in their writing.

Guide practice

Discuss why the author chose to use the words *breathless view* when writing about how the statue can be seen from Battery Park. Have students find other examples of specific word choices the author made to appeal to the readers senses.

On their own

Have students create a word web that shows specific word choices the author made to tell the reader what Emma does and how she feels. Have students discuss the word choice, as they build the word webs.

English Language Learners
Fact and opinion Provide support for students for distinguishing statements of fact from statements of opinion. Look at their statements together and ask questions such as,

- Does this statement have information that can be proved true?

- Does this statement tell a feeling?

- Are there any clue words in the sentence that tells you it is an opinion?

Articulation tip If students have trouble pronouncing words with vowel sounds /ü/ and /ủ/, demonstrate how to pronounce them by slowly repeating words. Have students pay close attention to the movement of your mouth when saying the words. Have students practice saying the words until they develop confidence.

Objectives
• Read aloud grade-level appropriate text with fluency.

Plan to Assess Fluency

☑ **This week assess Advanced students.**

☐ **Week 2** Assess Strategic Intervention students.

☐ **Week 3** Assess On-Level students.

☐ **Week 4** Assess Strategic Intervention students.

☐ **Week 5** Assess any students you have not yet checked during this unit.

Set individual goals for students to enable them to reach the year-end goal.

• Current Goal: 110–120 WCPM

• Year-End Goal: 120 WCPM

Assessment

Check words corrected per minute

Fluency Make two copies of the fluency passage on page 393k. As the student reads the text aloud, mark mistakes on your copy. Also mark where the student is at the end of one minute. To check the student's comprehension of the passage, have him or her retell what was read. To figure words correct per minute (WCPM), subtract the number of mistakes from the total number of words read in one minute.

WCPM

Corrective feedback

If... students cannot read fluently at a rate of 110–120 WCPM,

then... make sure they practice with text at their independent reading level. Provide additional fluency practice by pairing nonfluent readers with fluent readers.

If... students already read at 120 WCPM,

then... have them read a book of their choice independently.

Small Group Time

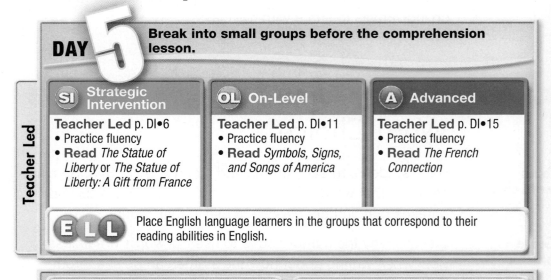

DAY 5 Break into small groups before the comprehension lesson.

SI Strategic Intervention
Teacher Led p. DI•6
• Practice fluency
• **Read** *The Statue of Liberty* or *The Statue of Liberty: A Gift from France*

OL On-Level
Teacher Led p. DI•11
• Practice fluency
• **Read** *Symbols, Signs, and Songs of America*

A Advanced
Teacher Led p. DI•15
• Practice fluency
• **Read** *The French Connection*

ELL Place English language learners in the groups that correspond to their reading abilities in English.

Practice Stations
• Words to Know
• Get Fluent
• Read for Meaning

Independent Activities
• Grammar Jammer
• Concept Talk Video
• Vocabulary Activities

Name _____

Grace's Place

Grace's class was putting on a play about famous places in the   12

United States. Each student was to choose his or her favorite place   24

and dress up to look like that place. Grace didn't know which place to   38

choose.   39

Her friend Nora was very tall. She was going to be the Washington   52

Monument. She was going to get a white suit and make a pointy white   66

hat with paper and glue. Grace couldn't think of anything as good as   79

that.   80

Grace had only a few days left to choose her place. She still had   94

no idea what to be. Grace went into her room and looked around.   107

She saw a crown from when she had dressed up as a princess. Then   121

she saw a flashlight that she had bought for camp. She looked in her   135

closet and saw a green dress that her mom had made her. She saw her   150

notebook on her desk.   154

Grace got an idea! She got all of the things together.   165

On the night of the play, all of Grace's friends showed up as   178

different famous places. There was a Mount Rushmore, a Craters of   189

the Moon, a White House, and of course the Washington Monument.   200

Grace unveiled her outfit last.   205

Grace's green dress became a gown. Her flashlight became a   215

torch, and her notebook became a tablet. She put the crown on top of   229

her head.   231

Grace was the Statue of Liberty!   237

MONITOR PROGRESS   • **Check Fluency**

Objectives
• Read grade-level text with comprehension.

Assessment

Check fact and opinion

Fact and Opinion Use "The Pony Express" on p. 393m to check students' understanding of fact and opinion.

1. Is this sentence a statement of fact or opinion? *There were no telephones, email, or television.* How do you know? (Possible response: I know it is a statement of fact because it is possible to prove whether those things existed before the 1850s.)

2. Is this sentence a statement of fact or opinion? *Pony Express riders were the bravest of all Americans alive in those days.* How do you know? (Possible response: I know it is a statement of opinion because it tells a feeling. The word *bravest* is also a clue that it is an opinion.)

3. Name two facts you learned about the Pony Express in this passage. (Possible response: The route was 1,800 miles long. Horses carried saddle bags filled with mail.)

Corrective feedback

If… students are unable to answer the comprehension questions, **then…** use the Reteach lesson in the *First Stop* book.

The Pony Express

Through much of American history, there wasn't an easy way to deliver mail around the country. There were no telephones, email, or televisions. It took a long time for information to get from one place to another.

By the 1850s, the telegraph started to be used. It allowed printed messages to be sent from place to place. Telegraph wires stretched across distant parts of America, but it took many, many years to get poles and wires up all over. In 1860, the Pony Express began to carry messages to some places where telegraph lines did not yet reach.

How did the Pony Express work? Horses and riders made up the Pony Express. The horses carried saddlebags filled with mail. A rider and horse started at one station and raced to the next. Then a new rider and horse would take the saddlebag and ride to the next station farther away.

The Pony Express could carry mail from Missouri to California in about 10 days. The route used was about 1,800 miles long. There were more than 150 stations along the way.

Pony Express riders were the bravest of all Americans alive in those days. Riders traveled alone on dangerous trails. They raced through icy rivers and along high cliffs. And Pony Express horses were America's fastest. They had to be in order to get the mail across those long distances.

In America's history, the Pony Express was one of the most important methods ever of getting and sending information.

MONITOR PROGRESS

• Fact and opinion

Objectives

- Communicate inquiry results.
- Administer spelling test.
- Review the use of capital letters.

Research and Inquiry
Communicate

Present ideas   Have students share their inquiry results by presenting their informational articles and giving a brief talk on their research and on-site inspections. Have students display any time lines that they created on Day 3.

Listening and speaking   Remind students how to be good speakers and how to communicate effectively with their audience.

- Respond to relevant questions with appropriate details.

- Speak clearly and loudly.

- Keep eye contact with audience members.

- Speak at an appropriate rate so that audience members can easily understand the ideas communicated.

Remind students of these tips for being a good listener.

- Wait until the speaker has finished before raising your hand to ask a relevant question or make a comment.

- Be polite, even if you disagree.

Spelling Test
Vowel Sounds in *moon* and *foot*

Spelling test
To administer the spelling test, refer to the directions, words, and sentences on p. 371c.

Conventions
Extra Practice

Teach
Remind students that days of the week, months of the year, titles and abbreviations of people, and the first word in a sentence or greeting are all capitalized.

Guide practice
Write the following sentences on the board. Have students tell which words should begin with capital letters, and why.

> senator smith was on the committee.
>
> does mr. mercer live in your neighborhood?
>
> the harlem renaissance is an interesting
>
> period in history.

Daily Fix-It
Use Daily Fix-It numbers 9 and 10 in the right margin.

On their own
Write these sentences. Have students look back in *The Story of the Statue of Liberty* to find the correct capitalized words to fill in the blanks. Students should complete *Let's Practice It!* page 370 on the *Teacher Resources DVD-ROM*.

1. **It was to be a present from the people of _____ to the people of America, as a remembrance of the old friendship between the two countries.** (France)

2. **Afterward, it stood in Madison Square in _____ for a number of years.** (New York City)

3. **As the huge statue grew, all of _____ watched with great fascination.** (Paris)

Daily Fix-It
9. When the Statue of Liberty was finaly presented, president Grover Cleveland gave a speech. *(finally; President)*
10. Mr. and mrs. Adams watched fireworks expload in the harbor. *(Mrs.; explode)*

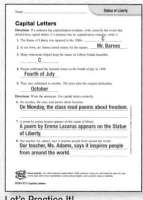

Let's Practice It!
TR DVD•370

Objectives
- Proofread notes, paying attention to spelling and capitalization.

Writing—Notes
Capital Letters

Review Revising

Remind students that yesterday they worked on revising their notes. Today they will proofread their notes.

MINI-LESSON

Proofread for Capitalization

■ **Teach** When we proofread, we look closely at our work, searching for errors in mechanics such as spelling, capitalization, punctuation, and grammar. Today we will focus on using capitalization.

■ **Model** Let's look at the notes we revised yesterday. Display Transparency 26C. Explain that you will look for errors in the spelling and capitalization of proper nouns. If you are unsure of a spelling, model how to check the spelling in the selection. I see a problem. My notes say that the pieces of the statue went across the *Atlantic Ochen.* Something doesn't look right. I'm going to check the selection to make sure I spelled this right. I can see that it should be spelled *O-c-e-a-n.*

Writing Transparency 26C, TR DVD

Continue to point out spelling and capitalization problems. Remind students that notes do not have to be in complete sentences. They can use sentences, sentence fragments, or a mixture of both. Then have students proofread their own notes.

Proofread

Display the Proofreading Tips. Ask students to proofread their notes, using the Proofreading Tips and paying particular attention to the spelling and capitalization of proper nouns. Circulate around the room answering students' questions. When students have finished editing their own work, have pairs proofread one another's notes.

Proofreading Tips

✔ Check to make sure that all proper nouns are capitalized and spelled correctly.

✔ Don't worry about punctuation.

✔ Remember, notes can be sentences or sentence fragments.

Present

Have students incorporate revisions and proofreading edits into their notes to create a final draft.

Give students two options for presenting their notes. Students may either compare their notes with a partner, or they can write a short summary of the selection based on their notes. Students who work with a partner should see how many of their notes are similar. Students who write a summary should read this aloud to a small group or to the class. When students have finished, have each complete the Writing Self-Evaluation Guide.

ROUTINE   Quick Write for Fluency   Team Talk

1. **Talk** Pairs discuss what they learned about taking notes.
2. **Write** Students write a sentence explaining one to two things that are important to remember when taking notes.
3. **Share** Students read aloud their paragraphs to their partners.

Routines Flip Chart

Teacher Note

Writing self-evaluation Make copies of the Self-Evaluation Guide on p. 39 of the *Reader's and Writer's Notebook* and hand out to students.

ELL

English Language Learners
Support proofreading Have students work with a partner to list proper nouns from their notes and practice pronouncing them correctly. Remind them to make sure they are capitalizing proper nouns, but not common nouns.

Poster preview Prepare students for next week by using Week 2, ELL Poster 27. Read the Poster Talk-Through to introduce the concept and vocabulary. Ask students to identify and describe objects and actions in the art.

Selection summary Send home the summary of *Happy Birthday Mr. Kang,* in English and the students' home languages, if available. Students can read the summary with family members.

Preview NEXT WEEK

What does it mean to grant freedom? Next week you read about Mr. Kang, an immigrant who left China to live in the United States.

Weekly Assessment

Use pp. 183–190 of *Weekly Tests* to check:

✔ **Phonics** Vowel Sounds in *moon* and *foot*

✔ **Comprehension Skill** Fact and Opinion

✔ **Lesson Vocabulary**

✔ Review **Comprehension Skill** Author's Purpose

crown	tablet
liberty	torch
models	unforgettable
symbol	unveiled

Weekly Tests

Differentiated Assessment

Use pp. 151–156 of *Fresh Reads for Fluency and Comprehension* to check:

✔ **Comprehension Skill** Fact and Opinion

✔ Review **Comprehension Skill** Author's Purpose

✔ **Fluency** Words Correct Per Minute

Fresh Reads for Fluency and Comprehension

Managing Assessment

Use *Assessment Handbook* for:

✔ **Weekly Assessment Blackline Masters for Monitoring Progress**

✔ **Observation Checklists**

✔ **Record-Keeping Forms**

✔ **Portfolio Assessment**

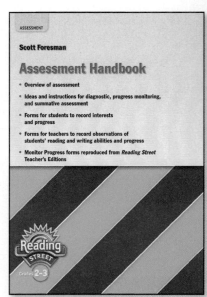

Assessment Handbook

Teacher Notes

Small Group Time

Pacing Small Group Instruction

5-Day Plan

DAY 1	• Reinforce the concept
	• Read Leveled Readers
	  Concept Literacy
	  Below Level

DAY 2	• ◉ Fact and Opinion • ◉ Questioning • Revisit Student Edition pp. 374–381
DAY 3	• ◉ Prefixes • Revisit Student Edition pp. 382–385
DAY 4	• Practice Retelling • Read/Revisit Student Edition pp. 390–391
DAY 5	• Reread for fluency • Reread Leveled Readers

3- or 4-Day Plan

DAY 1	• Reinforce the concept • Read Leveled Readers
DAY 2	• ◉ Fact and Opinion • ◉ Questioning • Revisit Student Edition pp. 374–381
DAY 3	• ◉ Prefixes • Revisit Student Edition pp. 382–385

DAY 4	• Practice Retelling
	• Read/Revisit Student
	  Edition pp. 390–391
	• Reread for fluency
	• Reread Leveled
	  Readers

3-Day Plan: Eliminate the shaded box.

Build Background

■ **Reinforce the Concept** Talk with students about the weekly question *Why do we have symbols that represent freedom?* A *symbol* is something that represents, or stands for, something else. What are some symbols that you know, such as symbols for holidays? *(Students may mention a turkey as a symbol for Thanksgiving and a heart shape as a symbol for Valentine's Day.)* Symbols such as the American flag and the bald eagle stand for the freedom that Americans share. **Add new words to the concept map.** This week we are going to learn about the Statue of Liberty. Even though the statue is a symbol of the United States, it actually came from France. We're going to learn who built the statue, why it was built, and how it got to New York.

Preview Decodable Practice Reader 26A

■ **Before Reading** Review the words on p. 121 of *Decodable Practice Readers 3.2*. Then have students blend these words from the text: *unruly, focus, shyly, zookeeper, gentle, traits, China,* and *picky*. Be sure students understand the meaning of such words as *unruly* and *traits.* Guide students through the text by doing a picture walk.

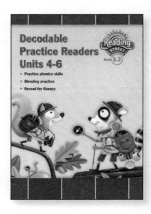

Objectives
• Participate in teacher-led discussions by answering questions with appropriate detail.

 SI *Strategic Intervention*

DAY 1

For a complete literacy instructional plan and additional practice with this week's target skills and strategies, see the **Leveled Reader Teaching Guide.**

Concept Literacy Reader

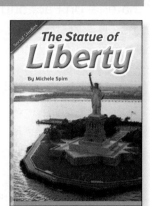

- **Read** *The Statue of Liberty*

- **Before Reading** Preview the book with students, focusing on key concepts and vocabulary. Then help students set a purpose for reading.

- **During Reading** Read the first two pages aloud while students track along with the print. Then have students finish reading the book with a partner.

- **After Reading** After students finish reading, ask: What idea does the Statue of Liberty help people remember? *(The United States and its people are free.)*

Below-Level Reader

- **Read** *The Statue of Liberty: A Gift from France*

- **Before Reading** Have students use the illustrations to preview the book. Then have students set a purpose for reading.

- **During Reading** Read pp. 3–5 aloud. Then do a choral reading of pp. 6–9. If students are able, have them read and discuss the remainder of the book with a partner. Ask: What did France want the Statue of Liberty to represent to the United States? *(the great friendship between the two nations)*

- **After Reading** Ask students to look at and discuss the concept map. Connect the Below-Level Reader to the weekly question *Why do we have symbols that represent freedom?* How do you think the Statue of Liberty makes immigrants to the United States feel? *(It probably makes them feel welcome, free, and hopeful.)*

MONITOR PROGRESS

If... students have difficulty reading the selection with a partner,

then... have them follow along as they listen to the Leveled Readers DVD-ROM.

If... students have trouble understanding what the Statue of Liberty represented for France,

then... reread pp. 6–8 and discuss where and how the statue was built.

Objectives
- Participate in teacher-led discussions by answering questions with appropriate detail.

Small **Group Time**

More Reading

Use additional Leveled Readers or other texts at students' instructional levels to reinforce this week's skills and strategies. For text suggestions, see the Leveled Reader Database or the Leveled Readers Skills Chart on pp. CL24–CL29.

SI *Strategic Intervention*

Reinforce Comprehension

Skill Fact and Opinion Review with students the *Envision It!* material on Fact and Opinion on p. EI•7. Then use p. 370 to review the definitions of *fact* and *opinion.* A statement of fact tells something that can be proved true or false. A statement of opinion tells someone's ideas or feelings. It cannot be proved true or false. Clue words and phrases such as *I believe, in my opinion, awful, great, best,* and *worst* often signal opinions.

Strategy Questioning Review the definition of questioning. As they read, remind students to ask themselves questions about the Statue of Liberty. Knowing which statements are facts and which statements are opinions can help them find answers to their questions. For additional support, refer students to *Envision It!* p. EI•23.

Revisit *The Story of the Statue of Liberty* on pp. 374–381. Have students begin reading aloud the story with a partner. As they read, have them apply the comprehension skill.

* Is the sentence "The Statue of Liberty stands on an island in New York Harbor" a fact or an opinion? *(fact)*

* How do you know the last statement is a fact? *(You can prove it.)* How? *(by looking in a reference book)*

* Is the sentence "She is a beautiful sight to all who pass by her" a fact or an opinion? *(opinion)*

* What clue word helped you identify the last sentence as an opinion? *(beautiful)*

Use the During Reading Differentiated Instruction for additional support.

> **MONITOR PROGRESS**
>
> **If...** students have difficulty reading along with the group,
> **then...** have them follow along as they listen to the AudioText.

Objectives

* Draw conclusions from facts presented in text.
* Ask literal questions of text.

 SI *Strategic Intervention*

DAY 3

Reinforce Vocabulary

■ **Reread for Fluency** Use Decodable Practice Reader 26A.

■ **Decoding Multisyllabic Words** Write the word *gleaming* and model how to use meaningful parts to read it. First, I look for parts I know. I see the ending *-ing*. I also notice the base word *gleam*. I say the parts of the word:
gleam ing. Then I read the word: *gleaming*.

Use the Multisyllabic Words routine on the *Routines Flip Chart* to help students read these other words from the selection: *liberty, sculptor, monuments, remembrance, models, symbol, engineers, skeleton, constructed, tablet, fascination, unveiled,* and *unforgettable.*

◉ **Prefix *un-*/Word Structure** Write and say the word *unwelcome.* Cover the prefix *un-* with your hand. When I cover the prefix *un-*, I see the base word *welcome.* I know the prefix *un-* means "not" or "the opposite of." I can use the meaning of the prefix to figure out that *unwelcome* means "not welcome."

■ **Revisit** *The Story of the Statue of Liberty* on pp. 382–385. Review *Words!* on p. W•5. Then have students finish reading *The Story of the Statue of Liberty.* Encourage them to use word structure to figure out the meaning of words with the prefix *un-*. Point out the word *unveiled* on p. 383. Ask: What prefix do you see in this word? *(un-)* The word *veil* means "to cover." What is the opposite of "to cover"? What do you think *unveiled* means? *("took the cover off")*

Use the During Reading Differentiated Instruction for additional support for struggling readers.

MONITOR PROGRESS

If... students need more practice with the lesson vocabulary,

then... use *Envision It! Pictured Vocabulary Cards.*

Student Edition p. W•5

More Reading

Use additional Leveled Readers or other texts at students' instructional levels to reinforce this week's skills and strategies. For text suggestions, see the Leveled Reader Database or the Leveled Readers Skills Chart on pp. CL24–CL29.

 **Objectives**
- Identify the meaning of common prefixes.
- Use word structure to analyze and decode new words.

Small Group Time

Practice Retelling

■ **Retell** Guide students in using the Retelling Cards to list events in the selection in order.

• Where and why was the Statue of Liberty built? *(in France as a gift to the United States to honor the friendship between the two countries)*

• What happened after the statue was completed? *(It was taken apart, put into 214 crates, shipped to America, and rebuilt on a pedestal on Bedloe's Island in New York Harbor.)*

If students struggle, model a fluent retelling.

Genre Focus

■ **Before Reading or Revisiting** "A Nation of Immigrants" on pp. 390–391, read aloud the genre information about textbooks on p. 390. A textbook is a source of information. A textbook can be about any subject taught in school. This textbook selection will explain in what way the United States is a nation of immigrants. Then have students preview the photographs and captions.

■ **During Reading or Revisiting** Have students perform a choral reading of the selection. When you get to the chart, point out the headings. The headings in a chart help you know what kind of information the chart contains and how it is organized. What are the headings in this article? *("Time Period" and "Where Many Were From")*

■ **After Reading or Revisiting** Have students share their reactions to the selection. Then guide them through the Reading Across Texts and Writing Across Texts activities. Why did immigrants come to the United States? *(to find freedom, opportunity, or work; because they had no choice)*

MONITOR PROGRESS

If... students have difficulty retelling the selection,

then... have them review the selection using the illustrations.

Objectives
• Draw conclusions from facts presented in text.

SI *Strategic Intervention*

DAY 5

For a complete literacy instructional plan and additional practice with this week's target skills and strategies, see the **Leveled Reader Teaching Guide.**

Concept Literacy Reader

■ **Model** Model the fluency skill of rate for students. Ask students to listen carefully as you read aloud the first two pages at an appropriate rate. Explain that reading too fast or too slowly can make it difficult to follow and understand ideas.

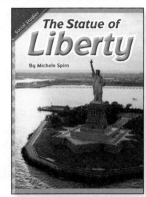

The Statue of Liberty

■ **Fluency Routine**

1. Have students reread passages from *The Statue of Liberty* with a partner.

2. For optimal fluency, students should reread three to four times.

3. As students read, monitor fluency and provide corrective feedback.

See *Routines Flip Chart* for more help with fluency.

■ **Retell** Have students retell *The Statue of Liberty*. Prompt as necessary.

Below-Level Reader

■ **Model** Ask students to listen carefully as you read aloud the first two pages of *The Statue of Liberty: A Gift from France,* emphasizing rate.

The Statue of Liberty: A Gift from France

■ **Fluency Routine**

1. Have students reread passages from *The Statue of Liberty: A Gift from France* with a partner.

2. For optimal fluency, students should reread three to four times.

3. As students read, monitor fluency and provide corrective feedback.

See *Routines Flip Chart* for more help with fluency.

■ **Retell** For additional practice, have students retell *The Statue of Liberty: A Gift from France* page by page, using the photographs and captions.

• Where is the Statue of Liberty? *(in New York Harbor)*

• Who created the statue? *(Frédéric Auguste Bartholdi)*

• Who designed the framework that supports the statue? *(Alexandre Gustave Eiffel)*

MONITOR PROGRESS

If... students have difficulty reading fluently,

then... provide additional fluency practice by pairing nonfluent readers with fluent ones.

Objectives
• Read aloud grade-level appropriate text with fluency.

Small **Group Time**

Pacing Small Group Instruction

15–20 min

5-Day Plan

DAY 1	• Expand the concept • Read On-Level Reader
DAY 2	• Fact and Opinion • Questioning • Revisit Student Edition pp. 374–381
DAY 3	• Prefixes • Revisit Student Edition pp. 382–385
DAY 4	• Practice Retelling • Read/Revisit Student Edition pp. 390–391
DAY 5	• Reread for fluency • Reread On-Level Reader

3- or 4-Day Plan

DAY 1	• Expand the concept • Read On-Level Reader
DAY 2	• Fact and Opinion • Questioning • Revisit Student Edition pp. 374–381
DAY 3	• Prefixes • Revisit Student Edition pp. 382–385
DAY 4	• Practice Retelling • Read/Revisit Student Edition pp. 390–391 • Reread for fluency • Reread On-Level Reader

3-Day Plan: Eliminate the shaded box.

OL On-Level

DAY 1

Build Background

■ **Expand the Concept** Explore with students the weekly question *Why do we have symbols that represent freedom?* Americans are proud of the American flag and the national anthem. Both are symbols of the freedom Americans enjoy. Knowing the facts about these and other symbols can make Americans feel patriotic and proud. Add new words to the concept map.

On-Level Reader

For a complete literacy instructional plan and additional practice with this week's target skills and strategies, see the **Leveled Reader Teaching Guide.**

■ **Before Reading** *Symbols, Signs, and Songs of America,* have students preview the book by looking at the title, cover, pictures, and headings.

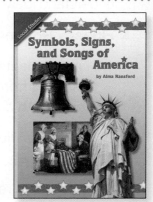

Symbols, Signs, and Songs of America

- What is the topic of this book? *(American symbols)*

- Why is it important to learn about these symbols? *(Knowing the symbols' history and meaning allows people to appreciate them more.)*

Have students create two-column charts with the headings *Symbols* and *Songs.* Explain that students will complete their two-column charts as they read.

■ **During Reading** Read aloud the first three pages of the book as students follow along. Then have them finish reading the book on their own. Remind students to add the names of symbols and songs to their two-column charts as they read. Ask: What are some of the ideas and ideals that these symbols represent? *(freedom, unity, innocence, and justice)*

■ **After Reading** Have partners compare their two-column charts.

- Which symbol did you most enjoy reading about? Why? *(Students should support their choices with evidence from the text.)*

- How does the topic relate to the weekly question *Why do we have symbols that represent freedom? (The text explains what the symbols mean and tells why they have those meanings.)*

Objectives
• Participate in teacher-led discussions by answering questions with appropriate detail.

 OL On-Level

DAY 2

Expand Comprehension

◉ Skill Fact and Opinion Use p. 370 to review the definitions of fact and opinion. For additional review, see Fact and Opinion on p. E•7 in *Envision It!* I will look for clue words that signal opinions, such as *believed, felt, must, should, most, best,* and *all.* Modifiers such as *amazing, wonderful,* and *great* can also signal opinions.

◉ Strategy Questioning Review the definition of questioning, and encourage students to ask questions as they read. For additional support, use the Extend Thinking questions during reading or refer students to p. El•23 of *Envision It!*

Revisit *The Story of the Statue of Liberty* on pp. 374–381. Then have students begin reading aloud. As they read, have them look for facts and opinions.

- On p. 376, what opinion does the author express about the Statue of Liberty? *(She is a beautiful sight to all who pass by her.)* What clue words do you notice? *(beautiful, all)*

- On p. 377, what facts does the author give about Bartholdi's work? *(Bartholdi made sketches and models. He called the woman Liberty, and he wanted her to be a symbol of freedom. He put a lamp in her hand to symbolize that immigrants were welcome. He called the statue* Liberty Enlightening the World.*)*

- Based on what you have read so far, what is your opinion of Bartholdi? What facts from the text support your opinion? *(Encourage students to supply facts in support of their opinions.)*

- What questions do you still have about the Statue of Liberty?

Student Edition p. El•7

More Reading

Use additional Leveled Readers or other texts at students' instructional levels to reinforce this week's skills and strategies. For text suggestions, see the Leveled Reader Database or the Leveled Readers Skills Chart on pp. CL24–CL29.

Objectives
- Draw conclusions from facts presented in text.
- Ask literal questions of text.

Student Edition p. W•5

More Reading

Use additional Leveled Readers or other texts at students' instructional levels to reinforce this week's skills and strategies. For text suggestions, see the Leveled Reader Database or the Leveled Readers Skills Chart on pp. CL24–CL29.

Expand Vocabulary

Prefix *un-*/Word Structure Write the word *unwelcome* as you say it aloud. Ask students to identify the prefix *(un-)*. Then ask:

- What word is the base word? *(welcome)*

- What does the prefix *un-* mean? Look it up in *Words!* or in a dictionary. *("not" or "the opposite of")*

- What meaning do you get when you combine the meaning of *welcome* with the prefix? *("not welcome, not wanted")*

Revisit *The Story of the Statue of Liberty* on pp. 382–385. As students read, encourage them to notice such word structures as the prefix *un-* and the base word *welcome* in *unwelcome*.

- The authors write that "Bartholdi himself unveiled Liberty's face." What does *unveiled* mean? *("took the veil off, uncovered")*

- On p. 385, the authors write that "The Statue of Liberty is a truly unforgettable sight." How can you break the word *unforgettable* into parts? (Un- *means "not" or "the opposite of."* Forget *means "not remember" or "slip from memory." The suffix* -able *means "able, can, may" or "capable."*) How can you put those parts together to figure out what *unforgettable* means? *("not able to forget" or "not capable of erasing from memory")*

- What are some words that have a similar meaning to *unforgettable*? *(remarkable, memorable, amazing)*

Objectives
- Identify the meaning of common prefixes.
- Use word structure to analyze and decode new words.

OL On-Level

DAY 4

Practice Retelling

- **Retell** To assess students' comprehension, use the Retelling Cards. Monitor students' retellings and prompt as needed.

Genre Focus

- **Before Reading or Revisiting** "A Nation of Immigrants" on pp. 390–391, read aloud the genre information about textbooks on p. 390. Explain that a textbook contains information on one subject. Help students preview "A Nation of Immigrants" and set a purpose for reading.

  - What features do you see that are different from stories you have read? *(photographs, captions, a chart)*

  - What does the chart show? *(dates when people from different countries came to the United States)* How do you know? *(by reading the chart title)*

- **During Reading or Revisiting** Have students read with you.

  - Why do you think the author used a chart to show information? *(The chart makes the long lists of dates and countries easier to read and understand.)*

  - What is the information in the chart—facts or opinions? *(facts)* How do you know? *(The information can be proved or disproved.)*

  - How is the textbook similar to and different from *The Story of the Statue of Liberty*? *(Both give facts and details. The textbook material is shorter and includes photographs, captions, and a chart. The narrative nonfiction selection contains opinions and many illustrations. Students may say that both selections are interesting and help them learn new things.)*

- **After Reading or Revisiting** Have students share their reaction to "A Nation of Immigrants." Then have them use dates from *The Story of the Statue of Liberty* to create a time line that could appear in a textbook article about the Statue of Liberty.

Objectives
- Draw conclusions from facts presented in text.

OL On-Level DAY 5

On-Level Reader

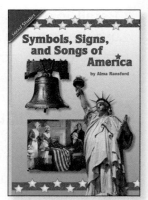

■ **Model** Read aloud p. 3 of the On-Level Reader *Symbols, Signs, and Songs of America,* emphasizing rate. If you wish, rush through the next page of text and discuss how reading too quickly makes it difficult for the listener and the reader to understand the text.

Symbols, Signs, and Songs of America

■ **Fluency Routine**

1. Have students reread passages from *Symbols, Signs, and Songs of America* with a partner.

2. For optimal fluency, students should reread passages three to four times.

3. As students read, monitor fluency and provide corrective feedback. Help students note the rate at which the reader reads. Then discuss how reading at an appropriate rate will help students understand and enjoy more of what they read.

See *Routines Flip Chart* if students need more help with fluency.

■ **Retell** For additional practice, have students use headings and pictures as a guide to retell *Symbols, Signs, and Songs of America.* Prompt as necessary.

• What are some important American symbols?

• What bird is a symbol of the United States? *(the bald eagle)* What bird did Benjamin Franklin want to be a symbol of the United States? *(the wild turkey)*

• How has the American flag changed over time? *(A new star is added with each new state.)*

• What did you learn from reading this selection? *(Encourage students to cite specific information from the text.)*

Objectives
• Read aloud grade-level appropriate text with fluency.

A Advanced **DAY 1**

Build Background

■ **Extend the Concept** Discuss the weekly question *Why do we have symbols that represent freedom?* For hundreds of years, people from other countries have been drawn to the United States by the promise of freedom and opportunity that such American symbols as the flag and the Statue of Liberty represent. How have the various cultures of these people become part of American culture? *(through music, food, art, architecture, and language)*

Advanced Reader

For a complete literacy instructional plan and additional practice with this week's target skills and strategies, see the **Leveled Reader Teaching Guide.**

■ **Before Reading** *The French Connection,* invite students to look at the photographs in the book. Help students set a purpose for reading.

■ **During Reading** Have students read the Advanced Reader independently.

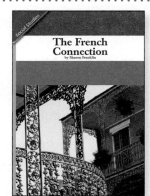

The French Connection

• The author includes journal entries, postcards, and an interview. How do these help make the text easier or harder to read? *(Although some students may find the different formats confusing, most will say that the format changes keep the text lively and varied.)*

• How did the French influence each place in the book? *(The French affected language, foods, place names, and celebrations.)*

■ **After Reading** Have students review the concept map and explain how *The French Connection* helps students answer the weekly question.

• How did the French contribute to the ideals of freedom and opportunity in America? *(They founded early governments, businesses, and communities in North America.)*

• How do you feel knowing that one of America's greatest symbols of freedom—the Statue of Liberty—came from France? Explain. *(Most students will say it seems fine and makes sense because France has affected the United States in many ways.)*

■ **Now Try This** Assign "Now Try This" at the end of the Advanced Reader.

Objectives
• Participate in teacher-led discussions by answering questions with appropriate detail.

Pacing Small Group Instruction

15–20 min

5-Day Plan	
DAY 1	• Extend the concept • Read Advanced Reader
DAY 2	• Fact and Opinion • Questioning • Revisit Student Edition pp. 374–381
DAY 3	• Prefixes • Revisit Student Edition pp. 382–385
DAY 4	• Textbook • Read/Revisit Student Edition pp. 390–391
DAY 5	• Reread for fluency • Reread Advanced Reader

3- or 4-Day Plan	
DAY 1	• Extend the concept • Read Advanced Reader
DAY 2	• Fact and Opinion • Questioning • Revisit Student Edition pp. 374–381
DAY 3	• Prefixes • Revisit Student Edition pp. 382–385
DAY 4	• Textbook • Read/Revisit Student Edition pp. 390–391 • Reread for fluency • Reread Advanced Reader

3-Day Plan: Eliminate the shaded box.

Small Group Time

More Reading

Use additional Leveled Readers or other texts at students' instructional levels to reinforce this week's skills and strategies. For text suggestions, see the Leveled Reader Database or the Leveled Readers Skills Chart on pp. CL24–CL29.

A Advanced   DAY 2

Extend Comprehension

◉ **Skill Fact and Opinion** Explain that narrative nonfiction often blends facts and opinions. A selection about an American symbol of freedom might contain facts about the history of the symbol and opinions about how people feel about the symbol. Then have students read the first page of *The Story of the Statue of Liberty,* tracking facts and opinions as they read.

◉ **Strategy Questioning** Review the definition of the strategy.

• What facts do you notice in the first paragraph of the selection? *(The statue stands on an island in New York Harbor. Millions of people visit the statue each year.)*

• What opinions do you notice in the first paragraph of the selection? *(The statue is "a beautiful sight to all." The view from the statue is stunning.)*

Revisit *The Story of the Statue of Liberty* on pp. 374–381. Remind students to look for facts and opinions and ask themselves questions as they read.

■ **Critical Thinking** Challenge students to think critically about the selection.

• How do the authors blend facts with opinions? Does the selection include more facts or more opinions? *(The selection is mostly factual, but the authors do also include their opinions of how beautiful the statue and the view from it are.)*

• On p. 381, the authors say "Then began the hard work of taking Liberty apart for the long voyage across the Atlantic Ocean." What facts do they give to support this statement? *(Each piece was marked and packed. There were 214 crates that were carried by train and then by ship.)*

During reading, use the Extend Thinking questions and the During Reading Differentiated Instruction for additional support.

Objectives
• Draw conclusions from facts presented in text.
• Ask literal questions of text.

A Advanced

DAY 3

Extend Vocabulary

👁 **Prefix *un-*/Word Structure** Read a sentence containing a word with the prefix *un-*, such as "When the crates reached the United States, the pieces of the Statue of Liberty had to be unpacked."

- The prefix *un-* means "not" or "the opposite of." So what does *unpacked* mean? *("took things out of boxes or cases")*

- How does knowing the meaning of the prefix help you understand the meaning of the word? *(It tells me that* unpacked *is the opposite of* packed.*)*

Challenge students to find other words with the prefix *un-*.

- What word on p. 383 contains the prefix *un-*? *(unveiled)* If *veiled* means "covered something," what does *unveiled* mean? *("took the cover off something")*

- What word do you see on p. 385 with the prefix *un-*? *(unforgettable)* What does the word mean? *("not able to be forgotten" or "staying in a person's memory")*

■ **Revisit** *The Story of the Statue of Liberty* on pp. 382–385.

■ **Creative Thinking** Encourage students to reflect on the selection. Say to students: Imagine that a group of people chose you to create a statue that symbolized our community. What would your statue show? Why? How large would the statue be and where would you put it? *(Accept all reasonable responses. Some students may say that they would create a large statue of a wild animal that lives in the region and that they would put the statue in a place where many people could see it. Other students might create a statue of a famous person from the community.)*

More Reading

Use additional Leveled Readers or other texts at students' instructional levels to reinforce this week's skills and strategies. For text suggestions, see the Leveled Reader Database or the Leveled Readers Skills Chart on pp. CL24–CL29.

Objectives
- Identify the meaning of common prefixes.
- Use word structure to analyze and decode new words.

Small Group Time

A Advanced

DAY **4**

Genre Focus

- **Before Reading or Revisiting** "A Nation of Immigrants" on pp. 390–391, have students read "A Nation of Immigrants" on their own. Read the panel information on textbooks. Then have students use the text features to set a purpose for reading.

- **During Reading or Revisiting** Have students read the selection. Point out the photographs, captions, and chart. *How is a textbook different from narrative nonfiction, such as* The Story of the Statue of Liberty? *(A textbook uses photographs, captions, headings, subheadings, charts, graphs, and other visual aids to support and expand the text; narrative nonfiction provides information as a story that has a beginning, middle, and end.)* As they read, have students consider how the text features increase understanding.

A Nation of Immigrants

- **After Reading or Revisiting** Have students discuss Reading Across Texts. Then have them do Writing Across Texts independently.

Objectives
- Draw conclusions from facts presented in text.

A Advanced

DAY **5**

- **Reread for Fluency** Have students silently reread passages from the Advanced Reader *The French Connection.* Then have them reread aloud with a partner or individually. As students read, monitor fluency and provide corrective feedback. If students read fluently on the first reading, they do not need to reread three to four times. Assess the fluency of students in this group using p. 393j.

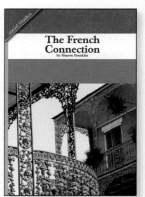

- **Retell** Have students summarize the main idea and key details from the Advanced Reader *The French Connection.*

- **Now Try This** Have students complete their projects and present them to classmates.

The French Connection

Objectives
- Read aloud grade-level appropriate text with fluency.

The ELL lessons are organized by strands. Use them to scaffold the weekly curriculum of lessons or during small group time instruction.

Academic Language

Students will hear or read the following academic language in this week's core instruction. As students encounter the vocabulary, provide a simple definition or concrete example. Then ask students to suggest an example or synonym of the word and identify available cognates.

Skill Words	fact	vowel (vocal)
	opinion (opinión)	prefix (prefijo)
Concept Words	represent	freedom
	(representar)	statue (estatua)

*Spanish cognates in parentheses

Concept Development

Why do we have symbols that represent freedom?

■ **Preteach Concept**

• **Prior Knowledge** Have students turn to pp. 366–367 in the Student Edition. Call attention to the picture of the American flag and tap into students' knowledge of the American flag. Do you recognize that flag? What country does that flag belong to? What is the flag a symbol of? Where have you seen that flag?

• **Discuss Concept** Elicit students' knowledge and experience of why we have symbols that represent freedom. Why is freedom important to Americans? Why do we have symbols like the flag and the Liberty Bell that represent freedom? Supply background information as needed.

• **Poster Talk-Through** Read the Poster Talk-Through on ELL Poster 26 aloud and work through the Day 1 activities.

■ **Daily Concept and Vocabulary Development** Use the daily activities on ELL Poster 26 to build concept and vocabulary knowledge.

Objectives
• Use prior knowledge and experiences to understand meanings in English.
• Learn new language structures, expressions, and basic and academic vocabulary heard during classroom instructions and interactions.
• Speak using grade-level content area vocabulary in context to internalize new English words and build academic language proficiency.

Content Objectives
• Use concept vocabulary related to symbols of freedom.

Language Objectives
• Express ideas in response to art and discussion.
• Derive meaning from media to build concept attainment.

Daily Planner	
DAY 1	• **Frontload Concept** • **Preteach** Comprehension Skill, Vocabulary, Phonics/Spelling, Conventions • **Writing**
DAY 2	• **Review** Concept, Vocabulary, Comprehension Skill • **Frontload Main Selection** • **Practice** Phonics/Spelling, Conventions/Writing
DAY 3	• **Review** Concept, Comprehension Skill, Vocabulary, Conventions/Writing • **Reread Main Selection** • **Practice** Phonics/Spelling
DAY 4	• **Review Concept** • **Read ELL/ELD Readers** • **Practice** Phonics/Spelling, Conventions/Writing
DAY 5	• **Review** Concept, Vocabulary, Comprehension Skill, Phonics/Spelling, Conventions • **Reread ELL/ELD Readers** • **Writing**

*See the ELL Handbook for ELL Workshops with targeted instruction.

Concept Talk Video

Have students build and reinforce concept attainment by listening to the Concept Talk Video to build background knowledge about symbols of freedom. Have students tell what they learned by listening.

Support for English Language Learners

Language Objectives

- Internalize, expand use basic vocabulary.
- Learn meanings of grade-level vocabulary.

Cognates

For Spanish learners, point out that the words for *represent* and *statue* are similar in English and Spanish. Reinforce the concept that these languages share many similar words.

English Opportunity

Have students internalize the high-frequency words. Have each student use a high-frequency word in a sentence that describes a person, place, or object. Students can use the ELL Poster or their Student Edition for ideas.

ELL *English Language Learners*

Basic Vocabulary

■ **High-Frequency Words** Use the ELL Vocabulary Routine on p. 471 of the *ELL Handbook* to systematically teach newcomers the first 300 sight words in English. Students who began learning ten words per week at the beginning of the year are now learning words 251–260 (*ELL Handbook,* p. 455). p. 446 of the handbook contains a bank of strategies that you can use to ensure students' mastery of high-frequency words.

Lesson Vocabulary

■ **Preteach** Preteach the Lesson Vocabulary using this routine:

1. Distribute copies of this week's Word Cards (*ELL Handbook,* p. 179).

2. Display ELL Poster 26 and reread the Poster Talk-Through.

3. Using the poster illustrations, model how a word's meaning can be expressed with other similar words: The statue was officially unveiled, or uncovered for all to see, in 1886.

4. Use these sentences to reveal the meaning of the other words.

- The *torch* is a symbol of freedom's light. **(a light usually carried by hand)**

- The date written on the *tablet* is July 4, 1776. **(a slab of stone or wood made for writing things on)**

- People always remember this *unforgettable* landmark. **(not easily forgotten)**

- The statue includes many *symbols* of freedom. **(representations)**

- The queen's *crown* was golden. **(royal head covering)**

- There were many *models* made of the statue before it was completed. **(small copies)**

- The statue stands for *liberty* to people all over the world. **(freedom)**

Objectives

- Expand and internalize initial English vocabulary by learning and using high-frequency English words necessary for identifying and describing people, places, and objects, by retelling simple stories and basic information represented or supported by pictures, and by learning and using routine language needed for classroom communication.

English Language Learners

■ **Reteach** Distribute a copy of the Word Cards to each student. Guide students in writing a clue for each word to help them recognize the word.

Point out that a *symbol* is something that stands for something else. Discuss each word's meaning.

Ask questions about the words. Students can read the correct Word Card to answer each question.

- What do kings and queens wear on their head? (crown)

- What can you write or carve a message on? (tablet)

- What is a synonym for *revealed*? (unveiled)

- If you were to build something, what might you make before you began? (models)

- What can represent light? (torch)

- What is another word for something that will always be remembered? (unforgettable)

- What is another word for *freedom*? (liberty)

■ **Writing** Have partners create their own picture/word cards using index cards. Assign words to students or have each student pick two words. Have them write the word on one side of an index card and write or draw the definition on the other side of the card. Then have students quiz their partners by showing the illustrated definition and asking their partner to guess which word it represents.

Beginning Have Beginning students illustrate and label their picture/word cards.

Intermediate Have students illustrate and write an example of the word on their picture/word cards.

Advanced Have students illustrate and write the word's meaning.

Advanced High Have students illustrate and write the word's meaning as well as provide a sample sentence using the word.

Language Objectives

- Produce drawings, phrases, or short sentences to show understanding of Lesson Vocabulary.

- Write newly acquired content-based vocabulary.

ELL Teacher Tip

According to ELL consultant Dr. Georgia Earnest García, "Students can transfer aspects of home-language literacy to their English literacy development, such as phonological awareness and reading (or listening) comprehension strategies." To help students grasp this week's topic and vocabulary, you might ask English learners to first think about what they have learned about the topic in their home language and then transfer this to English.

Support for English Language Learners

Content Objectives
- Monitor and adjust oral comprehension.
- Understand main points of spoken language that is unfamiliar.

Language Objectives
- Discuss oral passages.
- Use a graphic organizer to take notes.

Graphic Organizer

Main Idea		
Details	Details	Details

ELL Teacher Tip
Review with students that the main idea is what the text is mostly about and that the details support the main idea.

English Opportunity
Have students turn to p. E•19 in the Student Edition. Review the content on this page with students. Before students are familiar with the Liberty Bell, tell them the title of story and ask what they think the important ideas, or main points, of the story will be. Ask again after the first and second readings.

ELL English Language Learners

Listening Comprehension

The Liberty Bell

The Liberty Bell is the most famous bell in the world. It is a symbol of freedom of the United States. People see the bell and remember when and why America became a free country.

The Liberty Bell is now in Philadelphia, Pennsylvania. The bell that is there today is the third bell that was made. The first two bells did not work right. But the third bell worked just fine. The Liberty Bell weighs 13,000 pounds. This number stands for the first thirteen states in the United States. It weighs 1,000 pounds for each state.

The Liberty Bell now has a big crack in it. No one knows how it happened. As the crack got bigger, the sound got worse. Soon the bell grew silent. Until the bell cracked, it rang every year for sixty-one years. It was rung on July 4th. That day is the birthday of the United States.

For many years the Liberty Bell hung in a building called Independence Hall. A few years ago it was moved to a new building. The bell now hangs in Liberty Bell Center in Philadelphia. The building is open all year so people can visit the bell and learn more about it. The Liberty Bell is silent now. But it is still a symbol of freedom of the United States.

Prepare for the Read Aloud The modified Read Aloud above prepares students for listening to the oral reading "Let Freedom Ring" on p. 367b.

■ **First Listening: Listen to Understand** Write the title of the Read Aloud on the board. This is about a special bell in the United States that is a symbol of freedom. Listen to find out when and where the bell was made. Why it is so special? Afterward, ask the question again and have students share their answers.

■ **Second Listening: Listen to Check Understanding** Using a Main Idea and Details graphic organizer (*ELL Handbook,* p. 487) work with students to list the main idea and details from the Read Aloud.

Objectives
- Demonstrate listening comprehension of increasingly complex spoken English by following directions, retelling or summarizing spoken messages, responding to questions and requests, collaborating with peers, and taking notes commensurate with content and grade-level needs.

Phonics and Spelling

■ **Vowel Sounds for /ü/ and /u̇/** Use Sound-Spelling Cards 90, 68, 102, and 103 to teach the relationship between the sounds and letters, and spellings of *oo, ew, ue, ui.*

• Display Card 90. This is a moon, /m/ /oo/ /n/. What vowel sound do you hear in the word *moon*? Say it with me: /oo/ /oo/, *moon.* Repeat with cards 68, 102, and 103 to teach *ew, ue, ui.*

• Write *moon, newt, glue,* and *fruit* on the board. Underline the sound spellings in the words. The sound /oo/ can be spelled *oo, ew, ue,* or *ui.* Segment and blend each of the words as a class. Point out that /oo/ is usually spelled *ue* when it comes at the end of a word.

• Have students write the /oo/ sound spellings *oo, ew, ue,* and *ui* on index cards. Then read the following words aloud to the class: *food, flew, clue, suit, blue.* Pause after each word so students can find and hold up the card that contains the sound-spelling pattern that corresponds to the word.

Vocabulary Skill: Prefix *un-*

■ **Preteach and Model** Write these word pairs on the board:

happy, unhappy   *safe, unsafe*   *lucky, unlucky*

Read the words aloud with students and discuss their meanings. What do you notice about the words? Circle the prefix *un-* in each word. This syllable, *un-,* is a prefix. A prefix is a word part that is added to the beginning of a word. Adding a prefix changes the meaning of a word. The prefix *un-* means "not." So *unhappy* means "not happy."

■ **Practice** Display the words *kind, fair, fold,* and *true.* Discuss the meaning of each word with students. Then have students add the prefix *un-* to each word and ask volunteers to explain how each word's meaning has changed based on the addition of the prefix.

Beginning/Intermediate Guide students in figuring out the meaning of the following words: *unsure, unfamiliar, unlikely, unpopular.*

Advanced/Advanced High Once students determine the meaning of the new words, have them use each word in a sentence.

Content Objectives

• Read words with vowel sounds for /ü/ and /u̇/.

• Identify words with prefix *un-*.

Language Objectives

• Apply phonics and decoding skills to words with *oo, ew, ue,* and *ui.*

• Discuss meaning of words with prefix *un-*.

• Write words with prefix *un-*.

 Transfer Skills

Vowel Sounds In Spanish each vowel has only one sound. Spanish speakers may benefit from extra practice pronouncing and spelling words with variant vowel sounds in English.

ELL Teaching Routine

For more practice with prefixes, use the Multisyllabic Word Strategy Routine (*ELL Handbook,* p. 473).

Objectives
• Practice producing sounds of newly acquired vocabulary such as long and short vowels, silent letters, and consonant clusters to pronounce English words in a manner that is increasingly comprehensible.

Support for English Language Learners

Content Objectives

- Understand general meaning of spoken language and adapt for formal and informal purposes.

- Distinguish between facts and opinions.

- Identify facts and opinions to aid comprehension.

Language Objectives

- Discuss evidence for facts and opinions.

- Retell facts and opinions from a reading.

- Understand that opinions often express feelings.

ELL Workshop

Provide students with the opportunity to orally express their opinions and ideas. Express Opinions (*ELL Handbook,* pp. 414–415) supports student practice.

ELL *English Language Learners*

Comprehension
Fact and Opinion

- **Preteach** A statement of fact can be proven true or false. An opinion is someone's feeling about an idea, and people have different feelings about ideas. Have students turn to *Envision It!* on p. EI•7 in the Student Edition. Read the text aloud together so students understand general meaning. Have students identify how the first boy's statement can be proven true (you could check it in a book about ants) and how the second boy's statement is an opinion (he is stating his feeling about the ants).

- **Reteach** Distribute copies of Picture It! (*ELL Handbook,* p. 180). Before reading aloud, remind students to look for word clues about facts and opinions. (*Fact:* Most immigrants were men. Many left their families. Some made money by building railroads. Others did not want the job. The Chinese-American community has grown. *Opinion:* Life was hard for immigrants. That's a hard job! They have had great success.)

Beginning Reread the story to students. Have them raise their hand when you read an opinion, and have them nod when you read a fact. Take time to correct and explain mistakes.

Intermediate Tell students that adjectives are sometimes clues that a sentence contains an opinion. Have students work in pairs to underline all the adjectives in the reading and figure out if the sentence is an opinion.

Advanced/Advanced High Ask students to underline facts. Then, group students into groups of three. Assign each group a fact. Have students name two reference sources they could use to prove their fact.

MINI-LESSON

Social Language

Show students the picture of the two boys on the Envision It! above. Informal language is the way you speak to your friends. Formal language is the way you speak to adults. We also use formal language when we give facts: *Many ants collect seeds to feed other ants in the nest.* How do you say "Wow, this is awesome!" in a formal way?

Objectives

- Demonstrate an increasing ability to distinguish between formal and informal English and an increasing knowledge of when to use each one commensurate with grade-level learning expectations.

 English Language Learners

Reading Comprehension
The Story of the Statue of Liberty

Student Edition pp. 374–375

■ **Frontloading** Have students develop background knowledge by looking through *The Story of the Statue of Liberty,* pp. 374–385 in the Student Edition, and tell what they think makes it look like narrative nonfiction, or a story about real people and events. Distribute copies of the English summary of *The Story of the Statue of Liberty* (*ELL Handbook,* p.181). Have students read the summary aloud with you. Encourage them to ask questions about any ideas or unfamiliar words.

Sheltered Reading Have students demonstrate comprehension by responding to questions such as the following:

• p. 376: Where is the Statue of Liberty? (on an island in New York Harbor)

• p. 378: What does the Statue of Liberty hold in her right hand? (a torch) What does she hold in her left hand? (a tablet)

• p. 381: How was the Statue of Liberty sent to America? (It was taken apart, each piece was packed in a crate, then the crates were carried by train and ship to America.)

• p. 382: How was the Statue of Liberty built twice? (It was first built in France, then taken apart and built again in America.)

• p. 383: How was the Statue of Liberty important to immigrants coming to the United States? (They would see her when they arrived by ship. She was a symbol of their hopes and dreams.)

■ **Fluency: Rate** Remind students that it is important to read at a rate, or speed, that is fast enough to keep interest but slow enough to still understand the content. Read the first paragraph on p. 376, modeling how reading at different rates changes the effect of the story. Have pairs read a paragraph to each other and offer constructive feedback about each other's rate.

Have students turn to p. 386 in the Student Edition. Have partners work collaboratively by having one student use the visual support of the images to retell the story. The other student should take notes while listening and then summarize what he or she heard.

Content Objectives
• Monitor and adjust comprehension.

• Make and adjust predictions.

Language Objectives
• Expand reading skills by reading grade-level text at appropriate rate.

• Summarize text using visual support.

Audio Support
Students can prepare for reading *The Story of the Statue of Liberty* by using the eSelection or the Audio-Text CD. See the AudioText CD Routine (*ELL Handbook,* p. 477) for suggestions on using these learning tools.

ELL Workshop
Students can use the selection art to retell stories or information in selections. Support students with Retell or Summarize (*ELL Handbook,* pp. 409–410).

Objectives
• Demonstrate English comprehension and expand reading skills by employing basic reading skills such as demonstrating understanding of supporting ideas and details in text and graphic sources, summarizing text and distinguishing main ideas from details commensurate with content area needs.

Support for English Language Learners

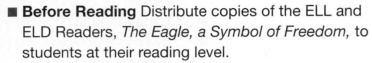

For additional leveled instruction, see the **ELL/ELD Reader Teaching Guide.**

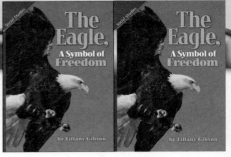

ELD Reader   ELL Reader

Comprehension
The Eagle, a Symbol of Freedom

■ **Before Reading** Distribute copies of the ELL and ELD Readers, *The Eagle, a Symbol of Freedom,* to students at their reading level.

 • **Preview** Read the title aloud with students: This is a nonfiction text about how the bald eagle became a symbol of freedom in the United States. Have students look through the pictures and predict why the eagle is a symbol of freedom.

 • **Set a Purpose for Reading** Let's read to figure out how bald eagles became a symbol of freedom.

■ **During Reading** Follow the Reading Routine for both reading groups.

1. Read the entire Reader aloud slowly.

2. Reread pp. 1–5, pausing to build background or model comprehension. Have Beginning students finger-point as you read. Use the questions in the chart to check students' comprehension.

3. Have students reread pp. 1–5 independently. They can read silently to increase comprehension.

4. Repeat steps 2–3 above for pp. 6–8.

■ **After Reading** Use the exercises on the inside back cover of each Reader and invite students to share their writing. In a whole-group discussion, ask students, How did the bald eagle become the symbol of American freedom? Record their answers on the board and invite them to point to pictures in the book to support their answers.

ELD Reader Beginning/Intermediate

■ **p. 2** What does the symbol of a heart mean? (love) Read the sentence that gives you the answer aloud. (A heart means love.)

■ **p. 6** What does the bald eagle stand for? (freedom) Read the sentence that gives you the answer aloud. (The bald eagle means or stands for freedom.)

Writing What fact about symbols is the most interesting to you? Find a sentence in the book that tells about it. Copy the sentence. Then read it aloud to your partner.

ELL Reader Advanced/Advanced High

■ **p. 2** What are symbols? (pictures, animals, or signs that mean something)

■ **p. 5** Why did leaders from the colonies want a national symbol? (They wanted something to stand for America's freedom.)

■ **p. 8** Where can you see symbols of the eagle today? (a one dollar bill, stamps, the president's flag)

Study Guide Distribute copies of the ELL Reader Study Guide (*ELL Handbook,* p. 184). Scaffold comprehension by helping students determine facts and opinions. Review their responses together. (See *ELL Handbook,* pp. 209–212.)

Objectives
• Express opinions, ideas, and feelings ranging from communicating single words and short phrases to participating in extended discussions on a variety of social and grade-appropriate academic topics.

 **ELL** English Language Learners

Conventions
Capital Letters

■ **Preteach** Display the following sentence on the board:
My brother's name is Mike.

Underline the capital *M* in *My* and *Mike.* Explain that these letters are capital letters, and that certain words in a sentence must always be capitalized. The first word in a sentence must always be capitalized. Names of people and places must also be capitalized.

■ **Practice** Display the following sentences: *juan was born in puerto rico. he has a sister named consuela. now juan and consuela live in new york.*

Have students write the sentences and underline the names of the people and places in the sentences. Have students rewrite the sentences correctly.

 Beginning/Intermediate Help students brainstorm a list of proper nouns. Help them use the nouns in oral sentences or short phrases. Record students' responses and have them identify which words should be capitalized.

Advanced/Advanced High Have students brainstorm a list of proper nouns. Have them write a paragraph that includes at least three proper nouns.

■ **Reteach** Some words in sentences must always be capitalized, including the names of people and places and the first word in a sentence. Display these sentences: *Sheri was born on July 4. She was born on Independence Day.*

Point out that *July and Independence Day* are capitalized. Months and dates must also be capitalized.

■ **Practice** Have students correct the capitalization errors in the sentences below.
new year's day is celebrated on january 1.
president grover Cleveland dedicated the statue of liberty.
the statue is a beautiful sight.

 Beginning Have students circle all the words that should be capitalized. Monitor words students identify.

Intermediate/Advanced/Advanced High Have students write two or three additional sentences that include proper nouns and dates.

Objectives
• Speak using a variety of grammatical structures, sentence lengths, sentence types, and connecting words with increasing accuracy and ease as more English is acquired.

Content Objectives
• Use capital letters.
• Correctly write phrases and sentences with capital letters.

Language Objectives
• Write phrases and sentences with capital letters.

 Transfer Skills

Capital Letters In languages including Spanish, French, Polish, and Vietnamese, the names of days and months are not usually capitalized.

Support for English Language Learners

Content Objectives
- Learn how to paraphrase a text.

Language Objectives
- Paraphrase a portion of text.
- Share feedback for editing and revising.

ELL Teaching Routine
For practice spelling words related to liberty, use the Spelling Routine (*ELL Handbook,* p. 476).

ELL Workshop
Students can collaborate with peers to discuss their writing. Discuss with Classmates (*ELL Handbook,* pp. 419–420) provides assistance with discussion.

ELL English Language Learners

Paraphrasing

■ **Introduce** Display the model and read it aloud. Explain that paraphrasing is explaining something in your own words. A paraphrase includes all of the author's ideas in the original text, but is simpler than the original. What happened in 1886? (Liberty was finally completed.) What did people do that day? (They held a celebration with speeches and songs.) Who unveiled the Statue of Liberty? (Frederic Auguste Bartholdi) Tell students that a paraphrase would include of all these ideas, written in their own words.

> **Writing Model**
>
> At last, in 1886, Liberty was standing where she belonged. A wonderful celebration was held. Boats and ships filled the harbor. Speeches were read, songs were sung. Bartholdi himself unveiled Liberty's face and she stood, gleaming in all her glory, for everyone to see. There was a great cheer from the crowd. Then President Grover Cleveland gave a speech.

■ **Practice** Work with students to paraphrase the model, using the following sentence frames.

> In 1886 _____. That day _____. Bartholdi _____.

■ **Write** Have students choose a page in *The Story of the Statue of Liberty.* Have them take notes and write a paraphrase of that page. Remind students to include only the most important ideas and include sentences of varying lengths.

Beginning Have students dictate to you one or two sentences about the page. Write out their sentences and have students copy them.

Intermediate Have students use sentence frames similar to what was used in Practice to write their paraphrase. Have them speak their frames when they are done.

Advanced/Advanced High Have students write their paraphrase independently. Then have pairs exchange papers and read the other's paragraph aloud, providing feedback for revising and editing. Encourage partners to check that all important ideas are included from the page.

Objectives
- Write using a variety of grade-appropriate sentence lengths, patterns, and connecting words to combine phrases, clauses, and sentences in increasingly accurate ways as more English is acquired.

Happy Birthday
Mr. Kang

This Week's ELL Overview

ELL Handbook

- Maximize Literacy and Cognitive Engagement
- Research Into Practice
- Full Weekly Support for Every Selection

Happy Birthday Mr. Kang
- Multi-Lingual Summaries in Five Languages
- Selection-Specific Vocabulary Word Cards
- Frontloading/Reteaching for Comprehension Skill Lessons
- ELD and ELL Reader Study Guides

- Transfer Activities
- Professional Development

Daily Leveled ELL Notes

ELL notes appear throughout this week's instruction and ELL Support is on the DI pages of your Teacher's Edition. The following is a sample of an ELL note from this week.

English Language Learners

Beginning Write several words with the schwa sound from the Decodable Practice Reader on the board, such as *seven, famous, moment, family, afraid,* and *breakfast.* Point to each word as you read it aloud. Then underline the vowel in each unaccented syllable that stands for /ə/. Have students repeat the words with you.

Intermediate After reading, have students list the words in the story with the schwa sound. Have them sort the words according to the vowel that stands for /ə/. Ask students to compare their lists with a partner.

Advanced Have students write sentences about the story, using at least five words with the schwa sound.

Advanced High After reading the story, have students write about another adventure that Ben goes on. Ask students to use at least four words in their writing that have the schwa sound.

ELL by Strand

The ELL lessons on this week's Support for English Language Learners pages are organized by strand. They offer additional scaffolding for the core curriculum. Leveled support notes on these pages address the different proficiency levels in your class. See pages DI•41–DI•50.

ELL Guy
Dr. Jim Cummins

The Three Pillars of ELL Instruction

ELL Strands	Activate Prior Knowledge	Access Content	Extend Language
Vocabulary pp. DI•42–DI•43	Preteach	Reteach	Leveled Writing Activities
Reading Comprehension p. DI•47	Frontloading	Sheltered Reading	After Reading
Phonics, Spelling, and Word Analysis p. DI•45	Preteach	Teach/Practice	Leveled Practice Activities
Listening Comprehension p. DI•44	Prepare for the Read Aloud	First Listening	Second Listening
Conventions and Writing pp. DI•49–DI•50	Preteach/Introduce	Practice	Leveled Practice Activities/ Leveled Writing Activities
Concept Development p. DI•41	Prior Knowledge	Discuss Concept	Daily Concept and Vocabulary Development

This Week's Practice Stations Overview

Six Weekly Practice Stations with Leveled Activities can be found at the beginning of each week of instruction. For this week's Practice Stations, see pp. 394h–394i.

Small Group Teacher-led

Classroom Management Handbook for Differentiated Instruction Practice Stations

Practice Stations

Daily Leveled Center Activities

○ Below   ☐ Advanced

△ On-Level   **ELL**

Practice Stations Flip Charts

	Word Wise	Word Work	Words to Know	Let's Write	Read For Meaning	Get Fluent
Objectives	• Spell words with the vowel sounds in *moon* and *foot*: *oo, ew, ue, ui,* and *oo, u.*	• Identify and pronounce words with the vowel sounds in *moon* and *foot*: *oo, ew, ue, ui,* and *oo, u.*	• Identify the meaning of words with the prefix *un-*.	• Take notes while reading a nonfiction selection.	• Identify fact and opinion in a nonfiction selection.	• Read aloud at an appropriate rate.
Materials	• *Word Wise* Flip Chart Activity 27 • Teacher-made word cards • paper • pencils	• *Word Work* Flip Chart Activity 27 • Teacher-made word cards • paper • pencils	• *Words to Know* Flip Chart Activity 27 • Teacher-made word cards • paper • pencils	• *Let's Write* Flip Chart Activity 27 • paper • pencils	• *Read for Meaning* Flip Chart Activity 27 • Leveled Readers • paper • pencils	• *Get Fluent* Flip Chart Activity 27 • Leveled Readers

This Week on Reading Street!

Freedom

Question of the Week
What does it mean to grant freedom?

Daily Plan

Don't Wait Until Friday

Whole Group

- ◉ Cause and Effect
- ◉ Antonyms
- • Fluency/Phrasing
- • Writing/Conventions
- • Research and Inquiry

MONITOR PROGRESS | **Success Predictor**

Day 1	Day 2	Day 3	Day 4	Day 5
Check Oral Vocabulary	Check Word Reading	Check Retelling	Check Fluency	Check Oral Vocabulary

Small Group

Teacher Led

- • Reading Support
- • Skill Support
- • Fluency Practice

Practice Stations

Independent Activities

Customize Literacy More support for a balanced literacy approach, see pp. CL•1–CL•47.

Customize Writing More support for a customized writing approach, see pp. CW•1–CW•10.

Whole Group

- • Writing: Poetry: Limerick
- • Conventions: Abbreviations
- • Spelling: Schwa

Assessment

- • Weekly Tests
- • Day 5 Assessment
- • Fresh Reads

You Are Here!
Unit 6
Week 2

This Week's Reading Selections

Main Selection
Genre: **Realistic Fiction**

Paired Selection
Genre: **Expository Text**

Decodable Readers

Leveled Readers

ELL and ELD Readers

Resources on Reading Street!

	Build Concepts	Phonics	Comprehension
Whole Group	 Let's Talk About pp. 394–395	 Phonics Skill Lesson pp. 396–397 / Decodable Readers / Sound-Spelling Cards	 Envision It! Skills/ Strategies / Comprehension Skill Lesson pp. 398–399
Go Digital	• Concept Talk Video	• Interactive Sound-Spelling Cards • Decodable eReaders	• Envision It! Animations • eSelections
Small Group and Independent Practice	 Happy Birthday Mr. Kang pp. 402–419 / ELL and ELD Readers Leveled Readers / Decodable Readers	 Decodable Readers / Practice Station Flip Chart	 Happy Birthday Mr. Kang pp. 402–419 / ELL and ELD Readers / Leveled Readers  Envision It! Skills/ Strategies / Reader's and Writer's Notebook / Practice Station Flip Chart
Go Digital	• eReaders • eSelection • Decodable eReaders	• Letter Tile Drag and Drop • Decodable eReaders	• Envision It! Animations • eSelection • eReaders
Customize Literacy	• Leveled Readers • Decodable Readers	• Decodable Readers	• Envision It! Skills/Strategies Handbook • Leveled Readers
Go Digital	• Concept Talk Video • Decodable eReaders • eReaders	• Decodable eReaders	• Envision It! Animations • eReaders • Decodable eReaders

Question of the Week
What does it mean to grant freedom?

Vocabulary	Fluency	Conventions and Writing

Vocabulary

Envision It! Vocabulary Cards

Vocabulary Skill Lesson pp. 400–401

Fluency

Let's Learn It! pp. 428–429

Decodable and Leveled Readers

Conventions and Writing

Let's Write It! pp. 422–423

Decodable Readers

- Envision It! Vocabulary Cards
- Vocabulary Activities

- eSelection
- Decodable eReaders
- eReaders

- Grammar Jammer

Envision It! Vocabulary Cards

Happy Birthday Mr. Kang pp. 402–419

Practice Station Flip Chart

Words!

Reader's and Writer's Notebook

Happy Birthday Mr. Kang pp. 402–419

Practice Station Flip Chart

Leveled Readers

ELL and ELD Readers

Reader's and Writer's Notebook

Happy Birthday Mr. Kang pp. 402–419

Practice Station Flip Chart

- Envision It! Vocabulary Cards
- Vocabulary Activities
- eSelection

- eSelection
- eReaders

- Grammar Jammer

- Envision It! Vocabulary Cards

- Leveled Readers
- Decodable Readers

- Reader's and Writer's Notebook

- Vocabulary Activities

- eReaders
- Decodable eReaders

- Grammar Jammer

You Are Here!
Unit 6
Week 2

My 5-Day Planner for Reading Street!

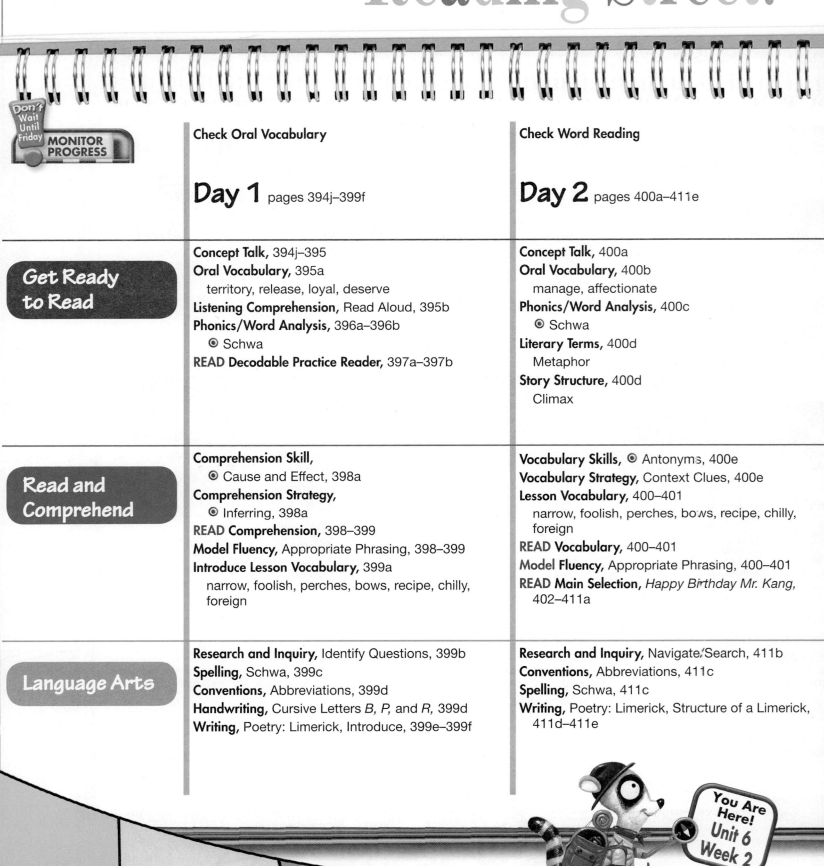

MONITOR PROGRESS — Don't Wait Until Friday

	Check Oral Vocabulary **Day 1** pages 394j–399f	Check Word Reading **Day 2** pages 400a–411e
Get Ready to Read	**Concept Talk,** 394j–395 **Oral Vocabulary,** 395a 　territory, release, loyal, deserve **Listening Comprehension,** Read Aloud, 395b **Phonics/Word Analysis,** 396a–396b 　◎ Schwa **READ Decodable Practice Reader,** 397a–397b	**Concept Talk,** 400a **Oral Vocabulary,** 400b 　manage, affectionate **Phonics/Word Analysis,** 400c 　◎ Schwa **Literary Terms,** 400d 　Metaphor **Story Structure,** 400d 　Climax
Read and Comprehend	**Comprehension Skill,** 　◎ Cause and Effect, 398a **Comprehension Strategy,** 　◎ Inferring, 398a **READ Comprehension,** 398–399 **Model Fluency,** Appropriate Phrasing, 398–399 **Introduce Lesson Vocabulary,** 399a 　narrow, foolish, perches, bows, recipe, chilly, 　foreign	**Vocabulary Skills,** ◎ Antonyms, 400e **Vocabulary Strategy,** Context Clues, 400e **Lesson Vocabulary,** 400–401 　narrow, foolish, perches, bows, recipe, chilly, 　foreign **READ Vocabulary,** 400–401 **Model Fluency,** Appropriate Phrasing, 400–401 **READ Main Selection,** *Happy Birthday Mr. Kang,* 　402–411a
Language Arts	**Research and Inquiry,** Identify Questions, 399b **Spelling,** Schwa, 399c **Conventions,** Abbreviations, 399d **Handwriting,** Cursive Letters *B, P,* and *R,* 399d **Writing,** Poetry: Limerick, Introduce, 399e–399f	**Research and Inquiry,** Navigate/Search, 411b **Conventions,** Abbreviations, 411c **Spelling,** Schwa, 411c **Writing,** Poetry: Limerick, Structure of a Limerick, 　411d–411e

You Are Here! Unit 6 Week 2

What does it mean to grant freedom?

Check Retelling	**Check Fluency**	**Check Oral Vocabulary**
Day 3 pages 412a–423c	**Day 4** pages 424a–429e	**Day 5** pages 429f–429q
Concept Talk, 412a	**Concept Talk,** 424a	**Concept Wrap Up,** 429f
Oral Vocabulary, 412b companion, nag	**Oral Vocabulary,** 424b retrieve, wandering	**Check Oral Vocabulary,** 429g territory, release, loyal, deserve, manage, affectionate, companion, nag, retrieve, wandering
Phonics/Word Analysis, 412c–412d ◉ Schwa	**Phonics/Word Analysis,** 424c–424f	**Amazing Ideas,** 429g
Decodable Story, 412d	[Review] Vowel Sounds /ü/ and /ů/	[Review] ◉ **Cause and Effect,** 429h
Comprehension Check, 412e	**Decodable Story,** 424f	[Review] ◉ **Antonyms,** 429h
Check Retelling, 412f	**Genre:** Expository Text, 424g	[Review] ◉ **Schwa,** 429i
		[Review] **Literary Terms,** 429i
READ Main Selection, *Happy Birthday Mr. Kang,* 412–419a	**READ Paired Selection,** "Once Upon a Constitution," 424–427a	**Fluency Assessment,** WCPM, 429j–429k
Retelling, 420–421	**Let's Learn It!** 428–429a	**Comprehension Assessment,**
Think Critically, 421a	Fluency: Appropriate Phrasing	◉ Cause and Effect, 429l–429m
Model Fluency, Appropriate Phrasing, 421b	Vocabulary: ◉ Antonyms	
Research and Study Skills, Maps, 421c	Listening and Speaking: Express an Opinion	
Research and Inquiry, Analyze, 421d	**Research and Inquiry,** Synthesize, 429b	**Research and Inquiry,** Communicate, 429n
Conventions, Abbreviations, 421e	**Conventions,** Abbreviations, 429c	**Conventions,** Abbreviations, 429o
Spelling, Schwa, 421e	**Spelling,** Schwa, 429c	**Spelling Test,** Schwa, 429o
Let's Write It! Poetry: Limerick, 422–423	**Writing,** Poetry: Limerick, Revising, 429d–429e	**Writing,** Poetry: Limerick, Abbreviations, 429p–429q
Writing, Poetry: Limerick, Structure, 423a–423c		**Quick Write for Fluency,** 429q

Week 2

Grouping Options for Differentiated Instruction
Turn the page for the small group time lesson plan.

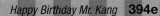

Planning Small Group Time on Reading Street!

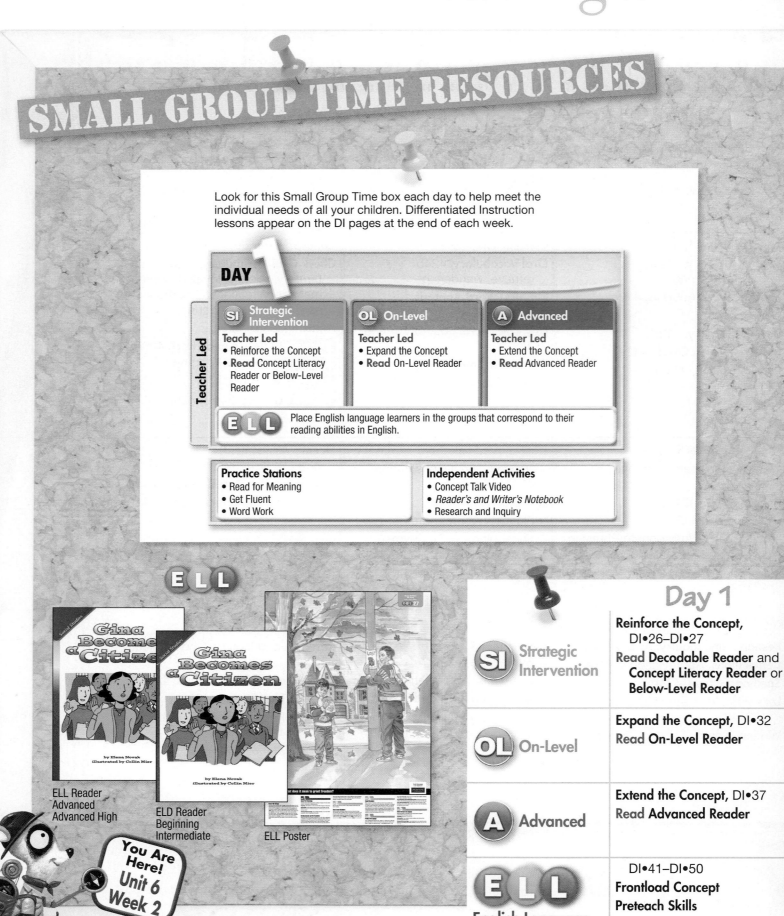

SMALL GROUP TIME RESOURCES

Look for this Small Group Time box each day to help meet the individual needs of all your children. Differentiated Instruction lessons appear on the DI pages at the end of each week.

DAY 1

Teacher Led

SI Strategic Intervention	**OL On-Level**	**A Advanced**
Teacher Led • Reinforce the Concept • **Read** Concept Literacy Reader or Below-Level Reader	**Teacher Led** • Expand the Concept • **Read** On-Level Reader	**Teacher Led** • Extend the Concept • **Read** Advanced Reader

ELL Place English language learners in the groups that correspond to their reading abilities in English.

Practice Stations
• Read for Meaning
• Get Fluent
• Word Work

Independent Activities
• Concept Talk Video
• *Reader's and Writer's Notebook*
• Research and Inquiry

ELL

ELL Reader
Advanced
Advanced High

ELD Reader
Beginning
Intermediate

ELL Poster

You Are Here! Unit 6 Week 2

Day 1

SI Strategic Intervention	**Reinforce the Concept,** DI•26–DI•27 **Read Decodable Reader** and **Concept Literacy Reader** or **Below-Level Reader**
OL On-Level	**Expand the Concept,** DI•32 **Read On-Level Reader**
A Advanced	**Extend the Concept,** DI•37 **Read Advanced Reader**
ELL English Language Learners	DI•41–DI•50 **Frontload Concept** **Preteach Skills** **Writing**

Reading Street
Response to
Intervention Kit

Reading Street
Practice Stations Kit

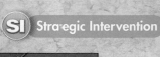

SI Strategic Intervention

Below-Level
Reader

Concept Literacy Reader

Happy Birthday Mr. Kang pp. 402–419

OL On-Level

On-Level Reader

A Advanced

Advanced
Reader

Decodable
Reader

Once Upon a Constitution pp. 424–427

Small Group Weekly Plan

Day 2	Day 3	Day 4	Day 5
Reinforce Comprehension, DI•28 **Revisit Main Selection**	**Reinforce Vocabulary,** DI•29 **Read/Revisit Main Selection**	**Reinforce Comprehension,** Practice Retelling, DI•30 Genre Focus **Read/Revisit Paired Selection**	**Practice Fluency,** DI•31 **Reread Concept Literacy Reader** or **Below-Level Reader**
Expand Comprehension, DI•33 **Revisit Main Selection**	**Expand Vocabulary,** DI•34 **Read/Revisit Main Selection**	**Expand Comprehension,** Practice Retelling, DI•35 Genre Focus **Read/Revisit Paired Selection**	**Practice Fluency,** DI•36 **Reread On-Level Reader**
Extend Comprehension, DI•38 **Revisit Main Selection**	**Extend Vocabulary,** DI•39 **Read/Revisit Main Selection**	**Extend Comprehension,** Genre Focus, DI•40 **Read/Revisit Paired Selection**	**Practice Fluency,** DI•40 **Reread Advanced Reader**
DI•41–DI•50 **Review Concept/Skills** **Frontload Main Selection** **Practice**	DI•41–DI•50 **Review Concept/Skills** **Reread Main Selection** **Practice**	DI•41–DI•50 **Review Concept** **Read ELL/ELD Readers** **Practice**	DI•41–DI•50 **Review Concept/Skills** **Reread ELL/ELD Reader** **Writing**

week 2

Practice Stations for Everyone on Reading Street!

Word Wise

Vowel sounds in *moon* and *foot: oo, ew, ue, ui,* and *oo, u*

Objectives
• Spell words with the vowel sounds in *moon* and *foot: oo, ew, ue, ui,* and *oo, u.*

Materials
• *Word Wise* Flip Chart Activity 27
• Teacher-made word cards
• paper   • pencils

Differentiated Activities

⬤ Choose five word cards. List your words. Write sentences using each word. List other words with the vowel sounds in *moon* and *foot (oo, ew, ue, ui,* and *oo, u).*

▲ Choose seven word cards. List your words. Write sentences using each word. List other words with the vowel sounds in *moon* and *foot (oo, ew, ue, ui,* and *oo, u).*

◼ Choose nine word cards, and write your words in a list. Write sentences using each word. Add other words with these vowel sounds.

Technology
• Online Dictionary

Word Work

Vowel sounds in *moon* and *foot: oo, ew, ue, ui,* and *oo, u*

Objectives
• Identify and pronounce words with the vowel sounds in *moon* and *foot: oo, ew, ue, ui,* and *oo, u.*

Materials
• *Word Work* Flip Chart Activity 27
• Teacher-made word cards
• paper   • pencils

Differentiated Activities

⬤ Choose eight word cards. List the words. Say each word. Circle the *moon* or *foot* vowel sound in each word. Write a silly, poem using some of the words.

▲ Choose ten word cards, and list the words. Say each word. Circle the *moon* or *foot* vowel sound in each. Write a silly, four- or eight-line poem with some of the words.

◼ Choose twelve word cards, and list your words. Say each word. Circle the *moon* or *foot* vowel sound in each. Write a silly, four- or eight-line poem using some of the words.

Technology
• Modeled Pronunciation Audio CD

Words to Know

Prefix *un-*

Objectives
• Identify the meaning of words with prefix *un-.*

Materials
• *Words to Know* Flip Chart Activity 27
• Teacher-made word cards
• paper   • pencils

Differentiated Activities

⬤ Choose four word cards. List the words. Circle the prefix in each. Use the dictionary to find each word's meaning. Write sentences using the words.

▲ Choose six word cards, and list the words. Circle the prefix in each word. Use the dictionary to find each word's meaning. Write sentences using each word.

◼ Choose eight word cards, and list the words. Use the dictionary to find each word's meaning. Write sentences for each word. Next, write sentences for each base word.

Technology
• Online Dictionary

You Are Here! Unit 6 Week 2

Use this week's materials from the Reading Street Leveled Practice Stations Kit to organize this week's stations.

Practice Station Flip Chart

Let's Write!
Take notes

Objectives
- Take notes while reading a nonfiction selection.

Materials
- *Let's Write!* Flip Chart Activity 27
- paper
- pencils

Differentiated Activities

● Choose and read your book. As you read take notes about the main idea and important details. Paraphrase ideas in the text. Include key words and phrases in your notes.

▲ Choose and read your book. Take notes about the main idea and some important details. Paraphrase the text in your own words. Include key phrases and words.

■ Choose your book. As you read, take notes about the main idea and important details. Paraphrase the text, using your own words. Include key words and phrases as well.

Technology
- Online Graphic Organizers
- Leveled Reader Database

Read for Meaning
Fact and opinion

Objectives
- Identify fact and opinion in a nonfiction selection.

Materials
- *Read for Meaning* Flip Chart Activity 27
- Leveled Readers
- paper
- pencils

Differentiated Activities

● Choose a book from those your teacher provided. Think about the information and ideas the author includes. Write one sentence that tells a fact from the selection. Write one sentence that gives an opinion.

▲ Read one of the books your teacher provided. Think about the facts and opinions the author includes. Write two sentences that give facts from the selection. Write two sentences that give opinions.

■ Choose and read a leveled reader. As you read it, distinguish statements of fact from statements of opinion. Write a paragraph telling about some of the facts and opinions the author includes.

Technology
- Leveled Reader Database

Get Fluent
Practice fluent reading

Objectives
- Read aloud at an appropriate rate.

Materials
- *Get Fluent* Flip Chart Activity 27
- Leveled Readers

Differentiated Activities

● Work with a partner. Choose a Concept Literacy Reader or Below-Level Reader. Take turns reading a page from the book. Use the readers to practice reading at an appropriate rate. Provide feedback as needed.

▲ Work with a partner. Choose an On-Level Reader. Take turns reading a page from the book. Use the reader to practice reading at an appropriate rate. Provide feedback as needed.

■ Work with a partner. Choose an Advanced Reader. Take turns reading a page from the book. Use the reader to practice reading at an appropriate rate. Provide feedback as needed.

Technology
- Leveled Reader Database
- Reading Street Readers CD-ROM

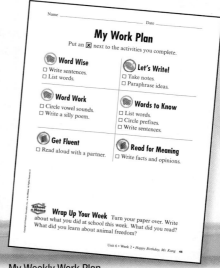

My Weekly Work Plan

Week 2

Objectives

- Introduce the weekly concept.
- Develop oral vocabulary.

Today at a Glance

Oral Vocabulary
territory, release, loyal, deserve

Phonics/Word Analysis
◉ Schwa

Comprehension
◉ Cause and effect
◉ Inferring

Reading
"A New Life"

Fluency
Appropriate phrasing

Lesson Vocabulary
Tested Vocabulary

Research and Inquiry
Identify questions

Spelling
Schwa

Conventions
Abbreviations

Handwriting
Cursive letters *B, P,* and *R*

Writing
Poetry: Limerick

Concept Talk

Question of the Week

What does it mean to grant freedom?

Introduce the concept

To further explore the unit concept of Freedom, this week students will read, write, and talk about what it means to grant freedom. Write the Question of the Week on the board.

ROUTINE **Activate Prior Knowledge** **Team Talk**

1. **Think** Have students think about some ways people might grant freedom to animals or other people.

2. **Pair** Have pairs of students discuss the Question of the Week. Remind them to ask relevant questions and listen attentively.

3. **Share** Call on a few students to share their ideas and comments with the group. Guide the discussion and encourage elaboration with prompts such as:

- Why is it important to be free?
- What are some ways that animals and people can be free?

Routines Flip Chart

Anchored Talk

Develop oral vocabulary

Have students turn to pp. 394–395 in their Student Editions. Look at each of the photos. Then, use the prompts to guide discussion and create the *What does it mean to grant freedom?* concept map. Remind students to speak coherently about the topic.

- How is the man granting the shark freedom? (by letting it go to swim freely) It's now free to swim in its own *territory,* or area of the sea.
- What are the children in the other pictures doing? (letting a seal out of a box and an insect out of a jar) They are *releasing* the seal and the insect into the wild, or letting them go *wandering* wherever they want to go.

Objectives
- Listen closely when someone speaks, ask questions about the topic he or she is talking about, and comment about the topic. • Work together with other students. Take part in discussions, ask and answer questions, and offer ideas that build on the ideas of others.

Oral Vocabulary

Let's **Talk** About

Granting Freedom
- Share ideas about how freedom is granted to people and animals.
- Ask questions about what it means to be granted freedom.
- Pose and answer questions about how freedom is granted through laws.

READING STREET ONLINE
CONCEPT TALK VIDEO
www.ReadingStreet.com

You've learned
2 5 6
Amazing Words ★
so far this year!

394   395

Student Edition pp. 394–395

Amazing Words

You've learned **2 5 6** words so far.

You'll learn **0 1 0** words this week!

territory	affectionate
release	companion
loyal	nag
deserve	retrieve
manage	wandering

Writing on Demand

Writing Fluency
Ask students to respond to the photos on pp. 394–395 by writing as well as they can and as much as they can about what it means to grant freedom.

- What do the shark, the seal, and the insect have in common? (They are all wild animals that people are letting go free.) Let's add *People can set wild animals free* to our concept map.

> What it means to grant freedom
>
> People can set wild animals free.

Connect to reading

Tell students that this week they will be reading about different ways that freedom can be granted. Encourage students to add concept-related words to this week's concept map.

ELL **Preteach Concepts** Use the Day 1 instruction on ELL Poster 27 to assess and build background knowledge, develop concepts, and build oral vocabulary.

ELL

English Language Learners
ELL support Additional ELL support and modified instruction is provided in the *ELL Handbook* and in the ELL Support lessons on pp. DI•41–DI•50.

Listening comprehension
English learners will benefit from additional visual support to understand the key terms in the concept map. Use the pictures on pp. 394–395 to scaffold understanding.

Frontload for Read Aloud
Use the modified Read Aloud on p. DI•44 of the ELL Support lessons to prepare students to listen to "A Little Freedom" (p. DI•44).

ELL   Poster 27

Oral Vocabulary
Amazing Words

Introduce Amazing Words

"A Little Freedom" on p. 395b is about two robots that want to be set free. Tell students to listen for this week's Amazing Words—*territory, release, loyal,* and *deserve*—as you read.

Model fluency

As you read "A Little Freedom," model appropriate phrasing by grouping words in a meaningful way and paying attention to punctuation cues.

Teach Amazing Words

Amazing Words Oral Vocabulary Routine

| territory |
| release |
| loyal |
| deserve |

1 **Introduce** Write the word *territory* on the board. Have students say the word aloud with you. In "A Little Freedom," we learn that *territory* is somewhere you can stand. Are there any other context clues that tell me the meaning of this word? Supply a student-friendly definition.

2 **Demonstrate** Have students answer questions to demonstrate understanding. Where is a *territory* where sharks might live? How might a dog protect its *territory*?

3 **Apply** Ask students to think of examples of different *territories* and who or what might live in each one.

See p. OV•2 to teach *release, loyal,* and *deserve.*

Routines Flip Chart

Apply Amazing Words

To build oral language, lead the class in a discussion about the Amazing Words' meanings. Remind students to listen attentively to speakers.

MONITOR PROGRESS **Introduce Amazing Words**

During discussion, listen for students' use of Amazing Words.

If... students are unable to use the Amazing Words to discuss the concept,

then... use Oral Vocabulary Routine in the Routines Flip Chart to demonstrate words in different contexts.

Day 1	**Day 2**	**Day 3**	**Day 4**	**Day 5**
Check Oral Vocabulary	Check Word Reading	Check Retelling	Check Fluency	Check Oral Vocabulary

Success Predictor

A Little Freedom

Ten-year-old Billy and Laury Norton have grown up under the care of two robots, JIL and JAK. Over the years, Billy and Laury have become quite fond of their robot friends. Tonight, JIL and JAK have an unusual request.

"Yes, JIL, JAK?" said Mr. Norton. He noticed the robots had been standing away from their usual territory near the children for several minutes. "Do you want something?"

JAK took one step forward. It seemed as though he were clearing his throat. "Dear Norton family," he began. "We would like our freedom. We would like you to release us."

"No-o-o-oo!" Bill and Laury wailed simultaneously.

"But why?" Mrs. Norton asked. "Don't you like us?"

"You're fine," answered JIL. "You've been very good employers."

"And of course we love Laury and Billy—," continued JAK.

"As much as robots can love," finished JIL.

"Well, then?" asked Mr. Norton.

JAK began, "Seven days ago, Billy mentioned freedom and how nice it is. And we've heard about freedom and read about it for years—"

JIL added, "Freedom of the press, freedom from slavery, religious freedom, freedom from underarm embarrassment—"

"'The land of the free, and the home of the brave.' It sounds like a nice thing, freedom," finished JAK.

"It's terribly important—to us humans," added Mr. Norton.

Billy said, "Our teacher Ms. Clive says our freedom is as important to us as the air we breathe."

Laury said, "But you can't be free—you're robots. And besides, we need you!"

"You're growing up, now," said JIL. "We're probably going to be too small for you in a year or so."

"And we know that we're out-of-date, technologically," added JAK. "We've been loyal to your family and served you for ten years, and we'd like to be free now."

"I guess you deserve it." Mrs. Norton looked back and forth between Billy and Laury and JIL and JAK. "But really," she said hesitatingly, "you belong to the children."

Laury and Billy seemed almost on the verge of tears.

"But—but—," began Billy.

"We'd miss you!" Laury burst out.

After a few days and a lot of thought, Billy and Laury finally agreed to set JAK and JIL free.

Oral Vocabulary

Success Predictor

Objectives

◎ Use word analysis to recognize unaccented syllables with schwa.

◎ Read words with the schwa sound spelled with an *a, e, i, o, u,* and *y.*

Skills Trace

◉ **Schwa**

Introduce U6W2D1

Practice U6W2D3; U6W2D4

Reteach/Review U6W2D5; U6W3D4

Assess/Test Weekly Test U6W2

Benchmark Test U6

Key: U = Unit, W = Week, D = Day

Word Analysis
 Schwa

ROUTINE **Word Parts Strategy**

1. **Connect** Connect today's lesson to previously learned multisyllabic words. Write *termite* and *remote.* You can already read words like these that have more than one syllable. Read these words. Today you will learn to read multisyllabic words that have an unaccented syllable.

2. **Model** Write *affect.* I know that *affect* is a two-syllable word. When I read words that have more than one syllable, I know that at least one of the syllables is accented, or spoken with more force than the others. The syllable or syllables that are unaccented often have a vowel sound that is different from its normal sound. I can hear that sound in the first syllable of *affect.* The name for the vowel sound is *schwa.* This vowel sound can be spelled by any vowel. When I am not sure how to pronounce a multisyllabic word, I can say the schwa sound for the vowel in each syllable until I recognize the word.

3. **Guide Practice** Have students read the words below with you, and identify the unaccented syllable and schwa sound.

almond	China	marble	cover
circus	April	occur	cardinal

4. **Review** What do you know about reading words with unaccented syllables? When you read a multisyllabic word, try stressing different syllables and using /ə/ in place of a vowel's normal sound until you recognize the word.

Routines Flip Chart

Model — Have students turn to p. 396 in their Student Editions. Each word on this page has an unaccented syllable with the schwa sound. The first word is *about.* I hear the schwa in the first syllable. The sound is spelled *a.*

Guide practice — For each word in Words I Can Blend, ask students to segment the word parts. Make sure that students identify the correct sound for schwa in unaccented syllables. Then have them read the words.

Corrective feedback — **If...** students have difficulty reading a word, **then...** model reading the parts and then the whole word, and then ask students to read it with you.

Student Edition pp. 396–397

Decode and Read

Read words independent of context

After students can successfully combine the word parts and read the words on p. 396 in their Student Editions, point to words in random order and ask students to read them naturally.

Read words in context

Have students read each of the sentences on p. 396. Have them identify words in the sentences that have the schwa sound.

Team Talk Pair students and have them take turns reading each of the sentences aloud.

Chorally read the I Can Read! passage on p. 397 with the students. Then have them read the passage aloud to themselves.

On their own

For additional practice, use the *Reader's and Writer's Notebook* p. 396.

Reader's and Writer's Notebook p. 396

Differentiated Instruction

A Advanced

Schwa Have students decode more challenging words with the schwa sound, such as *impossible, harmonica, information, kindergarten, convertible,* and *watermelon*. Students can consult a dictionary to confirm the unaccented syllable or vowel that stands for the schwa sound.

Vocabulary Support

You may wish to explain the meaning of these words.

almond a brown-skinned nut widely used in cooking

cardinal a North American songbird

ELL

English Language Learners

Pronunciation Many languages do not have the schwa sound, so English language learners may have difficulty pronouncing and spelling the unstressed syllable in words such as *along* and *upon*. Provide additional practice with these words. Try having students clap the rhythm of the words to identify the syllables.

Contrastive analysis chart See also the Contrastive Analysis Chart in the *First Stop* book.

Objectives

- Apply knowledge of sound-spellings to decode unknown multisyllabic words when reading.
- Decode and read words in context and independent of context.
- Practice fluency with oral rereading.

Decodable Practice Reader 27A
↻ Schwa

Read words independent of context

Have students turn to p. 133 in *Decodable Practice Readers 3.2*. Have students read each word.

Read high-frequency words

Have students read the high-frequency words *a, was, to, water, some, said, everywhere, of, you, the, one, have, into, what, there, wanted, would, coming, been, they,* and *were* on the first page.

Preview Decodable Practice Reader

Have students read the title and preview the story. Tell them that they will read words with the schwa sound spelled *a, e, i, o, u,* and *y*.

Read words in context

Pair students for reading and listen as they read. One student begins. Students read the entire story, switching readers after each page. Partners reread the story. This time the other student begins. Make sure that students are monitoring their accuracy when they decode words.

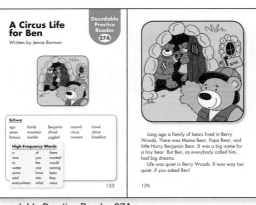

Decodable Practice Reader 27A

Corrective feedback

If... students have difficulty reading a word, **then...** refer them to the Sound-Spelling Cards to identify the word parts. Have them read the word parts individually and then together to say the word.

- What is the new word?
- Is the new word a word you know?
- Does it make sense in the story?

Check decoding and comprehension

Have students retell the story to include characters, setting, and events. Then have students find words in the story that have the schwa sound. Students should supply *ago, around, mountain, about, juggled, family, travel, afraid, famous, moment, Benjamin, seven, circus, marble,* and *breakfast.*

Reread for Fluency

Have students reread Decodable Practice Reader 27A to develop automaticity decoding words with the schwa sound.

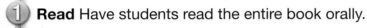 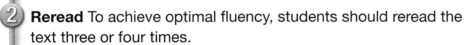

ROUTINE **Oral Rereading**

1. **Read** Have students read the entire book orally.

2. **Reread** To achieve optimal fluency, students should reread the text three or four times.

3. **Corrective Feedback** Listen as students read. Provide corrective feedback regarding their fluency and decoding.

Routines Flip Chart

English Language Learners
Schwa
Beginning Write several words with the schwa sound from the Decodable Practice Reader on the board, such as *seven, famous, moment, family, afraid,* and *breakfast.* Point to each word as you read it aloud. Then underline the vowel in each unaccented syllable that stands for /ə/. Have students repeat the words with you.

Intermediate After reading, have students list the words in the story with the schwa sound. Have them sort the words according to the vowel that stands for /ə/. Ask students to compare their lists with a partner.

Advanced/Advanced High After reading the story, have students write about another adventure that Ben goes on. Ask students to use at least four words in their writing that have the schwa sound.

Objectives
◎ Identify cause and effect relationships among ideas in texts.
◎ Make inferences to aid comprehension.
• Read grade-level text with appropriate phrasing.

Skills Trace
◎ **Cause and Effect**
Introduce U3W5D1; U4W5D1; U6W2D1
Practice U3W5D2; U3W5D3; U4W3D2; U4W5D2; U4W5D3; U5W1D2; U6W2D2; U6W2D3; U6W4D2; U6W4D3
Reteach/Review U3W5D5; U4W5D5; U6W2D5
Assess/Test Weekly Tests U3W5; U4W5; U6W2
Benchmark Tests U6
Key: U = Unit, W = Week, D = Day

Skill ↔ Strategy
⟳ Cause and Effect
⟳ Inferring

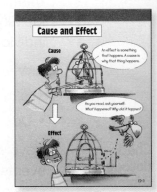
Student Edition p. EI•3

Introduce cause and effect

Envision It!

An effect is something that happens. What is a cause? (A cause is why a thing happens.) How many causes might an effect have? (It will have at least one, and possibly more.) Have students turn to p. EI•3 in the Student Edition to review cause and effect. Then read "A New Life" with students. Have students look for cause-and-effect clue words, such as *because* and *so,* as they read.

Model the skill

Think Aloud

Have students reread the first two paragraphs of the selection. What has caused immigrants to move to the United States? (They want to achieve their goals, to build better lives, and to experience freedom.) Can you identify any cause-and-effect clue words that show the relationship between immigrants coming to the United States and what causes them to do so? (so, because)

Guide practice

Have students finish reading "A New Life" on their own. After they read, have them use a graphic organizer like the one on p. 398 and explain cause and effect.

Strategy check

Inferring Tell students that to better understand cause and effect in "A New Life," they can make inferences.

Model the strategy

Envision It!

Think Aloud

I think immigrants can add to the richness of life in the United States. Making this inference helps me understand that, even though the population is increasing, the country will be more diverse. Have students review the strategy of inferring on p. EI•20 of the Student Edition.

Student Edition p. EI•20

On their own

Use p. 397 in the *Reader's and Writer's Notebook* for additional practice with inferring.

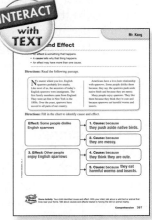
Reader's and Writer's Notebook p. 397

Objectives
• Identify the cause-and-effect relationships among ideas in the text.
• Use your prior knowledge and details from a text to make inferences about the text and support your inferences with evidence from the text.

Envision It! Skill/Strategy

Skill

Cause and Effect

Strategy

Inferring

READING STREET ONLINE
ENVISION IT! ANIMATIONS
www.ReadingStreet.com

Comprehension Skill

Cause and Effect

• An effect is something that happens.
• A cause is why that thing happens.
• An effect may have more than one cause.
• Use what you learned about cause and effect and a chart like the one below as you read "A New Life." Then write a short paragraph summarizing the cause-and-effect relationships.

Causes	⟶	Effects

Comprehension Strategy

Inferring

As you read a selection, you make inferences, or decisions that make sense after you combine the details or facts the author has included with what you already know. When you come up with your own ideas based on information in a text, you are inferring.

398

A New Life

An *immigrant* is a person who has moved from one country into another. According to the U.S. Census Bureau, in 1990, the foreign-born population in the United States was about 19.8 million. By the year 2000, that number had grown to 37.2 million! Immigrants make up about 12.5 percent of the United States population.

There are many reasons that people have immigrated to the United States. Many people view the United States as a place where people can achieve any goal if they put their minds to it and work hard. Some come here because of the opportunities to build better lives for themselves and their families. Some move here so they can experience the freedom that the United States offers.

Immigrants bring with them their cultural heritage, traditions, and new ideas. They have helped build the United States to make it what it is today.

Skill What has caused some people to move to the United States?

Strategy What are some of the benefits of people immigrating to the United States?

Your Turn!

Need a Review? See the *Envision It! Handbook* for help with cause and effect and inferring.

Ready to Try It? As you read *Happy Birthday Mr. Kang*, use what you've learned about cause and effect and inferring to understand the text.

399

Student Edition pp. 398–399

Skill People have moved to the U.S. to build better lives for themselves and their families. People have moved to experience more freedom.

Strategy People bring their cultural heritage and new ideas with them.

Academic Vocabulary

phrasing paying attention to punctuation when you read and pausing at appropriate places

Model Fluency
Appropriate Phrasing

Model fluent reading

Have students listen as you read the first paragraph of "A New Life." Explain that you will be careful to read with appropriate phrasing, which means that you will pay attention to all punctuation and pause at appropriate places.

Oral Rereading

1. **Read** Have students read paragraph 1 of "A New Life" orally.

2. **Reread** To achieve optimal fluency, students should reread the text three or four times.

3. **Corrective Feedback** Have students read aloud without you. Encourage them to read carefully and look for punctuation marks that must be followed. Listen to make sure students pause at punctuation marks and where it makes sense, and provide feedback as needed.

Routines Flip Chart

ELL

English Language Learners
Cause and effect Have students stand. What did you do? Why did you do it? (We stood because you said to stand.) To figure out cause and effect in a story, you should think about key ideas: Rosa was doing well. The store was doing well. The Garcías were happy. Which sentence is the result of the other two sentences? (the last sentence)

Objectives
- Activate prior knowledge of words.
- Identify questions for research.

Vocabulary
Tested Vocabulary

Lesson vocabulary

Use the following Question and Answer activity to help students acquire word knowledge that improves reading, speaking, listening, and writing vocabularies.

Activate prior knowledge

Display the lesson vocabulary words. Invite students to share any information they already know about the meaning of these words. Then have students answer and discuss oral questions such as the following:

- Is a *narrow* door easy or difficult to fit yourself through?
- If someone is *foolish,* does he or she make good decisions?
- What is an animal that *perches* in a tree?
- When someone *bows,* is he or she being polite or rude?
- Does using a *recipe* make cooking easier or harder?
- If you were *chilly,* would you put on or take off your coat?
- If a person is *foreign,* are they from a faraway country or from very nearby?

Preteach academic vocabulary

ELL **Academic Vocabulary** Write the following terms on the board:

abbreviation	limerick
period	letter spacing
metaphor	phrasing

Have students share what they know about this week's Academic Vocabulary. Use the students' responses to assess their prior knowledge. Preteach the Academic Vocabulary by providing a student-friendly description, explanation, or example that clarifies the meaning of each term. Then ask students to restate the meaning of the Academic Vocabulary term in their own words.

 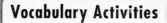
Research and Inquiry
Identify Questions

Teach

Discuss the Question of the Week: *What does it mean to grant freedom?* Tell students they will research granting freedom to animals. They will write a newspaper article to present to the class on Day 5.

Model

> **Think Aloud** I'll start by brainstorming a list of questions about different kinds of animals that might need to be granted freedom. Some possible questions could be *Where do baby chicks go after they have been hatched in a classroom? What happens to butterflies after a school butterfly release?* and *What happens to an injured wild animal, such as a seal, after an oil spill once it has been nursed back to health?*

Guide practice

After students have brainstormed inquiry questions, explain that tomorrow they will conduct an online research of their questions. Help students identify keywords that will guide their search.

On their own

Have students work individually, in pairs, or in small groups to write an inquiry question. Encourage them to generate their research topics from personal interests.

 INTERNET GUY
Don Leu

21st Century Skills

Weekly Inquiry Project

Day 1 Identify Questions

Day 2 Navigate/Search

Day 3 Analyze

Day 4 Synthesize

Day 5 Communicate

Differentiated Instruction

A Advanced

Set purpose Have students brainstorm a list of keywords for their research and set a purpose for what they expect to find.

Small Group Time

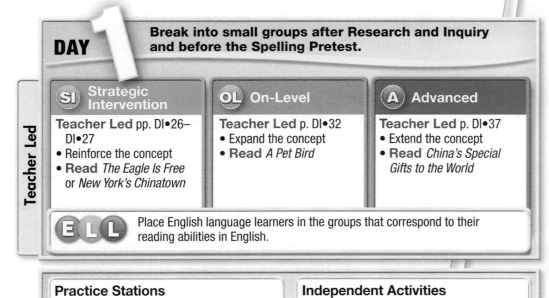

DAY 1

Break into small groups after Research and Inquiry and before the Spelling Pretest.

Teacher Led

SI Strategic Intervention	**OL On-Level**	**A Advanced**
Teacher Led pp. DI•26– DI•27	**Teacher Led** p. DI•32	**Teacher Led** p. DI•37
• Reinforce the concept	• Expand the concept	• Extend the concept
• **Read** *The Eagle Is Free* or *New York's Chinatown*	• **Read** *A Pet Bird*	• **Read** *China's Special Gifts to the World*

ELL Place English language learners in the groups that correspond to their reading abilities in English.

Practice Stations
• Read for Meaning
• Get Fluent
• Word Work

Independent Activities
• Concept Talk Video
• *Reader's and Writer's Notebook*
• Vocabulary Activities

ELL

English Language Learners
Multilingual vocabulary
Students can apply knowledge of their home languages to acquire new English vocabulary by using the Multilingual Vocabulary Lists (*ELL Handbook*, pp. 434–444).

Objectives
- Spell words with the schwa sound spelled correctly.
- Identify and understand abbreviations.
- Write cursive letters *B, P,* and *R* with proper letter spacing.

Spelling Pretest
Schwa

Introduce
Tell students to think of words with the *schwa* sound. *(oven, dozen, stomach)* Remind them that the schwa is an unaccented syllable. This week we will spell words with the *schwa* sound.

Pretest
Use these sentences to administer the spelling pretest. Say each word, read the sentence, and repeat the word.

1. above	Hold the ball **above** your head.	
2. another	Would you like **another** muffin?	
3. upon	Put your backpack **upon** the table.	
4. animal	I saw a striped **animal** at the zoo.	
5. paper	Can I borrow a sheet of **paper?**	
6. open	I can't wait to **open** my present!	
7. family	My brother is the youngest in the **family.**	
8. travel	I would like to **travel** to the mountains.	
9. afraid	Are you **afraid** of spiders?	
10. nickel	The eraser costs a **nickel.**	
11. sugar	Would you like **sugar** in your tea?	
12. circus	We saw clowns at the **circus.**	
13. item	Which **item** did you choose at the book fair?	
14. gallon	Mom dropped the **gallon** of milk.	
15. melon	Cantaloupe is my favorite **melon.**	

Challenge words

16. character	Mrs. Magoo is a **character** in a book.	
17. cardinal	The **cardinal** is the state bird of Ohio.	
18. Oregon	**Oregon** is a state in northwest United States.	
19. particular	My sister is very **particular** about her room.	
20. dinosaur	The museum has **dinosaur** bones on display.	

Self-correct
After the pretest, you can either display the correctly spelled words or spell them orally. Have students self-correct their pretests by rewriting misspelled words correctly.

On their own
For additional practice, use *Let's Practice It!* page 371 on the *Teacher Resources DVD-ROM.*

Let's Practice It!
TR DVD•371

Conventions
Abbreviations

Teach

Display Grammar Transparency 27, and read aloud the explanation and examples in the box. Explain that some titles for people, such as *Dr.* and *Mrs.*, are usually spelled as abbreviations. Point out the abbreviated titles, as well as the abbreviated days of the week and months of the year, in the transparency.

Model

Model capitalizing letters and using periods correctly to complete numbers 1 and 2. *Ms.* is an abbreviated title. It is pronounced /miz/. It begins with a capital letter and ends with a period.

Guide practice

Guide students to complete items 3–6. Remind them to capitalize the first letter and to use periods correctly. Record the correct responses on the transparency.

Daily Fix-It

Use Daily Fix-It numbers 1 and 2 in the right margin.

Connect to oral language

Have students read sentences 7–8 on the transparency and write the abbreviation to correctly complete each sentence.

Grammar Transparency 27,
TR DVD

Handwriting
Cursive letters *B, P,* and *R*

Model letter formation

Display the cursive uppercase letters *B, P,* and *R.* Follow the stroke instruction pictured to model letter formation.

Model letter spacing

Explain that using proper letter spacing means that the letters in a word are evenly spaced with the same amount of white space between each letter. Remind students that letters in a word should not be too close together or too far apart. Model writing these words with proper letter spacing: *Rob's Birthday Party.*

Guide practice

Have students write these titles: *Play Ball, Rusty!, Band Plays Rock, Plain Red Box.* Circulate around the room, guiding students.

Academic Vocabulary

An **abbreviation** is a shortened form of a word.

A **period** is a punctuation mark that signals the end of a sentence or is placed at the end of an abbreviation.

Letter spacing is the distance between the letters in a word.

Daily Fix-It

1. Did Mr Kang's pet fly all the way from China. (*Mr.; China?*)
2. Most birds cant' traval across the ocean. (*can't; travel*)

English Language Learners
Spanish cognates Tell Spanish-speaking students that the English word *abbreviate* shares the Latin root *brevis (short)* with the Spanish word *abrevie.*

Handwriting: Proper nouns To provide practice in handwriting the cursive capital letters *B, P,* and *R,* have students write the names of people and places they know that begin with each letter.

Objectives
- Understand and identify the features of a limerick.

Writing—Poetry: Limerick
Introduce

MINI-LESSON
5 Day Planner
Guide to Mini-Lessons

DAY 1	Read Like a Writer
DAY 2	Structure of a Limerick
DAY 3	Rhythm
DAY 4	Revising Strategy: Adding
DAY 5	Abbreviations

MINI-LESSON

Read Like a Writer

■ **Introduce** This week you will write a **limerick**. A limerick is a form of poetry with five lines and a special rhyme and rhythm structure.

Prompt	Write a limerick about the story *Happy Birthday Mr. Kang.*
Trait	Organization
Mode	Narrative

■ **Examine Model Text** Let's read an example of a limerick about a toad. Have students read "The Toad in the Shoe" on p. 398 of their *Reader's and Writer's Notebook.*

■ **Key Features** Limericks are poems made up of five lines and a fixed *a-a-b-b-a* rhyme scheme. Have students mark the *a-a-b-b-a* rhyme pattern on the model. Notice how lines 1, 2, and 5 rhyme. Have students identify the rhyming words *shoe, blue,* and *too.* Notice how lines 3 and 4 also rhyme. Have students identify the rhyming words *in* and *grin.*

Each line also has a set number of syllables with two or three accents per line. The accented syllables create rhythm, which is the beat you hear when a poem is read aloud. Lines 1, 2, and 5 not only rhyme but also have the same number of syllables and accents. Read the lines aloud and count the accented syllables. Lines 3 and 4 also have the same number of syllables and accents. Count aloud the syllables and accents in lines 3 and 4.

Limericks are often called nonsense poems because they are sometimes humorous or witty. Ask students why the limerick is funny. (The toad is hungry and lonely, so when a "friend" visits, he eats it.)

Reader's and Writer's Notebook p. 398

Review
key features

Review the key features of limericks with students. You may want to post the key features in the classroom for students to refer to as they work on their limericks.

Key Features of Limericks

- a form of poetry
- made up of five lines with a specific rhyme scheme (a-a-b-b-a)
- has rhythm created through the use of two or three accented syllables per line; each line contains a set number of syllables
- sometimes tells a humorous or witty story

ROUTINE **Quick Write for Fluency** **Team Talk**

1. **Talk** Pairs discuss the key features of limericks.

2. **Write** Each student writes a brief summary of the key features of limericks.

3. **Share** Partners read their summaries to each other.

Routines Flip Chart

Wrap Up Your Day

✔ **Build Concepts** Have students discuss what granting freedom to someone or something might mean.

✔ **Oral Vocabulary** Have students use the Amazing Words they learned in context sentences.

✔ **Homework** Send home this week's Family Times Newsletter, *Let's Practice It!* pages 372–373 on the *Teacher Resources DVD-ROM.*

Let's Practice It!
TR DVD•372–373

Write Guy
Jeff Anderson

What Do You Notice?

When students are examining the model text, ask, "What do you notice?" By giving students the responsibility of commenting on what they find effective in the text, they build self-confidence and often begin to notice features of the writing they might not have otherwise. Eventually they will start trying them in their writing.

Academic Vocabulary

A **limerick** is a type of poem with five lines and a fixed rhythm and rhyme scheme.

ELL

English Language Learners
Read the writing model aloud and help students understand it. Ask students to think about an experience that they have had that they could write about in a limerick.

Preview DAY 2

Tell students that tomorrow they will read about what it means to grant freedom to someone or something.

Objectives
- Expand the weekly concept.
- Develop oral vocabulary.

Today at a Glance

Oral Vocabulary
manage, affectionate

Phonics/Word Analysis
◉ Schwa

Literary Terms
Metaphor

Story Structure
Climax

Lesson Vocabulary
◉ Antonyms

Fluency
Appropriate phrasing

Reading
"Mr. Wang's Wonderful Noodles"
Happy Birthday Mr. Kang

Research and Inquiry
Navigate/Search

Conventions
Abbreviations

Spelling
Schwa

Writing
Poetry: Limerick

Concept Talk

Question of the Week

What does it mean to grant freedom?

Expand the concept

Remind students of the weekly concept question. Tell students that today they will begin reading *Happy Birthday Mr. Kang.* As they read, encourage students to think about what it means to grant freedom.

Anchored Talk

Develop oral vocabulary

Use the photos on pp. 394–395 and the Read Aloud, "A Little Freedom," to talk about the Amazing Words: *territory, release, loyal, deserve.* Add the words to the concept map to develop students' knowledge of the topic. Discuss the following questions. Remind students to listen attentively to others, ask relevant questions, and make pertinent comments during the discussion.

- Where are some *territories* into which people might *release* wild animals? (into the ocean, into the air, into a forest, into a desert)

- Discuss how being *loyal* to a person might affect the actions of a wild animal or a servant robot after being set free. (A wild animal might choose to become a pet and stay with the person, even though it could have gone off freely by itself. A servant robot might choose to remain close to its employer family as a friend because it, too, chooses to keep helping and supporting the family.)

- Give some examples why wild animals might *deserve* freedom. (Wild animals have as much right to land as people, so people should share space with animals and not keep them locked up.)

Oral Vocabulary
Amazing Words

Amazing Words

Amazing Words **Oral Vocabulary Routine**

territory	affectionate
release	companion
loyal	nag
deserve	retrieve
manage	wandering

Teach Amazing Words

1 Introduce Write the Amazing Word *manage* on the board. Have students say it aloud with you. Relate *manage* to the photographs on pp. 394–395 and "A Little Freedom." What are some ways people *manage* to keep animals as pets? How do these ways compare with how the Nortons have *managed* to keep their robots for so long? Have students determine the definition of the word. When you *manage* something, you handle, or deal with, it.

2 Demonstrate Have students answer questions to demonstrate understanding. How might a parent *manage* a crying baby? How could you *manage* to find your way around an unfamiliar place?

3 Apply Have students apply their understanding. What are some things you *manage* to do each day?

See p. OV•2 to teach *affectionate*.

Routines Flip Chart

Apply Amazing Words

As students read "Mr. Wang's Wonderful Noodles" on p. 401, have them think about how Mr. Wang *manages* to make the best noodles and how they can tell that his customers feel *affectionate* toward him.

Connect to reading

Explain that today students will read about a man who keeps a special pet bird. Help students establish a purpose for reading. As they read, they should think about how the Question of the Week and the Amazing Words *manage* and *affectionate* apply to the relationship between this man and his bird.

ELL **Reinforce Vocabulary** Use the Day 2 instruction on ELL Poster 27 to teach lesson vocabulary and the lesson concept.

ELL Poster 27

Objectives
- Apply knowledge of letter-sound correspondences to decode words in context and independent of context.

Check Word Reading
SUCCESS PREDICTOR

Word Analysis
 Schwa

Review   Review the schwa sound using Sound-Spelling Card 144.

Read words independent of context   Display these words. Have the class decode the words. Then point to the words in random order and ask students to read them quickly.

gadget	metal	lettuce	character
robin	commit	salad	another

Corrective feedback   Model reading the syllables and then have students read the whole word with you.

Read words in context   Display these sentences. Have the class read the sentences.

Team Talk   Have pairs take turns reading the sentences naturally.

> Put the **paper upon** the table.
> Which **item** did you **open**?
> A bear is a **circus animal.**

Don't Wait Until Friday

MONITOR PROGRESS   **Check Word Reading**

Words with Schwa

Write the following words and have the class read them. Notice which words students miss during the group reading. Call on individuals to read some of the words.

open	ripen	item	upon	sugar	
bugle	handle	trouble	hurdle	sparkle	**Spiral Review** Row 2 reviews words with a consonant + *le*.
redoing	disliked	together	cardinal	rewrite	Row 3 contrasts multisyllabic words with and without the schwa sound.

If... students cannot read words with the sound of schwa at this point,

then... use the Day 1 Word Parts Strategy on p. 396a to reteach the schwa sound. Use words from the Decodable Practice Passages (or Reader). Continue to monitor students' progress using other instructional opportunities during the week. See the Skills Trace on p. 396a.

Day 1	Day 2	Day 3	Day 4	Day 5
Check Oral Vocabulary	Check Word Reading	Check Retelling	Check Fluency	Check Oral Vocabulary

Success Predictor

Literary Terms
Metaphor

Teach metaphor

Tell students that a metaphor is when two things that are not very much like each other, but are alike in at least one way, are compared without using the words *like* or *as.* A metaphor says that one thing is the other thing, not just that it is like the thing. A metaphor is used to help the reader visualize what something is like and to draw attention to a quality or qualities that it possesses.

Model

 Think Aloud Let's look at "A New Life," on p. 399. It says that immigrants have made the United States what it is today by bringing their cultures and traditions with them. I can use the metaphor, "The United States is a melting pot," to help create an image of all the cultures coming together. The United States isn't really a melting pot, but they are similar because both are places where things are mixed together.

Guide practice

Find an example of a metaphor in the poem Mr. Kang writes on p. 407 of *Happy Birthday Mr. Kang.* Be sure to explain what comparison is being made and why the author (or Mr. Kang) might be making this comparison.

On their own

Have students look for examples of metaphors in other selections in their Student Edition.

Story Structure
Climax

Teach climax

The climax of a story is the moment when a character or characters take an action that will help solve the main problem of the story. Being able to identify the climax of a story shows that we understand the plot, or the series of events in the story.

Model the strategy

 Think Aloud Before we can identify the climax of a story, we must understand the main problem the characters face. Read "Mr. Wang's Wonderful Noodles," on page 401. The characters are afraid Mr. Wang will leave China to make noodles in America. The climax comes when Mr. Wang declares that he will stay in China.

Guide practice

Discuss with students how the climax resolves the problem, or conflict, in a story.

On their own

Have students identify the climax in another story they have read and explain why and how it resolves the story problem.

Word Reading

Success Predictor

Objectives

◎ Use context clues to determine the meanings of antonyms.

• Read aloud grade-level appropriate text with appropriate phrasing.

Vocabulary Strategy for

 Antonyms

Student Edition p. W•2

Teach antonyms

 Envision It!

Explain to students that when they encounter an unfamiliar word, they can use context clues to figure out the word's meaning. Point out that an author might have used antonyms, or words that have opposite meanings, in the text around the unfamiliar word. Refer students to *Words!* on p. W•2 in the Student Edition for additional practice.

Model the strategy

> Think Aloud

Write on the board: *The box was too wide to fit through the narrow doorway.* I can look for context clues to figure out the meaning of the word *narrow.* If I look in this sentence, I see the word *wide.* According to this sentence, something that is wide will not fit through something narrow. These words are antonyms—*wide* provides a clue to the meaning of the word *narrow.* Something narrow is not wide, or has sides that are not very far apart.

Guide practice

Write this sentence on the board: *Because the air was chilly, the girl put on a big coat to stay warm.* Have students determine the meaning of *chilly* using antonyms and context clues. If they are unable to use antonyms and context clues to define *chilly,* then have them look up the word in a dictionary, glossary, or thesaurus. Remind students that a thesaurus and some dictionaries list antonyms.

For additional support, use *Envision It! Pictured Vocabulary Cards* or *Tested Vocabulary Cards.*

On their own

Have students read "Mr. Wang's Wonderful Noodles" on p. 401. Have them use a thesaurus or dictionary to find antonyms to help them define the lesson vocabulary. For additional practice use *Reader's and Writer's Notebook,* p. 399.

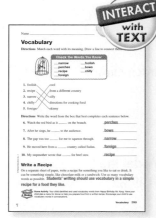

Reader's and Writer's Notebook p. 399

Objectives
• Use context clues to figure out words you don't know or words that have more than one meaning.
• Identify words that: re opposites, similar, have more than one meaning, and sound the same even though they mean different things:

Envision It | **Words to Know**

foreign

narrow

recipe

bows
chilly
foolish
perches

READING STREET ONLINE VOCABULARY ACTIVITIES
www.ReadingStreet.com

400

Vocabulary Strategy for

Antonyms

Context Clues Sometimes you will read a word you don't know. The author may include an antonym for the word. An antonym is a word that means the opposite of another word. For example, *hot* is the opposite of *cold*. Look for an antonym to figure out the meaning of the word.

1. Look at the words around the unfamiliar word. The author may have used an antonym.

2. Do you recognize a word that seems to have the opposite meaning of the unfamiliar word?

3. Use the antonym to help you figure out the meaning of the unfamiliar word.

Read "Mr. Wang's Wonderful Noodles" on page 401. Look for antonyms to help you understand the meanings of unfamiliar words.

Words to Write Reread "Mr. Wang's Wonderful Noodles." Write about your favorite food. How does it taste? Why do you like it? Use words from the Words to Know list and antonyms in your story.

MR. WANG'S WONDERFUL **Noodles**

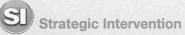

Mr. Wang is the best noodle maker in Shanghai, China. People who like wide, thick noodles may think people who like narrow, thin noodles are foolish. People who like narrow, thin noodles may think people who like wide, thick noodles are not very smart. But everyone agrees on one thing. Mr. Wang's noodles are the best.

One day, a stranger perches on a stool at the noodle shop. Mr. Wang bows his head in respect. The stranger says, "Mr. Wang, please bring your noodle recipe to the United States. Make noodles in my restaurant."

People stop slurping their noodles to listen to Mr. Wang's reply. The warm shop suddenly feels chilly.

Mr. Wang says, "Thank you. But I do not wish to go to a foreign land. I am happy making noodles in China."

Everyone heaves a sigh of relief. Everyone goes back to slurping Mr. Wang's wonderful noodles.

Your Turn!

Need a Review? For additional help with antonyms, see *Words!*

Ready to Try It? Read *Happy Birthday Mr. Kang*, pp. 402–419.

401

Student Edition pp. 400–401

Reread for Fluency
Appropriate Phrasing

Model fluent reading

Read paragraph 2 of "Mr. Wang's Wonderful Noodles" aloud, modeling how to pause at punctuation marks and read dialogue. Tell students that in order to comprehend what they read, it is important to pause where it makes sense.

ROUTINE **Oral Rereading**

1. **Read** Have students read paragraph 2 of "Mr. Wang's Wonderful Noodles" orally.

2. **Reread** To achieve optimal fluency, students should reread the text three or four times.

3. **Corrective Feedback** Have students read aloud without you. Listen for misread or omitted words and provide feedback.

Routines Flip Chart

Lesson Vocabulary

bows bends the head or body forward

chilly uncomfortably cold

foolish unwise; not making sense

foreign a place that is not your own country or homeland

narrow not wide

perches sits or rests on a bar, branch, or similar object

recipe ingredients and steps for making something to eat or drink

Differentiated Instruction

SI Strategic Intervention

Context clues Have students work in pairs to use context clues to find meanings for the words *foolish, bows,* and *foreign* from "Mr. Wang's Wonderful Noodles." Tell students to take turns making up sentences with these words.

ELL

English Language Learners
Build lesson vocabulary Use the lesson vocabulary pictured on p. 400 to teach the meanings of *narrow, recipe,* and *chilly.* Call on pairs to write the words on sticky notes and use them to label images of the words on the ELL Poster.

Objectives
- Understand the elements of realistic fiction.
- Use the title and illustrations to preview and predict.
- Set a purpose for reading.

Student Edition pp. 402–403

Build Background

Discuss birds

Team Talk Have students turn to a partner and discuss the Question of the Week and these questions about birds.

- How freely do birds in the wild live?
- How freely do pet birds live?
- How might a pet bird feel about living in the wild?

Connect to selection

Have students discuss their answers with the class. Remind them to listen attentively, make pertinent comments, and answer questions with appropriate detail. Possible responses: Birds in the wild are free to eat what they want and fly where they want. Pet birds must live in a cage and eat only what their masters give them. However, a pet bird might prefer to stay in its cage and not leave its master and the safe home it knows for the more dangerous wild. For additional opportunities to build background, use the Background Building Audio.

Prereading Strategies

Genre

Remind students that **realistic fiction** is a made-up story that could happen in real life. Explain that while all fiction is made up, the characters in realistic fiction behave as real people (or animals) do and face real problems. The main character in *Happy Birthday Mr. Kang* is a Chinese immigrant who works for 50 years in a restaurant, cutting noodles.

Preview and predict

Have students read the title of the selection and the name of the author/illustrator. Ask them to use the title and the illustrations to predict what they think the story will be about.

Set purpose

Prior to reading, have students set their own purpose for reading this selection based on their desire to comprehend more fully. To help students set a purpose, ask them to think about how a person, such as Mr. Kang, might feel caged and/or free the way a bird feels.

 INTERACT with TEXT

Strategy Response Log

Have students use p. 33 in the *Reader's and Writer's Notebook* to review the strategy of inferring. Then have them list their background knowledge of birds.

Small Group Time

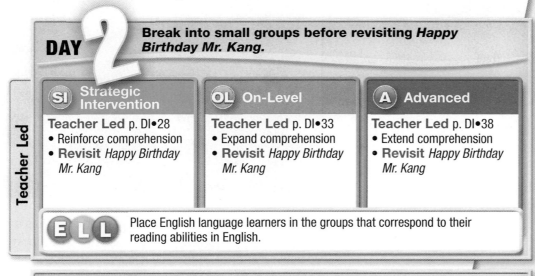

DAY 2 Break into small groups before revisiting *Happy Birthday Mr. Kang.*

Teacher Led

SI Strategic Intervention
Teacher Led p. DI•28
• Reinforce comprehension
• **Revisit** *Happy Birthday Mr. Kang*

OL On-Level
Teacher Led p. DI•33
• Expand comprehension
• **Revisit** *Happy Birthday Mr. Kang*

A Advanced
Teacher Led p. DI•38
• Extend comprehension
• **Revisit** *Happy Birthday Mr. Kang*

ELL Place English language learners in the groups that correspond to their reading abilities in English.

Practice Stations
• Words to Know
• Get Fluent
• Word Wise

Independent Activities
• Background Building Audio
• *Reader's and Writer's Notebook*
• Research and Inquiry

 **A** **Advanced**

Have students write a persuasive paragraph explaining why it is better to be either a pet bird in a safe cage or a free bird in the wild.

 Multidraft Reading

For **Whole Group** instruction, choose one of the reading options below. For each reading, have students set the purpose indicated.

Option 1
Day 2 Read the selection. Use Guide Comprehension to monitor and clairfy understanding.

Day 3 Reread the selection. Use Extend Thinking to develop higher-order thinking skills.

Option 2
Day 2 Read the first half of the selection, using both Guide Comprehension and Extend Thinking instruction.

Day 3 Read the second half of the selection, using both Guide Comprehension and Extend Thinking instruction.

 **ELL**

English Language Learners
Build background To build background, review the selection summary in English (*ELL Handbook*, p. 187). Use the Retelling Cards to provide visual support for the summary.

OPTION 1 Guide Comprehension Skills and Strategies

Teach Cause and Effect

🎯 **Cause and Effect** Remind students that characters, things, and events can cause certain things to happen. The effect is what happened and the cause is why it happened. Ask students what causes Mr. Kang to want to stop cooking. (He has been cooking every day for many years, so he is probably tired and wants to have time to do fun things.)

Corrective Feedback

If... students are unable to identify causes and effects,
then... use the model to help them to identify cause-and-effect relationships.

Let's Practice It!
TR DVD•374

Model the Skill

Think Aloud To figure out the cause and effect, I ask myself why Mr. Kang wants to stop cooking. This will give me the cause. (He has been cooking for many years.)

Student Edition pp. 404–405

404

OPTION 2 Extend Thinking Think Critically

Higher-Order Thinking Skills

🎯 **Cause and Effect • Analysis** Why does Mr. Kang want a bird? Possible response: His grandfather used to have one.

Genre • Evaluation How do you know the story is a realistic story and not a fantasy? Give an example to support your answer. Possible response: A fantasy is a story about something that could not happen, but events in this story could really happen. Mr. Kang could have come from China and lived in New York City.

What happens because he has been cooking for so many years? (He stops cooking on his 70th birthday.) This is the effect.

On Their Own

Have students reread pp. 404–405 to find another cause-and-effect relationship. For additional practice, use *Let's Practice It!* page 374 on the *Teacher Resources DVD-ROM*.

Forty-three years before his grandson, Sam, was born in the New World, Mr. Kang left China and came to America. Every day he chopped scallions, wrapped dumplings, and pulled noodle dough into long and perfect strands for the hungry people who ate at the Golden Dragon Restaurant in New York City.

When Mr. Kang turned seventy, Mrs. Kang had a birthday party for him.

"Make a wish!" said Sam as Mr. Kang shut his eyes, puffed his cheeks, and blew out all the candles on his cake. Everyone clapped and shouted hurray.

"What was your wish?" Sam asked.

"Three wishes," said Mr. Kang. "I want to read *The New York Times* every day. I want to paint poems every day. And I want a bird, a *hua mei*, of my own. I'll feed him every day, and on Sundays I'll take him to Sara Delano Roosevelt Park on Delancey Street. Enough cooking."

"Good idea," said Mrs. Kang. "I'll cook for you, and the Golden Dragon Restaurant can get a new cook."

"Grandpa, why do you want a bird in a cage? There are birds all over the place outside," said Sam.

"Sam," said Mr. Kang. "This is not just an American bird in a cage. This is a Chinese bird. My grandfather had a hua mei in a cage. Now I want a hua mei in a cage. And sometimes you and I will take him to Sara Delano Roosevelt Park on Delancey Street together."

And so it is that every morning Mr. Kang finds *The New York Times* on his doorstep. Every morning he reads it while he drinks his tea and eats his sweet and fragrant almond cakes, warm from the oven.

405

Sensory Details • Analysis How does the author use language that appeals to the reader's senses to help the reader understand the experience of eating an almond cake.

Possible response: The author describes how the cake feels warm from the oven, how it tastes sweet, and how it smells fragrant. These details help the reader picture what it would feel like if he or she were eating one of these cakes.

Differentiated Instruction

 Strategic Intervention

Graphic organizers If students need additional help identifying and understanding cause-and-effect relationships in this story, help them create a two-column graphic organizer that shows the cause-and-effect relationships. As they read, they should write down important events in the *effects* column and reasons for these events in the *causes* column.

ELL

English Language Learners

Activate prior knowledge Create a two-column chart to record students' prior knowledge of what a pet owner must do to keep a pet bird safely. We're going to read about how Mr. Kang gets a pet bird to keep in a cage. What do you know about the reasons that pet owners keep pet birds in cages? What do you know about how birds might feel about being kept in cages? Record students' answers in the chart, adding to them as they read the selection.

Objectives

◎ Use context clues to identify antonyms.

OPTION 1 ## Skills and Strategies, continued

Teach Antonyms

🔊 **Antonyms** Remind students that antonyms are words that have opposite meanings. Point out that if they encounter unfamiliar words in a text, they can use context clues to figure out the relevant meaning of the words and whether they are antonyms. Ask students to use textual evidence like context clues to determine the meaning of the words *chilly* and *warm* on p. 407.

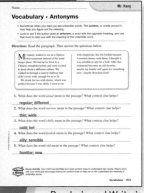

Reader's and Writer's Notebook p. 403

Corrective Feedback

If… students are unable to use context clues to figure out if words are antonyms,

then… use the model to help them use context clues.

Student Edition pp. 406–407

OPTION 2 ## Think Critically, continued

Higher-Order Thinking Skills

🔊 **Antonyms • Evaluation** How do the antonyms Mr. Kang uses in his poem (like *chilly* and *warm*) help him compare life in America to life in China? Possible response: In the beginning of the poem when Mr. Kang talks about life in America, he uses many words that mean "cold." This description contrasts with the *warm old days* he experienced when he lived in China and shows how the two places are opposites as well.

Model the Skill

Think Aloud I see that the *chilly* wind makes icy tears. I know that ice is cold, so *chilly* must mean "cold." Then the *warm* memories melt the tears. Since hot things melt ice, *warm* must mean "hot." *Chilly* and *warm* are antonyms.

Mr. Kang sits at the kitchen table and thinks about the sun showing through the trees in the park or the moon peeking into his window. He listens to words in his head, then he picks up his brush and paints a poem. Sometimes he paints a poem twice to practice his brushwork. Mrs. Kang hangs the poems on the kitchen cabinets.

And then, after making sure that the door and the windows are shut, Mr. Kang opens his hua mei's cage. Speaking softly, he invites the bird to stand on the table.

Mr. Kang cleans the cage with a damp towel and dries it with a soft cloth. He takes out the hand-painted ceramic water bowl, rinses it, and puts it back in its stand, full of cool, clear water. He washes the hand-painted ceramic food bowl and puts it back, full of his own special recipe of millet coated with egg yolks and mixed with chopped meat. These days this is the only cooking Mr. Kang does.

Last, Mr. Kang takes a small piece of silk cloth, dampens it with water not too hot, not too cold, and gently wipes the sleek gray feathers of his bird. The hua mei walks right back into his cage. He prefers to give himself a bath.

"Never mind, Birdie," says Mr. Kang. "Instead of the bath, I'll read you my poem. I know you can understand. We both left our homeland. We still speak the old language."

Compare and Contrast • Analysis Which two groups does Mr. Kang compare in his poem? How do the people in each group feel about where they live? Possible response: He compares the people who stayed home with those who immigrated to America. The people at home see and know their surroundings, while the people in America see a city but still remember what their old home was like.

Rushing to the Golden Dragon
against a chilly wind,
the icy tears on my cheeks melt
with memories of warm old days.

Those who never left their home
stay safe, wrapped
in the arms of their motherfather land.
When they look out
their narrow windows,
they see their own kitchen gardens.
They know every plum tree, every kumquat,
every blade of grass, each gray pebble.

We who long ago tossed on cold waters
looking only straight ahead
watch our city mountains
from wide windows, tall rooftops.
Yet our old hearts hold old places.
We save, in old, grown heads,
a full-blown rose in summer,
the sound of bamboo leaves when
the wind is gentle,
the taste of mooncakes.

The hua mei sings his own melody back
Mr. Kang. Mr. Kang closes his eyes to listen.
"Beautiful, Birdie. You are a good poet
a good friend to me," says Mr. Kang.

407

 Inferring • Synthesis How does Mr. Kang feel about living in America? What makes you think this? Possible response: He misses his old home, but he has seen things in America that he would never have seen if he had stayed in China. He thinks that people who have not left their homes have not seen as many things and look out of "narrow windows," while people who have left their homelands have seen more and look through "wide windows."

On Their Own

Have students use context clues to figure out if other words in the text are antonyms. For additional practice, use *Reader's and Writer's Notebook* p. 403.

Connect to Social Studies

Point out China and New York City on a world map or globe. Ask students on which continents they are located. (Asia; North America) In the late 1800s and early 1900s, people could travel from China to New York City by ship. They crossed the Pacific Ocean to North America and then traveled on land from the West Coast to the East Coast. Today people can travel much faster by airplane.

English Language Learners
Compound words Help students identify compound words on this spread, such as *brushwork* and *rooftops*. Have students draw a line between the two words in each compound.

Inferring Read aloud the second paragraph on p. 406. Why do you think Mr. Kang makes sure the door and window are shut? Have students use prior knowledge and information from the text to make an inference to answer the question. (Mr. Kang is about to open his bird's cage, and he does not want the bird to fly away.)

Objectives
- Identify the theme of a story to aid comprehension.

OPTION 1 Skills and Strategies, continued

Teach Theme

Review **Theme** Remind students that the theme of a text is its meaning, or what a reader learns from reading a story. Ask students to identify an important issue the story has presented so far. (whether Mr. Kang should keep his bird in a cage or not) Then ask them what they think the theme might be at this point. (the importance of being free)

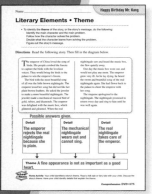

Corrective Feedback

If... students are unable to identify theme,

then... model how to figure out theme.

Let's Practice It!
TR DVD•375

Model the Skill

Think Aloud To figure out the theme of a story, I think about its most important parts and I try to see how they go together. Before, Mr. Kang stopped cooking so he would be free to do fun things.

> Sam usually comes to visit on Saturdays. If Mr. Kang is cleaning the cage, then the hua mei sings to Sam. Sam holds out his finger, and the hua mei holds on tightly. They stare at each other, each without blinking.
>
> "Did he really fly from China?" Sam asks one time.
>
> "In an airplane," says Mr. Kang. "China is so far, even for a bird."
>
> "You should let him go. Maybe he wants to fly home."
>
> "I don't think he could without an airplane. Anyway, he's like me. Home is here with you. If he went home now, I think he would miss his Sundays on Delancey Street." Mr. Kang puts his arm around Sam's shoulders and hugs him.
>
> "I have a very smart grandson," he sighs. "Maybe one day we can visit China together."
>
> And this is how Mr. Kang spends his days, except for Sundays.

408

Student Edition pp. 408–409

OPTION 2 Think Critically, continued

Higher-Order Thinking Skills

Review **Theme • Analysis** How does Sam feel about freedom? What is a detail that supports this idea? Possible response: He thinks birds should be free to fly outside, not be locked up in cages, even if they seem happy. One supporting detail that tells the reader this is that Sam suggests that Mr. Kang should let the hua mei fly home to China.

Make Predictions • Evaluation Do you think Sam will convince Mr. Kang to let his bird go free? What makes you think that? Possible response: Mr. Kang said Sam is very smart. Mr. Kang must respect and value Sam's opinion. I predict that Mr. Kang will decide to let the bird go.

Now Sam is telling him to let his bird go free, too. I think the theme of this story will have something to do with being free.

On Sundays Mr. Kang gets up when it's dark. He washes his face and puts on his clothes. When he is ready, he picks up the cage by the ring on top. The freshly ironed cover is tied shut, and the bird is still sleeping. As he opens the door to leave the apartment, Mrs. Kang is padding quickly behind him.

"Wait for me!" she calls.

"Shhhh!" says Mr. Kang, but he waits as she closes the door and turns her key.

Mr. Kang and his bird lead the way. He walks gingerly, holding onto the banister to steady himself as he goes down the stairs. Out the door, down the block, across the street he glides, to Sara Delano Roosevelt Park on Delancey Street.

Mrs. Kang follows, three steps behind. She sees her friends and slips away to join them.

Mr. Kang hangs the cage on the fence, stretches his arms, and breathes in the morning.

Mr. Lum arrives with a cage in each hand. "How are you, my friend? How is the bird?"

409

Inferring • Analysis Why might Mr. Kang tell Mrs. Kang "Shhhh!"? Possible response: The text says that the bird is still sleeping with the cover of its cage tied shut. Mr. Kang seems to care greatly for his bird, as is shown by the fact that the cover is freshly ironed. I think Mr. Kang does not want his bird disturbed, so he wants Mrs. Kang to be quiet for now.

On Their Own

Have students reread pp. 405–406 to find more details that support the theme of the story. For additional practice, use *Let's Practice It!* page 375 on the *Teacher Resources DVD-ROM.*

Differentiated Instruction

SI Strategic Intervention

Oral language Have students use the illustration on p. 408 to describe how Mr. Kang, Sam, and the bird feel about one another.

ELL

English Language Learners
Inferring Read aloud the first paragraph on p. 408. What do you think the hua mei thinks about Sam? How can you tell? Have students think about what they have read and what they already know to answer the question. (The hua mei seems to like Sam because it sings to him and holds tightly to his finger.)

Objectives
◎ Use the inferring strategy to aid comprehension.

OPTION 1 Skills and Strategies, continued

Teach Inferring

🔵 **Inferring** Remind students that when you infer, you use information from the story and information you already know to figure something out. Ask students why Mr. Kang greets Mr. Lum with this poem. (He wants to say that he enjoys their time in the park the same way he used to enjoy his time with his grandfather.)

Corrective Feedback

If... students are unable to make inferences,

then... use information from the text and from your prior knowledge to model how to make an inference.

Student Edition pp. 410–411

OPTION 2 Think Critically, continued

Higher-Order Thinking Skills

🔵 **Inferring • Analysis** Why might Mrs. Kang put almond cakes in Sam's pocket? Possible response: When Mr. Kang was a boy with his grandfather, his grandmother put almond cakes in his pocket. It is probably now a family tradition.

Model the Strategy

Think Aloud I know from what I read that Mr. Kang enjoyed the time he spent with his grandfather, who also had a bird. His poem tells how seeing Mr. Lum reminds him of this past time.

"We are enjoying the morning," smiles Mr. Kang.

"Mr. Lum!
When I see your cages
resting on the green ivy floor
of Sara Delano Roosevelt Park in New York,

I remember my arm is lifted up to hold
Grandfather's big hand
and that ivy is green
from the Shanghai sun
and that ginkgo tree is blowing
in the soft Shanghai breeze
and that heat in my breast
is from my sweet and fragrant almond cake.
Grandmother slipped it into my pocket,
and it is still there,
warm from her oven."

"Even when you speak a greeting to your friend you are painting a poem," says Mr. Lum. Mr. Kang bows his head.
Today is a special Sunday morning because Sam and Mr. Kang are going to the park together. Sam slept at his grandparents' house last night. It is still dark, and he is rubbing his eyes as he jumps from his bed. Just like Grandpa, he washes his face and puts on his clothes. Together, at dawn's first light, they lift the cage. The cover is still tied, the bird is still sleeping. Sam opens the front door. Grandpa steps out, and Grandma is there right behind him, just as she is every Sunday morning.
"Wait for me!" she says.

410

Character • Evaluation What kind of character is Mr. Kang? Possible response: He is thoughtful; he expresses his feelings in his poems; he likes to write poetry. He loves his grandson; he talks to him and spends time with him.

I know from my own life that sometimes friends have special ways of greeting each other. Mr. Lum seems to be a good friend; this is a way for Mr. Kang to greet him and tell him that.

On Their Own

Have students reread the text on these pages. Ask them why Sam might want to accompany his grandfather to the park.

"*Shhh!*" say Mr. Kang and Sam, but they wait as she closes the door. Mrs. Kang takes one extra minute to slip two warm almond cakes into Sam's pocket. Then Sam and Mr. Kang lead the way down the stairs, out the front door, on to the corner, across the street, all the way to Sara Delano Roosevelt Park on Delancey Street.

Background Knowledge • Evaluation • Text to Self Mr. Kang had a tradition of visiting the park with his grandfather, and now Sam visits the park with his grandfather. What are some family traditions you take part in? **Possible response:** My family takes fishing trips together.

Check Predictions Have students look back at the predictions they made earlier and discuss whether they were accurate. Then have students preview the rest of the selection and either adjust their predictions accordingly or make new predictions.

Differentiated Instruction

SI Strategic Intervention

Inferring Have pairs of students work together to make inferences about Mr. Kang's relationship with his bird and how important this relationship is to him and his life after he retires as a cook.

A Advanced

Inferring Have students find information about kinds of birds people keep as pets in China and some activities people do with these pets. Then have students make inferences about the importance pet birds hold for people in China.

ELL

English Language Learners
Antonyms Help students find a pair of antonyms on pp. 410–411, such as *dark/light* or *opens/closes*. Have students use context clues to create their own definitions for these words and to explain why they are antonyms.

If you want to teach this selection in two sessions, stop here.

Research and Inquiry
Navigate/Search

Teach

Have students generate a research plan to gather relevant information. Suggest that students search the Internet using their inquiry questions and keywords. Tell them to skim and scan each site for information that helps answer their inquiry question or leads them to specific information that will be useful. Bolded or italicized words may be clues to what kind of information the Web site will provide. Have students look for other features, such as headings, illustrations, captions, or highlighting. Remind students to take notes as they gather information.

Model

Think Aloud When looking for information on how animals are granted freedom, I found: *After the seals were nursed back to health, they were released back into the wild.* I will use the keywords from this information, such as *health,* to lead me to more specific information. One fact I found using these keywords states, *Workers from wildlife rescue centers take care of sick seals until they are in good health again.*

Guide practice

Have students continue their review of Web sites they identified. Explain that before accepting information from a Web site as reliable, students should check to see if the Web site contains spelling or grammatical errors. Remind them that Web addresses ending in *.gov, .org,* or *.edu* are more likely to have reliable information. Suggest they also check for the date when the Web site was last updated to make sure that the facts contained in the site are current.

On their own

Have students write down Web addresses, authors, and the dates the Web sites were last updated and create a Works Cited page.

Conventions
Abbreviations

Teach

Write this sentence on the board: *"Mr. Kang," says Mrs. Kang, "did you forget about your three birthday wishes already?"* *Mr.* and *Mrs.* are abbreviated titles, which are capitalized and end with a period.

Guide practice

Have students do the following:

- make a list of adults they know whom they call by a title, such as neighbors, parents of friends, teachers, or doctors.
- look up their birthdays on a calendar and write the date using abbreviations, including day of the week and the month.

Connect to oral language

Have students locate examples of abbreviations in the main selection. (*Mr. Kang, Mrs. Kang, Mr. Lum,* p. 409; *Mr. Wu,* p. 413)

Daily Fix-It

Use Daily Fix-It numbers 3 and 4 in the right margin.

On their own

For additional practice, use the *Reader's and Writer's Notebook* p. 400.

Spelling
Schwa

Teach

The schwa in unaccented syllables can be spelled several different ways, but it always has the same sound. Model how to spell words with the schwa sound. The parts in *another* are *a, no,* and *ther.* I spell the first syllable. If it is hard for me to spell the schwa sound, I'll check the spelling list. Then I write the second syllable. Then I write the last syllable. I may picture the word in my mind to help me spell *another, a-n-o-t-h-e-r.*

Guide practice

Have students write each spelling word and underline the unaccented syllable. Tell them to identify the vowels which form the schwa sound.

On their own

For additional practice, use the *Reader's and Writer's Notebook* p. 401.

Reader's and Writer's Notebook p. 401

Daily Fix-It

3. I always look at the bird's in the cage in dr. Robinson's office. (*birds; Dr.*)
4. Ms. Sanchez and him clean the cage dayly. (*he; daily*)

Reader's and Writer's Notebook p. 400

English Language Learners
Conventions To provide students with practice on abbreviations, use the modified grammar lessons in the *ELL Handbook* and the Grammar Jammer online at: www.ReadingStreet.com

Language transfer: Practice capitalization English learners often need help with capitalization. Vietnamese and Spanish speakers do not capitalize the names of days and months. Capital letters may even be new to some Chinese and Korean speakers. Provide examples in English and allow ample time for students to practice writing capital letters with abbreviations.

Objectives
- Understand and recognize the structure of a limerick.
- Generate a list of writing topics and rhyming words.

Writing—Poetry: Limerick
Writer's Craft: Structure of a Limerick

Introduce the prompt

Review the key features of limericks with students. Remind them that a limerick is a five-line poem that tells a silly, humorous story, has a fixed rhyme pattern, and that each line in a limerick contains a set number of syllables and accents that create rhythm. Remind students that they should think about these features as they are writing. Explain that they will begin the writing process for a limerick today. Read aloud the writing prompt.

> **Writing Prompt**
> Write a limerick about the story *Happy Birthday Mr. Kang.*

Select a topic

 Think Aloud Today you will begin writing a limerick about the main selection, *Happy Birthday Mr. Kang.* Start by reading the selection carefully several times. As you read, keep a list of topics that you could write about. Let's start a list now. Write the header "Topics" on the board. This story is about Mr. Kang's birthday. On his birthday, Mr. Kang makes three wishes. This could be a topic for a limerick. Write "Mr. Kang's three birthday wishes" at the top of the list. Mr. Kang writes poems and paints pictures for them with his grandson, Sam. This could also be a topic. Write "Mr. Kang writes poems/paints pictures with Sam." Mr. Kang has a bird from China. Every Sunday, he takes it to the park. These could also be topics. Add these topics to the list. Ask students for other suggestions from the story, adding viable topics to the list. Once you have a list of topics, think about how you can make that topic into a limerick. Create a T-chart by drawing a vertical line to the right of the list of topics. At the top of the new column, write the header "Limerick Ideas" and brainstorm with students ways of making the topic into a limerick.

Topics	Limerick Ideas
Mr. Kang's three birthday wishes	
Mr. Kang writes poems/paints pictures with Sam	
Mr. Kang's bird from China	
Mr. Kang takes his bird to the park every Sunday	

Corrective feedback

Circulate among students as they choose a topic to write about. Talk individually with students who are having difficulty understanding the assigment or making a choice. Ask students what their favorite part of the story was, and offer suggestions for making it into a limerick.

MINI-LESSON

Structure of a Limerick

■ Once you have chosen your topic and are ready to write, it's important to understand the structure of a limerick. Remember that a limerick has five lines. The rhyme pattern is *a-a-b-b-a*. Lines 1, 2, and 5 rhyme and lines 3 and 4 also rhyme.

■ Limericks are written with a certain rhythm. The lines that rhyme should have the same number of syllables and two or three accented syllables per line. **Read aloud the student model. Remind students to keep the rhythm in mind as they write.**

Now, use a T-chart to make a list of rhyming words to include in your limerick. You should have two lists—one list of rhyming words for the first, second, and fifth lines, and one list for the third and fourth lines. **Have students begin their lists using the form on p. 402 of their** *Reader's and Writer's Notebook.* **Guide students in creating lists of words around which they can build their limericks.**

ROUTINE   Quick Write for Fluency   Team Talk

1. **Talk** Have students discuss how they chose the rhyming words.

2. **Write** Each student should write a few sentences explaining his or her word choice.

3. **Share** Partners should read their writing to each other and then share their writing with other pairs.

Routines Flip Chart

Differentiated Instruction

 Advanced

Create a graphic Challenge students to create a graphic to go with their limerick, such as an illustration.

Teacher Tip

Work with students who have difficulty understanding the concept of rhythm. Read aloud the student model, emphasizing the accented syllables in lines 3 and 4. Read the model a second time, having students read chorally with you.

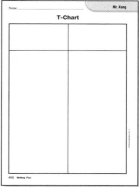

Reader's and Writer's Notebook p. 402

Wrap Up Your Day

✔ **Build Concepts** What did you learn about freedom?

✔ **Cause and Effect** How does knowing how to identify the cause and effect of an event help you understand your reading?

✔ **Inferring** How does using your own experience to infer something help you understand what you have read?

Preview DAY 3

Tell students that tomorrow they will read about why a person might feel that his or her pet deserves to be set free.

Objectives
- Expand the weekly concept.
- Develop oral vocabulary.

Today at a Glance

Oral Vocabulary
companion, nag

Comprehension Check/Retelling
Discuss questions

Phonics/Word Analysis
◉ Schwa

Reading
Happy Birthday Mr. Kang

Think Critically
Retelling

Fluency
Appropriate phrasing

Research and Study Skills
Maps

Research and Inquiry
Analyze

Conventions
Abbreviations

Spelling
Schwa

Writing
Poetry: Limerick

Concept Talk

Question of the Week

❓ What does it mean to grant freedom?

Expand the concept

Remind students of the weekly concept question. Discuss how the question relates to keeping a pet bird. Tell students that today they will read about a decision a pet owner must make about whether to let his bird go free or not. Encourage students to think about why a person might think his or her pet companion deserves to be released into the wild.

Anchored Talk

Develop oral vocabulary

Use text features—illustrations and italic text—to review pp. 404–415 of *Happy Birthday Mr. Kang.* Discuss the Amazing Words *manage* and *affectionate.* Add these words to the concept map. Use the following questions to develop students' understanding of the concept.

- Mr. Kang *manages* to keep his pet bird happy by taking very good care of it. Think of other ways that people *manage* pets to keep them content.

- Mr. Kang is *affectionate* with his pet bird as he takes care of it, and the bird is *affectionate* with Sam. What are some ways that people are *affectionate* with different kinds of pets for which they care?

Oral Vocabulary
Amazing Words

Teach Amazing Words

Amazing Words Oral Vocabulary Routine

1. **Introduce** Write the word *companion* on the board. Have students say it with you. Yesterday, we read about a man who keeps a bird as a *companion*. Have students determine a definition of *companion*. (A *companion* is someone who spends time with another person.)

2. **Demonstrate** Have students answer questions to demonstrate understanding. What are some reasons that Mr. Kang's bird is a good *companion* for him? (The bird is a good *companion* for Mr. Kang because it reminds him of his homeland and his past. Also, the bird and Mr. Kang can spend fun time together being artists, with the bird singing and Mr. Kang writing poems.)

3. **Apply** Have students apply their understanding. What are some personality traits that someone might look for in a good *companion*?

See p. OV•2 to teach *nag.*

Routines Flip Chart

Apply Amazing Words

As students read pp. 415–419 of *Happy Birthday Mr. Kang,* have them consider how the Amazing Words *companion* and *nag* apply to Mr. Kang's relationship with his bird and how Sam feels about this relationship.

Connect to reading

Explain that today students will read about how and why Mr. Kang tries to change the relationship between himself and his bird. As they read, students should think about how the Question of the Week and the Amazing Words *companion* and *nag* apply to Mr. Kang's actions.

ELL **Expand Vocabulary** Use the Day 3 instruction on ELL Poster 27 to help students expand vocabulary.

ELL Poster 27

Objectives

◎ Read and sort words with the schwa sound.

• Decode and read words in context and independent of context.

Word Analysis
Sort Words

Model word sorting

Write *schwa* and *no schwa* as heads in a two-column chart. Now we are going to sort words. We'll put words with the schwa sound in the first column. Words without the schwa sound will go in the second column. I will start. Write *pretzel* and model how to read it, using the Word Parts Strategy Routine on p. 396a. Since the second syllable in *pretzel* is an unaccented syllable, I wlll write *pretzel* in the first column. Model reading *nickel* and *redo* in the same way.

Guide practice

Use the following words for the sort: *sister, meadow, profile, decorate, robin,* and *gadget.* Point to a word. Have students read the word, identify its syllables, and tell where it should be written on the chart.

Corrective feedback

For corrective feedback, model identifying the syllables and whether or not they have the sound of schwa.

schwa	no schwa			
pretzel	redo			
nickel	meadow			
sister	profile			
decorate				
robin				
gadget				

Fluent Word Reading

Model

Write *family.* I know this word has three syllables. (fam/i/ly) The middle syllable, *i,* is unaccented, so I use the schwa sound to represent *i.* I read the word as *family.*

Guide practice

Write the words below. Look for the word parts you know. When I point to the word, we'll read it together. Allow one second per word part previewing time for the first reading.

vitamin	envelope	balcony	camera	local	customer

On their own

Have students read the list above three or four times, until they can read one word per second.

Decode and Read

Read words independent of context

Have students turn to p. 141 in *Decodable Practice Readers 3.2* and find the first list of words. Each word in this list has the schwa sound. Let's read these words. Be sure that students pronounce the vowel that stands for the schwa sound correctly.

Next, have students read the high-frequency words.

Preview Decodable Practice Passage

Have students read the title and preview the story. Tell them that they will read words that have the schwa sounds.

Read words in context

Chorally read the story along with the students. Have students identify words in the story that have the schwa sound. Make sure that students are monitoring their accuracy when they decode words.

 Team Talk Pair students and have them take turns reading the story aloud to each other. Monitor students as they read to check for proper pronunciation and appropriate pacing.

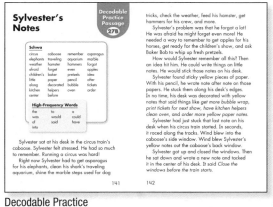

Decodable Practice Passage 27B

Differentiated Instruction

SI Strategic Intervention

Sort words Help students divide each word in the chart into syllables. Write each word on the board and show students how to indicate which syllable is stressed using an accent mark. For example, *pret´zel*. Then have children underline the vowel in the unstressed syllable that stands for the schwa sound.

Comprehension Check

Have students discuss each question with a partner. Ask several pairs to share their responses.

☑ **Genre • Analysis**

How are the characters in *Happy Birthday Mr. Kang* appropriate for a piece of realistic fiction? **Possible response: They experience feelings and act the way people in real life would.**

☑ **Cause and effect • Analysis**

What causes Mr. Kang to want to read the newspaper every day, paint poems, and buy a bird? **Possible response: He has retired. It has been his dream to do these things. Now that he is no longer working, he will do them.**

☑ **Inferring • Evaluation**

Why does the author provide details about how Mr. Kang takes care of his bird, such as the fact that the bird's water bowl is hand-painted and ceramic, that Mr. Kang cooks the bird's food himself, and that he bathes it with a silk cloth? **Possible response: These details all show how much Mr. Kang treasures his bird.**

☑ **Antonyms • Analysis**

Use context clues and antonyms to define the word *dampens.* Check your definition in a dictionary. **Possible response: *Dampens* means "makes a little wet." Mr. Kang cleans the cage with a damp towel and dries it with another one. I can tell that *damp* and *dry* are antonyms, which helps me determine the meaning of *dampen.***

☑ **Connect text to self**

Mr. Kang keeps a special pet that his grandson feels should be set free. Are there any animals you have cared for that other people might have felt should live in the wild? **Possible response: I have a dog I care for, but my dog is much better off living with me than being completely free and having to take care of itself outside.**

Strategy Response Log

Have students use their background knowledge and clues from the text to make inferences about being free to do what you like. Use p. 33 in the *Reader's and Writer's Notebook* to list clues students found in the text.

INTERACT with TEXT

Check Retelling

Have students retell the first part of *Happy Birthday Mr. Kang,* summarizing the plot's main events.

Corrective feedback

If... the students leave out important details,

then... have students look back through the illustrations in the selection.

Small Group Time

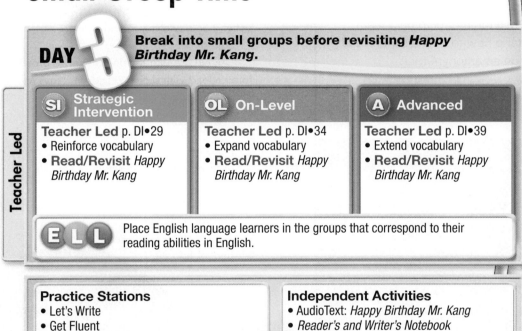

DAY 3

Break into small groups before revisiting *Happy Birthday Mr. Kang*.

Teacher Led

SI Strategic Intervention

Teacher Led p. DI•29
• Reinforce vocabulary
• **Read/Revisit** *Happy Birthday Mr. Kang*

OL On-Level

Teacher Led p. DI•34
• Expand vocabulary
• **Read/Revisit** *Happy Birthday Mr. Kang*

A Advanced

Teacher Led p. DI•39
• Extend vocabulary
• **Read/Revisit** *Happy Birthday Mr. Kang*

ELL Place English language learners in the groups that correspond to their reading abilities in English.

Practice Stations
• Let's Write
• Get Fluent
• Word Work

Independent Activities
• AudioText: *Happy Birthday Mr. Kang*
• *Reader's and Writer's Notebook*
• Research and Inquiry

English Language Learners

Check retelling To support retelling, review the multilingual summary for *Happy Birthday Mr. Kang* with the appropriate Retelling Cards to scaffold understanding.

Objectives

◎ Identify antonyms.

OPTION 1 Skills and Strategies, continued

Teach Antonyms

 Antonyms Review with students that antonyms are words that have opposite meanings. Point to the word *foreign* on p. 412. Ask students to use the context to figure out the meaning of this word and an antonym for it. (A foreign land is one that is strange to a person. An antonym for *foreign* would be *familiar*.)

Corrective Feedback

If... students are unable to find antonyms,

then... use the model to help them understand how to define a word and decide on an antonym for it.

Multidraft Reading

If you chose . . .

Option 1 Return to Extend Thinking instruction starting on p. 404–405.

Option 2 Read pp. 412–419. Use the Guide Comprehension and Extend Thinking instruction.

Student Edition pp. 412–413

OPTION 2 Think Critically, continued

Higher-Order Thinking Skills

 Antonyms • Analysis What antonyms does the author use to describe how Mr. Kang feels in a foreign land and how Sam thinks the birds' songs sound? What do these antonyms tell the reader about the difference between Mr. Kang's situation and that of the birds? Mr. Kang says he is happy in this strange land, but Sam says the birds' songs sound sad. Using antonyms helps the author make the difference clear between how Mr. Kang feels about his life and how the birds might feel about theirs.

Model the Skill

Think Aloud I know that Mr. Kang came to America from China, so the land where he is growing old is not his original land. I think *foreign* means "unfamiliar."

As usual, Mrs. Kang follows until she sees her friends. Sam sets the bird cage gently on the ground. Mr. Lum's cages are already hanging.

"Look who's here!" says Mr. Lum. "How are you, Sam? You're getting so big. How old are you?"

"Seven," says Sam.

"Only seven?" says Mr. Lum. "You're handling that cage better than a twelve-year-old would!"

Sam smiles.

"An old grandfather does not mind growing old in a foreign land with such a grandson," says Mr. Kang.

"I am happy in this strange land:
I see my grandson planted
in the new, rich earth,
growing straight and smart and tall.
I water him.
The sun shines on his
firm young leaves
as I watch for his flowers
and for his fruit."

412

Confirm Prediction • Evaluation Can you confirm the prediction you made on page 409? Possible response: I predicted that Mr. Kang would value Sam's opinion and decide to let his bird go. Since he says that Sam may be right, it seems like he is definitely considering letting the bird go.

I am sure this is the right definition, because Mr. Kang uses *strange* in the same way in his poem. An antonym for *foreign* would be *familiar.*

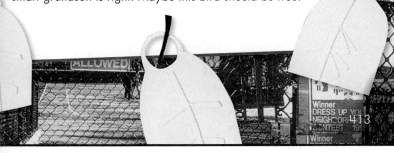

"More poems, Mr. Kang," says Mr. Lum. "I think you always speak in poems."

"Your ears are kind to my words, my friend," says Mr. Kang. Two more men with two more cages arrive, then another and yet another. Soon there are twenty-seven cages in the park.

Mr. Kang lets Sam untie the cover. A strand of light passes through the bamboo bars. As the sun climbs, the men and Sam open all the curtains, inch by inch.

A bird calls and is answered by another.

"They sing sad songs," says Sam.

"They sing of their strong young years," says Mr. Lum.

"They sing about their grandfathers," says Mr. Wu.

"Maybe they sing about their grandsons," says Sam.

"They sing about being in their cages," says Mr. Wu. "Probably they want to fly out."

"Like me in my cage," says Mr. Kang. "Like me, making noodles every day for fifty years."

"I would fly out if I were a bird," says Sam.

Mr. Kang stands away from the fence. "Maybe my smart grandson is right. Maybe this bird should be free."

Metaphors • Analysis To what does Mr. Kang compare Sam in his poem? How does he use language to create an image in the reader's mind? (He compares Sam to a plant that is growing well in this new land, while Mr. Kang helps him grow and looks after him. He builds a picture in the reader's mind of Sam being a growing plant by using descriptive phrases like *growing straight and smart and tall* and talking about how the sun shines on his firm young leaves.)

On Their Own

Have students pick another word from this spread and think of an antonym for it.

Differentiated Instruction

A Advanced

Similes and metaphors Have students identify examples of similes and metaphors on this spread. Then have them use these examples of figurative language as models for writing their own similes and metaphors about the process of growing up.

E L L

English Language Learners

Inferring Read aloud the dialogue on p. 413 where each character explains what topic he thinks the birds are singing about. Ask students to use prior knowledge and what they have learned about each character to explain what the characters think the topics of the songs are.

Objectives
◎ Make inferences about a text to aid comprehension.

OPTION 1 Skills and Strategies, continued

Teach Inferring

Inferring Ask students why they think Mr. Kang uses English after he lets his bird go free. (Mr. Kang realizes that keeping the bird in the cage is like his working in the restaurant every day when he didn't want to be there. Mr. Kang thinks that America is the land of the free and the *hua mei* deserves freedom. Speaking English shows his acceptance of a new way of thinking and his new life.)

Corrective Feedback

If… students are unable to make inferences,

then… use the model to help them understand how to infer.

Model the Strategy

Think Aloud From what I have read, I know that Mr. Kang cares deeply about his past in China. Mrs. Kang speaks Chinese to him here, so they must speak Chinese to each other often.

> Mr. Kang walks slowly toward his cage.
>
> "Stop!" Mr. Lum puts a hand on his friend's arm. "Mr. Kang, do not be foolish!" The men form a circle around Mr. Kang, and everyone is talking at once. The women rush over.
>
> "Mr. Kang," says Mrs. Kang, "did you forget about your three birthday wishes already? What will you do when you finish painting your poems and there is no bird to sing to you afterwards?"
>
> "Ever since my birthday, I am a free man," says Mr. Kang. "Maybe this hua mei wants to be a free bird. America is the land of the free. Sam says . . ."
>
> "Sam is a seven-year-old American boy," interrupts Mrs. Kang. "He cannot understand old ways."
>
> "But Grandma, it's not fair."
>
> "Sam." Mrs. Kang turns to her grandson. "Sam. This is not something you can understand."
>
> Mr. Kang just shakes his head. He brushes away Mrs. Kang's hands. He brushes away the hands of his friends.
>
> 414

Student Edition pp. 414–415

OPTION 2 Think Critically, continued

Higher-Order Thinking Skills

Inferring • Synthesis Why does Mr. Kang take off his cap and cover his heart with his hand after his bird flies away? Possible response: Both of these actions are things people do to show respect. Mr. Kang loves his bird very much and is showing the *hua mei* how he feels about it as it flies away.

Cause and Effect • Evaluation Why does Mr. Kang let his bird fly free? Possible response: Mr. Kang compares the bird's life to his life and decides that the bird should be as free as he is now.

By listening to Sam and speaking in English, Mr. Kang is showing that he is accepting American ways.

On Their Own

Have students infer why Mrs. Kang thinks Sam doesn't understand why Mr. Kang shouldn't let his bird go free.

Suddenly Sam is frightened. What if Grandma is right? What if Grandpa is sorry after the hua mei flies away? What if the hua mei gets lost? What if he starves? What if he dies?

"Grandpa, wait," says Sam. But Grandpa does not hear. Mr. Kang cannot hear any voice except the voice inside his own head, inside his own heart. He opens the bamboo door.

Mr. Kang's hua mei perches on the threshold of his cage. Perhaps he thinks it's cage-cleaning time. He slowly steps out. He stops to sing a long, sweet note, turns his head to the breeze, and flies into the sky.

Mr. Kang takes off his cap and covers his heart with his hand. For a moment there is silence. Mrs. Kang bends her head and hugs herself. Her mouth is a thin straight line. "Oh, Mr. Kang," she whispers in Chinese. "What can you be thinking?" Sam starts to cry.

"Sam and I are going home to paint poems," says Mr. Kang loudly, in English.

He lifts his empty cage, takes Sam's hand, and together they walk out of the park. Onto the sidewalk, over to the corner, across the street, up the block they walk.

SARA D. ROOSEVELT PARK

415

Compare and Contrast • Synthesis How does the way the other people feel about Mr. Kang letting his bird go free compare with the way Mr. Kang thinks about it? **Possible response:** The other people think it's a foolish idea to let the bird go, especially because Mr. Kang wanted it so much in the first place. They don't care whether it's fair to keep a bird in a cage as long as the bird's owner is happy. Sam and Mr. Kang think the bird should have a choice about where it lives.

Differentiated Instruction

SI Strategic Intervention

Character Have students compare how Sam feels about letting the bird go at the beginning of this spread with how he feels at the end. Ask them to explain why Sam's feelings change.

ELL

English Language Learners

Metaphor Point out the metaphor on p. 415: *Her mouth is a thin, straight line.* Discuss how her mouth is not actually a line and how a metaphor makes a comparison without using *like* or *as.*

DAY 3 Read and Comprehend

Objectives
• Identify the theme of a story to aid comprehension.

Skills and Strategies, continued

Teach Theme

Review **Theme** Remind students that the message of a story is its theme. Ask students how Mr. Kang's action of letting his bird fly free relates to this story's theme. (Possible response: The theme is that we all should have the freedom to make choices for ourselves, and Mr. Kang let his bird choose whether it was going to live in a cage or not.)

Corrective Feedback

If... students have trouble identifying how this action relates to the theme, **then...** model how to determine the theme of a story.

Model the Skill

 To figure out the theme, I ask myself, "What is the message of this story?" I read that the bird was free to fly away, but it came back to the apartment.

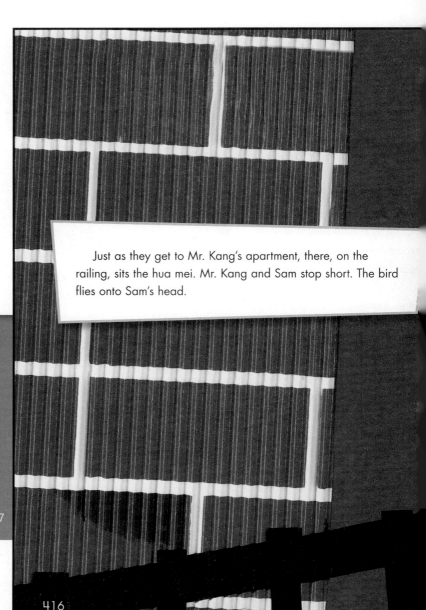

Just as they get to Mr. Kang's apartment, there, on the railing, sits the hua mei. Mr. Kang and Sam stop short. The bird flies onto Sam's head.

416

Student Edition pp. 416–417

Cause and Effect • Analysis Why is the bird back at Mr. Kang's apartment? Possible response: It chose to fly back and live there instead of in the wild.

Think Critically, continued

Higher-Order Thinking Skills

Review **Theme • Evaluation** Why do you think Mr. Kang's bird came back after being set free? How does this relate to the theme? Possible response: The bird was free to fly away, but it came back on its own. It is still free after that, even though it is living in a cage. It is free because it was free to make that choice. This relates to the theme because the bird has the freedom to decide where and how to live.

Nobody made it come back, so it was free to do it on its own. The theme is that we all, including Mr. Kang's bird, should have freedom to decide where and how we live.

On Their Own

Have students paraphrase the theme in their own words.

Differentiated Instruction

A **Advanced**

Have students write a paragraph discussing what it means to be free and to allow others to be free.

English Language Learners

Idioms Reread the sentence where Mr. Kang and Sam "stop short." Explain that when a person "stops short," he or she stops suddenly, taking a very short distance to do so. Have students stand up and act out walking and "stopping short."

417

Inferring • Evaluation How do you think Mr. Kang and Sam will react to having the bird back? Do you think Mr. Kang will let it go free again? Possible response: Mr. Kang and Sam will probably welcome the bird back. Mr. Kang set the bird free and it chose to stay. Mr. Kang is probably very happy that the bird likes its life with him.

Objectives
◎ Identify cause-and-effect relationships.

OPTION 1 Skills and Strategies, continued

Teach Cause and Effect

Cause and Effect Remind students that an effect is what happens and a cause is why it happened. Point out that seeing the bird again causes Mr. Kang and Sam to sit at the table with their coats and caps on because they are so excited. Ask students why Mrs. Kang starts smiling when she enters the kitchen. (She is excited to see the bird back too.)

Corrective Feedback

If... students are unable to identify a cause and effect,
then... use the model to help them identify an effect and then identify its cause.

Student Edition pp. 418–419

OPTION 2 Think Critically, continued

Higher-Order Thinking Skills

Cause and Effect • Synthesis Why does Mr. Kang say that no one needs to see his face to know he did not come over on the Mayflower? Possible response: He looks Asian and speaks English with a Chinese accent, so it is clear he is from China.

Model the Skill

Think Aloud I see from the text that Mrs. Kang starts smiling. I think back to what happened just before this that might have made her happy. She just entered the kitchen and saw the bird. I think that is what caused her to smile.

Then up the stairs and into the kitchen they run. They sit at the table, coats and caps still on. The hua mei hops onto Sam's paper. Mr. Kang paints his poem as Sam paints his picture. The bird helps.

After forty-three American years
I still speak my native tongue,
but any Chinese ear can hear
that I no longer speak
like a native. Sometimes

even I can hear
the familiar sounds bending
by themselves in my own throat,
coming out strangely,
sounding a little American. Yet

those same words in English suffer more.
I open up
my American mouth and
no one needs to see my face to know
my ship was never Mayflower. But

at home, with even you, my hua mei, peeping
a little like a sparrow,
I sit at my kitchen table, and I paint these words.
They sing out without accent:
We are Americans, by choice.

418

Review **Theme • Evaluation** Paraphrase the theme of the poem on page 418. How does it connect to the theme of the unit? Possible response: The poem says that Mr. Kang was born in China but became an American by choice. The theme is that America is a land of choices and freedoms and that we are Americans by choice. The poem relates to the unit theme of freedom.

On Their Own

Have students reread pp. 414–415 to find other related causes and effects.

"This is your poem, Birdie," says Mr. Kang, "and Sam, it's your poem too."

Then Mr. Kang looks at Sam's painting. "My grandson is a great artist," he says. He hangs the paintings on the kitchen cabinet and sits back to admire them.

Mrs. Kang walks into the kitchen with her mouth still in that thin straight line, but there is the bird, and suddenly she is smiling

"Today I'll cook for both of you, and for your hua mei," she says.

And she makes tea, and more sweet and fragrant almond cakes, warm from the oven.

Differentiated Instruction

SI **Strategic Intervention**

Summarize To make sure students understand the meaning of Mr. Kang's last poem, have them write what it means to them.

A **Advanced**

Poetry Have students use Mr. Kang's poem as a model for writing their own poem celebrating how they feel about growing up in America.

Comprehension Check

Spiral Review

Draw Conclusions • Evaluation Think about what you have read. How has Mr. Kang changed? Possible response: Mr. Kang wanted a bird (a *hua mei*) for his birthday to keep up a tradition from his home country. Later, he realizes that like himself, the bird may long for freedom, so he decides to let the bird go free.

Author's Purpose • Evaluation What reasons might the author have had for writing this story?

Possible response: The author might have wanted to entertain readers but also to convince her audience how important the freedom to make our own choices is and how lucky people who live in America are to have this freedom.

Check Predictions Have students return to the predictions they made earlier and confirm whether they were accurate.

E L L

English Language Learners
Graphic organizer Have students use a Venn diagram to compare and contrast Mr. Kang and his bird. Help them locate important details in the text and record them in the appropriate sections of the diagram.

Objectives

◎ Identify causes and effects to aid in comprehension.

◎ Make inferences to aid in comprehension.

Check Retelling

SUCCESS PREDICTOR

Plan to Assess Retelling

☑ **Week 1** Assess Strategic Intervention students.

☑ **This week assess Advanced students.**

☐ **Week 3** Assess Strategic Intervention students.

☐ **Week 4** Assess On-Level students.

☐ **Week 5** Assess any students you have not yet checked during this unit.

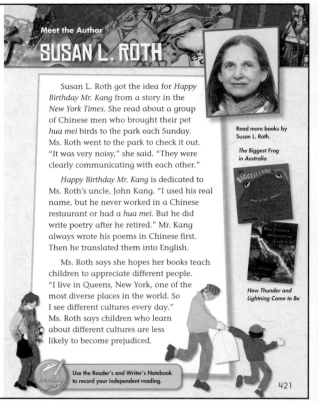

Student Edition pp. 420–421

Retelling

Envision It! Have students work in pairs to retell the selection, using the Envision It! Retelling Cards as prompts. Remind students that they should accurately describe the main events in a logical order and use key vocabulary as they summarize. Monitor students' retellings.

Scoring rubric

> **Top-Score Response** A top-score response makes connections beyond the text, describes the plot's main events using accurate information, evaluates cause-and-effect relationships, and draws conclusions from the text.

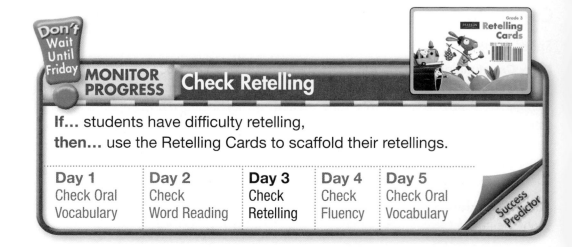

Don't Wait Until Friday

MONITOR PROGRESS Check Retelling

If... students have difficulty retelling,

then... use the Retelling Cards to scaffold their retellings.

Day 1	Day 2	Day 3	Day 4	Day 5
Check Oral Vocabulary	Check Word Reading	**Check Retelling**	Check Fluency	Check Oral Vocabulary

Success Predictor

Think Critically

Text to text

1. They are alike because they both tell about places, people, and events that are like places, people, and events in real life. They are different because "Me and Uncle Romie" tells about the main character's life when he was younger, while "Happy Birthday Mr. Kang" tells about the main character's life now.

Think like an author

2. Possible Response: On p. 418, the artist drew Sam's drawing, Mr. Kang's poem, and the bird's painting. It is important to include all of these to show how the characters share their time making art together.

Cause and effect

3. Sam helped Mr. Kang realize that like him, the bird is not free to live its life the way it chooses. The effect was that he let the bird go free so it could make its own choice about how to live.

Inferring

4. Sam says the birds' songs sound sad and that if he were a bird he would want to fly free. Mr. Kang shows that he is happy with his decision to listen to Sam by speaking English and holding Sam's hand as they leave.

5. **Look Back and Write** To build writing fluency, assign a 10–15 minute time limit.

Suggest that students use a prewriting strategy, such as brainstorming or using a graphic organizer, to organize their ideas. Remind them to establish a topic sentence and support it with facts, details, or explanations. As students finish, encourage them to reread their responses, revise for organization and support, and proofread for errors in grammar and conventions.

Scoring rubric

Top-Score Response A top-score response uses details to tell why Mr. Kang's birthday is special and how it influences future events in the plot.

A top-score response should include:

- Mr. Kang spent years not being free to do what he wanted.

- Mr. Kang announces on his birthday that his birthday wishes are to stop cooking and do what he wants.

- After his birthday, Mr. Kang does what he wants, including getting a Chinese bird as a companion.

Differentiated Instruction

SI Strategic Intervention

Cause-and-effect Have students describe what Mr. Kang's life was like and what he did to pass the time before and after his birthday. Help them use this information to figure out why his birthday is special and marks a turning point in his life.

Meet the Author

Have students read about author Susan L. Roth on page 421. Ask them how she expresses her beliefs about how to live freely in *Happy Birthday Mr. Kang*.

Independent Reading

After students enter their independent reading information into their Reading Logs, have them paraphrase a portion of the text they just read. Remind students that when we paraphrase, we express the meaning of a passage, using other words and maintaining logical order.

ELL

English Language Learners
Retelling Use the Retelling Cards to discuss the selection with students. Place the cards in an incorrect order and have volunteers correct the mistake. Then have students explain where each card should go as they describe the sequence of the selection.

 Retelling

Success Predictor

Objectives

- Read aloud grade-level text with appropriate phrasing.
- Reread for fluency.
- Read and interpret information displayed in a map.

Model Fluency
Appropriate Phrasing

Model fluent reading

Have students turn to p. 412 of *Happy Birthday Mr. Kang.* Have students follow along as you read this page. Tell them to listen to where you pause for punctuation and as you read the dialogue. Point out places where the text breaks naturally into groups of words, or phrases.

Guide practice

Have students follow along as you read the page again. Then have them read the page as a group without you until they read with correct phrasing and with no mistakes. Ask questions to be sure students comprehend the text. Continue in the same way on p. 413.

Reread for Fluency

Corrective feedback

If... students are having difficulty reading with correct phrasing, **then...** prompt:

- Where can we break up this sentence? Which words are related?
- Read the sentence again. Pause after each group of words.
- Tell me the sentence. Now read it with pauses after each group of words.

ROUTINE Oral Rereading

1. **Read** Have students read the dialogue on p. 415 of *Happy Birthday Mr. Kang* orally.

2. **Reread** To achieve optimal fluency, students should reread the text three or four times.

3. **Corrective Feedback** Have students read aloud without you. Listen to ensure that words are read correctly and that no words or lines are omitted, and provide feedback.

Routines Flip Chart

Research and Study Skills
Maps

Teach

Ask students what kind of texts use maps. Students may mention atlases, encyclopedias, newspapers, magazines, textbooks, or stories. Note that maps may show road systems, state boundaries, the geography of an area, weather, or products produced in an area. Show a map from a content-area text and use it to review these terms:

- Every map has a **legend,** or a key that explains the things the map shows. You must look at the legend before using the map for the first time.
- Each legend contains a **compass rose** that shows the directions north, south, east, and west on the map.
- Each legend has a **scale** that shows distance on the map and provides information such as how many inches equal a mile or a kilometer.
- Each legend contains **symbols,** or small pictures that show landmarks such as airports, schools, or campgrounds.

Provide groups with examples of different kinds of maps. Have each group show its map to the class, telling what kind of map it is, and using the legend to explain what it shows and how it is shown.

Guide practice

Discuss these questions:

How do you know what the symbols on a map represent? (The legend explains the meaning of the symbols.)

How are maps alike or different? (They all show information about a place, but they show different kinds of information, such as area boundaries, geographical features, or manmade features such as roads or buildings.)

After groups describe their maps, ask specific questions about the information depicted on the map and how it is represented visually.

On their own

Have students review and complete p. 404 of the *Reader's and Writer's Notebook.*

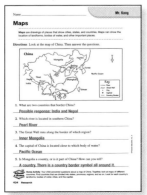

Reader's and Writer's
Notebook p. 404

English Language Learners
Professional Development: What ELL experts say about using visuals "Visuals enable students to 'see' the basic concepts we are trying to teach more effectively than if we rely only on words. Among the visuals we can use are… maps."—Dr. Jim Cummins

Maps Help students create and draw a classroom map that includes a legend with a scale, a compass rose, and symbols to represent typical classroom objects such as desks and bookcases.

Objectives
• Analyze data for usefulness.
• Identify and correctly use abbreviations.
• Spell frequently misspelled words.

Research and Inquiry
Analyze

Teach

Tell students that today they will analyze their research findings. Have students sort the information from their notes into an outline. Remind students that an outline is a plan for writing. Then explain that students may have to improve the focus of their research by interviewing a local expert.

Model

Think Aloud Originally I thought that it would be easy for people to nurse animals back to health and release them into the wild if they were hurt by oil spills and other causes. When I talked to a local animal rescue worker, however, I found that sometimes people are not able to heal animals enough for them to be able to stay safe if they are returned to the wild. Now my inquiry question is *What must people do to be able to grant freedom to animals?*

Guide practice

Have students analyze their findings. They may need to refocus their inquiry question to better fit the information they found. Remind students that if they have difficulty improving their focus they can ask a reference librarian or the local expert for guidance.

Remind students that they can use a map to provide a visual representation of their findings about places where animals might be able to be released safely.

On their own

Have students scan their information and decide if it is credible, reliable, and useful to their purposes. Suggest that they print out their research and highlight relevant information.

Conventions
Abbreviations

Review

Remind students that this week they learned about abbreviations. An abbreviation is a shortened version of a word.

- Certain titles, such as *Dr.* and *Mrs.,* are spelled as abbreviations.
- Days of the week and months of the year are often abbreviated.
- People's initials are often abbreviated.
- Abbreviations often begin with a capital letter and end with a period.

Daily Fix-It

Use Daily Fix-It numbers 5 and 6 in the right margin.

Connect to oral language

Have students name the initials of each president.

> **Franklin D. Roosevelt** (F.D.R.)
>
> **John F. Kennedy** (J.F.K.)
>
> **Lyndon Baines Johnson** (L.B.J.)

On their own

For additional support, use *Let's Practice It!* page 376 on the *Teacher Resources DVD-ROM.*

Let's Practice It!
TR DVD•376

Spelling
Schwa

Frequently misspelled words

The words *upon, again,* and *beautiful* are words that students often misspell. Think carefully before you write these words. Have students practice writing the words *upon, again,* and *beautiful* by writing sentences using each word.

On their own

For additional support, use the *Reader's and Writer's Notebook* p. 405.

Reader's and Writer's Notebook p. 405

Differentiated Instruction

 Strategic Intervention

Abbreviations Provide struggling students with extra practice working with abbreviations. Have each student write his or her name on a slip of paper, then exchange papers with a partner to identify each other's initials.

Daily Fix-It

5. This bird has bright fethers and it sings a cheerfull song. (*feathers, and; cheerful*)
6. It's musick makes me feel happy. (*Its; music*)

Objectives
- Understand the criteria for writing a limerick.
- Begin draft of a limerck.

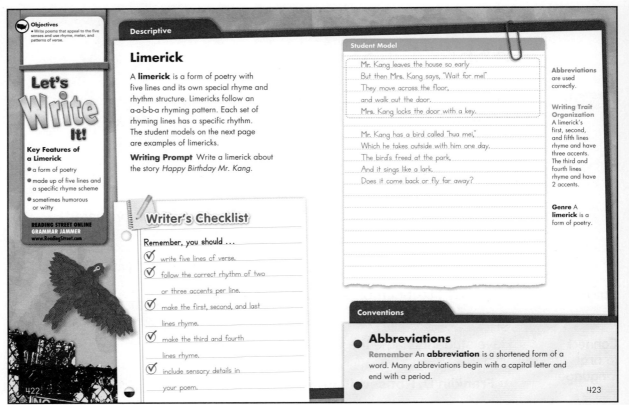

Student Edition pp. 422–423

Let's Write It!
Poetry: Limerick

Teach

Use pp. 422–423 in the Student Edition. Direct students to read the key features of a limerick, which appear on p. 422. Remind students that they can refer to the information in the Writer's Checklist as they write their own limericks.

Read the student models on p. 423. Point out that lines 1, 2, and 5 rhyme, as do lines 3 and 4. Read the models aloud so that students can identify the accents and hear the rhythm.

Connect to conventions

Remind students that an abbreviation is a shortened form of a word that often begins with a capital letter and ends with a period. Point out the correct use of abbreviations in the models.

Writing—Poetry: Limerick
Writer's Craft: Structure

Display rubric

Display Scoring Rubric 27 from the *Teacher Resources DVD-ROM* and go over the criteria for each trait under each score. Then, using the model in the Student Edition, choose students to explain why the model should score a 4 for one of the traits and why. If a student offers that the model should score below 4 for a particular trait, the student should offer support for that response. Remind students that this is the rubric that will be used to evaluate the limericks they write.

Scoring Rubric: Limerick

	4	3	2	1
Focus/Ideas	Clear, focused limerick	Most details in limerick are clear	Some details in limerick unclear	Limerick lacks clarity and development
Organization	Correct use of limerick structure	Mostly correct use of the limerick structure	Some attempt to use limerick structure	No attempt to use limerick structure
Voice	Engaged, lively voice throughout	Writer engaged with topic	Writer not very engaged	Uninterested tone
Word Choice	Strong use of sensory details	Adequate use of sensory details	Weak use of sensory details	No use of sensory details
Sentences	Energetic; tied cleverly by rhythm and rhyme	Good balance between structure and rhyme scheme	Simple, but mostly connected by rhyme	Simple, error-filled; confused
Conventions	Few, if any, errors; correct use of abbreviations	Several minor errors; mostly correct use of abbreviations	Many errors; incorrect use of abbreviations	Numerous errors; no use of abbreviations

Rhyming word list

Have students get out the lists of rhyming words that they worked on yesterday. If their lists are incomplete or if they have not yet chosen a topic, provide them additional time to do so.

Write

You will use your lists of rhyming words as you write the first draft of your limerick. When you are drafting, don't worry if your limerick doesn't sound exactly how you want it. You will have a chance to revise it tomorrow.

Differentiated Instruction

 Advanced

Abbreviations Challenge students to include a variety of abbreviations in their limericks, such as the days of the week or months of the year.

English Language Learners
Rhyming words If beginning English language learners have difficulty identifying rhyming words, pair students with native English speakers. Have partners work together to develop lists of rhyming words. Instruct students to use a dictionary to find the meaning of unfamiliar words.

Objectives
- Understand rhythm in poetry.
- Write a first draft of a limerick.

Writing, continued
Writer's Craft: Structure

MINI-LESSON

Rhythm

■ **Introduce** Explain that rhythm is the beat heard when reading a poem aloud. The words you choose and the structure of the poem create rhythm. Remind students that a limerick has a set structure of five lines. Lines 1, 2, and 5 rhyme and have the same number of syllables and accents, or beats, and lines 3 and 4 rhyme and have the same number of syllables and beats. Display the Drafting Tips for students. Remind them that the goal of drafting is to get their ideas down in an organized way. Then display Writing Transparency 27A.

"It should be free,
free," mr Kang said, "just like me."
mister Lum called out "No!"
But Kang let him go.
When he went home, what did he see?

Unit 6 Happy Birthday Mr. Kang   Writing Model **27A**

Writing Transparency 27A,
TR DVD

Drafting Tips

✔ Review lists of rhyming words.

✔ Write with proper rhyme and rhythm—read lines aloud periodically to check for rhythm.

✔ Don't worry about grammar and mechanics while drafting. You'll have a chance to revise during the proofreading stage.

Think Aloud I am going to write my limerick about the story *Happy Birthday Mr. Kang.* When I draft, I develop my ideas. I won't worry about using correct grammar and mechanics right now, but I will make sure to choose words that create rhythm and rhyme. I will refer to my lists of rhyming words as I write.

Have students use the Drafting Tips as a guide as they draft their limericks. Remind students to include the key features of limericks in their writing.

Differentiated Instruction

 Advanced

Peer review Have partners review each other's limericks to ensure that proper rhyme and rhythm have been used. Monitor feedback partners provide to each other.

ROUTINE **Quick Write for Fluency** **Team Talk**

1. **Talk** Pairs discuss how they created rhythm in their drafts.

2. **Write** Students write a sentence or two discussing the challenges of creating rhythm, using appropriate abbreviations.

3. **Share** Partners read each other's writing. Then partners check each other's writing for the correct use of abbreviations.

Routines Flip Chart

Wrap Up Your Day

✔ **Build Concepts** What did you learn about what it might mean to set a pet free?

✔ **Cause and Effect** How does knowing how to identify the cause and effect of an event help you understand your reading?

✔ **Inferring** How does using your own experience to infer something help you understand what you have read?

Preview DAY 4

Tell students that tomorrow they will read about the freedoms given to us by the U.S. Constitution.

Objectives
- Expand the weekly concept.
- Develop oral vocabulary.

Today at a Glance

Oral Vocabulary
retrieve, wandering

Phonics/Word Analysis
Vowel Sounds /ü/ and /ú/

Genre
Expository text

Reading
"Once Upon a Constitution"

Let's Learn It!
Fluency: Appropriate phrasing
Vocabulary: ⊙ Antonyms
Listening/speaking: Express an opinion

Research and Inquiry
Synthesize

Conventions
Abbreviations

Spelling
Schwa

Writing
Poetry: Limerick

Concept Talk

Question of the Week

What does it mean to grant freedom?

Expand the concept

Remind students that this week they have read about different ways that freedom can be granted and reasons why this might be done. Tell students that today they will read a piece of expository text that will inform them about the freedoms granted to people by the Constitution of the United States.

Anchored Talk

Develop oral vocabulary

Use text features—illustrations and italic text—to review pp. 412–419 of *Happy Birthday Mr. Kang.* Discuss the Amazing Words *companion* and *nag.* Add these words to the concept map. Use the following questions to develop students' understanding of the concept. Remind students to ask and answer questions with appropriate detail and to build on other students' answers.

- Think about the ways that Mr. Kang's bird was a good *companion* to him. How might a person feel about the possibility of losing such a good *companion* by setting it free?

- Sam *nags* Mr. Kang to let the pet bird go free. When are some times that a person might *nag* others to do the right thing and let someone or something be free?

Strategy Response Log

Have students interpret or make new inferences about *Happy Birthday Mr. Kang.* Then have them complete p. 33 in *Reader's and Writer's Notebook.*

INTERACT with TEXT

Oral Vocabulary
Amazing Words

Amazing Words

territory	affectionate
release	companion
loyal	nag
deserve	retrieve
manage	wandering

Teach Amazing Words

Amazing Words Oral Vocabulary Routine

1 Introduce Write the word *retrieve* on the board. Have students say it aloud with you. We read about how Mr. Kang did not have to *retrieve* his bird because it returned to his home on its own. What is something that a bird might *retrieve*? (It might *retrieve* its own food.) Have students determine a definition of *retrieve*. (When you *retrieve* something, you find it and then carry it back with you.)

2 Demonstrate Have students answer questions to demonstrate understanding. What is something you might have to *retrieve* from your bedroom? (a backpack)

3 Apply Have students apply their understanding. What word might be an antonym for *retrieve*?

See p. OV•2 to teach *wandering*.

Routines Flip Chart

Apply Amazing Words

As students read "Once Upon a Constitution" on pp. 424–427, have them think about how the Constitution gives people rights, such as the freedom to *wander* to certain places and *retrieve* things that they might want.

Connect to reading

Help students establish a purpose for reading. As they read today's selection about the Constitution, have them think about how the Question of the Week and the Amazing Words *retrieve* and *wandering* apply to the Constitution.

ELL Produce Oral Language Use the Day 4 instruction on ELL Poster 27 to extend and enrich language.

ELL Poster 27

Objectives

• Read and identify words with /ü/ spelled *oo, ew, ue, ui* and /u̇/ spelled *oo, u.*

• Read words fluently independent of context.

Phonics Review
Vowel Sounds /ü/ and /u̇/

Review sound-spellings

To review last week's phonics skill, write the following words: *school, took, full, statue, look, true, few, wool, suit, cushion, glue,* and *smooth.* We studied different spellings for the sounds /ü/ and /u̇/. Let's review the spellings by looking at these words. Have students identify all the words with /ü/. *(school, statue, true, few, suit, glue, smooth).* What letters can stand for this sound? *(oo, ew, ue, ui)* Continue in the same way for words with /u̇/. *(took, full, look, cushion)* Remind students that *oo* can stand for both /ü/ and /u̇/, so they must look at the context of the word to determine the sound.

Corrective feedback

If students are unable to answer the questions about the spellings of /ü/ and /u̇/, refer them to Sound-Spelling Cards 68, 89, 90, 101, 102 and 103.

Guide practice

Draw a two-column chart with the headings /ü/ and /u̇/. Write the following words on the board: *fruit, grew, took, bloom, push, shook, new, good, blue,* and *hook.* Have students read the words and sort them into the correct column. Ask volunteers to underline the letters that stand for /ü/ or /u̇/ in each word.

/ü/	/u̇/
fruit	took
grew	push
bloom	shook
new	good
blue	hook

On their own

For additional practice, use *Let's Practice It!* page 377 on the *Teacher Resources DVD-ROM.*

Let's Practice It! DVD
TR DVD•377

Fluent Word Reading
Spiral Review

Read words independent of context

Display these words. Tell students that they can decode some words on this list. Explain that other words they should know because they appear often in reading.

Have students read the list three or four times until they can read at the rate of two to three seconds per word.

Word Reading

very	because	neither	weight	clothes
all	warm	saw	always	from
sunny	childhood	friends	taught	receive
stylish	refreshment	eight	pretty	bought

Corrective feedback

If... students have difficulty reading whole words,
then... have them use sound-by-sound blending for decodable words or chunking for words that have word parts, or have them say and spell high-frequency words.

If... students cannot read fluently at a rate of two to three seconds per word,
then... have pairs practice the list until they can read it fluently.

Differentiated Instruction

 Strategic Intervention

Vowel Sounds /ü/, / u̇/ To assist students having difficulty with the vowel sounds /ü/ and /u̇/, focus on only one sound at a time. Assist students in writing words with /ü/ spelled *oo* on separate cards. Repeat with /ü/ words spelled *ew, ue,* and *ui* and /u̇/ words spelled *oo* and *u.*

Spiral Review

These activities review

- previously taught high-frequency words *very, warm, friends, pretty, clothes, from.*

- vowel patterns *a, au, aw, al, augh, ough;* vowel patterns *ei, eigh;* suffixes (*-y, -ish, -hood, -ment*).

English Language Learners
Fluent word reading Have students listen to a more fluent reader say the words. Then have them repeat the words.

Objectives

- Read words fluently in context.
- Apply knowledge of sound-spellings to decode unknown words when reading.
- Practice fluency with oral rereading.

Read words in context

Display these sentences. Call on individuals to read a sentence. Then randomly point to review words and have students read them. To help you monitor word reading, high-frequency words are underlined and decodable words are italicized.

MONITOR PROGRESS | **Sentence Reading**

Ice cream is a <u>very</u> good *refreshment* on a <u>warm</u> *sunny* day.

Mom *bought* <u>pretty</u>, *stylish* <u>clothes</u> <u>from</u> the boutique.

The *eight childhood* <u>friends</u> *saw* each other once a year.

Dad *taught all* of us to *always* say "thank you."

We did not *receive either* package *because* of its *weight*.

If... students are unable to read an underlined high-frequency word,

then... read the word for them and spell it, having them echo you.

If... students have difficulty reading an italicized decodable word,

then... guide them in using sound-by-sound blending or chunking.

Reread for Fluency

Have students reread the sentences to develop automaticity decoding words.

ROUTINE | **Oral Rereading**

 Read Have students read all the sentences orally.

 Reread To achieve optimal fluency, students should reread the sentences three or four times.

 Corrective Feedback Listen as students read. Provide corrective feedback regarding their fluency and decoding.

Routines Flip Chart

Decode and Read

Read words independent of context

Have students turn to p. 143 in *Decodable Practice Readers 3.2* and find the first list of words. Each word in this list has the schwa sound. Let's read these words. Be sure that students pronounce the vowel that stands for the schwa sound correctly.

Next, have students read the high-frequency words.

Preview Decodable Practice Passage

Have students read the title and preview the story. Tell them that they will read words with the schwa sound.

Read words in context

Chorally read the story along with the students. Have students identify words in the story that have the schwa sound. Make sure that students are monitoring their accuracy when they decode words.

Team Talk Pair students and have them take turns reading the story aloud to each other. Monitor students as they read to check for proper pronunciation and appropriate pacing.

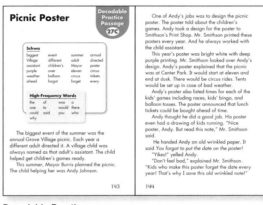

Decodable Practice Passage 27C

Differentiated Instruction

A Advanced

Decodable and high-frequency words Have students write a short paragraph about a favorite memory using some of the decodable and high-frequency words found in the sentences on p. 424e.

Let's Think About Genre
Expository Text

Introduce expository text

Explain to students that what we read is structured differently depending on the author's reasons for writing and what kind of information he or she wishes to convey. Different types of texts are called genres. Expository text is one type of genre, and one purpose a writer might have for writing expository text is to inform an audience about a topic.

Discuss the genre

Discuss with students how authors write with different purposes in mind, such as to inform, to persuade, or to entertain. Ask students to share some examples of informative expository text they have read before. (Possible responses: biographies, encyclopedia articles, articles or books about things in nature)

On the board, draw a word web like the one below. Label the center oval *Features that Inform.* Help students brainstorm some features of expository text, such as facts, details, technical vocabulary, graphic sources such as photographs and illustrations, and text features such as labels. Record responses on the word web.

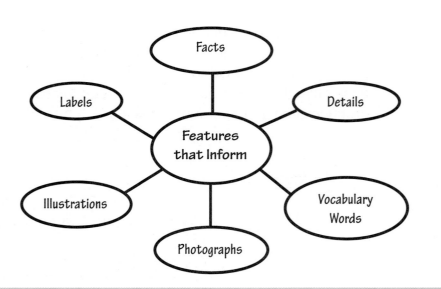

Guide practice

Have students work in pairs to describe how each text feature helps the author inform an audience about a topic. Invite them to share their ideas with the class. Encourage students to listen attentively and ask any relevant questions.

Connect to reading

Tell students that they will now be reading an expository text whose purpose is to inform about the Constitution and the rights it grants. Have the class pay attention to how the author uses text features to inform.

Small Group Time

DAY 4

Break into small groups before reading or revisiting "Once Upon a Constitution."

Teacher Led

SI Strategic Intervention
Teacher Led p. DI•30
- Practice retelling
- Genre focus
- **Read/Revisit** "Once Upon a Constitution"

OL On-Level
Teacher Led p. DI•35
- Practice retelling
- Genre focus
- **Read/Revisit** "Once Upon a Constitution"

A Advanced
Teacher Led p. DI•40
- Genre focus
- **Read/Revisit** "Once Upon a Constitution"

ELL Place English language learners in the groups that correspond to their reading abilities in English.

Practice Stations
- Read for Meaning
- Get Fluent
- Words to Know

Independent Activities
- AudioText: "Once Upon a Constitution"
- *Reader's and Writer's Notebook*
- Research and Inquiry

Objectives

- Introduce features of expository text.
- Evaluate features of expository text.

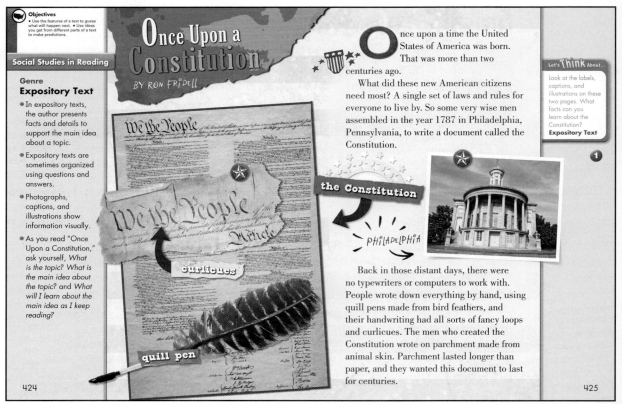

Student Edition pp. 424–425

Guide Comprehension

Teach expository text

Expository Text: Labels Have students preview "Once Upon a Constitution" on pp. 424–425. Have them identify and describe any labels they see, noting any unusual fonts or text treatments used. Then ask: What purpose do these labels serve and how do they fulfill this purpose?

Corrective feedback

If... students are unable to identify the purpose of the labels and how they fulfill this purpose,
then... use the model to guide students in interpreting labels.

Model the skill

Think Aloud I see words connected by arrows to the picture of the Constitution and the photo of Philadelphia. I think these words are telling me what I am looking at. To make it clear what exactly is being labeled, the arrows point to specific parts of the pictures and a different font is used for the labels for each graphic source.

On their own

Have students work in pairs to think up another system of labeling the parts of a picture.

Extend Thinking
Think Critically

Higher-order thinking skills

 Cause and Effect • Analysis Why did people write the Constitution? Possible response: Because the United States of America was a new country, it needed laws for everyone to follow.

 Inferring • Evaluation Why would it be important for the document to last for centuries? Possible response: The men who wrote the Constitution wanted the laws to last a long time, so writing these laws on parchment that would hold up over time would show how strong the laws were too.

Let's Think About...

1 Possible response: You can learn facts about how, when, and where it was written.

Differentiated Instruction

SI Strategic Intervention

Text structure Give students extra practice with how the author presents information in a question and answer format. Have them pick out and rewrite in simpler form, the questions the author asks and the answers he provides. Then have them write a short summary of the information contained in the reading.

A Advanced

Draw conclusions Have students discuss reasons why it is important for a country to have one set of agreed-upon and clear laws for everyone to follow and what might happen to a country and its people if such a system of laws were not in place.

 ELL

English Language Learners
Social studies vocabulary
Work with students to make a list of History-Social Science vocabulary words from this reading, such as *rights, democracy,* and *citizens.* Have students use context and dictionaries to write definitions for each.

Objectives

- Identify the main idea or topic of a text.
- Identify details or facts that support the main idea.

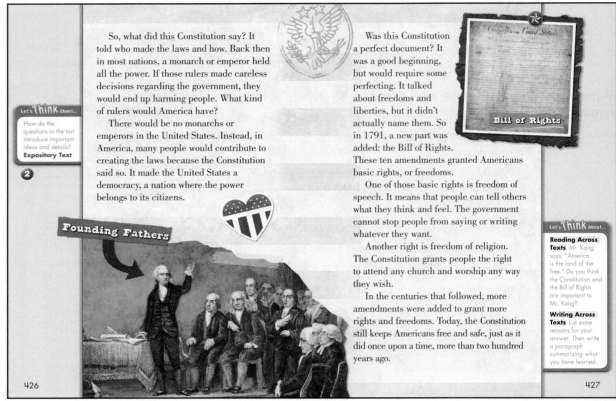

Student Edition pp. 426–427

Guide Comprehension

Teach main idea

Main Idea Explain that to understand what an author is talking about in an informational article, the reader must be able to distinguish between main ideas and details. Then ask: What is the main idea of the information on these pages?

Corrective feedback

If... students are unable to distinguish the main idea from the details, then... use the model to guide students in identifying the main idea.

Model the skill

Think Aloud Authors include many pieces of information, so I need to figure out which piece of information is the most important, or the main idea. The questions the author asks give me clues as to what the author thinks are the most important ideas. They talk about what the Constitution says and how it works. The information about the specific freedoms is interesting, but I think the main idea of this article is that the Constitution is a single set of laws and rules for all Americans to live by.

On their own

Have students identify and summarize details that support this main idea.

Extend Thinking
Think Critically

Higher-order thinking skills

Compare and Contrast • Analysis How was the government of the new United States of America different from the way many other nations were ruled at the time? Possible response: Where other nations were ruled by monarchs or emperors who held all the power and could make decisions for everyone else, America gave power to its citizens and let many people help create its laws.

Draw Conclusions • Synthesis Why was the Constitution only a beginning? Possible response: The people who wrote the Constitution couldn't predict what would happen to the country over time or imagine and write down every single freedom that would end up needing to be protected.

Let's Think About...

2 Possible response: The questions form the main ideas he will discuss. The author draws the reader's attention to these points and helps the reader understand what the most important ideas in this informational article are. The author then follows up with details about what words would ensure a fair government and what kind of leadership or government Americans would want.

Reading Across Texts

Have students create a T-chart of facts about freedom learned from each selection.

Writing Across Texts

Have students use what they have learned about the main idea and details of this informational article to list reasons why they think these documents are important to Mr. Kang. Then have them write a paragraph summarizing what the author has taught them about the Constitution and its importance.

Connect to Social Studies

Amendments are changes or clarifications that are added to the Constitution. There have been 27 amendments to the U.S. Constitution. The first 10 were done collectively and called the Bill of Rights. Other amendments include the 13th amendment to abolish slavery, the 22nd amendment to limit the length of time a president can serve, and the 26th amendment to set the voting age at 18.

ELL

English Language Learners
Graphic organizer Help students use a main idea and details graphic organizer to organize and record their ideas about the main idea and details of this informational article.

Objectives

- Read with fluency and comprehension.
- Use context clues to identify and define antonyms.
- Deliver a speech to express an opinion.

Check Fluency WCPM

SUCCESS PREDICTOR

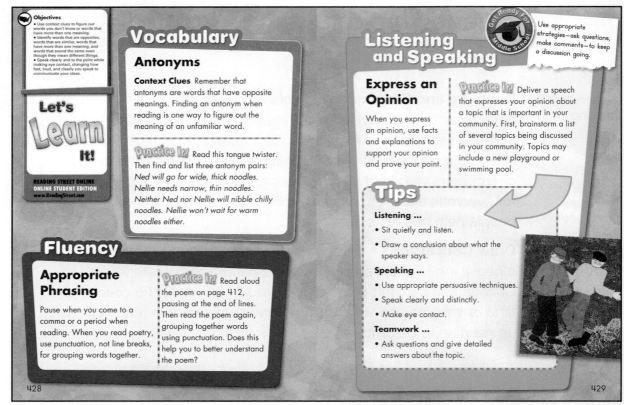

Student Edition pp. 428–429

Fluency
Appropriate Phrasing

Guide practice

Use the Student Edition activity as an assessment tool. Make sure the reading passage is at least 200 words in length. As students read aloud with partners, walk around to make sure their phrasing is appropriate and that they pause after groups of words when it makes sense.

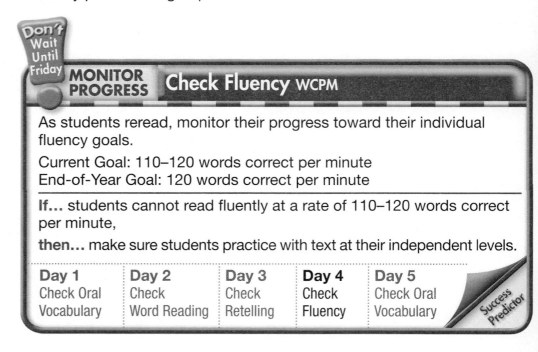

Don't Wait Until Friday

MONITOR PROGRESS Check Fluency WCPM

As students reread, monitor their progress toward their individual fluency goals.

Current Goal: 110–120 words correct per minute
End-of-Year Goal: 120 words correct per minute

If... students cannot read fluently at a rate of 110–120 words correct per minute,

then... make sure students practice with text at their independent levels.

Day 1	Day 2	Day 3	Day 4	Day 5
Check Oral Vocabulary	Check Word Reading	Check Retelling	Check Fluency	Check Oral Vocabulary

Success Predictor

Vocabulary
 Antonyms

Teach antonyms

Context Clues Write the following sentence on the board: *Jan liked quiet, so she left the house when Mark and his loud band began to practice.*

Discuss how *quiet/loud* are an antonym pair of words with opposite meanings. Note how students can use context clues to figure out the meaning of each word.

Guide practice

Provide students with other sentences that contain antonym pairs such as *tall/short, fast/slow,* and *dark/light* and help students use context clues to identify and define each antonym pair.

On their own

Walk around the room as students work with partners to make sure they can use context clues to identify and define the antonym pairs in the tongue twisters. Suggest that students use dictionaries and thesauruses to check their work.

Listening and Speaking
Express an Opinion

Teach

Tell students that to express their opinions effectively in a speech, they must gather evidence to support their view and organize the evidence in a logical manner. Point out the importance of listening to other viewpoints and asking questions when gathering evidence.

Guide practice

As students prepare to present their speeches, remind them to make eye contact with their audience and to use appropriate speaking rate, volume, and enunciation to communicate their ideas. Tell them to use opinion phrases such as *I believe, I think,* and *my point of view* when presenting their thoughts about the topic.

On their own

Have students present their speeches to the class. Invite the class to identify each speaker's opinion and evaluate how well the speaker convinced the audience to share this opinion. Tell students to listen attentively, ask relevant questions, and make pertinent comments.

Expressing an Opinion

Remind students that when presenting a speech that expresses an opinion, they should pick a viewpoint to support and explain it clearly with specific examples and details. Encourage them to use an organizational pattern that fits the information included in their speech. Tell listeners to identify the viewpoint being expressed, analyze the evidence the speaker uses to support this viewpoint, and then evaluate the worth of the overall opinion. Remind them that their judgment will be affected by their own viewpoint on the topic.

Fluency

Success Predictor

Objectives

- Use a map to present information.
- Review abbreviations.
- Spell words with the schwa sound correctly.

Research and Inquiry
Synthesize

Teach

Have students synthesize their research findings and results. Students may choose to use a map to help show areas where animals might be granted their freedom and released. Suggest that students use a map to visually present information they found while researching. Review how to choose relevant information from a number of sources and organize it logically.

Guide practice

Have students use a word processing program to create a short article for a school newspaper on Day 5. If students are using maps, check to see that they have included a legend that explains what all the symbols on the map mean and to include map parts such as a compass rose and a scale.

On their own

Have students write a brief explanation of their research findings. Then have them organize and combine information and plan their presentations.

Conventions
Abbreviations

Test practice
Remind students that grammar skills, such as abbreviations, are often assessed on important tests. Remind students that an abbreviation is a shortened form of a word. It often begins with a capital letter and ends with a period.

Daily Fix-It
Use Daily Fix-It numbers 7 and 8 in the right margin.

On their own
For additional practice, use the *Reader's and Writer's Notebook* p. 406.

Reader's and Writer's
Notebook p. 406

Spelling
Schwa

Practice spelling strategy
Supply pairs of students with index cards on which the spelling words have been written. Have one student read a word while the other writes it. Then have students switch roles. Have them use the cards to check their spelling and correct any misspelled words.

On their own
For additional practice, use *Let's Practice It!* page 378 on the *Teacher Resources DVD-ROM.*

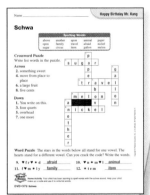

Let's Practice It!
TR DVD•378

Daily Fix-It

7. The women was afriad the bird would fly away. *(were; afraid)*

8. The bird dissappeared on Feb 2. *(disappeared; Feb.)*

Writing—Poetry: Limerick
Revising Strategy

MINI-LESSON

Revising Strategy: Adding

■ Yesterday we wrote limericks about the story *Happy Birthday Mr. Kang.* Today we will revise our drafts. The goal is to make your writing clearer and more interesting.

■ Display Writing Transparency 27B. Remind students that revising does not include corrections of grammar and mechanics. Tell them that this will be done during the lesson as they proofread their work. Then introduce the revising strategy of adding.

Writing Transparency 27B, TR DVD

■ When you revise, ask yourself, *What important information about the topic is missing*? Let's look at the first line of the limerick. What should be free, and why? I will revise the first line to read *This bird in its cage should be free.* Now I know that a bird should be free, and that it should be free because it is in a cage.

Revising Tips

✔ Make sure the ideas are clear and focused.
✔ Review writing to make sure that it maintains rhythm and includes rhyme.
✔ Add information to support the central idea and make writing more detailed.

Peer conferencing

Peer Revision Have pairs of students exchange papers for peer revision. Students should write two questions about the partner's writing. Tell students that their questions should focus on where the partner could revise by adding relevant information. Refer to the *Teacher Resources DVD-ROM* for more information about peer conferencing.

Have students revise their limericks using the questions their partner wrote during Peer Revision as well as the key features of limericks to guide them. Be sure that students are using the revising strategy of adding.

Corrective feedback

Circulate around the room to monitor and confer with students as they revise. Remind students correcting errors that they will have time to edit tomorrow. They should be working on content and organization today.

Write Guy
Jeff Anderson

Show Off—in a Good Way

Post students' successful sentences or short paragraphs. Celebrate them as writers. Select a sentence of the week, and write it large! Display it as a poster inside or outside the classroom door. Students learn from each others' successes.

ROUTINE — Quick Write for Fluency — Team Talk

1. **Talk** Have pairs discuss Mr. Kang's character in *Happy Birthday Mr. Kang.*

2. **Write** Each student writes a brief description of Mr. Kang's character that includes rhyme.

3. **Share** Partners read each another's writing. Then partners check each other's writing for rhyme.

Routines Flip Chart

Wrap Up Your Day

✔ **Build Concepts** What did you learn about the freedoms given to us by the U.S. Constitution?

✔ **Oral Vocabulary** Monitor students' use of oral vocabulary as they respond: How does the U.S. Constitution allow us to *wander* where we want or give away and *retrieve* things that were ours?

✔ **Story Structure** Discuss how knowing about a story's climax helps you understand text.

ELL

English Language Learners
Creating rhyme Beginning language learners may have trouble using the correct number of syllables in each line of their limericks. Allow these students to disregard the syllable pattern and focus instead on creating rhyme.

Preview DAY 5

Remind students to think about what it means to grant freedom.

Objectives
- Review the weekly concept.
- Review oral vocabulary.

Today at a Glance

Oral Vocabulary

Comprehension
◉ Cause and effect

Lesson Vocabulary
◉ Antonyms

Phonics/Word Analysis
◉ Schwa

Literary Terms
Metaphor

Assessment
Fluency
Comprehension

Research and Inquiry
Communicate

Spelling
Schwa

Conventions
Abbreviations

Writing
Poetry: Limerick

Check Oral Vocabulary
SUCCESS PREDICTOR

Concept Wrap Up

Question of the Week

❓ What does it mean to grant freedom?

Review the concept

Have students look back at the reading selections to find examples that best demonstrate what it means to grant freedom.

Review Amazing Words

Display and review this week's concept map. Remind students that this week they have learned ten Amazing Words related to granting freedom. Have students use the Amazing Words and the concept map to answer the question *What it means to grant freedom?*

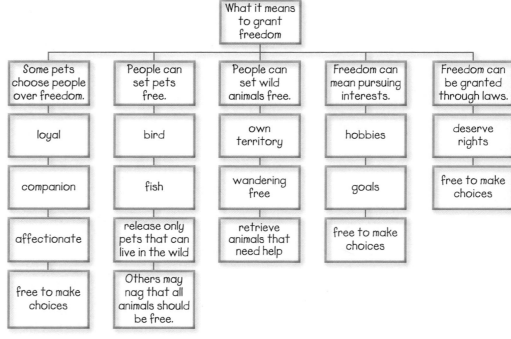

What it means to grant freedom

Some pets choose people over freedom.	People can set pets free.	People can set wild animals free.	Freedom can mean pursuing interests.	Freedom can be granted through laws.
loyal	bird	own territory	hobbies	deserve rights
companion	fish	wandering free	goals	free to make choices
affectionate	release only pets that can live in the wild	retrieve animals that need help	free to make choices	
free to make choices	Others may nag that all animals should be free.			

ELL Check Concepts and Language Use the Day 5 instruction on ELL Poster 27 to monitor students' understanding of the lesson concept.

ELL Poster 27

Amazing Ideas

Connect to the Big Question

Have pairs of students discuss how the Question of the Week connects to the Big Question: *What does freedom mean?* Tell students to use the concept map and what they have learned from this week's Anchored Talks and reading selections to form an Amazing Idea—a realization or "big idea" about Freedom. Remind partners to pose and answer questions with appropriate detail and to give suggestions that build on each other's ideas. Then ask pairs to share their Amazing Ideas with the class.

Amazing Ideas might include these key concepts:

- Both people and animals can enjoy freedom.
- An important part of freedom is being able to make choices for yourself.
- Laws can protect people's freedom and the right to make choices for themselves.

Write about it

Have students write a few sentences about their Amazing Idea, beginning with "This week I learned...." Remind them to include supporting sentences with details.

Amazing Words

territory	affectionate
release	companion
loyal	nag
deserve	retrieve
manage	wandering

It's Friday

MONITOR PROGRESS | **Check Oral Vocabulary**

Have individuals use this week's Amazing Words to describe how freedom can be granted. Monitor students' ability to use the Amazing Words and note which words you need to reteach.

If... students have difficulty using the Amazing Words,

then... reteach using the Oral Vocabulary Routine, pp. 395a, 400b, 412b, 424b, OV•2.

Day 1	Day 2	Day 3	Day 4	Day 5	
Check Oral Vocabulary	Check Word Reading	Check Retelling	Check Fluency	**Check Oral Vocabulary**	Success Predictor

ELL

English Language Learners
Concept map Work with students to add new words to the concept map.

Oral Vocabulary **Success Predictor**

Objectives
◎ Review cause and effect.
◎ Review antonyms.
◎ Review schwa spelled *a, e, I, o, u,* and *y.*
• Review metaphor.

Comprehension Review
Cause and Effect

Teach cause and effect

Envision It!

Review the definition of cause and effect on p. 398. Remind students that an effect is something that happens and a cause is why that thing happens. Review how sometimes an effect may have more than one cause. For additional support have students review p. EI•3 on cause and effect.

Student Edition p. EI•3

Guide practice

Have partners identify related causes and effects. Have student pairs find an example of a cause-and-effect relationship in *Happy Birthday Mr. Kang.* Then have pairs identify which is the cause and which is the effect and tell whether the effect has any other causes.

On their own

For additional practice with cause and effect, use *Let's Practice It!* page 379 on the *Teacher Resources DVD-ROM.*

Let's Practice It!
TR DVD•379

Vocabulary Review
Antonyms

Teach antonyms

Remind students that antonyms are words with opposite meanings.

Guide practice

Look back at p. 407 of *Happy Birthday Mr. Kang* and review with students how to use context clues and antonyms to figure out the correct meaning of the lesson vocabulary word *chilly.*

On their own

Have students work with a partner to write sentences using antonym pairs that include this week's lesson vocabulary words. Partners can trade sentences and identify the antonym pairs and the context clues that help them determine each word's meaning.

Word Analysis Review
↻ Schwa

Teach schwa

Write the following sentences on the board. Have students read each one, first quietly to themselves and then aloud as you track the print.

> 1. We stayed at a log cabin at the bottom of a canyon.
> 2. I like to put lots of lettuce in my salad.
> 3. Would you buy a pretzel for a nickel?
> 4. The firefighters saw that the garage was ablaze.
> 5. We will travel to seven cities this year.

Team Talk Have students discuss with a partner which words have the schwa sound. Then call on individuals to identify the vowel in each word that stands for /ə/.

Literary Terms Review
Metaphor

Teach metaphor

Have students reread p. 412 of *Happy Birthday Mr. Kang,* focusing on Mr. Kang's poem. Remind students that a metaphor is when two things are compared with each other, but without the use of the word *like* or *as.* Metaphors often use sensory words.

Guided practice

Find an example of a metaphor in Mr. Kang's poem on this page. Discuss what two things the metaphor is comparing and why the author (and Mr. Kang) might be making this comparison. Have students find other examples of metaphors from this poem or other parts of the selection and discuss them.

On their own

Have students list examples of different metaphors from the selection and write a sentence or two explaining what each metaphor is comparing and why this comparison is being made. Tell students to identify words that appeal to the senses.

Lesson Vocabulary

bows bends the head or body forward

chilly uncomfortably cold

foolish unwise; not making sense

foreign from a place that is not your own country or homeland

narrow not wide

perches sits or rests on a bar, branch, or similar object

recipe ingredients and steps for making something to eat or drink

English Language Learners
Articulation tip If students have trouble pronouncing words with the sounds of schwa, demonstrate how to pronounce them by slowly repeating words. Have students practice saying them until they develop confidence.

Metaphors If students have trouble identifying metaphors, work with them to identify examples of figurative language. Then ask, How is each comparison made? Does it use the words *like* or *as*? Is it comparing two unlike things? What is being compared?

Objectives
- Read grade-level text with fluency and comprehension.

Plan to Assess Fluency

☑ **Week 1** Assess Advanced students.

☑ **This week assess Strategic Intervention students.**

☐ **Week 3** Assess On-Level students.

☐ **Week 4** Assess Strategic Intervention students.

☐ **Week 5** Assess any students you have not yet checked during this unit.

Set individual goals for students to enable them to reach the year-end goal.

- Current Goal: 110–120 WCPM
- Year-End Goal: 120 WCPM

Assessment

Check words correct per minute

Fluency Make two copies of the fluency passage on p. 429k. As the student reads the text aloud, mark mistakes on your copy. Also mark where the student is at the end of one minute. To check the student's comprehension of the passage, have him or her retell what was read. To figure words correct per minute (WCPM), subtract the number of mistakes from the total number of words read in one minute.

WCPM

Corrective feedback

If... students cannot read fluently at a rate of 110–120 WCPM,
then... make sure they practice with text at their independent reading level. Provide additional fluency practice by pairing nonfluent readers with fluent readers.

If... students already read at 120 WCPM,
then... have them read a book of their choice independently.

Small Group Time

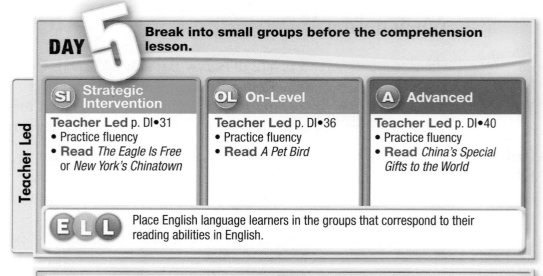

DAY 5

Break into small groups before the comprehension lesson.

Teacher Led

SI Strategic Intervention	**OL On-Level**	**A Advanced**
Teacher Led p. DI•31	Teacher Led p. DI•36	Teacher Led p. DI•40
• Practice fluency	• Practice fluency	• Practice fluency
• **Read** *The Eagle Is Free* or *New York's Chinatown*	• **Read** *A Pet Bird*	• **Read** *China's Special Gifts to the World*

ELL Place English language learners in the groups that correspond to their reading abilities in English.

Practice Stations	**Independent Activities**
• Words to Know	• Grammar Jammer
• Get Fluent	• Concept Talk Video
• Read for Meaning	• Vocabulary Activities

The Secret Recipe

When it's chilly out, I like to bake. My favorite recipe is a cookie	14
recipe that came from my aunt. When she is free, she travels. My aunt	28
says she found the recipe on one of her travels in a foreign country. She	43
bought a book that had the recipe.	50

When my aunt got home from that trip, she tried the cookie recipe. 63
It is very odd. Besides the other ingredients, she had to use a gallon 77
of milk. The recipe made more than seven dozen cookies. The cookies 89
baked for a long time in the oven. After a while, my aunt felt foolish. 104
Could this be right? When the cookies were done, though, we all loved 117
them. 118

Now, my family makes the cookies every year. We all have different 130
kinds of shapes we like to make. My brother likes animals. He makes 143
cats, dogs, bears, and tigers. Sometimes he makes so many animals he 155
could have his own circus. My cousin likes to make stars. She also likes 169
the color pink, so she colors all the stars pink. My younger cousin likes 183
to make dinosaurs. I like to make circles. I use the bottom of a plastic 198
drinking glass to get a perfect circle shape. 206

All of our friends like the cookies. They think they are the best treats 220
ever. My family laughs. We all know the secret. The famous cookies 232
have vinegar in them! 236

MONITOR PROGRESS

• Check Fluency

Objectives
• Read grade-level text with comprehension.

Assessment

Check cause and effect

Cause and Effect Use "Yosuke Returns" on p. 429m to check students' understanding of cause and effect.

1. Given the choice, where was Yosuke the happiest to live? (Yosuke chose to return to his family instead of remaining free in the wild.)

2. Why do many parrots not survive in the wild? (They do not have the skills to survive alone without people to take care of them.)

3. What had to happen so that the vet could return Yosuke to his family? (He had to start talking and tell the vet his name and address.)

Corrective feedback

If... students are unable to answer the comprehension questions, **then...** use the Reteach lesson in the *First Stop* book.

Yosuke Returns

There are amazing stories of real lost pets and how they returned to their owners. For example, here's the entertaining tale of a parrot named Yosuke.

Yosuke lived with a Japanese family in a town near Tokyo. From his birth, Yosuke was raised as a pet. His human family took excellent care of him. Like many intelligent parrots, Yosuke was taught to repeat words and phrases. Yosuke could recite his name and address among other things.

One day Yosuke escaped from his cage. That probably wasn't too unusual, but he escaped from his family's house as well. Yosuke had flown to freedom!

The family searched, but couldn't find their Yosuke. How long could he survive without being fed and cared for?

Is a lost parrot happy to be free? There is no way to know what a parrot thinks. But most pet parrots don't have the skills to survive alone. They may not live very long once they have escaped. However, some birds figure out how to stay alive.

Yosuke was gone for two weeks when police noticed a gray parrot on the roof of a house. When they rescued the parrot, they didn't know it could talk. It said nothing to them. The police did know that the parrot needed help. They took it to a vet.

Once the parrot got a little care, it must have felt better. It started talking. It told the vet its name and address. It was Yosuke! Soon Yosuke was back home again.

MONITOR PROGRESS

• **Cause and effect**

Objectives
- Communicate inquiry results.
- Administer spelling test.
- Review abbreviations.

Research and Inquiry
Communicate

Present ideas　Have students share their inquiry results by presenting their articles and giving a brief talk on their research. Have students display any graphic sources they created on Day 4.

Listening and speaking　Remind students how to be good speakers and how to communicate effectively with their audience.

- Respond to relevant questions with appropriate details.
- Speak clearly and loudly.
- Keep eye contact with audience members.

Remind students of these tips for being a good listener.

- Wait until the speaker has finished before raising your hand to ask a relevant question.
- Be polite, even if you disagree.

Spelling Test
Schwa

Spelling test   To administer the spelling test, refer to the directions, words, and sentences on p. 399c.

Conventions
Extra Practice

Teach   Remind students of the week's grammar skill, abbreviations. Explain that an abbreviation is a shortened form of a word, and that it often begins with a capital letter and ends with a period.

Guide practice   Write these sentences on the board and have students point to words that can be abbreviated. Invite volunteers to rewrite the sentences with abbreviations.

> **Mister Coleman's birthday party is on Saturday, January 11.** (Mr., Sat., Jan.)
>
> **Some birds fly south in October or November.** (Oct., Nov.)
>
> **I am writing a report on Doctor Martin Luther King, Junior.** (Dr., Jr.)

Daily Fix-It   Use Daily Fix-It numbers 9 and 10 in the right margin.

On their own   Have students complete these sentence frames with relevant abbreviations. You may want to list common abbreviations on the board for students to reference. Students should complete *Let's Practice It!* page 380 on the *Teacher Resources DVD-ROM.*

> 1. My teacher, _____ Wilman, was born in _____.
>
> 2. I am sick, so I am going to see _____ Carey.
>
> 3. _____ and _____ Lewis are my neighbors.
>
> 4. Today is _____ and the date is _____.
>
> 5. I was born on _____.
>
> 6. My friend was born on _____.

Daily Fix-It

9. The old man feel selfesh because the bird wants its freedom. *(feels; selfish)*

10. Can the bird live out side in the Winter safely? *(outside; winter)*

Let's Practice It!
TR DVD•380

Objectives

- Edit drafts for correct use of abbreviations.
- Proofread drafts for correct spelling, capitalization, punctuation, and grammar.
- Publish and present a final draft.

Writing—Poetry: Limerick
Abbreviations

Review Revising

Remind students that yesterday they revised their limericks, using the revising strategy adding to include important information about the topic. Today, students will proofread their writing.

MINI-LESSON

Abbreviations

▪ **Teach** When we proofread, we look closely at our work, searching for errors in mechanics such as spelling, capitalization, punctuation, and grammar. Today we will focus on abbreviations.

▪ **Model** Let's look at the limerick we revised yesterday. Display Writing Transparency 27C and explain that you will look for errors in the use of abbreviations. In line 2, *mr* is not abbreviated correctly. The first letter needs to be capitalized and the abbreviation needs to end with a period. In line 3, *mister* should be abbreviated. I will correct this by writing *Mr.* with an initial capital letter and ending it with a period. Then point out *Kang* in line 4. Explain that the writer intentionally left out the title in order to achieve the correct number of syllables in the line. Explain to students that they should reread their limericks a number of times, looking for errors in spelling, punctuation, capitalization, and grammar.

Writing Transparency 27C, TR DVD

Proofread

Display the Proofreading Tips. Ask students to proofread their compositions, using the tips and paying attention to abbreviations. Circulate around the room answering students' questions. When students have finished editing their own work, have pairs proofread one another's limericks.

Proofreading Tips

✔ Be sure that all abbreviations are used correctly.

✔ Check for correct spelling, punctuation, capitalization, and grammar.

✔ Make sure that each line contains the correct number of syllables.

Present

Have students incorporate revisions and proofreading edits into their limericks to create a final draft.

Have students give an oral presentation of their limericks to the class. Have students find or create art and graphics to accompany their limericks. For oral presentations, students should create art large enough for the class to view, and explain why they chose the art or graphics they included. When students have finished, have each complete the Writing Self-Evaluation Guide.

ROUTINE Quick Write for Fluency **Team Talk**

 Talk Pairs discuss what they learned about writing limericks.

 Write Each student writes a paragraph summarizing what he or she learned.

 Share Partners read their summaries to each other.

Routines Flip Chart

Teacher Note

Writing self-evaluation Make copies of the Writing Self-Evaluation Guide on p. 39 of the *Reader's and Writer's Notebook*.

English Language Learners

Support proofreading Provide practice with abbreviations. Students may benefit from practice with converting words to abbreviations.

Poster preview Prepare students for next week by using Week 3, ELL Poster 28. Read the Poster Talk-Through to introduce the concept and vocabulary. Ask students to identify and describe objects and actions in the art.

Selection summary Send home the summary of *Talking Walls: Art for the People* in English and the students' home languages, if available. Students can read the summary with family members.

Preview NEXT WEEK

Why is freedom of expression important? Read about how some artists express their beliefs and feelings on painted wall murals.

Weekly Assessment

Use pp. 191–198 of *Weekly Tests* to check:

✔ **Phonics** Schwa

✔ **Comprehension Skill** Cause and Effect

✔ **Lesson Vocabulary**

✔ **Review** **Comprehension Skill**
Literary Element: Theme

bows	narrow
chilly	perches
foolish	recipe
foreign	

Weekly Tests

Advanced

On-Level

SI

Strategic Intervention

Differentiated Assessment

Use pp. 157–162 of *Fresh Reads for Fluency and Comprehension* to check:

✔ **Comprehension Skill** Cause and Effect

✔ **Review** **Comprehension Skill** Literary Element: Theme

✔ **Fluency** Words Correct Per Minute

Fresh Reads for Fluency and Comprehension

Managing Assessment

Use *Assessment Handbook* for:

✔ **Weekly Assessment Blackline Masters for Monitoring Progress**

✔ **Observation Checklists**

✔ **Record-Keeping Forms**

✔ **Portfolio Assessment**

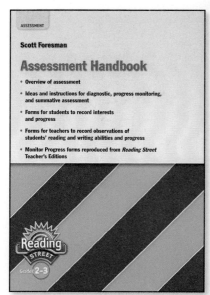

Assessment Handbook

Teacher Notes

Small Group Time

Pacing Small Group Instruction

15–20 min

5-Day Plan

DAY 1	• Reinforce the concept • Read Leveled Readers Concept Literacy Below Level
DAY 2	• ◉ Cause and Effect • ◉ Inferring • Revisit Student Edition pp. 402–411
DAY 3	• ◉ Antonyms • Revisit Student Edition pp. 412–419
DAY 4	• Practice Retelling • Read/Revisit Student Edition pp. 424–427
DAY 5	• Reread for fluency • Reread Leveled Readers

3- or 4-Day Plan

DAY 1	• Reinforce the concept • Read Leveled Readers
DAY 2	• ◉ Cause and Effect • ◉ Inferring • Revisit Student Edition pp. 402–411
DAY 3	◉ Antonyms • Revisit Student Edition pp. 412–419
DAY 4	• Practice Retelling • Read/Revisit Student Edition pp. 424–427 • Reread for fluency • Reread Leveled Readers

3-Day Plan: Eliminate the shaded box.

SI Strategic Intervention

DAY 1

Build Background

■ **Reinforce the Concept** Talk about the weekly question *What does it mean to grant freedom?* When people are free, they are allowed to live where and how they choose. In the United States, people are free to practice the traditions that are part of their culture. For example, they may celebrate certain holidays, eat certain foods, or dress a certain way. When wild animals are free, they live in their natural habitat. **Add new words to the concept map.** This week we are going to read about people and animals that are free. What does freedom mean to you? *(Some students may mention being able to do as they please. Others may mention freedom to travel or vote.)*

Preview Decodable Practice Reader 27A

■ **Before Reading** Review the words on p. 133 of *Decodable Practice Readers 3.2*. Then have students blend these words from the text: *spout, jungle, performer, trapeze, balanced, juggled, gracefully,* and *gasped.* Be sure students understand the meaning of such words as *spout, trapeze,* and *gasped.* Guide students through the text by doing a picture walk.

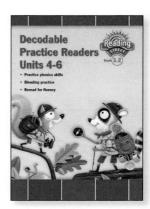

Decodable Practice Readers Units 4-6
• Practice phonics skills
• Blending practice
• Reread for fluency

Objectives

• Participate in teacher-led discussions by answering questions with appropriate detail.

For a complete literacy instructional plan and additional practice with this week's target skills and strategies, see the **Leveled Reader Teaching Guide.**

Concept Literacy Reader

- **Read** *The Eagle Is Free*

- **Before Reading** Preview the book with students, focusing on key concepts and vocabulary. Then help them set a purpose for reading.

- **During Reading** Read the first two pages aloud while students track along with the print. Then have students finish reading the book with a partner.

- **After Reading** After students finish reading, ask: What freedom does the American bald eagle have? *(the freedom to fly free)* In what way is the bald eagle a symbol of freedom? *(It is on the seal of the United States, as shown in* The Eagle Is Free.*)*

Below-Level Reader

- **Read** *New York's Chinatown*

- **Before Reading** Help students use the illustrations to preview the book. Then help students set a purpose for reading.

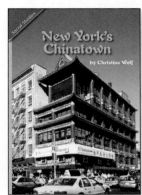

- **During Reading** Read pp. 3–5 aloud. Then do a choral reading of pp. 6–9. If students are able, have them read and discuss the remainder of the book with a partner. Ask: How do the people of Chinatown keep Chinese traditions alive? *(They speak Chinese, cook and eat traditional foods, and celebrate Chinese holidays.)*

- **After Reading** Ask students to look at and discuss the concept map. Connect the Below-Level Reader to the weekly question *What does it mean to grant freedom?* What might happen if Asian Americans were not granted the freedom to practice their traditions? *(Places like Chinatown might not exist or might be kept secret from outsiders.)*

MONITOR PROGRESS

If... students have difficulty reading the selection with a partner,

then... have them follow along as they listen to the Leveled Readers DVD-ROM.

If... have trouble understanding how Chinese traditions are kept alive,

then... reread pp. 10–13 and discuss the different customs.

Objectives
- Participate in teacher-led discussions by answering questions with appropriate detail.

Reinforce Comprehension

◉ **Skill Cause and Effect** Review with students the *Envision It!* material on cause and effect on p. EI•3. Then use p. 398 to review the definitions of cause and effect. An *effect* is something that happens. A *cause* is why that thing happens. Look for clue words such as *so* and *then* to find effects. Look for clue words such as *because* and *since* to find causes.

◉ **Strategy Inferring** Review inferring on p. 398. Remind students to use details in the text and what they already know to make inferences about what causes characters to act as they do and why certain events happen. For additional support, refer students to *Envision It!* p. EI•20.

Revisit *Happy Birthday Mr. Kang* on pp. 402–410. Have students begin reading aloud *Happy Birthday Mr. Kang* with a partner. As they read, have them apply the comprehension skill to the realistic fiction.

• At the beginning of the story, why does everyone clap and shout hurray? *(Mr. Kang blows out all the candles on his birthday cake.)*

• What is going to happen because Mr. Kang says, "Enough cooking"? *(Mrs. Kang will cook for her husband, and the restaurant will get a new cook.)*

• What happens every morning as a result of Mr. Kang's wishes? *(He reads* The New York Times.)

• What clue words in the text helped you answer the previous question? *(and so)*

Use the During Reading Differentiated Instruction for additional support for struggling readers.

Student Edition p. EI•3

More Reading

Use additional Leveled Readers or other texts at students' instructional levels to reinforce this week's skills and strategies. For text suggestions, see the Leveled Reader Database or the Leveled Readers Skills Chart on pp. CL24–CL29.

MONITOR PROGRESS

If... students have difficulty reading along with the group,

then... have them follow along as they listen to the AudioText.

Objectives
• Identify explicit cause and effect relationships among ideas in texts.
• Make inferences about text.

 **Strategic Intervention**

DAY 3

Reinforce Vocabulary

■ **Reread for Fluency** Use Decodable Practice Reader 27A.

■ **Decoding Multisyllabic Words** Write *tightly* and model how to use meaningful parts to read it. First, I cover the suffix *-ly* and read the base word: *tight.* Then I uncover the suffix and blend the base word and the suffix to read the whole word: *tight ly, tightly.*

Use the Multisyllabic Words routine on the *Routines Flip Chart* to help students read other words from the realistic fiction, such as *fragrant* and *ceramic.*

⊚ **Antonyms/Context Clues** Read the following sentence from p. 406: "Mr. Kang cleans the cage with a damp towel and dries it with a soft cloth." I'm not sure of the meaning of the word *damp.* I will look at the words around it to figure out its meaning. Maybe the author used an antonym as a clue. In this sentence, I see that Mr. Kang "dries" the cage after he uses the damp cloth. In the next paragraph, I see that Mr. Kang dampens a cloth "with water." *Damp* must mean "slightly wet." An antonym for *damp* would be *dry.*

■ **Revisit** *Happy Birthday Mr. Kang* on pp. 411–419. Then review *Words!* on pp. W•2 and W•7. Encourage students to use antonyms as context clues to figure out the meanings of unfamiliar words.

Use the During Reading Differentiated Instruction for additional support for struggling readers.

MONITOR PROGRESS

If... students need more practice with the lesson vocabulary,

then... use *Envision It! Pictured Vocabulary Cards*.

Student Edition p. W•2

More Reading

Use additional Leveled Readers or other texts at students' instructional levels to reinforce this week's skills and strategies. For text suggestions, see the Leveled Reader Database or the Leveled Readers Skills Chart on pp. CL24–CL29.

Objectives
- Identify antonyms.
- Use context to determine the relevant meaning of unfamiliar words.

Small Group Time

SI Strategic Intervention

DAY 4

Practice Retelling

■ **Retell** Guide students in using the Retelling Cards to list events in the selection.

- What does Mr. Kang wish for on his birthday?

- What problem does the bird cause between Sam and Mr. Kang? What happens because of this problem?

If students struggle, model a fluent retelling.

Genre Focus

■ **Before Reading or Revisiting** "Once Upon a Constitution" on pp. 424–427, read aloud the genre information about expository nonfiction on p. 424. In expository nonfiction, the author presents facts and details to support the main idea. This selection will tell about our Constitution and the freedoms it grants Americans. Then have students find the arrows on the first three pages and read the labels.

■ **During Reading or Revisiting** Help students do a choral reading of the article. Ask questions to help students recognize explicit and implicit causes and effects, such as "What happened because Americans needed laws and rules?"

■ **After Reading or Revisiting** Have students share their reactions to the selection. Then guide them through the Reading Across Texts and Writing Across Texts activities.

- What American rights and freedoms does Mr. Kang enjoy? *(saying what he thinks and feels; living and working where and when he chooses; practicing Chinese traditions)*

- Why does Mr. Kang change his mind about setting his bird free? *(Sam reminds his grandfather that he had felt caged before he stopped cooking.)*

MONITOR PROGRESS

If... students have difficulty retelling the selection,

then... have them review the story using the illustrations.

Objectives
- Make connections between literary and informational texts with similar ideas.

For a complete literacy instructional plan and additional practice with this week's target skills and strategies, see the **Leveled Reader Teaching Guide.**

Concept Literacy Reader

The Eagle Is Free

- **Model** Model the fluency skill of appropriate phrasing for students. Ask students to listen carefully as you read aloud the first two pages of *The Eagle Is Free.* Have students note the difference between grouping your words in a meaningful way and reading word by word with no phrasing or expression.

- **Fluency Routine**

  1. Have students reread passages from *The Eagle Is Free* with a partner.

  2. For optimal fluency, students should reread three to four times.

  3. As students read, monitor fluency and provide corrective feedback. Have students note how you read entire groups of words together.

  See *Routines Flip Chart* for more help with fluency.

- **Retell** Have students retell *The Eagle Is Free.* Prompt as necessary.

Below-Level Reader

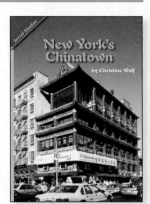

New York's Chinatown

- **Model** Ask students to listen carefully as you read aloud the first two pages of *New York's Chinatown,* emphasizing appropriate phrasing.

- **Fluency Routine**

  1. Have students reread passages from *New York's Chinatown* with a partner or individually.

  2. For optimal fluency, students should reread three to four times.

  3. As students read, monitor fluency and provide corrective feedback. Discuss how reading in meaningful phrases helps readers better understand what they read.

  See *Routines Flip Chart* for more help with fluency.

- **Retell** For additional practice, have students retell *New York's Chinatown* page by page, using the headings and photographs.

  - What traditions are you likely to see on a trip to Chinatown? *(people bowing to elders to show respect, working hard, and practicing Tai Chi)*

  - What did you learn about the Chinese culture from reading this book? *(It is rich, colorful, and full of traditions.)*

MONITOR PROGRESS

If... students have difficulty reading fluently,

then... provide additional fluency practice by pairing nonfluent readers with fluent ones.

Objectives
- Read aloud grade-level text with fluency.

Pacing Small Group Instruction

15–20 min

5-Day Plan

DAY 1	• Expand the concept • Read On-Level Reader
DAY 2	• Cause and Effect • Inferring • Revisit Student Edition pp. 402–411
DAY 3	• Antonyms • Revisit Student Edition pp. 412–419
DAY 4	• Practice Retelling • Read/Revisit Student Edition pp. 424–427
DAY 5	• Reread for fluency • Reread On-Level Reader

3- or 4-Day Plan

DAY 1	• Expand the concept • Read On-Level Reader
DAY 2	• Cause and Effect • Inferring • Revisit Student Edition pp. 402–411
DAY 3	• Antonyms • Revisit Student Edition pp. 412–419
DAY 4	• Practice Retelling • Read/Revisit Student Edition pp. 424–427 • Reread for fluency • Reread On-Level Reader

3-Day Plan: Eliminate the shaded box.

OL On-Level

DAY 1

Build Background

■ **Expand the Concept** Discuss the weekly question *What does it mean to grant freedom?* Have you ever heard the saying "free as a bird"? What does it mean? *(completely free, able to go almost anywhere)* This week you will learn about a bird that is not free. You will also learn more about what freedom means to people. Discuss the meaning of the words on the concept map on p. 395.

On-Level Reader

For a complete literacy instructional plan and additional practice with this week's target skills and strategies, see the **Leveled Reader Teaching Guide.**

■ **Before Reading** *A Pet Bird,* have students preview the book by looking at the title, cover, pictures, and headings. Why is it important to learn about pet birds? *(The book provides helpful information to anyone interested in owning a pet bird.)*

A Pet Bird

Help students create a KWL chart. Have them write what they already know about caring for pet birds in the *K* column. Have them write three questions about bird care in the *W* column. Explain that students will complete their KWL charts as they read.

■ **During Reading** Read aloud the first three pages of the book as students follow along. Remind students to write answers to the questions in their KWL charts as they finish reading the book. What is the first thing you learned about getting a pet bird? *(buy only birds bred in the United States)* Why is this important? *(Taking birds from foreign habitats can make them become endangered.)*

■ **After Reading** Have partners compare their KWL charts.

• Where did you find details to answer your questions? What new facts did you learn?

• How does the topic relate to the weekly question? *(When we take away a bird's freedom to make it a pet, we are responsible for meeting all the bird's needs.)*

Objectives
• Participate in teacher-led discussions by answering questions with appropriate detail.

 On-Level DAY 2

Expand Comprehension

Skill Cause and Effect Use p. 398 to review cause and effect. For additional review, see Cause and Effect on *Envision It!* p. EI•3. Sometimes a cause will have more than one effect. Because you forget your homework, you have to miss recess, and you get a lower grade. Sometimes an effect will have more than one cause. Hitting a home run in a baseball game may be the result of both extra practice and good coaching.

Strategy Inferring Review the definition of inferring, and encourage students to make inferences as they read. For additional support, use the Extend Thinking questions during reading or refer students to p. EI•20 of *Envision It!*

- Based on what you have read so far, what can you infer about Mr. Kang? *(He worked every day for many years, so he must be a hard worker. He paints poems, which must mean that he is creative.)*

- Based on what you have read, what can you infer about the author? *(Possible answer: She describes Chinese American customs very precisely, so they must interest her.)*

Revisit *Happy Birthday Mr. Kang* on pp. 402–410. Then have students begin reading aloud. As they read, have them look for causes and effects.

- What reasons does Mr. Kang give for wanting a caged bird? *(It's a special Chinese bird. His grandfather had a* hua mei *in a cage.)*

- What are three effects of Mr. Kang's birthday wishes? *(He gets to read the paper every day. He paints poems every day. He gets a* hua mei *as a pet.)*

Student Edition p. EI•3

More Reading

Use additional Leveled Readers or other texts at students' instructional levels to reinforce this week's skills and strategies. For text suggestions, see the Leveled Reader Database or the Leveled Readers Skills Chart on pp. CL24–CL29.

Objectives
- Identify explicit cause and effect relationships among ideas in texts.
- Make inferences about text.

DAY 3

Expand Vocabulary

🔊 **Antonyms/Context Clues** Read the following sentence from the second stanza of Mr. Kang's first poem: "When they look out / their narrow windows, / they see their own kitchen gardens." Write the word *narrow* as you say it aloud. Then model the process of using an antonym as a context clue. Later in this poem, "wide windows" are described. The view from narrow windows is only a kitchen garden, but from the view from wide windows is an entire city. So it seems that *wide* means the opposite of *narrow*. *Wide* is an antonym that provides a context clue for *narrow*.

Revisit *Happy Birthday Mr. Kang* on pp. 411–419. Read the first stanza of the first poem: "Rushing to the Golden Dragon / against a *chilly* wind, / the icy tears on my cheeks melt / with memories of warm old days." Write the word *chilly* as you say it aloud. Ask:

• What does the chilly wind cause Mr. Kang to do? *(He cries icy tears.)*

• What effect do his "memories of warm old days" have? *(They melt the icy tears.)*

• What do you think *warm* means—the same as *chilly* or the opposite? *(opposite)*

Encourage students to use context clues as they read this selection, other selections, and textbooks in their other classes.

Student Edition p. W•2

More Reading

Use additional Leveled Readers or other texts at students' instructional levels to reinforce this week's skills and strategies. For text suggestions, see the Leveled Reader Database or the Leveled Readers Skills Chart on pp. CL24–CL29.

Objectives
• Identify antonyms.
• Use context to determine the relevant meaning of unfamiliar words.

 **OL** On-Level

DAY 4

Practice Retelling

■ **Retell** To assess students' comprehension, use the Retelling Cards. Monitor retelling and prompt students as needed.

Genre Focus

■ **Before Reading or Revisiting** "Once Upon a Constitution" on pp. 424–427, read aloud the genre information about expository nonfiction on p. 424. Explain that expository nonfiction can help readers learn facts about a topic. Help students preview "Once Upon a Constitution" and set a purpose for reading. Ask:

- What features do you see that are different from most stories you have read? *(photographs, arrows, and labels)*

- Why do you think the opening words of the document are enlarged on the first page? *(to show the importance of "We the People" in a democracy and to help explain the word curlicue)*

■ **During Reading or Revisiting** Have students read along with you. Ask:

- How does the author use the questions and answers? *(Questions introduce main ideas; answers explain the ideas with supporting details.)*

- How would a fictional story about the Constitution be different than the expository nonfiction? *(A fictional story could have made-up characters, events, and details.)*

■ **After Reading or Revisiting** Have students share their reactions to "Once Upon a Constitution." Then have them write a brief conversation between Mr. Kang and Sam in which the two discuss why the Constitution and Bill of Rights are important to them.

Objectives
• Make connections between literary and informational texts with similar ideas.

OL On-Level

DAY 5

On-Level Reader

■ **Model** Read aloud p. 3 of the On-Level Reader *A Pet Bird,* emphasizing appropriate phrasing.

■ **Fluency Routine**

1. Have students reread passages from *A Pet Bird* with a partner.

2. For optimal fluency, students should reread passages three to four times.

3. As students read, monitor fluency and provide corrective feedback. Have students note how you read entire groups of words instead of reading word by word. Then discuss how reading with appropriate phrasing leads to greater understanding.

See *Routines Flip Chart* for more help with fluency.

A Pet Bird

■ **Retell** For additional practice, guide students on how to use headings and photographs to retell *A Pet Bird.* Prompt students as necessary.

• What important details about keeping birds as pets does this book explain? *(choosing a pet bird, preparing the bird's cage, and feeding and caring for the bird)*

• What do you think would be best about keeping a pet bird? *(Students may mention spending time with the bird or teaching it to do tricks.)*

Objectives
• Read aloud grade-level text with fluency.

A Advanced **DAY 1**

Build Background

■ **Extend the Concept** Discuss the weekly question *What does it mean to grant freedom?* If you were not allowed to be free, what do you think you would miss most? *(Students may say the ability to do what they want to do or to say what they want to say.)* What freedoms do you think confined or caged animals miss most? *(Students may say hunting or traveling.)* What reasons can you think of for not setting an animal free? *(Many pets cannot survive in the wild because of the harsh weather and because they do not know how to find their own food.)*

Advanced Reader

For a complete literacy instructional plan and additional practice with this week's target skills and strategies, see the **Leveled Reader Teaching Guide.**

China's Special Gifts to the World

■ **Before Reading** *China's Special Gifts to the World,* ask students to preview the book. Based on the title, cover art, and contents page, what do you think the book is about? *(the Chinese language)* Have students use the chapter titles and illustrations in the book to predict what they will learn. Then have students set a purpose for reading.

■ **During Reading** Have students read the Advanced Reader independently.

● What are the "four treasures"? *(brushes, ink sticks, ink stones, fine paper)*

● What are the benefits of using written language instead of spoken language? *(Written language can be preserved for many years.)*

■ **After Reading** Have students review the concept map and explain how *China's Special Gifts to the World* helps students answer the weekly question. How is the power to grant or deny freedom different in the United States today from China in the time of Li Po? *(No one in the United States today can simply take away a person's freedom like the Chinese emperor could.)*

■ **Now Try This** Assign "Now Try This" at the end of the Advanced Reader.

Pacing Small Group Instruction

15–20 min

5-Day Plan	
DAY 1	● Extend the concept ● Read Advanced Reader
DAY 2	● Cause and Effect ● Inferring ● Revisit Student Edition pp. 402–411
DAY 3	● Antonyms ● Revisit Student Edition pp. 412–419
DAY 4	● Expository Nonfiction ● Read/Revisit Student Edition pp. 424–427
DAY 5	● Reread for fluency ● Reread Advanced Reader

3- or 4-Day Plan	
DAY 1	● Extend the concept ● Read Advanced Reader
DAY 2	● Cause and Effect ● Inferring ● Revisit Student Edition pp. 402–411
DAY 3	● Antonyms ● Revisit Student Edition pp. 412–419
DAY 4	● Expository Nonfiction ● Read/Revisit Student Edition pp. 424–427 ● Reread for fluency ● Reread Advanced Reader

3-Day Plan: Eliminate the shaded box.

Objectives

→ Participate in teacher-led discussions by answering questions with appropriate detail.

More Reading

Use additional Leveled Readers or other texts at students' instructional levels to reinforce this week's skills and strategies. For text suggestions, see the Leveled Reader Database or the Leveled Readers Skills Chart on pp. CL24–CL29.

A Advanced **DAY 2**

Extend Comprehension

◎ **Skill Cause and Effect** Explain that authors do not always use clue words, such as *because* and *therefore,* to signal causes and effects. Sometimes readers have to figure out on their own what happened and why. Think of the book that you just read, *China's Special Gifts to the World.*

• In your opinion, why has calligraphy survived since ancient times? *(Students might mention the beauty and usefulness of calligraphy.)*

• What effects has the gift of calligraphy had on the world? *(Beautiful works of art have been created, and great literature has been preserved.)*

◎ **Strategy Inferring** Review the definition of *infer,* and ask students to make inferences about characters and events as they read. During reading, use the Extend Thinking questions and the During Reading Differentiated Instruction for additional support.

Revisit *Happy Birthday Mr. Kang* on pp. 402–410. Ask students to track causes and effects and make inferences as they read.

• On p. 405, why does Mr. Kang say, "Enough cooking"? *(After fifty years of working as a cook, he has grown tired.)*

• What are the effects of his decision? *(He retires from work at the Golden Dragon and spends his days reading the newspaper, writing poems, and tending to his bird.)*

■ **Critical Thinking** Encourage students to reflect on what they have read so far.

• Think about Mr. Kang's three wishes. Why do you think he asked for simple things and not riches or excitement? What can you infer about him based on his wishes? *(He is a simple and practical person. He enjoys the little things in life. He wants a quiet but enjoyable retirement.)*

• What can you infer about Mr. Kang based on how he treats his bird? *(Some students will say that he loves the bird because he takes good care of it and calls it a good friend.)*

Objectives
• Identify explicit cause and effect relationships among ideas in texts.
• Make inferences about text.

 A |  Advanced

DAY 3

Extend Vocabulary

More Reading

Use additional Leveled Readers or other texts at students' instructional levels to reinforce this week's skills and strategies. For text suggestions, see the Leveled Reader Database or the Leveled Readers Skills Chart on pp. CL24–CL29.

Antonyms/Context Clues Read the following sentence: "Sometimes even I can hear the familiar sounds bending by themselves in my own throat, coming out strangely, sounding a little American." Write the word *familiar* as you say it aloud. Then ask:

- What does Mr. Kang think is happening to the "familiar sounds" of his native Chinese? *(He has lived in the United States for so long that his Chinese is "bending" or sounding different in his throat and beginning to sound "a little American" to him.)*

- What context clue does the author give for the meaning of *familiar?* *("coming out strangely")*

- Why does *strangely* mean—the same as *familiar* or the opposite? *(opposite)*

Revisit *Happy Birthday Mr. Kang* on pp. 411–419. Challenge students to use antonyms as clues to the meaning of other words in the text. For example, ask:

- In the first stanza of Mr. Kang's first poem, what does *chilly* mean? *(unpleasantly cold)*

- What antonym can you use as a context clue to figure out its meaning? *(warm)*

- What does *narrow* mean in the second stanza? *(small in width)*

- What antonym can you use as a context clue to figure out its meaning? *(wide)*

Objectives
- Identify antonyms.
- Use context to determine the relevant meaning of unfamiliar words.

Small Group Time

A — Advanced

Genre Focus

Once Upon a Constitution

■ **Before Reading or Revisiting** "Once Upon a Constitution" on pp. 424–427, have students read the panel information on expository nonfiction. Then have students use the text features to set a purpose for reading.

■ **During Reading or Revisiting** Point out that the article is organized into three sections. What pattern does the author repeat in each section? *(Each section begins with a question that introduces the main idea. That is followed by an answer that explains the main idea and gives supporting details.)* Why do you think the author used this organization? *(It's attention getting and prepares the reader for what is going to follow.)*

■ **After Reading or Revisiting** Have students discuss Reading Across Texts. Then have them do Writing Across Texts independently.

Objectives
• Make connections between literary and informational texts with similar ideas.

A — Advanced

■ **Reread for Fluency** Have students silently reread passages from the Advanced Reader *China's Special Gifts to the World.* Then have them reread aloud with a partner or individually. As students read, monitor fluency and provide corrective feedback. If students read fluently on the first reading, they do not need to reread three to four times. Assess the fluency of students in this group using p. 429j.

■ **Retell** Ask students to summarize the main ideas and key details from the Advanced Reader *China's Special Gifts to the World.*

■ **Now Try This** Have students share their calligraphy with classmates.

China's Special Gifts to the World

Objectives
• Read aloud grade-level text with fluency.

The ELL lessons are organized by strands. Use them to scaffold the weekly curriculum of lessons or during small group time instruction.

Academic Language

Students will hear or read the following academic language in this week's core instruction. As students encounter the vocabulary, provide a simple definition or concrete example. Then ask students to suggest an example or synonym of the word and identify available cognates.

Skill Words	limerick	cause *(causa)*
	abbreviation *(abreviatura)*	effect *(efecto)*
	monitor	predict
Concept Words	citizen	freedom
	grandson	robot

*Spanish cognates in parentheses

Concept Development

What does it mean to grant freedom?

■ **Preteach Concept**

• **Prior Knowledge** Have students turn to pp. 394–395 in the Student Edition. Call attention to the man and children letting the animals go free and tap into students' knowledge of letting something go free. Why do you think the people are letting the animals go free? Why should we let some animals go free?

• **Discuss Concept** Elicit students' knowledge and experience of granting freedom. What are some ways people can grant freedom? Is the girl granting freedom to the dragonfly? How? Why is freedom important? Supply background information as needed.

■ **Poster Talk-Through** Read aloud the Poster Talk-Through on ELL Poster 27 and work through the Day 1 activities.

■ **Daily Concept and Vocabulary Development** Use the daily activities on ELL Poster 27 to build concept and vocabulary knowledge.

Objectives
• Learn new language structures, expressions, and basic and academic vocabulary heard during classroom instruction and interactions.

Content Objectives
• Use concept vocabulary related to the idea of granting freedom.

Language Objectives
• Express ideas in response to art and discussion.

Daily Planner

DAY 1	• **Frontload Concept** • **Preteach** Comprehension Skill, Vocabulary, Phonics/Spelling, Conventions • **Writing**
DAY 2	• **Review** Concept, Vocabulary, Comprehension Skill • **Frontload Main Selection** • **Practice** Phonics/Spelling, Conventions/Writing
DAY 3	• **Review** Concept, Comprehension Skill, Vocabulary, Conventions/Writing • **Reread Main Selection** • **Practice** Phonics/Spelling
DAY 4	• **Review Concept** • **Read ELL/ELD Readers** • **Practice** Phonics/Spelling, Conventions/Writing
DAY 5	• **Review** Concept, Vocabulary, Comprehension Skill, Phonics/Spelling, Conventions • **Reread ELL/ELD Readers** • **Writing**

*See the ELL Handbook for ELL Workshops with targeted instruction.

Concept Talk Video

Use Concept Talk Video Routine (*ELL Handbook,* p. 477) to build background knowledge about granting freedom. For listening practice, see Use Classroom Resources (*ELL Handbook,* pp. 406–407).

Support for English Language Learners

Language Objectives

- Understand and use basic vocabulary.
- Learn meanings of grade-level vocabulary.

Mini-Lesson

Have students write the ten high-frequency words on cards. These are words that you will see many times as you read. Have students work in pairs to write a sentence using one of the high-frequency words. Students can use the illustration on ELL Poster 27 for sentence ideas.

ELL Workshop

Students may need extra assistance deriving meaning from basic vocabulary in environmental print. Support them with Read the Words Around You (*ELL Handbook,* pp. 422–423).

ELL *English Language Learners*

Basic Vocabulary

■ **High-Frequency Words** Use the vocabulary routines and the High-Frequency Word list on p. 455 of the *ELL Handbook* to systematically teach newcomers the first 300 sight words in English. Students who began learning ten words per week at the beginning of the year are now learning words 261–270. The *ELL Handbook* (p. 446) contains a bank of strategies that you can use to ensure students' mastery of High-Frequency Words.

Lesson Vocabulary

■ **Preteach** Introduce the Lesson Vocabulary using this routine:

1. Distribute copies of this week's Word Cards (*ELL Handbook,* p. 185).

2. Display ELL Poster 27 and reread the Poster Talk-Through.

3. Using the poster illustrations, model how a word's meaning can be expressed with other similar words: The boy puts his head down, or *bows,* because his dog is missing.

4. Use these sentences to reveal the meaning of the other words.

   - She *bows* her head in sadness. (bends down)

   - He felt *foolish* when he made a mistake. (not showing good sense)

   - The new student is from a *foreign* country. (from another country)

   - The wooden bridge is *narrow.* (not broad or wide)

   - The little parakeet *perches* on the ledge. (rests)

   - My mom tried a new *recipe* for lasagna last night. (instructions for preparing or cooking food)

   - The weather was *chilly,* so I wore my warm coat. (feeling slightly cold)

Objectives

- Use strategic learning techniques such as concept mapping, drawing, memorizing, comparing, contrasting, and reviewing to acquire basic and grade-level vocabulary.
- Internalize new basic and academic language by using and reusing it in meaningful ways in speaking and writing activities that build concept and language attainment.
- Use accessible language and learn new and essential language in the process.

ELL *English Language Learners*

■ **Reteach** Distribute a copy of the Word Cards and six blank cards to each pair of students. Have partners write a clue or simple picture on a blank card for each word.

Have students mix the Word Cards and clue cards together and lay them face down, spread out on a table. Students can take turns choosing two cards, trying to match a word with its clue. Have students explain their choices.

■ **Writing** Write the following sentences on the board. Have students write the vocabulary words to fill in the blanks.

- He _____ his head out of respect. (bows)

- The _____ wind makes my cheeks red. (chilly)

- Marcus felt _____ for trying to trick his brother. (foolish)

- The colorful bird came from a _____ country. (foreign)

- The stone path was long and _____. (narrow)

- The proud eagle _____ at the top of the tree. (perches)

- My grandmother likes to try new _____ when she cooks. (recipes)

 Leveled LS Support

Beginning/Intermediate Have students draw pictures and label the clue words.

Advanced/Advanced High Have students generate and write their own sentences using the vocabulary words for the week.

Language Objectives

- Produce drawings, phrases, or short sentences using Lesson Vocabulary.

ELL Teacher Tip

Help English learners to learn new words by grouping words that are related to a specific theme, quality, or activity. Have students make a word grid to group related words and create a visual reference that can be used in future lessons.

ELL Workshop

As students speak using new vocabulary, they may need assistance knowing how to adapt spoken English for informal purposes. *Use Informal English (ELL Handbook,* pp. 390–391) provides extra support.

Objectives

- Develop basic sight vocabulary, derive meaning of environmental print, and comprehend English vocabulary and language structures used routinely in written classroom materials.
- Demonstrate an increasing ability to distinguish between formal and informal English and an increasing knowledge of when to use each one commensurate with grade-level learning expectations.

Support for English Language Learners

Content Objectives
- Monitor and adjust oral comprehension.

Language Objectives
- Discuss oral passages.
- Understand implicit information.
- Use a graphic organizer to take notes.

English Opportunity: Setting

Help students understand the setting of the Read Aloud. Use Student Edition p. EI•20 to review inferring. Have students listen again for clues in the text to answer the following question. How do you know the story is set into the future? (People have robots.)

ELL Workshop

Encourage students to demonstrate listening comprehension of the Read Aloud and other spoken messages. Provide Retell or Summarize (*ELL Handbook,* pp. 408–409) for practice.

Listening Comprehension

JAK and JIL Ask for Freedom

The Norton family has two kids and two robots. The robots are named *JAK* and *JIL.* JAK and JIL care for the children. The children's names are *Bill* and *Laury.*

One day, JAK and JIL ask the Nortons to set them free. They have read about freedom. They want to find out what it is like. Bill and Laury are sad. They love the robots. They do not want to see JAK and JIL go away.

The family talks about freedom and how important it is to humans. JAK and JIL tell the children that they don't need robots any more to take care of them. They are growing up.

Finally, the Nortons decide to let JAK and JIL have their freedom.

Prepare for the Read Aloud The modified Read Aloud above prepares students for listening to the oral reading "A Little Freedom" on p. 395b.

■ **First Listening: Listen to Understand** Write the title of the Read Aloud on the board. This is a story about freedom. Who are the characters? Listen to find out what happens. What does the family decide? Afterward, ask the questions again and have students share their answers.

■ **Second Listening: Listen to Check Understanding** Using a Story Map, work with students to identify the characters in the story, the setting, and the events. Record their ideas in the Story Map graphic organizer (*ELL Handbook,* p. 484). Listen again to check that you have included the most important events.

Objectives
- Understand implicit ideas and information in increasingly complex spoken language commensurate with grade-level learning expectations.
- Demonstrate listening comprehension of increasingly complex spoken English by following directions, retelling or summarizing spoken messages , reponding to questions and requests collaborating with peers. and taking notes commensurate with content and grade-level needs.

Phonics and Spelling

■ **Schwa (/ə/)** Copy and distribute *ELL Handbook,* p. 266.

- **Preteach** Hold up a pencil and say its name. This is a pencil. The second syllable is unstressed. Listen to the vowel sound. It sounds like this: /ə/ Listen for the schwa sound in these words: *afraid, dragon.*

- **Teach** Write the words *alarm, seven, pencil, lemon, minus, oxygen* on the board. The schwa sound can come in the beginning or middle of a word. It can be spelled with any vowel. Say the words aloud and have students identify its spelling. Circle the vowels so the relationship is clear.

- **Schwa Sound** Read a practice sentence aloud. Have students raise a finger each time they hear a word with the schwa sound. *I put a pretzel on the table next to the apple and a bagel.*

To provide students additional instruction and practice for the schwa sound, use the lessons in the *ELL Handbook* (p. 267).

Selection Vocabulary: Antonyms

■ **Preteach** Write the words *night/day, up/down, open/closed,* and *enter/exit* on the board. Each of these words is an antonym of the other. That means each word has the opposite meaning. Draw or act out each word if necessary.

■ **Reteach** Give examples of words you can think of that are antonyms, or opposites. Write each example they think of on the board. Read each set of words aloud. Complete a set if necessary.

■ **Practice** Listen to these sentences: *At the library, Sue was very quiet. At the park, Sue was very ____.* Have students fill in the missing word. Repeat with other antonym pairs.

Beginning Have students draw and label pictures of five antonym pairs.

Intermediate Have students work in pairs to make a list of antonym pairs.

Advanced/Advanced High Have students generate a list of antonym pairs and write sentences with them.

Content Objectives

- Schwa spelled with *an a, e, i, o, u,* and *y.*

- Learn relationships between schwa sounds and spellings.

- Identify antonyms.

Language Objectives

- Apply phonics and decoding skills to vocabulary.

- Identify, pronounce, words that contain the schwa sound.

 Transfer Skills

Schwa The schwa sounds like the /u/ sound in *up.* You say it quickly and without any stress on the syllable: /ə/. Try these words with a schwa sound: *about, around, final, little, taken, pencil, jungle, able.*

ELL Teaching Routine

For more practice with the schwa sound, use the Nondecodable Words Routine (*ELL Handbook,* p. 472).

Objectives

- Use visual and contextual support from peers and teachers to read grade-appropriate content area text, enhance and confirm understanding, and develop vocabulary, grasp of language structures, and background knowledge needed to comprehend increasingly challenging language.
- Learn relationships between sounds and letters of the English language to represent sounds when writing in English.

Support for English Language Learners

Content Objectives

- Distinguish cause and effect.
- Identify cause and effect to aid comprehension.

Language Objectives

- Discuss the connections between causes and effects.
- Pronounce transition words that suggest cause and effect relationships.
- Write about causes and effects from personal experience.

ELL Workshop

Encourage students to ask questions to monitor their understanding of instruction of comprehension skills. Use Ask Clarifying Questions (*ELL Handbook*, pp. 404–405) for practice.

ELL *English Language Learners*

Comprehension
Cause and Effect

- **Preteach** An effect is something that happens. A cause is why that thing happens. Have students turn to *Envision It!* on p. EI•3 in the Student Edition. Read aloud the text together. What clue word do you see in sentence 2? (because) The effect is Benito cannot answer. What is the cause in sentence 2? (He does not speak English yet.)

- **Reteach** Give each student a copy of Picture It! (*ELL Handbook,* p. 186). Look at the pictures first. Read the directions aloud. Point out that the paragraph describes two effects: Benito cannot answer and Carmen tells Benito what the teacher said. Students need to find causes for each. Guide students in completing the graphic organizer on the page at their language proficiency level. (*Causes:* does not speak English yet; Carmen is bilingual. *Effects:* cannot answer; tells Benito what teacher said.)

Beginning/Intermediate Reread the paragraph with students and guide them as they underline clue words. After each sentence, ask: *What is the effect? What is the cause?*

Advanced/Advanced High Have students write the causes and effects in the organizer.

MINI-LESSON

Social Language

Tell students that certain words signal a cause and effect relationship. List some of them on the board, such as *because, therefore, if, then, consequently,* and so on. Give examples of how each word can be used in a cause and effect situation. Provide this sentence frame: If I learn to speak English, then _____.

Objectives

- Internalize new basic and academic language by using it and reusing it in meaningful ways in speaking and writing activities that build language attainment.
- Express opinions, ideas, and feelings ranging from communicating single words and short phrases to participating in extended discussions on a variety of social and grade-appropriate academic topics.
- Narrate, describe, and explain with increasing specificity and detail as more English is acquired.

Reading Comprehension
Happy Birthday Mr. Kang

Student Edition pp. 402–419

■ **Frontloading** Read aloud the title and discuss what a birthday is. Who has the birthday in the story? Guide students on a picture walk through *Happy Birthday Mr. Kang.* Point out the present Mr. Kang gets for his birthday. What do you think Mr. Kang will do with his gift? During reading, pause and invite students to adjust their predictions. Distribute a Story Predictions Chart graphic organizer and fill out the first two columns before you read.

Sheltered Reading Ask questions such as the following to guide students' comprehension.

- **p. 405:** What did Mr. Kang wish for when he blew out his birthday candles? (to read a newspaper, to paint poems, and to have a *hua mei* bird)

- **p. 406:** What does Mr. Kang do to care for his bird? (wash the cage and the bird's feathers)

- **p. 409:** Where does Mr. Kang go on Sundays? (to the park with his bird)

- **pp. 413–414:** What does Sam think his grandfather should do with the bird? (set the bird free)

- **p. 415:** What does the *hua mei* do when Mr. Kang opens the cage door? (it flies away)

- **p. 419:** How does the family feel at the end of the story? (happy)

■ **Fluency: Appropriate Phrasing** Explain to students that reading paragraphs is different than reading poetry. When you read a poem, you often pause at the end of a line, although a poet often continues through from one line to the next. Read the poem on p. 412, pausing at the end of lines. Have pairs of students read parts of the poem on p. 418. Have them adjust their reading to have appropriate phrasing of the poetic lines. For more practice, use the Fluency: Oral Rereading Routine (*ELL Handbook,* p. 474).

After Reading Help students summarize the text with the Retelling Cards. Give each student a Retelling Card. As a group, have them decide which card comes first. Have students explain their own Retelling Card in the correct order.

Content Objectives
- Monitor and adjust comprehension.
- Make and adjust predictions.

Language Objectives
- Practice appropriate phrasing.
- Summarize text using visual support.

Graphic Organizer

What might happen?	What clues do I have?	What did happen?

Audio Support

Students can prepare for reading *Happy Birthday Mr. Kang* by using the eSelection or the AudioText Routine (*ELL Handbook,* p. 477).

ELL Workshop

Have students work with peers to ask questions about the content. Use Ask Clarifying Questions (*ELL Handbook,* pp. 404–405).

Objectives
- Understand the general meaning, main points, and important details of spoken language ranging from situations in which topics, language, and contexts are familiar to unfamiliar.
- Narrate, describe, and explain with increasing specificity and detail as more English is acquired.
- Demonstrate English comprehension and expand reading skills by employing analytical skills such as evaluating written information and performing critical analyses commensurate with content area and grade level needs.

Support for English Language Learners

ELD Reader   ELL Reader

For additional leveled instruction, see the **ELL/ELD Reader Teaching Guide.**

Comprehension
Gina Becomes a Citizen

■ **Before Reading** Distribute copies of the ELL and ELD Readers, *Gina Becomes a Citizen,* to students at their reading level.

• **Preview** Read the title aloud with students: This is a story about a girl who becomes a citizen. Invite students to look through the pictures and name what they see. Have them predict what will happen if Gina studies very hard in her classes.

• **Set a Purpose for Reading** Let's read to find out what Gina does to become a citizen.

■ **During Reading** Follow the Reading Routine for both reading groups.

1. Read the entire Reader aloud slowly.

2. Reread pp. 2–5, pausing to build background or model comprehension. Have Beginning students finger-point as you read. Use the questions in the chart to check students' comprehension.

3. Have students read pp. 2–5 independently.

4. Repeat steps 2–3 above for pp. 6–9 of the Reader.

■ **After Reading** Have students demonstrate comprehension by analyzing the character of Gina. In a whole-group discussion, ask students: Why was it important for Gina to go to school? Record their answers on the board and invite them to point to pictures in the book to support their answers.

ELD Reader Beginning/Intermediate

■ **pp. 2–3** Who is Gina? (a girl from another country) What does she want to become? (a U.S. citizen)

■ **pp. 4–6** What did Gina learn in her classes? (English and US government and history)

Writing The story tells how Gina studies hard. Her studying causes something important to happen. Write a sentence that tells the effect of all her studies. Read your sentence aloud to your partner.

ELL Reader Advanced/Advanced High

■ **pp. 4–5** How did Gina learn English? (by working hard and practicing in class)

■ **p. 8** Why is Gina happy to be a U.S. citizen? (She has freedom to make her own choices and vote.)

Study Guide Distribute copies of the ELL Reader Study Guide (*ELL Handbook,* p. 190). Scaffold comprehension of cause and effect by helping students look back through the Reader in order to complete the page. Review their responses together. (See *ELL Handbook,* pp. 209–212.)

Objectives

• Demonstrate comprehension of increasingly complex English by participating in shared reading, retelling or summarizing material, responding to questions, and taking notes commensurate with content area and grade level needs.
• Use visual, contextual, and linguistic support to enhance and confirm understanding of increasingly complex and elaborated spoken language.
• Demonstrate English comprehension and expand reading skills by employing analytical skills such as evaluating written information and performing critical analyses commensurate with content area and grade level needs.

Conventions
Abbreviations

■ **Preteach** Display the following sentences on the board:

Mister Morales is my science teacher.

My birthday is in February.

Read each sentence aloud. Underline *Mister* in the first sentence. Explain that *Mister* is a word that can be shortened into an abbreviation. Write *Mr.* on the board. Point out the capital letter and the period. Repeat with the other sentence with February (Feb.).

■ **Practice** Display these sentences:

I live on Strawn <u>Street</u>.

He lives on Good Hope <u>Drive</u>.

We went on vacation in <u>December</u>.

Beginning/Intermediate Have students read the sentences aloud, clarifying language as needed. Then help students change each underlined word into an abbreviation.

Advanced/Advanced High Have students write the sentences. Then help students change the underlined words into abbreviations.

■ **Reteach** Help students change the underlined words into abbreviations. Then have students write the abbreviations on index cards for additional practice.

■ **Practice** Display a chart to illustrate forming abbreviations.

Word or Category	Abbreviation
Mister, Missus	Mr., Mrs.
State Names	ME, NY, CA, TX
Month Names	Jan., Feb., Aug., Sept.
Street, Avenue, Drive	St., Ave., Dr.

Beginning/Intermediate Have students point to each abbreviation in the chart and tell what word it is an abbreviation for.

Advanced/Advanced High Have students expand the chart by adding other words that are often abbreviated.

Objectives
• Speak using a variety of grammatical structures, sentence lengths, sentence types, and connecting words with increasing accuracy and ease as more English is acquired.

Content Objectives
• Identify abbreviations in reading.
• Decode abbreviations in reading.

Language Objectives
• Read aloud sentences that contain abbreviations.
• Write abbreviations accurately.

 Transfer Skills

Abbreviations English learners may be able to pronounce the abbreviation, but may not easily connect it to the word that it represents. Conversely, some words, such as *Mr.* or *Mrs.,* are rarely seen unabbreviated. Offer plenty of examples to help comprehension.

Support for English Language Learners

Content Objectives
- Identify the structure of a limerick.

Language Objectives
- Write about the structure of limericks.
- Share feedback for editing and revising.

ELL Workshops
Students can collaborate with peers to discuss their writing. Discuss with Classmates (*ELL Handbook,* pp. 418–419) provides assistance with discussion.

Students may use classroom resources to respond to questions they have about their writing. Use Classroom Resources (*ELL Handbook,* pp. 406–407) provides extra support.

Structure of a Limerick

■ **Introduce** Display the limerick model and read it aloud. Review that a limerick has five lines with a predictable rhyme pattern: *a-a-b-b-a.* A limerick is a funny poem. In a limerick, each line has a certain number of syllables. Lines 1, 2, and 5 have 8 syllables. Line 3 has 5 and line 4 has 6 syllables. Use the model to demonstrate the structure.

> **Writing Model**
>
> There was a young girl from Lepore
>
> Who rode an old yak to the store.
>
> She got to the town
>
> But her yak did fall down.
>
> So she lived in town evermore.

■ **Practice** Use what you learned about the language structure of a limerick. Review the number of lines, rhyme scheme, and syllable count using the model as an example.

■ **Write** Write a sentence that tells how this limerick follows the correct structure. Use this sentence frame. *This poem is a limerick because _____.*

Beginning/Intermediate Write a description of the limerick structure and allow students to refer directly to it as they complete their writing assignment.

Advanced As part of their writing assignment, have students compare the structure of a limerick with the poetry in *Happy Birthday Mr. Kang.* Have them explain three differences in the structures.

Advanced High Have students extend their writing assignment by writing their own limericks. Explain that sometimes syllables go uncounted if they are unstressed at the beginning or end of the line.

Objectives
- Develop and expand repertoire of learning strategies such as reasoning inductively or deductively, looking for patterns in language, and analyzing sayings and expressions commensurate with grade-level learning expectations.
- Demonstrate English comprehension and expand reading skills by employing analytical skills such as evaluating written information and performing critical analyses commensurate with content area and grade level needs.
- Write using a variety of grade-appropriate sentence lengths, patterns, and connecting words to combine phrases, clauses, and sentences in increasingly accurate ways as more English is acquired.

This Week's ELL Overview

ELL Handbook

- Maximize Literacy and Cognitive Engagement
- Research Into Practice
- Full Weekly Support for Every Selection

Talking Walls: Art for the People
- Multi-Lingual Summaries in Five Languages
- Selection-Specific Vocabulary Word Cards
- Frontloading/Reteaching for Comprehension Skill Lessons
- ELD and ELL Reader Study Guides

- Transfer Activities
- Professional Development

Daily Leveled ELL Notes

ELL notes appear throughout this week's instruction and ELL Support is on the DI pages of your Teacher's Edition. The following is a sample of an ELL note from this week.

English Language Learners

Beginning Have students make a set of flashcards with the *-tion, -ion, -ture, -ive,* and *-ize* words from the Decodable Practice Reader: *active, decision, station, future, vacation, inventive, substitution, adventures, picture,* and *visualize.* Have students work with a partner to gain fluency in reading the words by using the flashcards.

Intermediate After reading, have students orally use each of the words with these syllables from the Decodable Practice Reader in a sentence.

Advanced Have students write sentences about Henry, using words with final syllables *-tion, -ion, -ture, -ive,* and *-ize.*

Advanced High After reading, have students write about a future adventure they would like to have. Remind them to use words with final syllables *-tion, -ion, -ture, -ive,* and *-ize* and high-frequency words from the Decodable Practice Reader in their writing.

ELL by Strand

The ELL lessons on this week's Support for English Language Learners pages are organized by strand. They offer additional scaffolding for the core curriculum. Leveled support notes on these pages address the different proficiency levels in your class. See pages DI•66–DI•75.

ELL Guy
Dr. Jim Cummins

The Three Pillars of ELL Instruction

ELL Strands	Activate Prior Knowledge	Access Content	Extend Language
Vocabulary pp. DI•67–DI•68	Preteach	Reteach	Leveled Writing Activities
Reading Comprehension p. DI•72	Frontloading	Sheltered Reading	After Reading
Phonics, Spelling, and Word Analysis p DI•70	Preteach and Model	Practice	Leveled Practice Activities
Listening Comprehension p DI•69	Prepare for the Read Aloud	First Listening	Second Listening
Conventions and Writing pp. DI•74–DI•75	Preteach/Introduce	Teach/Model and Practice	Leveled Practice Activities/ Leveled Writing Activities
Concept Development p DI•66	Prior Knowledge	Discuss Concept	Daily Concept and Vocabulary Development

This Week's Practice Stations Overview

Six Weekly Practice Stations with Leveled Activities can be found at the beginning of each week of instruction. For this week's Practice Stations, see pp. 430h–430i.

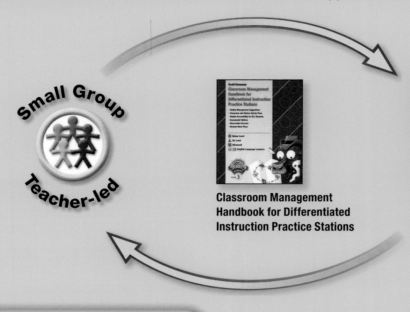

Practice Stations

Small Group Teacher-led

Classroom Management Handbook for Differentiated Instruction Practice Stations

Daily Leveled Center Activities

○ Below   ▢ Advanced   △ On-Level   **ELL**

Practice Stations Flip Charts

	Word Wise	**Word Work**	**Words to Know**	**Let's Write**	**Read For Meaning**	**Get Fluent**
Objectives	• Spell words with schwa sound spelled with *a, e, i, o, u,* and *y.*	• Identify and pronounce words with schwa sound spelled with *a, e, i, o, u,* and *y.*	• Identify and define antonyms.	• Write a limerick.	• Identify cause and effect.	• Read aloud with appropriate phrasing.
Materials	• *Word Wise* Flip Chart Activity 28 • Teacher-made word cards • paper • pencils	• *Word Work* Flip Chart Activity 28 • Teacher-made word cards • paper • pencils	• *Words to Know* Flip Chart Activity 28 • Teacher-made word cards • paper • pencils	• *Let's Write* Flip Chart Activity 28 • paper • pencils	• *Read for Meaning* Flip Chart Activity 28 • Leveled Readers • paper • pencils	• *Get Fluent* Flip Chart Activity 28 • Leveled Readers

This Week on Reading Street!

Freedom

Question of the Week
Why is freedom of expression important?

Daily Plan

Don't Wait Until Friday

Whole Group
- ◉ Graphic Sources
- ◉ Unknown Words
- • Fluency/Accuracy
- • Writing/Conventions
- • Research and Inquiry

MONITOR PROGRESS	Success Predictor			
Day 1 Check Oral Vocabulary	Day 2 Check Word Reading	Day 3 Check Retelling	Day 4 Check Fluency	Day 5 Check Oral Vocabulary

Small Group

Teacher Led

- • Reading Support
- • Skill Support
- • Fluency Practice

Practice Stations

Independent Activities

Customize Literacy More support for a balanced literacy approach, see pp. CL•1–CL•47.

Customize Writing More support for a customized writing approach, see pp. CW•1–CW•10.

Whole Group
- • Writing: Description
- • Conventions: Combining Sentences
- • Spelling: Final Syllables

Assessment
- • Weekly Tests
- • Day 5 Assessment
- • Fresh Reads

You Are Here!
Unit 6 Week 3

This Week's Reading Selections

Main Selection
Genre: **Photo Essay**

Paired Selection
Genre: **Palindromes**

Decodable Readers

Leveled Readers

ELL and ELD Readers

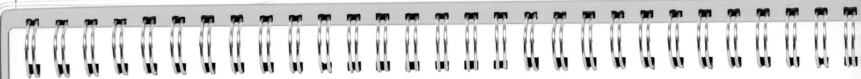

	Build Concepts	Phonics	Comprehension
Whole Group	 Let's Talk About pp. 430–431	 Phonics Skill Lesson pp. 432–433 / Decodable Readers / Sound-Spelling Cards	 Envision It! Skills/ Strategies / Comprehension Skill Lesson pp. 434–435
Go Digital	• Concept Talk Video	• Interactive Sound-Spelling Cards • Decodable eReaders	• Envision It! Animations • eSelections
Small Group and Independent Practice	 Talking Walls pp. 438–451 / ELL and ELD Readers Leveled Readers / Decodable Readers	 Decodable Readers / Practice Station Flip Chart	Talking Walls pp. 438–451 / ELL and ELD Readers / Leveled Readers Envision It! Skills/ Strategies / Reader's and Writer's Notebook / Practice Station Flip Chart
Go Digital	• eReaders • eSelections • Decodable eReaders	• Letter Tile Drag and Drop • Decodable eReaders	• Envision It! Animations • eSelection • eReaders
Customize Literacy	• Leveled Readers • Decodable Readers	• Decodable Readers	• Envision It! Skills and Strategies Handbook • Leveled Readers
Go Digital	• Concept Talk Video • Decodable eReaders • eReaders	• Decodable eReaders	• Envision It! Animations • eReaders • Decodable eReaders

Vocabulary

Envision It!
Vocabulary
Cards

Vocabulary Skill Lesson
pp. 436–437

- Envision It! Vocabulary Cards
- Vocabulary Activities

Envision It!
Vocabulary
Cards

Talking Walls
pp. 438–451

Practice Station
Flip Chart

Words!

Reader's
and Writer's
Notebook

- Envision It! Vocabulary Cards
- Vocabulary Activities
- eSelection

- Envision It! Vocabulary Cards

- Vocabulary Activities

Fluency

Let's Learn It!
pp. 458–459

Decodable and Leveled
Readers

- eSelection
- Decodable eReaders
- eReaders

Talking Walls
pp. 438–451

Practice Station
Flip Chart

Leveled
Readers

ELL and ELD
Readers

- eSelection
- eReaders

- Leveled Readers
- Decodable Readers

- eReaders
- Decodable eReaders

Conventions and Writing

Let's Write It!
pp. 454–455

Decodable
Readers

- Grammar Jammer

Reader's
and Writer's
Notebook

Talking Walls
pp. 438–451

Practice Station
Flip Chart

- Grammar Jammer

- Reader's and Writer's Notebook

- Grammar Jammer

You Are Here! Unit 6 Week 3

My 5-Day Planner for Reading Street!

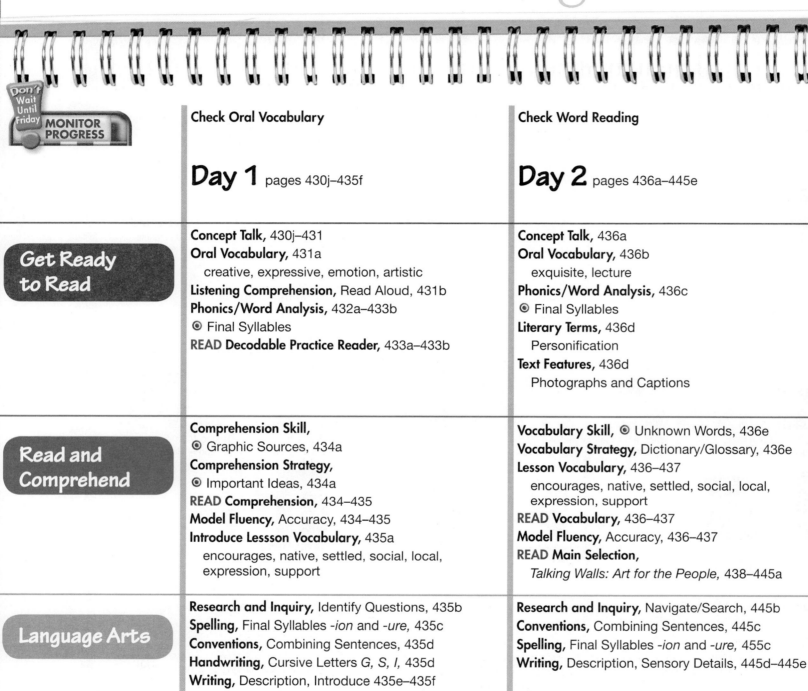

MONITOR PROGRESS

	Check Oral Vocabulary **Day 1** pages 430j–435f	Check Word Reading **Day 2** pages 436a–445e

Get Ready to Read	**Concept Talk,** 430j–431
	Oral Vocabulary, 431a
	  creative, expressive, emotion, artistic
	Listening Comprehension, Read Aloud, 431b
	Phonics/Word Analysis, 432a–433b
	◉ Final Syllables
	READ Decodable Practice Reader, 433a–433b
		Concept Talk, 436a
		Oral Vocabulary, 436b
		  exquisite, lecture
		Phonics/Word Analysis, 436c
		◉ Final Syllables
		Literary Terms, 436d
		  Personification
		Text Features, 436d
		  Photographs and Captions

Read and Comprehend	**Comprehension Skill,**
	◉ Graphic Sources, 434a
	Comprehension Strategy,
	◉ Important Ideas, 434a
	READ Comprehension, 434–435
	Model Fluency, Accuracy, 434–435
	Introduce Lessson Vocabulary, 435a
	  encourages, native, settled, social, local, expression, support
		Vocabulary Skill, ◉ Unknown Words, 436e
		Vocabulary Strategy, Dictionary/Glossary, 436e
		Lesson Vocabulary, 436–437
		  encourages, native, settled, social, local, expression, support
		READ Vocabulary, 436–437
		Model Fluency, Accuracy, 436–437
		READ Main Selection,
		  Talking Walls: Art for the People, 438–445a

Language Arts	**Research and Inquiry,** Identify Questions, 435b **Spelling,** Final Syllables *-ion* and *-ure,* 435c **Conventions,** Combining Sentences, 435d **Handwriting,** Cursive Letters *G, S, I,* 435d **Writing,** Description, Introduce 435e–435f	**Research and Inquiry,** Navigate/Search, 445b **Conventions,** Combining Sentences, 445c **Spelling,** Final Syllables *-ion* and *-ure,* 455c **Writing,** Description, Sensory Details, 445d–445e

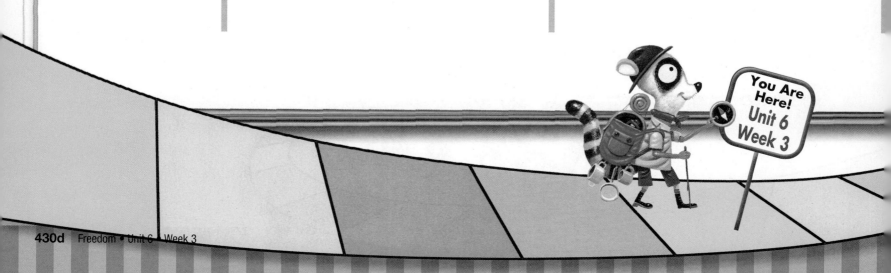

You Are Here! Unit 6 Week 3

Check Retelling	Check Fluency	Check Oral Vocabulary
Day 3 pages 446a–455c	**Day 4** pages 456a–459e	**Day 5** pages 459f–459q

Concept Talk, 446a
Oral Vocabulary, 446b
  significant, pause
Phonics/Word Analysis, 446c–446d
◉ Final Syllables
Decodable Story, 446d
Comprehension Check, 446e
Check Retelling, 446f
	Concept Talk, 456a
	Oral Vocabulary, 456b
	  view, lyrics
	Phonics/Word Analysis, 456c–456f
	Review Schwa
	Decodable Story, 456f
	Genre: Palindromes, 456g
		Concept Wrap Up, 459f
		Check Oral Vocabulary, 459g
		  creative, expressive, emotion, artistic, exquisite, lecture, significant, pause, view, lyrics
		Amazing Ideas, 459g
		Review ◉ **Graphic Sources,** 459h
		Review ◉ **Unknown Words,** 459h
		Review ◉ **Final Syllables,** 459i
		Review **Literary Terms,** 459i

READ Main Selection,
  Talking Walls: Art for the People, 446–451a
Retelling, 452–453
Model Fluency, Accuracy, 453b
Research and Study Skills, 453c
  Alphabetical Order
	READ Paired Selection,
	  "The History of Palindromes," 456–457a
	Let's Learn It! 458–459a
	  Fluency: Accuracy
	  Vocabulary: ◉ Unknown Words
	  Media Literacy: Talk Show
		Fluency Assessment, WCPM, 459j–459k
		Comprehension Assessment,
		  ◉ Graphic Sources, 459l–459m

Research and Inquiry, Analyze, 453d **Conventions,** Combining Sentences, 453e **Spelling,** Final Syllables *-ion* and *-ure,* 453e **Let's Write It!** Description, 454–455 **Writing,** Description, Word Choice, 455a–455c	**Research and Inquiry,** Synthesize, 459b **Conventions,** Combining Sentences, 459c **Spelling,** Final Syllables *-ion* and *-ure,* 459c **Writing,** Description, Revising 459d–459e	**Research and Inquiry,** Communicate, 459n **Conventions,** Combining Sentences, 459o **Spelling Test,** Final Syllables *-ion* and *-ure,* 459o **Writing,** Description, Voice, 459p–459q **Quick Write for Fluency,** 459q

Grouping Options for Differentiated Instruction
Turn the page for the small group time lesson plan.

Week 3

Planning Small Group Time on Reading Street!

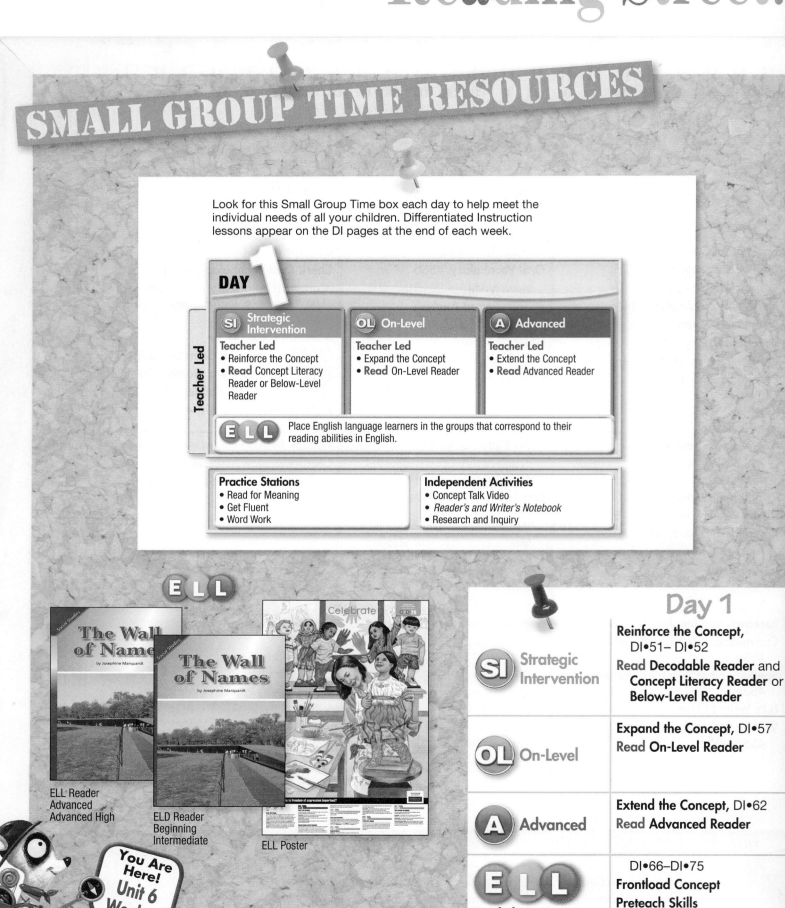

SMALL GROUP TIME RESOURCES

Look for this Small Group Time box each day to help meet the individual needs of all your children. Differentiated Instruction lessons appear on the DI pages at the end of each week.

DAY 1

Teacher Led

SI Strategic Intervention	**OL** On-Level	**A** Advanced
Teacher Led • Reinforce the Concept • **Read** Concept Literacy Reader or Below-Level Reader	**Teacher Led** • Expand the Concept • **Read** On-Level Reader	**Teacher Led** • Extend the Concept • **Read** Advanced Reader

ELL Place English language learners in the groups that correspond to their reading abilities in English.

Practice Stations	**Independent Activities**
• Read for Meaning • Get Fluent • Word Work	• Concept Talk Video • *Reader's and Writer's Notebook* • Research and Inquiry

ELL

Social Studies
The Wall of Names
by Josephine Marquardt

ELL Reader
Advanced
Advanced High

Social Studies
The Wall of Names
by Josephine Marquardt

ELD Reader
Beginning
Intermediate

Celebrate

ELL Poster

You Are Here!
Unit 6
Week 3

		Day 1
SI	Strategic Intervention	Reinforce the Concept, DI•51– DI•52 **Read Decodable Reader** and **Concept Literacy Reader** or **Below-Level Reader**
OL	On-Level	Expand the Concept, DI•57 **Read On-Level Reader**
A	Advanced	Extend the Concept, DI•62 **Read Advanced Reader**
ELL	English Language Learners	DI•66–DI•75 **Frontload Concept** **Preteach Skills** **Writing**

Reading Street
Response to
Intervention Kit

Reading Street
Practice Stations Kit

SI Strategic Intervention

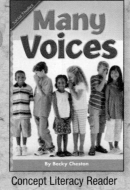

Concept Literacy Reader

OL On-Level

On-Level Reader

A Advanced

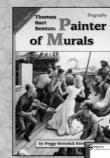

Advanced Reader

Decodable Practice Readers Units 4-6
• Practice phonics skills
• Blending practice
• Reread for fluency

Decodable Reader

Below-Level Reader

Talking Walls pp. 438–451

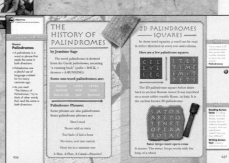

The History of Palindromes pp. 456–457

Week 3

Small Group Weekly Plan

Day 2	Day 3	Day 4	Day 5
Reinforce Comprehension, DI•53 **Revisit Main Selection**	**Reinforce Vocabulary,** DI•54 **Read/Revisit Main Selection**	**Reinforce Comprehension,** Practice Retelling, DI•55 Genre Focus **Read/Revisit Paired Selection**	**Practice Fluency,** DI•56 **Reread Concept Literacy Reader** or **Below-Level Reader**
Expand Comprehension, DI•58 **Revisit Main Selection**	**Expand Vocabulary,** DI•59 **Read/Revisit Main Selection**	**Expand Comprehension,** Practice Retelling, DI•60 Genre Focus **Read/Revisit Paired Selection**	**Practice Fluency,** DI•61 **Reread On-Level Reader**
Extend Comprehension, DI•63 **Revisit Main Selection**	**Extend Vocabulary,** DI•64 **Read/Revisit Main Selection**	**Extend Comprehension,** Genre Focus, DI•65 **Read/Revisit Paired Selection**	**Practice Fluency,** DI•65 **Reread Advanced Reader**
DI•66–DI•75 **Review Concept/Skills** **Frontload Main Selection** **Practice**	DI•66–DI•75 **Review Concept/Skills** **Reread Main Selection** **Practice**	DI•66–DI•75 **Review Concept** **Read ELL/ELD Readers** **Practice**	DI•66–DI•75 **Review Concept/Skills** **Reread ELL/ELD Reader** **Writing**

Practice Stations for Everyone on Reading Street!

Word Wise
Schwa sound spelled with *a, e, i, o, u,* and *y*

Objectives
• Spell words with schwa sound spelled with *a, e, i, o, u,* and *y*.

Materials
• *Word Wise* Flip Chart Activity 28
• Teacher-made word cards
• paper   • pencils

Differentiated Activities

⬤ Choose five word cards. Write your words in a list. Write sentences using each word. List other words with the *schwa* sound spelled with *a, e, i, o, u,* or *y*.

▲ Choose seven word cards. Write your words in a list. List other words with the *schwa* sound spelled with *a, e, i, o, u,* or *y*, and add them to your list. Write sentences for each of word.

■ Choose nine word cards. Write your words in a list, and write a sentence for each. List other words with the *schwa* sound spelled with *a, e, i, o, u,* or *y*.

Technology
• Online Dictionary

Word Work
Schwa sound spelled with *a, e, i, o, u,* and *y*

Objectives
• Identify and pronounce words with schwa sound spelled with *a, e, i, o, u,* and *y*.

Materials
• *Word Work* Flip Chart Activity 28
• Dictionary
• paper   • pencils

Differentiated Activities

⬤ Find five words in the dictionary with the schwa sound. Write the words in a list. Say each word. Write their pronunciations and circle the schwa.

▲ Find eight words in the dictionary with the schwa sound. Write the words in a list, and say each word. Write their pronunciations and circle the schwa.

■ Find ten words in the dictionary with the schwa sound—four words with the schwa in the first syllable, four in the last syllable, and two in the middle syllable. Write the words in a list, and say each word. Write the pronunciations and circle the schwa.

Technology
• Modeled Pronunciation Audio CD

Words to Know
Antonyms

Objectives
• Identify and define antonyms.

Materials
• *Words to Know* Flip Chart Activity 28
• Teacher-made word cards
• paper   • pencils

Differentiated Activities

⬤ Choose three pairs of word cards that are antonyms. Use the dictionary to check word meaning. Write sentences for each word and its antonym to show the opposite meanings.

▲ Choose five pairs of word cards that are antonyms. Use the dictionary if you need to check word meaning. Write sentences for each word and its antonym.

■ Choose seven pairs of antonym word cards, and write a sentence for each pair to show the opposite meanings. Make a list of other words and their antonyms.

Technology
• Online Dictionary

You Are Here!
Unit 6 Week 3

Let's Write!
Limericks

Objectives
• Write a limerick.

Materials
• *Let's Write!* Flip Chart Activity 28
• paper   • pencils

Differentiated Activities

⬤ Write a funny limerick. Remember that a limerick is a humorous, five-line poem. The first, second, and fifth lines rhyme. The third line rhymes with the fourth line.

△ Write a humorous limerick. Remember a limerick is a funny, five-line poem. The first, second, and fifth lines rhyme. The third line rhymes with the fourth line.

■ Write a funny limerick that rhymes the first, second, and fifth lines. Remember that a limerick also rhymes the third line with the fourth line. Include rebuses, or pictures, for some of the words.

Technology
• Online Graphic Organizers

Read for Meaning
Cause and effect

Objectives
• Identify cause and effect.

Materials
• *Read for Meaning* Flip Chart Activity 28
• Leveled Readers
• paper   • pencils

Differentiated Activities

⬤ Choose a book from those your teacher provided. Think about something that happens in the story. What caused this to happen? Write one sentence telling what happened. Write one sentence telling what caused this to happen.

△ Read one of the books your teacher provided. Make a two-column chart labeled *Cause* and *Effect*. Write about what happens in the *Effects* column. Write about the reason in the *Cause* column.

■ Choose and read a leveled reader. As you read, think about the causes and effects of story events. Make a two-column chart with the headings *Cause* and *Effect*. Fill in your chart with examples each from the story.

Technology
• Leveled Reader Database

Get Fluent
Practice fluent reading

Objectives
• Read aloud with appropriate phrasing.

Materials
• *Get Fluent* Flip Chart Activity 28
• Leveled Readers
• Reading Street Readers CD-ROM

Differentiated Activities

⬤ Work with a partner. Choose a Concept Literacy Reader or Below-Level Reader. Take turns reading a page from the book. Use the reader to practice appropriate phrasing. Provide feedback as needed.

△ Work with a partner. Choose an On-Level Reader. Take turns reading a page from the book. Use the reader to practice appropriate phrasing. Provide feedback as needed.

■ Work with a partner. Choose an Advanced Reader. Take turns reading a page from the book. Use the reader to practice appropriate phrasing. Provide feedback as needed.

Technology
• Leveled Reader Database

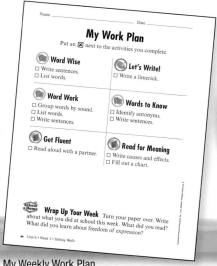

My Weekly Work Plan

Week 3

Objectives
- Introduce the weekly concept.
- Develop oral vocabulary.

Today at a Glance

Oral Vocabulary
creative, expressive, emotion, artistic

Phonics/Word Analysis
◉ Final syllables

Comprehension
◉ Graphic sources
◉ Important ideas

Reading
"Ancient Cave Murals"

Fluency
Accuracy

Lesson Vocabulary
Tested Vocabulary

Research and Inquiry
Identify questions

Spelling
Final syllables *-ion, -ure*

Conventions
Combining sentences

Handwriting
Cursive letters *G, S,* and *I*

Writing
Description

Concept Talk

Question of the Week

Why is freedom of expression important?

Introduce the concept

To further explore the unit concept of Freedom, this week students will read, write, and talk about why freedom of expression is important. Write the Question of the Week on the board.

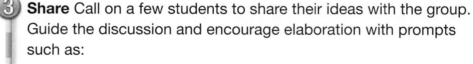

ROUTINE — Activate Prior Knowledge — Team Talk

1. **Think** Have students think about why freedom of expression is important to them.
2. **Pair** Have pairs of students discuss the Question of the Week.
3. **Share** Call on a few students to share their ideas with the group. Guide the discussion and encourage elaboration with prompts such as:
   - Why are basic rights such as freedom of speech important in your life?
   - How would you feel if you could not freely express your opinions or beliefs?

Routines Flip Chart

Anchored Talk

Develop oral vocabulary

Have students turn to pp. 430–431 in their Student Editions. Look at each of the photos. Then, use the prompts to guide discussion and create the *Why is freedom of expression important?* concept map. Remind students to ask and answer questions with appropriate detail.

- Why is it important for the boy to be able to speak in front of his class? **(Freedom of speech is important so the boy can share his ideas.)** Freedom of expression allows us to *share ideas publicly.* Let's add this to our concept map.

- What emotion are the children in the top photo on pages 430–431 expressing? **(enthusiasm/joy)** Freedom of expression allows us to *express our feelings.* Let's add this to the concept map.

Objectives
• Listen closely when someone speaks, ask questions about the topic he or she is talking about, and comment about the topic. • speak clearly and to the point while making eye contact, changing how fast, loud, and clearly you speak to communicate your ideas.

Oral Vocabulary

Let's **Talk** About

Freedom of Expression
• Ask what people can gain from freedom of expression.
• Share ideas about how to express ideas or feelings constructively.
• Pose and answer questions about how to best convey a message.

READING STREET ONLINE
CONCEPT TALK VIDEO
www.ReadingStreet.com

430

431

Student Edition pp. 430–431

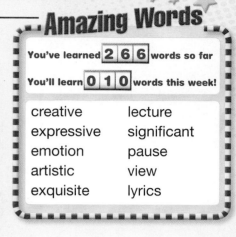

Amazing Words

You've learned **2 6 6** words so far
You'll learn **0 1 0** words this week!

creative	lecture
expressive	significant
emotion	pause
artistic	view
exquisite	lyrics

 **Writing on Demand**

Writing Fluency
Ask students to respond to the photos on pp. 430–431 by writing as well as they can and as much as they can about why freedom of expression is important.

• Which photos show artistic expression? (the photos of the girls singing and playing the piano and the boy reading his writing) Let's add *Artistic expression* to our concept map.

• After discussing the photos, ask: Why is freedom of expression important?

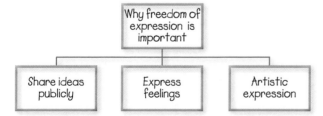

Connect to reading Tell students that this week they will be reading about why freedom of expression is important. Throughout the week, encourage students to add concept related words to this week's concept map.

ELL **Preteach Concepts** Use the Day 1 instructions on ELL Poster 28 to assess and build background knowledge, develop concepts, and build oral vocabulary.

English Language Learners
ELL support Additional ELL support and modified instruction is provided in the *ELL Handbook* and in the ELL support sessons on pp. 66–75.

Listening comprehension
English learners will benefit from additional visual support to understand the key terms in the concept map. Use the pictures on pp. 430–431 to scaffold understanding.

Frontload for Read Aloud Use the modified Read Aloud on p. DI•69 of the *ELL support lessons* to prepare students to listen to "Toothpicks, Bottles, Tin, and Rocks" (p. 429b).

 **ELL** Poster 28

Objectives
• Develop listening comprehension.
• Build oral vocabulary.

Check Oral Vocabulary
SUCCESS PREDICTOR

Oral Vocabulary
Amazing Words

Introduce Amazing Words

"Toothpicks, Bottles, Tin, and Rocks" on p. 431b is about artistic expression. Tell students to listen for this week's Amazing Words—*creative, expressive, emotion,* and *artistic*—as you read.

Model fluency

As you read "Toothpicks, Bottles, Tin, and Rocks," model accuracy with smooth, fluent reading.

Amazing Words Oral Vocabulary Routine

creative
expressive
emotion
artistic

Teach Amazing Words

1 Introduce Write the word *creative* on the board. Have students say the word aloud with you. In the story, we learn that the artists have all been *creative* in making their art forms. What does *creative* mean? Supply a student-friendly definition.

2 Demonstrate Have students answer questions to demonstrate understanding. What *creative* material does Wayne Kusy use in his art? Why do artists need to be *creative*?

3 Apply Ask students what elements they might find in a *creative* story.

See pp. OV•3 to teach *expressive, emotion,* and *artistic*.

Routines Flip Chart

Apply Amazing Words

To build oral language, lead the class in a discussion about the Amazing Words' meanings.

MONITOR PROGRESS Check Oral Vocabulary

During discussion, listen for students' use of the Amazing Words.

If... students are unable to use the Amazing Words to discuss the concept,

then... use Oral Vocabulary Routine Card x to demonstrate words in different contexts.

Day 1	Day 2	Day 3	Day 4	Day 5
Check Oral Vocabulary	Check Word Reading	Check Retelling	Check Fluency	Check Oral Vocabulary

Toothpicks, Bottles, Tin, and Rocks

Close your eyes and picture an artist at work. What do you see? Do you see someone brushing paints on a canvas or molding clay? Many artists use paints or clay, but some become very creative with their materials.

Whenever Wayne Kusy sees a toothpick, he thinks of a huge ship. To Wayne, a toothpick is not just a sliver of wood. It's a way for him to express himself.

Wayne has been making model ships out of toothpicks since he was ten years old. He includes tiny details on his ships, such as portholes, stairways, and even lifeboats with teeny oars for rowing. Wayne once used 75,000 toothpicks to build a ten-foot model of the famous ocean liner *Titanic*.

In the art world, Wayne Kusy is known as an outsider artist. That means that he never went to art school. Outsider artists often work with unlikely materials, such as recycled trash, chunks of cardboard, burnt matchsticks, used chewing gum, and hunks of scrap metal.

Tressa Prisbrey, known as "Grandma," spent 25 years turning old bottles into something she calls Bottle Village. For many years, Grandma collected old bottles. She decided to make walls of bottles held together with concrete. Those walls eventually turned into a quirky village with buildings, gardens, shrines, walkways, and even wishing wells. Through the years Grandma added all sorts of other expressive objects to her village, including doll heads, TV screens, and car headlights— all recovered from the garbage dump.

Grandma's Bottle Village has been declared a historical treasure by the United States government. It never made Grandma rich, but that was fine with her. The emotion people felt while walking through her whimsical village was enough for her.

Charlie Lucas is another artist who spends lots of time at the dump. But instead of bottles, Charlie looks for scrap metal. He makes sculptures and statues out of the metal that others have thrown away. That's why people call him the "Tin Man."

Charlie's yard has metal sculptures of enormous birds and prehistoric dinosaurs, and even a big rusty handmade airplane. People from all around the world buy Charlie's art and exhibit his sculptures in museums. But Charlie still says his sculptures are his toys. "If I called them anything else, I wouldn't know what I was talking about," said the Tin Man.

Artists like Wayne, Grandma, and the Tin Man see toothpicks, bottles, and tin in brand-new ways. They use these everyday objects to make artistic creations that amaze us all.

Oral Vocabulary

Success Predictor

Objectives

◎ Use word analysis to recognize words with final syllables (-tion, -ion, -ture, -ive, -ize).

◎ Read words with final syllables (-tion, -ion, -ture, -ive, -ize).

Skills Trace

◎ **Final Syllables**

Introduce U6W3D1

Practice U6W3D3; U6W3D4

Reteach/Review U6W3D5; U6W4D4

Assess/Test Weekly Test U6W3

Benchmark Test U6

Key: U = Unit, W = Week, D = Day

Word Analysis
◉ Final Syllables

> ### ROUTINE Word Parts Strategy
>
> **①** **Connect** Connect today's lesson to previously learned suffixes -y, -ish, -hood, and -ment. Write *childhood* and *babyish.* You already can read words like these. Each is a base word with an ending. Read these words. Today you will learn to read words with final syllables -tion, -ion, -ture, -ive, and -ize.
>
> **②** **Model** Write *collection. Collection* is a three syllable word. I recognize the syllable *-tion.* When I see this word, I break it into parts. Cover the *-tion.* When I cover the *-tion,* I recognize the word collect. Uncover the *-tion.* Then I read the word ending: *-tion.* I put these parts together to read the word collection. Word endings change how a word is used. For example, to collect something is to gather something. *I collect toy cars.* A *collection* is a group of similar objects. *My toy car collection won a prize.*
>
> **③** **Guide practice** Continue the process in step 2. This time have students read the words with you. Identify each final syllable.
>
> | culture | active | realize | adventure | education |
> |---------|--------|---------|-----------|-----------|
> | native | summarize | celebration | direction | expression |
>
> **④** **Review** What do you know about reading words with these final syllables? When you recognize one of these final syllables, break the word into parts, read each part, and then put the parts together to read the whole word.

Routines Flip Chart

Model

Have students turn to p. 432 in their Student Editions. Each word on this page has one of the above final syllables. The first word is *contraction.* I recognize the ending *-tion,* and I recognize the first part: *contrac.* I put the parts together and read the whole word: *contraction.*

Guide practice

For each word in Words I Can Blend, ask for the word parts. Make sure that students identify the final syllables. Then have them read the words.

Corrective feedback

If... students have difficulty reading a word,

then... model reading the parts and then the whole word, and then ask students to read it with you.

Envision It! | Sounds to Know

festive

lotion

syllable -ive

onion

syllable -tion

syllable -ion

furniture

organize

syllable -ture

syllable -ize

READING STREET ONLINE
SOUND-SPELLING CARDS
www.ReadingStreet.com

Phonics

Final Syllables *-tion, -ion, -ture, -ive, -ize*

Words I Can Blend

contrac**tion**
cush**ion**
punc**ture**
fest**ive**
specia**lize**

Sentences I Can Read

1. The word *I'll* is a contraction.
2. The scissors created a puncture mark on the cushion.
3. Party planners specialize in festive occasions.

432

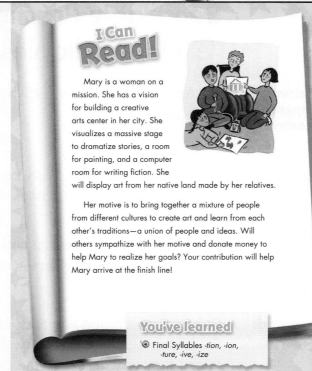

I Can Read!

Mary is a woman on a mission. She has a vision for building a creative arts center in her city. She visualizes a massive stage to dramatize stories, a room for painting, and a computer room for writing fiction. She will display art from her native land made by her relatives.

Her motive is to bring together a mixture of people from different cultures to create art and learn from each other's traditions—a union of people and ideas. Will others sympathize with her motive and donate money to help Mary to realize her goals? Your contribution will help Mary arrive at the finish line!

You've learned

● Final Syllables *-tion, -ion, -ture, -ive, -ize*

433

Student Edition pp. 432–433

Decode and Read

Read words independent of context

After students can successfully combine the words parts to read the words on p. 432 in their Student Editions, point to words in random order and ask students to read them naturally.

Read words in context

Have students read each of the sentences on p. 432. Have them identify words in the sentences that have final syllables *-tion, -ion, -ture, -ive,* and *-ize*.

Team Talk Pair students and have them take turns reading each of the sentences aloud.

Chorally read the I Can Read! passage on p. 433 with the students. Then have them read the passage aloud to themselves.

On their own

For additional practice, use the *Reader's and Writer's Notebook* p. 407.

Reader's and Writer's
Notebook p. 407

Differentiated Instruction

SI Strategic Intervention

Final syllables Have students write the words from the Guide practice activity on p. 432 on strips of paper. Then have students cut off the final syllable at the end of each word. Once the words are cut apart, have students use them like puzzle pieces to put all of the words back together.

Vocabulary Support

You may wish to explain the meaning of these words.

culture the beliefs, practices, and customs of a particular people

native a person born in a certain place or country

adventure an exciting series of events

ELL

English Language Learners

Final syllables The suffix *-tion* has similar forms in other languages, including French (*-tion*), Spanish (*-scion, -sión*), Haitian Creole (*-syon*), and Portuguese (*ção*). For example, the English word *direction* is *direction* in French, *dirección* in Spanish, *direksyon* in Haitian Creole, and *direção* in Portuguese.

Objectives

◎ Apply knowledge of sound-spellings and common syllables to decode unknown multisyllabic words when reading.

• Decode and read words in context and independent of context.

• Practice fluency with oral rereading.

Decodable Practice Reader 28A
Final Syllables

Read words independent of context

Have students turn to p. 145 in *Decodable Practice Readers 3.2*. Have students read each word.

Read high-frequency words

Have students read the high-frequency words *was, the, wasn't, a, would, have, of, to, only, could, gone, there, said, very, wanted,* and *water* on the first page.

Preview Decodable Practice Reader

Have students read the title and preview the story. Tell them that they will read words with final syllables *-tion, -ion, -ture, -ive,* and *-ize*.

Read words in context

Pair students for reading and listen as they read. One student begins. Students read the entire story, switching readers after each page. Partners reread the story. This time the other student begins. Make sure that students are monitoring their accuracy when they decode words.

Decodable Practice Reader 28A

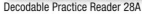

Corrective feedback

If... students have difficulty reading a word, **then...** refer them to the Sound-Spelling Cards to identify the word parts. Have them read the word parts individually and then together to read the word.

- What is the new word?
- Is the new word a word you know?
- Does it make sense in the story?

Check decoding and comprehension

Have students retell the story to include characters, setting, and events. Then have students find words in the story that have final syllables *-tion, -ion, -ture, -ive,* and *-ize.* Students should find *active, vacation, adventures, decision, inventive, picture, station, substitution, visualize,* and *future.*

Reread for Fluency

Have students reread Decodable Practice Reader 28A to develop automaticity decoding words with final syllables *-tion, -ion, -ture, -ive,* and *-ize.*

Oral Rereading

1. **Read** Have students read the entire book orally.
2. **Reread** To achieve optimal fluency, students should reread the text three or four times.
3. **Corrective Feedback** Listen as students read. Provide corrective feedback regarding their fluency and decoding.

Routines Flip Chart

E L L

English Language Learners
Final syllables
Beginning Have students make a set of flashcards with the *-tion, -ion, -ture, -ive,* and *-ize* words from the Decodable Practice Reader: *active, decision, station, future, vacation, inventive, substitution, adventures, picture,* and *visualize.* Have students work with a partner to gain fluency in reading the words by using the flashcards.

Intermediate After reading, have students orally use each of the words with these syllables from the Decodable Practice Reader in a sentence.

Advanced/Advanced High After reading, have students write about a future adventure they would like to have. Remind them to use words with final syllables *-tion, -ion, -ture, -ive,* and *-ize* and high-frequency words from the Decodable Practice Reader in their writing.

Objectives

- ⊙ Use graphic sources to aid comprehension.
- ⊙ Identify important ideas to aid comprehension.
- • Read grade-level text with accuracy.

Skills Trace

⊙ **Graphic Sources**

Introduce U3W3D1; U4W2D1; U6W3D1

Practice U3W3D2; U3W3D3; U4W1D3; U4W2D2; U4W2D3; U6W3D2; U6W3D3

Reteach/Review U3W3D5; U4W2D5; U6W3D5

Assess/Test Weekly Tests U3W3; U4W2; U6W3

Benchmark Tests

Key: U = Unit, W = Week, D = Day

Skill ↔ Strategy

Graphic Sources
Important Ideas

Introduce graphic sources

Graphic sources are ways of showing information in a way you can see. What are some examples of graphics? (charts, photos, diagrams, and maps. You begin reading. How might graphics help you understand the text? (Graphics provide more information.) Have students turn to pp. EI•10–EI•11 in the Student Edition to review graphic sources. Then read "Ancient Cave Murals" with students.

Student Edition p. EI•10–EI•11

Model the skill

Think Aloud Today we are going to read about some murals painted in caves long ago. Which graphic shows what the murals looked like? (the photo of the cave paintings) What information does the color wheel provide? (primary colors red, yellow, and blue, as well as purple, orange, and green)

Guide practice

Have students finish reading "Ancient Cave Murals" on their own. Tell students to ask questions, clarify what's read, look for key words, and find facts and other details as they read. Have students explain the multi-step directions for making green paint.

Strategy check

Important Ideas Remind students that if they have difficulty identifying important ideas in "Ancient Cave Murals," they can look at the graphic sources. Model using graphic sources to find important ideas.

Model the strategy

Envision It!

Think Aloud One important idea in this article is that two or more colors of paint can be mixed together to make a different color. The color wheel helped me to see how the primary colors can be mixed to get many other colors. Have students review the strategy of important ideas on p. EI•19 of the Student Edition.

Student Edition p. EI•19

On their own

Have partners use the color wheel to explain multi-step directions for making orange paint and to follow the directions in art class. Use p. 408 in the *Reader's and Writer's Notebook* for more practice with graphic sources.

Reader's and Writer's Notebook p. 408

Objectives
• Look for and use information found in graphics.
• Find and use information by following and explaining a set of written directions with many steps.

Envision It! | Skill / Strategy

Skill
Graphic Sources

Strategy
Important Ideas

READING STREET ONLINE
ENVISION IT! ANIMATIONS
www.ReadingStreet.com

Comprehension Skill
Graphic Sources

• Graphic sources are ways of showing information visually, or in a way you can see. They provide additional information to the text.

• Charts, photos, diagrams, and maps are all graphic sources.

• Use what you learned about graphic sources as you read "Ancient Cave Murals." Then, using the procedural text and the color wheel, write a paragraph explaining the steps to make purple paint.

Comprehension Strategy
Important Ideas

Active readers look for graphic sources and text features that often present important ideas. An author's most important ideas can be emphasized in graphic sources. Graphic sources help readers better understand the text.

434

Ancient Cave Murals

In 1940, four teenage boys discovered a cave covered with murals of animals. People had painted the murals about 17,000 years ago. Scientists studied the cave paintings and found that the ancient artists made their paint using pigment, which is a powder that gives paint its color. They were able to make very few colors of paint.

There are only three primary colors that, along with black and white, make all other colors. Today we can buy or make any color of paint we want!

How to Make Green Paint
1. Choose yellow and blue paint pigment.
2. Add water or oil and mix it together.
3. Add black or white pigment to make the green darker or lighter.
4. Add more blue or more yellow until you have a green you like!

Skill What colors do you see in the murals?

Strategy What important idea is shown by the color wheel?

*red *yellow *blue *primary color

Skill What colors would you add together to make orange? Try it in art class!

Your Turn!

 Need a Review? See the *Envision It! Handbook* for information about graphic sources and important ideas.

 Ready to Try It? As you read *Talking Walls,* use what you've learned about graphic sources and important ideas to understand the text.

435

Student Edition pp. 434–435

Model Fluency
Accuracy

Model fluent reading

Have students listen as you read paragraph 1 of "Ancient Cave Murals" with accuracy. Explain that you will read each individual word correctly. Tell students that if any of the words were unknown, you would have looked them up before you began reading.

ROUTINE

Oral Rereading

1. **Select a passage** Use paragraph 1 of "Ancient Cave Murals."
2. **Model** Have students listen as you read with accuracy.
3. **Guide practice** Have students read along with you.
4. **On their own** For optimal fluency, students should reread three or four times with accuracy.

Routines Flip Chart

Skill Orange, yellow, black, white, gray
Strategy There are only three primary colors.
Skill Red and yellow.

Differentiated Instruction

SI Strategic Intervention

Graphic sources Have students work with partners to find all of the graphic sources in the passage. Say: Explain what type of information each graphic source contains. Discuss why each one is helpful.

A Advanced

Graphic sources Ask students to look carefully at the photo of the Lascaux cave paintings. Ask: How can you tell these paintings were done in ancient times?

Academic Vocabulary

accuracy reading without errors or mistakes

chart a diagram or table showing information

ELL

English Language Learners
Graphic sources Provide practice in having students use a map to locate cities and countries. Have students answer the question: Why are maps useful when reading about a place?

Objectives
- Activate prior knowledge of words.
- Identify questions for research.

Vocabulary
Tested Vocabulary

Lesson vocabulary

Have students create word rating charts using the categories *Know, Have Seen,* and *Don't Know.*

Word Rating Chart

Word	Know	Have Seen	Don't Know
encourages		✔	
expression			✔
local			
native			
settled	✔		
social		✔	
support			✔

Activate prior knowledge

Read each word to students and have them rate their knowledge of the word by putting a checkmark in one of the three columns on the graphic organizer: *Know* (know and can use); *Have Seen* (have seen or heard the word; don't know meaning); *Don't Know* (don't know the word).

Have students provide sentences for the words they checked in the *Know* column. By the end of the week, have them revise their charts and demonstrate their understanding by using each word in a sentence.

Preteach Academic Vocabulary

 Academic Vocabulary Write the following terms on the board:

chart	photo essay
caption	palindrome
accuracy	personification

Have students share what they know about this week's Academic Vocabulary. Use the students' responses to assess their prior knowledge. Preteach the Academic Vocabulary by providing a student-friendly description, explanation, or example that clarifies the meaning of each term. Then ask students to restate the meaning of the Academic Vocabulary term in their own words.

Research and Inquiry
Identify Questions

Teach

Discuss the Question of the Week: *Why is freedom of expression important?* Tell students they will research why freedom of expression is important. They will write a review or definition to present to the class on Day 5.

Model

Think Aloud I'll start by brainstorming a list of questions about freedom of expression. I know that the First Amendment of the Constitution deals with free speech. Possible related questions could be *What does free speech mean? How can people express themselves non-verbally? What are some symbolic expressions of freedom?*

Guide practice

After students have brainstormed inquiry questions, suggest they list them on a chart. Then explain that tomorrow they will conduct online research using their questions. Help students identify keywords that will guide their search.

On their own

Have students work individually, in pairs, or in small groups to write an inquiry question.

INTERNET GUY
Don Leu

21st Century Skills

Weekly Inquiry Project

Day 1 Identify Questions

Day 2 Navigate/Search

Day 3 Analyze

Day 4 Synthesize

Day 5 Communicate

Academic Vocabulary

chart a sheet of information arranged in lists, pictures, tables, or diagrams

Small Group Time

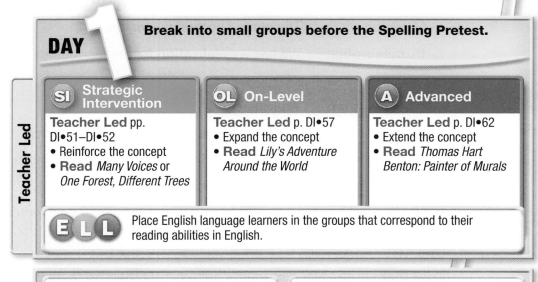

Break into small groups before the Spelling Pretest.

DAY 1

Teacher Led

SI Strategic Intervention

Teacher Led pp. DI•51–DI•52
• Reinforce the concept
• **Read** *Many Voices* or *One Forest, Different Trees*

OL On-Level

Teacher Led p. DI•57
• Expand the concept
• **Read** *Lily's Adventure Around the World*

A Advanced

Teacher Led p. DI•62
• Extend the concept
• **Read** *Thomas Hart Benton: Painter of Murals*

ELL Place English language learners in the groups that correspond to their reading abilities in English.

Practice Stations
• Read for Meaning
• Get Fluent
• Word Work

Independent Activities
• Concept Talk Video
• *Reader's and Writer's Notebook*
• Vocabulary Activities

 **ELL**

English Language Learners
Multilingual vocabulary
Students can apply knowledge of their home languages to acquire new English vocabulary by using Multilingual Vocabulary Lists (*ELL Handbook,* pp. 433–444).

Objectives
- Spell words with common final syllables *-ion* and *-ure*.
- Practice combining sentences.
- Write cursive letters *G*, *S*, and *I*.

Spelling Pretest
Final Syllables *-ion, -ure*

Introduce   Tell students to think of words with the final syllables *-ion* and *-ure*. This week we will spell words with the syllables *-ion* and *-ure*.

Pretest   Use these sentences to administer the spelling pretest. Say each word, read the sentence, and repeat the word.

1. **question**	She had a **question** for the teacher.
2. **creature**	A rabbit is a tiny **creature.**
3. **furniture**	We moved the **furniture** out of the room.
4. **division**	We learned about **division** in math.
5. **collision**	Two cars just had a **collision!**
6. **action**	There was a lot of **action** in the play.
7. **direction**	Do you know what **direction** we are traveling?
8. **culture**	I studied Chinese **culture** and food.
9. **vacation**	Where would you like to travel on **vacation?**
10. **mansion**	The **mansion** had a pool and a tennis court.
11. **fiction**	Where are the **fiction** books in the library?
12. **feature**	What **feature** of the game is your favorite?
13. **sculpture**	The **sculpture** is in the museum garden.
14. **vision**	The nurse checked my **vision.**
15. **celebration**	We had a **celebration** for my graduation.

Challenge words

16. **fascination**	We listened to the story in **fascination.**
17. **legislature**	The **legislature** passed the law yesterday.
18. **manufacture**	At the factory, they **manufacture** light bulbs.
19. **possession**	They took **possession** of the new house.
20. **declaration**	I made a **declaration** that I would be a writer.

Self-correct   After the pretest, you can either display the correctly spelled words or spell them orally. Have students self-correct their pretests by rewriting misspelled words correctly.

On their own   For additional practice, use *Let's Practice It!* p. 381 on the *Teacher Resources DVD-ROM.*

Let's Practice It!!
TR DVD•381

Conventions
Combining Sentences

Teach
Display Grammar Transparency 28, and read aloud the explanation and examples in the box. Explain that repeated words and ideas in sentences are clues that the sentences can be combined.

Grammar Transparency 28, TR DVD

Model
Model combining sentences by completing number 1. Point out that the two sentences have the same subject (*People in France; They*) and so can be combined.

Guide practice
Guide students to complete item 2. Remind them to use the underlined words only once in each new sentence. Record the correct responses on the transparency.

Daily Fix-It
Use Daily Fix-It numbers 1 and 2 in the right margin.

Connect to oral language
Have students read sentences 3–4 on the transparency and combine the pairs of sentences to form grammatically correct sentences.

Handwriting
Cursive Letters *G, S,* and *I*

Model letter formation
Display the capital cursive letters *G, S,* and *I.* Follow the stroke instructions pictured to model letter formation.

Model word spacing
Explain that writing legibly means words are spaced correctly. Model writing this sentence with appropriate spacing between words: *Greg goes sailing with Sue and Iris.* Make sure the letters aren't too light, dark, or jagged.

Guide practice
Have students write these sentences: *Stop singing! I give Giselle eggs. Ina is in India.* Circulate around the room, guiding students.

Daily Fix-It
1. Carlos and Maria created a mural about they're cullture. *(their; culture)*
2. The class helped Carlos and she with the desine. *(her; design)*

ELL

English Language Learners
Options for grammar support: Coordinating conjunctions
Display these pairs of sentences:
I like to play soccer. I enjoy watching baseball.
I want to play soccer. I need to do my homework first.

Read each sentence aloud. Explain to students that each set of sentences can be combined using a conjunction and a comma. Write *and* and *but* on the board. Identify them as conjunctions. Explain that *and* joins two sentences that are similar. *But* joins sentences that are different. Help students use *and* to join the first set of sentences and *but* to join the second set.

Objectives

- Identify the key features of description.
- Understand and use sensory details.

Writing—Description
Introduce

MINI-LESSON

5 Day Planner
Guide to Mini-Lessons

DAY 1	Read Like a Writer
DAY 2	Main Idea and Details
DAY 3	Choosing Descriptive Words
DAY 4	Revising Strategy: Consolidating
DAY 5	Proofread for Voice

MINI-LESSON

Read Like a Writer

■ **Introduce** This week you will write a **description.** Your description will be nonfiction. A description explains what a person, place, or thing is like, so the reader can imagine it.

Prompt	Think about a piece of art that you know from the selection or your own life. Describe it, using sensory details.
Trait	Word choice
Mode	Expository

■ **Examine Model Text** Let's read an example of a nonfiction description that describes a piece of art. Have students read "Description of 'Girl with a Pearl Earring,'" on p. 409 of their *Reader's and Writer's Notebook.*

■ **Key Features** Descriptions **explain what a person, place, or thing is like**. What is being described here? Find the topic of this description and circle it. Point out to students that the topic sentence appears at the beginning of a description and that everything else in the description is a supporting detail that tells the reader something about that topic.

Descriptions help readers visualize something by using vivid words that **appeal to the senses—taste, touch, smell, hearing, and sight.** A description is full of strong details, such as the size, color, shape, smell, and texture of the person, place, or thing. Help students identify and underline sensory details in the model.

Good description contains vivid language. Writing a good description means **choosing your words carefully.** Have students draw a box around other strong details in the model that show careful word choice.

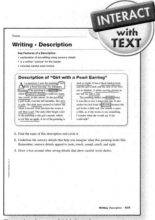

Reader's and Writer's Notebook, p. 409

Review
key features

Review the key features of a description with students. You may want to have students write the key features on index cards to tape to their desktops to refer to as they work on their descriptive passages.

Key Features of a Description

- uses sensory details to explain something
- is a written "picture" for the reader
- includes careful precise word choice

ROUTINE **Quick Write for Fluency**　　Team Talk

1 **Talk** Students choose a person or object in your classroom and describe it to a partner, using sensory details.

2 **Write** Students write their descriptions without identifying the person or object they are describing.

3 **Share** Students read their descriptions out loud to a new partner and have that partner guess what or who it is they are describing.

Routines Flip Chart

Wrap Up Your Day

✔ **Build Concepts** Have students discuss why freedom of expression is important.

✔ **Oral Vocabulary** Have students use the Amazing Words they learned in context sentences.

✔ **Homework** Send home this week's Family Times Newsletter, *Let's Practice It!* pages 382–383 on the *Teacher Resources DVD-ROM.*

Let's Practice It!
TR DVD•382–383

Write Guy
Jeff Anderson

Details, Details

Ask students to notice details in mentor text—but not just any details. Rather than pointing out many details, select a detail that is beyond the obvious. (*It was hot* versus *The sun melted my crayons that sat on the long window sill in the kitchen.*) What evocative description reveals something new to readers? With guidance, students can learn how to include *details that matter* rather than obvious details or simply longer and longer lists of details.

ELL

English Language Learners
Visual learning Invite students to talk about which mural from the selection is their favorite. Help them describe the murals.

Preview DAY 2

Tell students that tomorrow they will read about talking walls.

Objectives
- Expand the weekly concept.
- Develop oral vocabulary.

Today at a Glance

Oral Vocabulary
exquisite, lecture

Phonics/Word Analysis
◉ Final syllables

Literary Terms
Personification

Text Features
Photographs and captions

Lesson Vocabulary
◉ Unknown words

Reading
"Class Art"

Talking Walls: Art for the People

Fluency
Accuracy

Research and Inquiry
Navigate/Search

Spelling
Final syllables *-ion* and *-ure*

Conventions
Combining sentences

Writing
Description

Concept Talk

Question of the Week

Why is freedom of expression important?

Expand the concept

Remind students of the weekly concept question. Tell students that today they will begin reading *Talking Walls: Art for the People*. As they read, encourage students to think about freedom of expression.

Anchored Talk

Develop oral vocabulary

Use the photos on pp. 430–431 and the Read Aloud, "Toothpicks, Bottles, Tin, and Rocks," to talk about the Amazing Words: *emotion, artistic, creative,* and *expressive*. Add the words to the concept map to develop students' knowledge of the topic. Discuss the following questions. Remind students to listen attentively to other students and to answer with appropriate detail. Encourage students to build upon the ideas of others.

- Why is freedom of expression important to someone who is *artistic* or *creative*?
- What *expressive* creations have you made?
- What *emotion* comes to mind when you think of freedom?

Oral Vocabulary
Amazing Words

Amazing Words

creative	lecture
expressive	significant
emotion	pause
artistic	view
exquisite	lyrics

Teach Amazing Words

 Amazing Words Oral Vocabulary Routine

1. **Introduce** Write the Amazing Word *exquisite* on the board. Have students say it aloud with you. Relate *exquisite* to the photographs on pp. 430–431 and *"Toothpicks, Bottles, Tin, and Rocks."* Why might some people say the painting of the American flag is *exquisite*? What makes Wayne Kusy's creations *exquisite*? Have students determine the definition of the word. (*Exquisite* means lovely, beautiful, excellent, or of high quality.)

2. **Demonstrate** Have students answer questions to demonstrate understanding. Which is *exquisite*, an old jacket or a painting of a sunset? What would make a day at school *exquisite*?

3. **Apply** Have students apply their understanding. Make a list of things you think are *exquisite*.

See p. OV•3 to teach *lecture*.

Routines Flip Chart

Apply Amazing Words

As students read "Class Art" on p. 437, have them think about what would make an *exquisite* class mural and about a *lecture* they could prepare to explain the mural.

Connect to reading

Explain that today students will read about muralists who create large paintings on buildings. As they read, students should think about how the Question of the Week and the Amazing Words *exquisite* and *lecture* apply to the story.

ELL **Reinforce Vocabulary** Use the Day 2 instruction on ELL Poster 28 to teach lesson vocabulary and discuss the lesson concept.

ELL Poster 28

Talking Walls: Art for the People **436b**

Objectives

◎ Apply knowledge of letter-sound correspondences and final syllables to decode words in context and independent of context.

Check Word Reading
⚑ SUCCESS PREDICTOR

Word Analysis
 Final Syllables

Review

Review the final syllables *-tion, -ion, -ture, -ive,* and *-ize,* pointing out that these word parts appear at the end of words.

Read words independent of context

Display these words. Have the class read the words. Then point to the words in random order and ask students to read them quickly.

fiction	expansion	signature	comprehension
structure	reflective	reactive	agonize

Corrective feedback

Model reading the word parts and then ask students to read the whole word with you.

Read words in context

Display these sentences. Have the class read the sentences.

Team Talk Have pairs take turns reading the sentences naturally.

They stayed in a **mansion** on their **vacation.**
Since Dad had bad **vision,** he could not see the **sculpture.**
I did not **realize** that Lynn is not a **native** of this area.

Don't Wait Until Friday

MONITOR PROGRESS | **Check Word Reading**

Words with final syllables *-tion, -ion, -ture, -ive, -ize*

Write the following words and have the class read them. Notice which words students miss during the group reading. Call on individuals to read some of the words.

expansion	exhaustion	adventure	active	**Spiral Review** Row 2 reviews compound words.
football	homework	scarecrow	earring	Row 3 contrasts compound words with words with final syllables *-tion, -ion, -ture, -ive,* and *-ize.*
lifeboat	champion	brainstorm	failure	

If... students cannot read words with common syllables at this point,

then... use the Day 1 Word Parts Strategy routine on p. 432a to reteach final syllables *-tion, -ion, -ture, -ive,* and *-ize.* Use words from the Decodable Practice Passages (or Reader). Continue to monitor students' progress using other instructional opportunities during the week. See the Skills Trace on p. 432a.

Day 1	Day 2	Day 3	Day 4	Day 5	
Check Oral Vocabulary	Check Word Reading	Check Retelling	Check Fluency	Check Oral Vocabulary	Success Predictor

Literary Terms
Personification

Teach personification

Tell students that personification is a figure of speech in which human traits are given to animals or objects. Personification is used in fiction and nonfiction to make things seem more real and make writing livelier.

Model personification

 Think Aloud Let's look at "Ancient Cave Murals" on page 435. I don't see an example of personification in this passage. Since the passage is about murals, can you think of a way to personify these paintings? **(Answers will vary.)**

Guide practice

Have students find an example of personification in *Talking Walls: Art for the People.* Ask them to think about the title. Ask them if walls actually talk.

On their own

Have students find examples of personification in other selections of their Student Edition.

Text Features
Photographs and Captions

Teach photographs and captions

Nonfiction text often uses photographs and captions to help readers increase their understanding. The photographs present information visually and the captions give additional information about the photos.

Model the strategy

Think Aloud I see many photographs in *Talking Walls: Art for the People.* If I look on page 442, I see a photograph of a building with a mural painted on it. The caption below the photo tells me the title of the mural. Then the photos on page 443 show a close-up of that mural. These photos help me better understand the description of the mural presented in the text.

Guide practice

Point out another mural photograph and caption in *Talking Walls: Art for the People.* Discuss with students how the photo and caption make the text easier to understand.

On their own

Have students preview *Talking Walls: Art for the People* to find other photographs and captions. Ask students to tell what they learn from each.

Academic Vocabulary

personification a figure of speech in which human traits are given to animals or to inanimate objects or abstract ideas

Word Reading

Success Predictor

Objectives

- ◎ Use a dictionary or glossary to find the meaning, syllabication, and pronunciation of unknown words.
- • Read grade-level text with accuracy.

Vocabulary Strategy for
◌ Unknown Words

Teach unknown words

Envision It!

Tell students that when they encounter an unknown word, they should use a dictionary or glossary to look up the meaning. Explain how a dictionary or glossary can help students understand the meaning, syllabication, and pronunciation of unknown words. Refer students to *Words!* on p. W•14 in the Student Edition for additional practice.

Student Edition W•14

Model the strategy

Think Aloud

Write on the board: *Our town's cultural celebration encourages people to share their customs.* I can't figure out the meaning of *encourages* by using context clues, so I'll look in a dictionary or glossary. When I look up *encourages* in the dictionary, the definition is "increases confidence." Now I understand that the town's cultural celebration increases people's confidence in sharing their customs. Each word in a dictionary or glossary is divided into syllables, and the pronunciation of each word is shown in parentheses right after it. The pronunciation key helps me understand the pronunciations.

Guide practice

Write this sentence on the board: *Volunteers develop art projects in their local neighborhoods.* Have students determine the meaning of *local* using context clues. If they are unable to define the word, have them look up the word in a dictionary or glossary. Have students determine the syllabication and pronunciation of *local*. For additional support, use *Envision It! Pictured Vocabulary Cards* or *Tested Vocabulary Cards.*

On their own

Read "Class Art" on p. 437. Have students use a dictionary or glossary to make a list of definitions for the Words to Know. For additional practice, use *Reader's and Writer's Notebook* p. 410.

Reader's and Writer's Notebook p. 410

Objectives
• Put a series of words in alphabetical order up to the third letter. Use a dictionary or glossary to look up the meanings, syllable patterns, and ways to say words you do not know.

Envision It! Words to Know

encourages

expression

native

local
settled
social
support

READING STREET ONLINE
VOCABULARY ACTIVITIES
www.ReadingStreet.com

436

Vocabulary Strategy for

🔍 Unknown Words

Dictionary/Glossary When you read an unknown word, ask yourself if it's a noun, verb, or adjective. Knowing what part of speech a word is can help you find and understand its meaning. Then use a dictionary or glossary to find the correct meaning and how the word is pronounced.

1. Use the first letter in the word to find it in the dictionary or glossary.

2. Look at the pronunciation key and each syllable to pronounce the word correctly.

3. Read the definitions of the word. Choose a meaning for the correct part of speech.

4. Try your meaning in the sentence. Does it make sense? If not, try another meaning.

Read "Class Art" on page 437. Use a dictionary or glossary to find the meanings and pronunciations of the Words to Know.

Words to Write Reread "Class Art." Sort the Words to Know into three groups: nouns, adjectives, and verbs, according to how each is used in the selection.

Class Art

Ms. Ramsey's students are excited. They are planning to paint a mural on one wall in their classroom. Ms. Ramsey encourages the students to talk about what they will paint on the mural. Everyone has a different idea. Julio's family came to the United States from Mexico. He wants to paint something about his native country. Mary wants to paint something about the community's history. Her family settled here a long, long time ago. Gerrard thinks the mural should show the social life of the people who live in the community. Diana thinks the mural should be more about global, not local, issues. It should show how the community is part of the world. How can the students get all these ideas on one mural? Ms. Ramsey points out that the mural should be an expression of the group's interests and beliefs. She says that with a little planning, the students can paint a mural that will support everyone's ideas.

Your Turn!

 Need a Review? For additional help with unknown words, see *Words!*

▶ **Ready to Try It?** Read *Talking Walls: Art for the People,* on pp. 438–451.

437

Student Edition pp. 436–437

Reread for Fluency
Accuracy

Model fluent reading

Read the first half of "Class Art" aloud, making sure you accurately read each individual word. Tell students that you are reading the passage with accuracy, focusing on understanding what you are reading.

ROUTINE **Oral Rereading**

1. **Select a passage** Read the first half of "Class Art" aloud.

2. **Model** Have students listen as you read with accuracy.

3. **Guide practice** Have students read along with you.

4. **On their own** For optimal fluency, students should reread three or four times with accuracy.

Routines Flip Chart

Lesson Vocabulary

encourages increases confidence

expression act of putting into words or visual medium

local of a certain place

native belonging to you because of your birth

settled made a home in a new place

social about people as a group

support to help or assist; to back

Differentiated Instruction

SI Strategic Intervention

Dictionary Work with a small group of students. Demonstrate how to find the definition of two of the vocabulary words using a dictionary.

 **ELL**

English Language Learners
Build Academic Vocabulary
Use the lesson vocabulary pictured on p. 436 to teach the meanings of *encourages, native,* and *expression*. Call on pairs to write the words on sticky notes and use them to label images of the words on the ELL Poster.

Objectives

• Understand elements of a photo essay.

• Use photographs and captions to preview and predict.

• Set a purpose for reading.

Talking Walls
Art for the People

by Katacha Díaz

Genre A photo essay relies on photographs to help give factual information. What information do you get from the photos in this selection?

438

Question of the Week
Why is freedom of expression important?

439

Student Edition pp. 438–439

Build Background

Discuss murals

Team Talk Have students turn to a partner and discuss the Question of the Week and these questions about murals.

• What murals have you seen painted on buildings?

• Why do you think artists like to paint murals?

• Have you ever painted a mural? Describe it.

Connect to selection

Have students discuss their answers with the class. Possible responses: I saw a sports scene painted on the outside of a gymnasium. People might paint murals to make buildings look better or to tell a story. Our class once painted a mural of our community. We included roads, parks, houses, schools, houses, and other important buildings. For additional opportunities to build background, use the Background Building Audio.

Prereading Strategies

Genre

Tell students that a **photo essay** is a collection of photographs that share a common topic or theme. A photo essay has text to tell about the events and people in the photographs. The essay might have an introduction that explains the topic or purpose of the photo essay. Also, each photo may have a caption that gives additional information about it.

Preview and predict

Have students preview the title, photographs, and photo captions for *Talking Walls: Art for the People.* Ask students to predict what they will discover as they read.

Set purpose

Prior to reading, have students set their own purpose for reading this selection. To help students set a purpose, ask them to think about why freedom of expression is important.

Strategy Response Log

Have students use p. 34 in the *Reader's and Writer's Notebook* to identify the characteristics of a photo essay.

Small Group Time

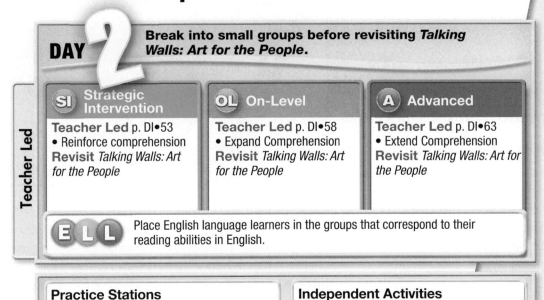

DAY 2

Break into small groups before revisiting *Talking Walls: Art for the People.*

SI Strategic Intervention
Teacher Led p. DI•53
• Reinforce comprehension
Revisit *Talking Walls: Art for the People*

OL On-Level
Teacher Led p. DI•58
• Expand Comprehension
Revisit *Talking Walls: Art for the People*

A Advanced
Teacher Led p. DI•63
• Extend Comprehension
Revisit *Talking Walls: Art for the People*

ELL Place English language learners in the groups that correspond to their reading abilities in English.

Practice Stations
• Words to Know
• Get Fluent
• Word Wise

Independent Activities
• Background Building Audio
• *Reader's and Writer's Notebook*
• Research and Inquiry

Differentiated Instruction

A Advanced
Brainstorm a list of things you might see on public murals.

 **Multidraft Reading**

For **Whole Group** instruction, choose one of the reading options below. For each reading, have students set the purpose indicated.

Option1
Day 2 Read the selection. Use Guide Comprehension to monitor and clairfy understanding.

Day 3 Reread the selection. Use Extend Thinking to develop higher-order thinking skills.

Option 2
Day 2 Read the first half of the selection, using both Guide Comprehension and Extend Thinking instruction.

Day 3 Read the second half of the selection, using both Guide Comprehension and Extend Thinking instruction.

Academic Vocabulary

photo essay a collection of photographs that go together

English Language Learners
Build background To build background, review the selection summary in English (*ELL Handbook,* p. 193). Use the Retelling Cards to provide visual support for the summary.

Objectives

◎ Use a dictionary or glossary to find the meanings of unknown words.

OPTION 1 Guide Comprehension Skills and Strategies

Teach Unknown Words

🔊 **Unknown Words** Have students look at the highlighted words on p. 440. Ask them to look up each word in the glossary in the back of this book or in a dictionary and write its definition. (Possible definitions: *native:* related to the place of one's birth; *expression:* the communication of thoughts or feelings; *settled:* became permanent residents of a place)

Corrective Feedback

If... students are unable to use a glossary or a dictionary to look up unknown words,

then... model using a glossary or a dictionary to find the meaning of unknown words.

Reader's and Writer's Notebook p. 414

Model the Skill

Think Aloud The first word I see is *native.* That is a new word for me. I check the dictionary I keep nearby when I read. My dictionary has *native* on a page with the guide words *nationalism* and *naturalize.*

Immigrants travel to America from all over the world. They leave behind homes and villages in their native countries for the promise of a better life and for the freedom this country has to offer.

The people in America enjoy many different kinds of freedom, including the freedom of artistic expression. Writers, musicians, dancers, and artists are free to speak their minds through their art—in any way they choose. Do you know that some painters use walls as their canvas? These painted walls are called murals and are often painted in public places for all the people of the community to see.

Muralists are asked by a town, school, or business to create a work of art on a wall. Muralists paint many different kinds of murals. Some are inside, some are outside. Some tell the history of a town and everyday life of the people who settled there. Others show special celebrations and community festivals. Still others depict symbols of American freedom and democracy at work. All are great examples of artistic expression at its best.

"Community of Music," Long Beach, California ▶

440

Student Edition pp. 440–441

OPTION 2 Extend Thinking Think Critically

Higher-Order Thinking Skills

🔊 **Unknown Words • Analysis** How can context clues help you figure out the meaning of the word *artistic* on page 440, paragraph 2? Use a dictionary to check your response. Possible response: The author is talking about artists speaking their minds through art. When I look in a dictionary it says *artistic* means "typical of art or artists."

Review **Fact and Opinion • Analysis** Find one statement of opinion from the last paragraph on page 440. How do you know it is an opinion? Possible response: The sentence *All are great examples of artistic expression at its best* is the author's judgment or feeling that the murals are great examples of artistic expression. It can't be proved true or false.

The definition given that fits the context of the sentence is "related to the place of one's birth."

441

Main Idea and Details • Synthesis What is the main idea of the last paragraph on page 440? What details or facts support that idea? Possible response: Main idea: Muralists paint many different kinds of murals. Supporting details: Some are inside, some are outside. Some tell the history of a town and everyday life of the people who settled there. Others show special celebrations and community festivals.

On Their Own

Have students reread pp. 440–441 and use classroom dictionaries to check the meaning of other unknown words. For additional practice with unknown words, see *Reader's and Writer's Notebook* p. 414.

Differentiated Instruction

 Strategic Intervention

Context clues Remind students that in addition to finding the meanings of unknown words by using a dictionary or a glossary, context clues also can help readers figure out a new word. Have students discuss which context clues can help them figure out the meaning of *immigrants* in paragraph 1 on p. 440.

A **Advanced**

Critical thinking Remind students that some artists use walls as their canvas. Have students discuss what kinds of artists would probably like to have their murals publicly displayed. Then have students answer the question: Would you like to be a famous muralist? Why or why not?

Connect to Social Studies

Murals often bring members of a community together. What kind of mural would you expect to see in your community?

ELL

English Language Learners
Activate prior knowledge Begin a word web with the word *mural* in the center. Have students activate their prior knowledge by adding related words to the word web. Record students' answers on the web, adding to it as they read the selection.

Objectives
◎ Understand and use graphic sources to aid comprehension.

OPTION 1 Skills and Strategies, continued

Teach Graphic Sources

🔊 **Graphic Sources** Have students look at the photograph on p. 442 and read the caption. Then ask students how the photograph and caption help them better understand the text in the first paragraph.

Corrective Feedback

If... students are unable to explain how the photograph and caption aid to their understanding of the text, **then...** model how to use a graphic source.

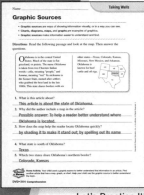

Let's Practice It!
TR DVD•384

Model the Skill

Think Aloud I know that a graphic source is a way of showing information visually. Photos and captions are examples of graphic sources. As I read I can ask myself how the photos and captions help me understand the text.

Immigrant

On the walls of a meat market in Los Angeles is a mural about immigrants painted by Hector Ponce. It tells the history of the people who live in the Pico and Hoover neighborhood. This mural, titled "Immigrant," shows the Statue of Liberty just beyond reach and Latin American immigrants working hard to provide for their families. Do you see a woman with young children, a man selling bags of oranges, a seamstress, and a man looking for cans to recycle?

Hector Ponce, the artist, came from El Salvador more than 15 years ago. He says, "My mural shows what's in the hearts of many people who come to this country looking for a better life."

▲ "Immigrant," Los Angeles, California ▶

442

Student Edition pp. 442–443

OPTION 2 Think Critically, continued

Higher-Order Thinking Skills

🔊 **Graphic Sources • Evaluation** This photo essay contains pictures of the murals the artist painted, but no photographs of the actual artists. Would it be better if the artists' photographs were also included in the text? Possible response: Yes, it would make the story more interesting to see actual photographs of the artists named in the text.

Compare and Contrast • Evaluation If you were going to paint a mural of your own neighborhood, how would it compare to Hector Ponce's mural "Immigrant"? Possible response: My mural would also show various people who live in my neighborhood but they would probably be doing very different things than the people shown in "Immigrant."

Objectives

◎ Understand and use graphic sources to aid comprehension.

OPTION 1 Skills and Strategies, continued

Teach Graphic Sources

Graphic Sources Have students look at the photograph on p. 442 and read the caption. Then ask students how the photograph and caption help them better understand the text in the first paragraph.

Corrective Feedback

If... students are unable to explain how the photograph and caption aid to their understanding of the text, **then...** model how to use a graphic source.

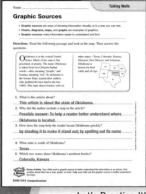

Let's Practice It!
TR DVD•384

Model the Skill

Think Aloud I know that a graphic source is a way of showing information visually. Photos and captions are examples of graphic sources. As I read I can ask myself how the photos and captions help me understand the text.

Immigrant

On the walls of a meat market in Los Angeles is a mural about immigrants painted by Hector Ponce. It tells the history of the people who live in the Pico and Hoover neighborhood. This mural, titled "Immigrant," shows the Statue of Liberty just beyond reach and Latin American immigrants working hard to provide for their families. Do you see a woman with young children, a man selling bags of oranges, a seamstress, and a man looking for cans to recycle?

Hector Ponce, the artist, came from El Salvador more than 15 years ago. He says, "My mural shows what's in the hearts of many people who come to this country looking for a better life."

▲ "Immigrant," Los Angeles, California ▶

442

Student Edition pp. 442–443

OPTION 2 Think Critically, continued

Higher-Order Thinking Skills

Graphic Sources • Evaluation This photo essay contains pictures of the murals the artist painted, but no photographs of the actual artists. Would it be better if the artists' photographs were also included in the text? Possible response: Yes, it would make the story more interesting to see actual photographs of the artists named in the text.

Compare and Contrast • Evaluation If you were going to paint a mural of your own neighborhood, how would it compare to Hector Ponce's mural "Immigrant"? Possible response: My mural would also show various people who live in my neighborhood but they would probably be doing very different things than the people shown in "Immigrant."

The definition given that fits the context of the sentence is "related to the place of one's birth."

On Their Own
Have students reread pp. 440–441 and use classroom dictionaries to check the meaning of other unknown words. For additional practice with unknown words, see *Reader's and Writer's Notebook* p. 414.

441

Main Idea and Details • Synthesis What is the main idea of the last paragraph on page 440? What details or facts support that idea? Possible response: Main idea: Muralists paint many different kinds of murals. Supporting details: Some are inside, some are outside. Some tell the history of a town and everyday life of the people who settled there. Others show special celebrations and community festivals.

Differentiated Instruction

 Strategic Intervention
Context clues Remind students that in addition to finding the meanings of unknown words by using a dictionary or a glossary, context clues also can help readers figure out a new word. Have students discuss which context clues can help them figure out the meaning of *immigrants* in paragraph 1 on p. 440.

A Advanced
Critical thinking Remind students that some artists use walls as their canvas. Have students discuss what kinds of artists would probably like to have their murals publicly displayed. Then have students answer the question: Would you like to be a famous muralist? Why or why not?

Connect to Social Studies

Murals often bring members of a community together. What kind of mural would you expect to see in your community?

 ELL

English Language Learners
Activate prior knowledge Begin a word web with the word *mural* in the center. Have students activate their prior knowledge by adding related words to the word web. Record students' answers on the web, adding to it as they read the selection.

Objectives

◎ Use a dictionary or glossary to find the meanings of unknown words.

Reader's and Writer's
Notebook p. 414

OPTION 1 Guide Comprehension Skills and Strategies

Teach Unknown Words

👁 **Unknown Words** Have students look at the highlighted words on p. 440. Ask them to look up each word in the glossary in the back of this book or in a dictionary and write its definition. (Possible definitions: *native:* related to the place of one's birth; *expression:* the communication of thoughts or feelings; *settled:* became permanent residents of a place)

Corrective Feedback

If... students are unable to use a glossary or a dictionary to look up unknown words,

then... model using a glossary or a dictionary to find the meaning of unknown words.

Model the Skill

Think Aloud The first word I see is *native.* That is a new word for me. I check the dictionary I keep nearby when I read. My dictionary has *native* on a page with the guide words *nationalism* and *naturalize.*

> Immigrants travel to America from all over the world. They leave behind homes and villages in their native countries for the promise of a better life and for the freedom this country has to offer.
>
> The people in America enjoy many different kinds of freedom, including the freedom of artistic expression. Writers, musicians, dancers, and artists are free to speak their minds through their art—in any way they choose. Do you know that some painters use walls as their canvas? These painted walls are called murals and are often painted in public places for all the people of the community to see.
>
> Muralists are asked by a town, school, or business to create a work of art on a wall. Muralists paint many different kinds of murals. Some are inside, some are outside. Some tell the history of a town and everyday life of the people who settled there. Others show special celebrations and community festivals. Still others depict symbols of American freedom and democracy at work. All are great examples of artistic expression at its best.

"Community of Music," Long Beach, California ▶

440

Student Edition pp. 440–441

OPTION 2 Extend Thinking Think Critically

Higher-Order Thinking Skills

👁 **Unknown Words • Analysis** How can context clues help you figure out the meaning of the word *artistic* on page 440, paragraph 2? Use a dictionary to check your response. Possible response: The author is talking about artists speaking their minds through art. When I look in a dictionary it says *artistic* means "typical of art or artists."

Review Fact and Opinion • Analysis Find one statement of opinion from the last paragraph on page 440. How do you know it is an opinion? Possible response: The sentence *All are great examples of artistic expression at its best* is the author's judgment or feeling that the murals are great examples of artistic expression. It can't be proved true or false.

Prereading Strategies

Genre

Tell students that a **photo essay** is a collection of photographs that share a common topic or theme. A photo essay has text to tell about the events and people in the photographs. The essay might have an introduction that explains the topic or purpose of the photo essay. Also, each photo may have a caption that gives additional information about it.

Preview and predict

Have students preview the title, photographs, and photo captions for *Talking Walls: Art for the People.* Ask students to predict what they will discover as they read.

Set purpose

Prior to reading, have students set their own purpose for reading this selection. To help students set a purpose, ask them to think about why freedom of expression is important.

Strategy Response Log

Have students use p. 34 in the *Reader's and Writer's Notebook* to identify the characteristics of a photo essay.

Small Group Time

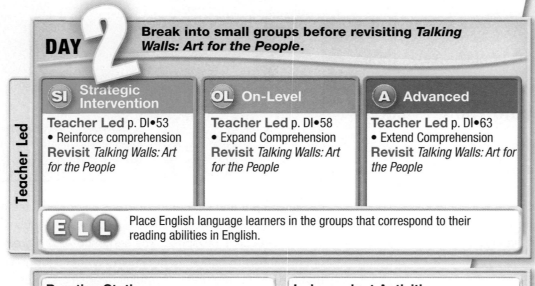

DAY 2 Break into small groups before revisiting *Talking Walls: Art for the People.*

Teacher Led

SI Strategic Intervention	OL On-Level	A Advanced
Teacher Led p. DI•53 • Reinforce comprehension **Revisit** *Talking Walls: Art for the People*	**Teacher Led** p. DI•58 • Expand Comprehension **Revisit** *Talking Walls: Art for the People*	**Teacher Led** p. DI•63 • Extend Comprehension **Revisit** *Talking Walls: Art for the People*

ELL Place English language learners in the groups that correspond to their reading abilities in English.

Practice Stations
• Words to Know
• Get Fluent
• Word Wise

Independent Activities
• Background Building Audio
• *Reader's and Writer's Notebook*
• Research and Inquiry

Differentiated Instruction

A **Advanced**

Brainstorm a list of things you might see on public murals.

 **Multidraft Reading**

For **Whole Group** instruction, choose one of the reading options below. For each reading, have students set the purpose indicated.

Option1
Day 2 Read the selection. Use Guide Comprehension to monitor and clairfy understanding.

Day 3 Reread the selection. Use Extend Thinking to develop higher-order thinking skills.

Option 2
Day 2 Read the first half of the selection, using both Guide Comprehension and Extend Thinking instruction.

Day 3 Read the second half of the selection, using both Guide Comprehension and Extend Thinking instruction.

Academic Vocabulary

photo essay a collection of photographs that go together

ELL

English Language Learners
Build background To build background, review the selection summary in English (*ELL Handbook,* p. 193). Use the Retelling Cards to provide visual support for the summary.

The photograph and caption on p. 442 help me see where this mural appears—on the side of a meat market in Los Angeles.

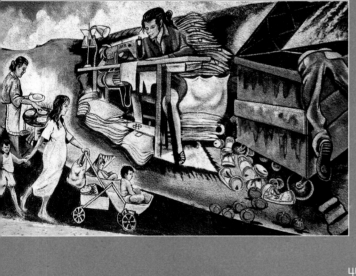

443

Draw Conclusions • Analysis Why does the photo essay include information about where muralist Hector Ponce was from? **Possible response: Knowing that Hector Ponce came to the United States from El Salvador means that he knows what it is like to be an immigrant.**

On Their Own

Have students look at the photographs on p. 443. Ask them to explain how these pictures help them understand what the author means when he says, *My mural shows what's in the hearts of many people who come to this country looking for a better life.* For additional practice, see *Let's Practice It!* page 384 on the *Teacher Resources DVD-ROM.*

Differentiated Instruction

 Strategic Intervention

Summarize Have students work in small groups and summarize the text on p. 442. Have the groups share their summaries with each other.

Connect to Social Studies

Artists often create images that reflect their cultures. They can depict the world around them or paint scenes from their history or mythology. Hector Ponce uses art to show the everyday lives of immigrants. Have students look at the murals on pp. 442–443. Ask why they think Hector Ponce painted these murals.

ELL

English Language Learners
Vocabulary: Idioms Focus students' attention on the expression "what's in the hearts" on p. 442. This is an idiom that means "what people feel." Ask students to share "what's in their hearts" when they think about the freedoms they have today.

Graphic sources Have students look closely at the illustrations on p. 443. What details in the pictures support the text *Latin American immigrants working hard to provide for their families*? Have students share their answers. (man selling oranges, seamstress working, man recycling cans)

Objectives
- Identify facts and opinions to improve comprehension.

Teach Fact and Opinion

Review **Fact and Opinion** Write the following sentences on the board and have students determine which of the statements is a fact, and which is an opinion: *Before artist Joshua Sarantitis creates a mural, he talks with the people of the community.* (fact) *It's a good thing Joshua Sarantitus talks with members of the community.* (opinion)

Corrective Feedback

If... students are unable to distinguish between statements of fact and statements of opinion,
then... model guiding students in identifying facts and opinions.

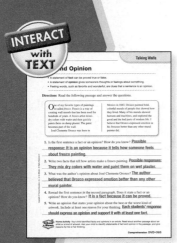

Let's Practice It!
TR DVD•385

Model the Skill

Think Aloud How could I check or verify whether the first sentence is a fact? (ask the artist) What can I conclude from this fact? (that the murals reflect real life)

Reach High and You Will Go Far

Before artist Joshua Sarantitis creates a mural, he talks with the people of the community. He listens to the stories about the neighborhood. He interprets their stories by making sketches, and then he makes plans for the painting of the mural.

Over the years, Sarantitis has created many public murals across America, including "Reach High and You Will Go Far." This mural honors the hopes and dreams of the many children who live in a downtown neighborhood in Philadelphia. The painting is beautiful. It shows a young girl with her arms held high. Her hands and fingers become a tree rising over the building. The artist fashioned the top of the tree as a billboard extending above the roof to show how people can grow and change. The mural encourages children to reach for the future through education.

444

Student Edition pp. 444–445

OPTION 2 Think Critically, continued

Higher-Order Thinking Skills

Review **Fact and Opinion • Analysis** Find one more statement of opinion on page 444. How do you know it is an opinion? Possible response: *The painting is beautiful.* It is the author's feeling or judgment that the painting is beautiful. It can't be proved true or false.

Sequence • Analysis Why do you think Joshua Sarantitis follows the steps he does to create a mural? Possible response: Since he wants his murals to reflect real life in the community, he needs to first talk with people to come up with ideas. It makes sense that he sketches his ideas before he actually paints the mural.

Visualize • Evaluation What do you think about the description of "Reach High and You Will Go Far? on page 444? When you look at the mural on page 445, is it what you visualized the mural to be? Possible response: Yes, I knew it would be of a young girl with her hands held high. I also knew that her fingers would become a tree at the top of the mural.

What words in the second sentence tell me that this might be an opinion? *(it's a good thing)* A statement of opinion is someone's judgment, belief, or way of thinking about something. It cannot be proved true or false.

"Reach High and You Will Go Far," Philadelphia, Pennsylvania

445

On Their Own

Have students reread p. 444 to find more statements of fact about Joshua Sarantitis's murals. For additional practice with fact and opinion, see *Let's Practice It!* page 385 on the *Teacher Resources DVD-ROM.*

Background Knowledge • Evaluation • Text to Self The text states that *The mural encourages children to reach for the future through education.* Does the mural personally encourage you to do this? Why or why not? Possible response: Yes, I find the mural very encouraging and I recognize the importance of education to my future.

Check Predictions Have students look back at the predictions they made earlier and discuss whether they were accurate. Then have students preview the rest of the selection and either adjust their predictions accordingly or make new predictions.

Differentiated Instruction

 Strategic Intervention

Fact and opinion Arrange students in small groups. Have groups write statements of fact and opinion about the mural "Reach High and You Will Go Far." Groups can share their statements. Other groups can decide which statements are fact and which are opinions.

A Advanced

Fact and opinion Have students find examples of other murals that inspire children. Ask them to write a fact and an opinion about each mural.

ELL

English Language Learners
Vocabulary: Compound words Have students find a compound word on p. 442 *(neighborhood, downtown, billboard).* In pairs, have students look at one of the sentences with these words. Have students use context clues to determine the meaning of the words. Have students restate the meanings to the class.

 If you want to teach this selection in two sessions, stop here.

Objectives
- Find pertinent information from online sources.
- Correctly combine sentences.
- Practice correctly spelling words with final syllables *ion* and *ure*.

Research and Inquiry
Navigate/Search

Teach

Have students generate a research plan for gathering relevant information about their research questions. Encourage them to search the Internet using their inquiry questions and keywords. Tell them to skim and scan each site for information that helps answer their inquiry question or leads them to specific information that will be useful. Bolded or italicized words may be clues to the kind of information the Web site will provide. Have students look for other features, such as headings, illustrations, captions, or highlighting. Remind students to take notes as they gather information.

Model

Think Aloud When searching for information on the importance of freedom of expression, I found links to the First Amendment. I will scan and bookmark Web sites that contain information on the First Amendment because I know that this amendment deals with freedom of speech.

Guide practice

Have students continue their review of Web sites they identified. Have students weed out any Web sites that are out-of-date or that are not relevant to their inquiry question.

On their own

Have students write down Web addresses, authors, and the dates the Web sites were last updated and create a Works Cited page.

Conventions
Combining Sentences

Teach

One way to learn about compound sentences is to know how to identify them when you read. Write this sentence: My cat likes to play at night, and he is always running and meowing at my feet. Have students break it into two sentences.

Guide practice

Have students identify the compound sentence in the following paragraph:

> **Parents, students, and teachers enjoy art. Teachers provide art materials, and students make creative art projects. Parents come to school and enjoy the art that students create.**

Daily Fix-It

Use Daily Fix-It numbers 3 and 4 in the right margin.

Connect to oral language

Have students identify sentences in *Talking Walls: Art for the People* that can be broken into two simple sentences. (*These painted walls are called murals and are often painted in public places for all the people of the community to see.* p. 440.)

On their own

For additional practice, use the *Reader's and Writer's Notebook* p. 411.

Spelling
Final Syllables *-ion* and *-ure*

Teach

Remind students that their spelling words have the final syllables *-tion, -ion, -ture, -ive,* and *-ize.* Model how to spell those words. The parts in *creature* are *crea* and *ture.* First I write the first syllable, *crea.* Then I write the second syllable, *ture.* Then I spell *creature, c-r-e-a-t-u-r-e.*

Guide practice

Have students write each spelling word and underline the final syllables.

On their own

For additional practice, use the *Reader's and Writer's Notebook* p. 412.

Reader's and Writer's Notebook p. 411

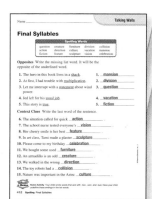

Reader's and Writer's Notebook p. 412

Daily Fix-It

3. The classes paints the mural on a large wall of the shcool. (*paint; school*)

4. We didnt know what great artests we had. (*didn't; artists*)

ELL

English Language Learners
Conventions To provide students with practice on combining sentences, use the modified grammar lessons in the *ELL Handbook* and the Grammar Jammer online at: www.ReadingStreet.com

Language transfer: Clauses
Students may have difficulty recognizing the clauses in a compound sentence. Give them additional practice finding the subject and verb within each independent clause.

Objectives
- Generate ideas to prepare for writing.
- Choose a topic.
- Organize ideas to prepare for writing.
- Practice using sensory details.

Writing—Description
Writer's Craft: Sensory Details

Introduce the prompt

Review the key features of a description. Remind students that a description explains what something is like. A description uses words that appeal to the senses—taste, touch, smell, hearing, and sight. Point out that when describing a piece of art, a writer might use many sensory images that appeal to sight and touch, rather than taste, smell, or hearing.

Writing Prompt

Think about a piece of art that you know from the selection or your own life. Describe it, using sensory details.

Select a topic

 To help me choose a topic, first I'm going to look through the photos in *Talking Walls: Art for the People.* Art often causes our feelings to come to the surface. I'm going to see how these murals make me feel and what details make me feel that way. I'm going to write these details in a chart. **Display a three-column chart.** This mural on p. 441 gives me a magical, mysterious feeling, because of the colors and the way the people look. How does the mural on p. 449 make you feel? **Fill in the descriptions based on student responses.** But my favorite piece of art is a collage my friend Ori made of a cat. It makes me feel really happy. **Have students complete their own charts.**

Gather information

Remind students that they can do research to help them find additional images of artwork. Have students keep this chart, as they will refer to it again tomorrow as they draft.

Name of Art	My Feeling	Sensory Details
"Community of Music"	magical, mysterious	green grass, blue and purple rocks, shadows, straight, tall people
"Dreams of Flight"	light, like I want to move	animals and a plane flying, people swinging and jumping
My friend Ori's collage	happy	bright colors, bottle caps for eyes, glitter, bumpy yarn fur

Corrective feedback

Move around the room as students complete their charts. If students seem to have trouble finding a piece of art that interests them, help them find a print resource or Web site that shows different styles of visual art. Encourage students to choose a piece of art that evokes strong emotion.

MINI-LESSON

Main Idea and Details

■ Knowing your main idea helps you keep your composition focused. When you know your main idea, you can make sure that each one of your details supports that idea. I've decided that my topic will be my friend Ori's cat collage, because I like it so much. I will use a chart to organize the details I will use to describe Ori's collage. Draw a main idea chart, but draw only two boxes for supporting details. In the main idea box, I will write, *My friend Ori made a collage of a cat.*

■ Explain that each supporting detail will be a sensory detail about the collage. I will use the sensory details from my earlier chart to describe Ori's collage. In the first box, I will describe how it looks: *It has bright colors, bottle caps for eyes, glitter, and yarn fur.* In the second box, I will describe how it makes me feel: *It makes me feel happy.*

Have students begin their own chart using the form on p. 413 of their *Reader's and Writer's Notebook.*

ROUTINE — Quick Write for Fluency — Team Talk

1 **Talk** Pairs of students exchange images of the art they will be describing.

2 **Write** Students brainstorm a list of words and phrases that describe their partner's piece of art.

3 **Share** Students read their lists to each other. Make clear that students can use their partner's list to help them write their description.

Routines Flip Chart

Wrap Up Your Day

✔ **Build Concepts** Have students discuss how artists express themselves by painting murals.

✔ **Graphic Sources** How do the photographs help you understand the selection?

✔ **Important Ideas** What important ideas do the murals represent?

Differentiated Instruction

A Advanced

Creative extension Invite students to plan their own mural or to create another work of art that expresses an important idea.

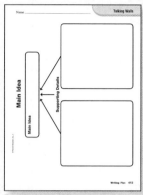

Reader's and Writer's Notebook p. 413

Teacher Tip
Check that each student has written a short, clear topic sentence in the main idea box of the graphic organizer.

Preview DAY 3

Tell students that tomorrow they will read about more interesting murals.

Objectives
- Expand the weekly concept.
- Build oral vocabulary.

Today at a Glance

Oral Vocabulary
significant, pause

Comprehension Check/Retelling
Discuss Questions

Phonics/Word Analysis
◉ Final syllables *-tion, -ion, -ture, -ive, -ize*

Reading
Talking Walls: Art for the People

Think Critically
Retelling

Fluency
Accuracy

Research and Study Skills
Alphabetical order

Research and Inquiry
Analyze

Spelling
Final syllables *-ion* and *-ure*

Conventions
Combining sentences

Writing
Description

Concept Talk

Question of the Week
Why is freedom of expression important?

Expand the concept

Remind students of the weekly concept question. Discuss how the question relates to *Talking Walls: Art for the People.* Tell students that today they will read about some artists. Encourage students to think about the *exquisite* murals they painted.

Anchored Talk

Develop oral vocabulary

Use text features—graphic sources—to review pp. 438–445 of *Talking Walls: Art for the People.* Discuss the Amazing Words *exquisite* and *lecture.* Add these and other concept-related words to the concept map. Use the following questions to develop students' understanding of the concept. Remind students to listen attentively, make pertinent comments, and answer questions with appropriate detail.

- Many of the murals in the story have *exquisite* details and colors. Think about what *exquisite* means. What makes freedom of expression *exquisite*?

- Think about the artists and why they painted the murals they did. If these artists were going to prepare a *lecture* for an art class, what would they say?

Oral Vocabulary
Amazing Words

★ **Amazing Words** ★

emotion	lecture
artistic	significant
creative	pause
expressive	view
exquisite	lyrics

★ **Amazing Words** ★ **Oral Vocabulary Routine**

Teach Amazing Words

1 Introduce Write the word *significant* on the board. Have students say it with you. Yesterday, we read about and looked at photos of some *significant* murals. Have students determine a definition of *significant*. (*Significant* means having importance.)

2 Demonstrate Have students answer questions to demonstrate understanding. How is an artist's personal life *significant* to what they paint? (Many artists paint murals showing where they came from or where they now live.)

3 Apply Have students apply their understanding. What is a synonym for *significant*?

See p. OV•3 to teach *pause*.

Routines Flip Chart

Apply Amazing Words

As students read pp. 446–451 of *Talking Walls: Art for the People*, have them consider how the Amazing Words *significant* and *pause* apply to the artists and murals pictured in the rest of the story.

Connect to reading

Explain that today students will read about murals that show the importance of education and following your dreams. As they read, students should think about how this week's Question of the Week and the Amazing Words *significant* and *pause*, apply to the murals.

ELL Expand Vocabulary Use the Day 3 instruction on ELL Poster 28 to help students expand vocabulary.

ELL Poster 28

Objectives

◎ Read and sort words with final syllables *-tion, -ion, -ture, -ive, -ize.*

◎ Apply knowledge of sound-spellings and syllable patterns to decode unknown words when reading.

• Decode and read words in context and independent of context.

Word Analysis
Sort Words

Model word sorting

Write *-tion, -ion, -ture, -ive,* and *-ize* as heads in a five-column chart. Now we are going to sort words. We'll put words with the syllable *-tion* in the first column. Words with the syllable *-ion* will go in the second column. Words with the syllable *-ture* will go in the third column, words with the syllable *-ive* will go in the fourth column, and words with the syllable *-ize* will go in the last column. I will start. Write *structure* and model how to read it, using the Word Parts Strategy Routine on p. 432a. *Structure* ends with the final syllable *-ure,* so I will write *structure* in the third column. Model reading *expansion* and *subtraction* in the same way.

Guide practice

Use practice words from the activity on p. 432a for the word sort. Point to a word. Have students read the word, identify its parts, and tell where it should be written on the chart.

Corrective feedback

For corrective feedback, model reading each word the same way you read *structure.*

-tion	-ion	-ture	-ive	-ize
subtraction	expansion	structure	active	realize
education	expression	culture	native	
celebration		adventure		
direction				

Fluent Word Reading

Model

Write *motorize.* I recognize the syllable *-ize* at the end. I combine that with the two other syllables *mo/tor* to read the whole word, *motorize.*

Guide practice

Write the words below. Look for word parts you know. When I point to the word, we'll read it together. Allow one second per word part previewing time for the first reading.

mature	civilize	positive	confusion	intervention	nature

On their own

Have students read the list above three or four times, until they can read one word per second.

Decode and Read

Read words independent of context

Have students turn to p. 153 in *Decodable Practice Readers 3.2* and find the first list of words. Each word in this list has the final syllable *-tion, -ion, -ture, -ive,* or *-ize.* Let's read these words. Be sure that students pronounce each final syllable correctly.

Next, have students read the high-frequency words.

Preview Decodable Practice Passage

Have students read the title and preview the story. Tell them that they will read words with final syllables *-tion, -ion, -ture, -ive,* and *-ize.*

Read words in context

Chorally read the story along with the students. Have students identify words in the story with final syllables *-tion, -ion, -ture, -ive,* and *-ize.* Make sure that students are monitoring their accuracy when they decode words.

Team Talk Pair students and have them take turns reading the story aloud to each other. Monitor students as they read to check for proper pronunciation and appropriate pacing.

Decodable Practice Passage 28B

Differentiated Instruction

A Advanced

Sort words Have students choose four words from the word sort activity and write a paragraph about school. Have students trade paragraphs with a partner and identify the words used that have final syllables *-tion, -ion, -ture, -ive,* and *-ize.*

Objectives

◎ Use graphic sources to aid comprehension.

◎ Identify important ideas.

◎ Use a dictionary or glossary to determine the meanings of unknown words.

Comprehension Check

Have students discuss each question with a partner. Ask several pairs to share their responses.

☑ **Genre • Analysis**

Why do you think the author chose to use photos and captions in *Talking Walls: Art for the People*? **Possible response: Having images of the actual murals makes it easier for the readers to visualize the selection.**

☑ **Graphic sources • Evaluation**

How do you think this story would be different if there were no photographs and captions? Would the author's words be enough to tell about the murals? **Possible response: The story would not be as visual. I don't think I would understand it as well.**

☑ **Important ideas • Evaluation**

What do you think are a few of the most important ideas the author wants to share, up until this point in the story? How do you know? **Possible response: Artists paint many different kinds of murals. The murals tell about different things such as about the neighborhoods and history of the people who live there. The illustrations help me realize the most important ideas.**

☑ **Unknown words • Synthesis**

Use what you have learned about murals to define the word *canvas*. Check your definition in a dictionary or glossary. **Possible response: *Canvas* means "something you paint on." I arrived at this definition because the text says muralists use walls as a canvas.**

☑ **Connect text to self**

Muralists are asked by a town, school, or business to paint a mural. Do you think you have the characteristics to be a good muralist? Why or why not? **Responses will vary.**

Strategy Response Log

Have students revisit p. 34 in their *Reader's and Writer's Notebook* to add additional information about photo essays.

INTERACT with TEXT

Check Retelling

Have students retell *Talking Walls: Art for the People.* Ask
students to use details and name specific information in
the graphic sources that helps them retell the text.

**Corrective
feedback**

If... the students leave out important details,
then... have students look back through the illustrations and
photographs in the selection.

Small Group Time

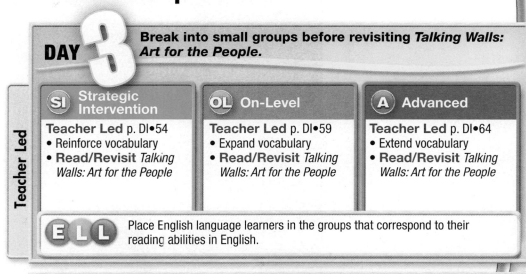

DAY 3 Break into small groups before revisiting *Talking Walls:
Art for the People.*

Teacher Led

SI Strategic Intervention	**OL On-Level**	**A Advanced**
Teacher Led p. DI•54 • Reinforce vocabulary • **Read/Revisit** *Talking Walls: Art for the People*	**Teacher Led** p. DI•59 • Expand vocabulary • **Read/Revisit** *Talking Walls: Art for the People*	**Teacher Led** p. DI•64 • Extend vocabulary • **Read/Revisit** *Talking Walls: Art for the People*

ELL Place English language learners in the groups that correspond to their
reading abilities in English.

Practice Stations
• Let's Write
• Get Fluent
• Word Work

Independent Activities
• AudioText: *Talking Walls: Art for the People*
• *Reader's and Writer's Notebook*
• Research and Inquiry

Objectives

◎ Identify important ideas to aid comprehension.

OPTION 1 Skills and Strategies, continued

Teach Important Ideas

 Important Ideas Ask students to state one important idea from the first paragraph on page 446.

Corrective Feedback

If... students have difficulty stating an important idea,

then... model how to identify the important idea.

Model the Strategy

Think Aloud I know that important ideas are the facts and details that the author most wants me to learn from the text.

Multidraft Reading

If you chose . . .

Option 1 Return to the Extend Thinking instruction starting on p. 440–441.

Option 2 Read pp. 446–451. Use the Guide Comprehension and Extend Thinking instruction.

Student Edition pp. 446–447

OPTION 2 Think Critically, continued

Higher-Order Thinking Skills

 Important Ideas • Analysis How does the page heading "A Shared Hope" support the important ideas on pages 446–447? Possible response: One of the important ideas the author conveys is that people immigrate to the United States because they share a hope for a better life. Also, Paul Botello's mural is called "A Shared Hope."

A Shared Hope

Paul Botello was 8 years old when he began helping his older brother, David, paint murals. Paul loved painting murals and was inspired to become an artist like his brother. When Paul graduated from high school, he went on to college to study art. Today he creates and paints murals, and he teaches art too!

Paul painted a special mural called "A Shared Hope" for an elementary school in Los Angeles, California. Most of the students at Esperanza School are immigrants from Central America. The mural speaks to the schoolchildren. It tells them that education is the key to success.

446

Cause and Effect • Analysis What caused Paul Botello to become an artist? Possible response: As a child, Paul Botello loved painting murals with his brother. That must be why he became an artist.

When I read the first paragraph, I read many details about Paul Botello, but the most important idea the author wants me to know is that he creates and paints murals. What do you think the most important idea is in paragraph 2 on page 446?

On Their Own

Have students find the important ideas in the text on p. 447. Remind them that there can be more than one important idea.

At the top of the mural, a teacher helps guide her students over the building blocks of life. Students are standing at the bottom of the painting holding objects that symbolize their future. Their parents stand behind to help guide and support them. Teachers, students, and parents from the school posed for the artist and his assistants as they created the mural.

"Education, hope, and immigration are my themes," says Paul Botello. "People immigrate to the United States because they hope for a better life. Through education, a better life can be accomplished."

"A Shared Hope," Los Angeles, California

447

Fact and Opinion • Evaluation What is your opinion of Paul Botello? Based on facts you read, would you like to have him as an art teacher? Possible response: Paul is a talented artist. He would be a good art teacher because he cares about art, children, and education.

Differentiated Instruction

Advanced

Important ideas One of Paul Botello's important ideas is that education is the key to success. In small groups, have students discuss this idea and tell whether or not they agree with it.

Connect to Social Studies

One freedom of all Americans is the freedom of speech. Many people think that is our most important right. Discuss the effect of freedom of speech: How does it benefit our country? How does it not benefit our country? Make a list to discuss as a class.

ELL

English Language Learners

Fact and opinion Provide oral practice by having students share facts and opinions about their favorite artists or musicians. Then write these sentences on the board and read them aloud. Have students tell whether each sentence is a fact or an opinion, then support their answers.

- It would be fun to be an art teacher.
- "A Shared Hope" is the name of a mural on a building in Los Angeles.
- It's a good idea to paint murals for children.

DAY 3 Read and Comprehend

Objectives

◎ Use a dictionary or glossary to find the meanings of unknown words.

OPTION 1 Skills and Strategies, continued

Teach Unknown Words

🔊 **Unknown Words** Have students use a dictionary or glossary to determine the meaning of the word *speak* on p. 448, paragraph 3.

Corrective Feedback

If... students are unable to figure out the meaning of *speak*,

then... model using a dictionary or glossary to figure out the meaning of the unknown word.

Model the Skill

Think Aloud Can anyone tell me what we call words like *speak*? (multiple-meaning words) When I look up the word *speak* in a dictionary it gives two meanings: "to talk" and "to express opinions and ideas."

Student Edition pp. 448–449

OPTION 2 Think Critically, continued

Higher-Order Thinking Skills

🔊 **Unknown Words • Synthesis** What is the meaning of the word *inspire* in the last sentence on page 449? Use a dictionary or glossary to check the definition. Then create a sentence of your own using *inspire*. Possible response: encourage; response sentences will vary.

Dreams of Flight

David Botello—the older brother of Paul—loved to paint and dreamed of becoming an artist. When he was in the third grade, he and his art partner, Wayne Healy, painted a mural of a dinosaur in art class. Little did David know that that dinosaur mural was the first of many murals he would paint with Wayne.

Years later, the childhood friends, now both artists, decided to go into business together painting murals. David and Wayne often create and paint murals together, but not always.

David painted a large mural called "Dreams of Flight" at Estrada Courts, a public housing project in Los Angeles. He says, "I've always wanted this mural to speak to the children who see it, and to say, 'Your dreams can come true.'"

ARTIST	LOCATION	TITLE
Hector Ponce	Los Angeles, California	"Immigrant"
Joshua Sarantitis	Philadelphia, Pennsylvania	"Reach High and You Will Go F
Paul Botello	Los Angeles, California	"A Shared Hope"
Allyn Cox	U.S. Capitol, Washington, D.C.	"Declaration of Independence,

448

Compare and Contrast • Analysis How are David Botello's murals different from his brother's murals? Possible response: The people in Paul's work seem more realistic.

Which meaning do you think the author means? (Possible response: "to express opinions and ideas")

On Their Own

Have students use a dictionary to figure out the meaning of the word *originally* on p. 449, paragraph 1 (first).

Differentiated Instruction

SI **Strategic Intervention**

Have students describe what the people in the mural "Dreams of Flight" are doing.

It's interesting to note that when the artist repainted the mural seventeen years after it was originally completed, he changed one of the children from a boy to a girl. Much had changed over the years, and the artist wanted all children to know that girls can dream of flying model airplanes too. It is the artist's hope that over time the mural will inspire many of the children who see it to work hard and follow their dreams.

"Dreams of Flight," Los Angeles, California

Draw Conclusions • Evaluation What conclusion can you draw from the fact that the artist David Botello changed one of the children from a boy to a girl when he repainted "Dreams of Flight"? Possible response: The artist wanted to be more sensitive to showing girls realizing their dreams and not just boys.

Objectives

◎ Understand and use graphic sources to aid comprehension.

OPTION 1 Skills and Strategies, continued

Teach Graphic Sources

Graphic Sources Ask students to look at the photo on p. 450 and read the caption below it. Have students explain what they can tell about this mural just by looking at the photo. (Possible response: The mural shows something that happened long ago. The hair styles and clothing that people are wearing are not popular today.)

Corrective Feedback

If... students are unable to explain how the photograph aids their understanding of the text,
then... use the Model to help them understand graphic sources.

Model the Skill

Think Aloud Graphic sources include charts, tables, diagrams, maps, or photographs with captions. When I read, I can look for graphic sources to help me understand information presented visually.

Talking Walls

Cities, large and small, invite artists to paint special murals in public places for everyone to see. Murals are talking walls; they speak to the people.

Community murals tell stories of personal, political, and social beliefs of the local residents. Some murals inspire or amuse us, while others stir our hearts.

"Declaration of Independence, 1776" was painted by Allyn Cox in the United States Capitol, Washington, D.C.

450

Student Edition pp. 450–451

OPTION 2 Think Critically, continued

Higher-Order Thinking Skills

Graphic Sources • Evaluation How would you rate the murals pictured in the story? Which one most clearly shows the theme of "Freedom?" Possible response: I would give the murals a high rating. They are colorful and many showed children whom I liked. I think the "American Flag" mural best expresses the theme of "Freedom."

Important Ideas • Evaluation Reread the last sentence on page 450. Why do you think the author used the words *stir our hearts*? Possible response: to tell that some murals touch people very deeply

When I look at the picture on page 450, I can tell that this mural shows an important event that took place a long time ago. Reading the caption confirms this.

On Their Own

Have students look at the photo and caption at the top of p. 451. Ask what they learn from the caption.

From sea to shining sea, the artists who create art for the people are instrumental in reminding Americans everywhere of the freedoms that help our democracy work.

Muralists use scaffolding to reach large murals.

The "American Flag" mural was painted by Meg Saligman in Philadelphia, Pennsylvania. ▼

451

Differentiated Instruction

SI Strategic Intervention

Have children work in small groups to create their own mural symbolizing freedom.

A Advanced

Compare and contrast Ask students to compare and contrast all of the murals in the story. Have them create a T chart detailing their findings.

Comprehension Check

Spiral Review

Compare and Contrast • Analysis How are the murals "A Shared Hope" and "Reach High and You Will Go Far" alike? Possible response: They both show the importance of education.

Draw Conclusions • Evaluation What conclusion can you draw about how the author of *Talking Walls: Art for the People* feels about the murals in the story? Possible response: The author likes the murals and thinks they remind Americans of the freedoms in our country.

Check Predictions Have students return to the predictions they made earlier and confirm whether they were accurate.

ELL

English Language Learners
Professional Development:
Shelter instruction "English language learners benefit when teachers shelter, or make comprehensible their literacy instruction. One way to do this is to use consistent, simplified, clearly enunciated, and slower-paced oral language to explain literacy concepts or activities."
—Dr. Georgia Ernest García

Objectives

◎ Use graphic sources to aid comprehension.

◎ Identify important ideas.

Check Retelling
SUCCESS PREDICTOR

Plan to Assess Retelling

☑ **Week 1** Assess Strategic Intervention students.

☑ **Week 2** Assess Advanced students.

☑ **Week 3 This week assess Strategic Intervention students.**

☐ **Week 4** Assess On-Level Students.

☐ **Week 5** Assess any students you have not yet checked during this unit.

Objectives • Ask questions, clear up anything you don't understand, and look for facts and details. Support your answers with details from the text. • Look for and use information found in graphics. • Identify the details or facts that support the main idea.

Envision It! Retell

Think Critically

1. In the story, the author uses a map to illustrate several mural locations in the United States. See if there is a mural in your city. If you were a muralist, where might you paint a mural? What would you paint a mural to celebrate? **Text to Self**

2. The subtitle of this selection is *Art for the People*. Why do you think the author used this subtitle? What topics does the author write about and why? Read "Meet the Author" on page 453 to find out. **Think Like an Author**

3. Look back at pages 448–449. What are the graphic sources on these pages? What information do they convey to the reader? **Graphic Sources**

4. What are the three most important ideas in the story? Explain your answers using evidence from the story. **Important Ideas**

5. **Look Back and Write** Look back at each artist and mural in the selection. Think about the reasons why the artists painted the murals. What do the murals represent, or stand for? Provide evidence to support your answer.

TEST PRACTICE Extended Response

READING STREET ONLINE STORY SORT www.ReadingStreet.com

452

Meet the Author

Katacha Díaz

Katacha Díaz grew up in Peru and immigrated to the United States when she was 15. She was one of seven daughters. Her parents moved to the United States so that the girls could get a good education. Moving to a new country as a teenager was hard. "My sister Ana María and I were the only Spanish-speaking students in our new school. There was a lot of peer pressure to get rid of the accent," she says.

Ms. Díaz wrote about murals because they have always fascinated her. She especially loves the murals by Paul and David Botello because they speak of education, immigration, and hope. These themes are a big part of her own life. "Education is important in my family," she points out.

Read more books about murals.

The School Mural by Sarah Vázquez

Murals: Walls That Sing by George Ancona

Use the Reader's and Writer's Notebook to record your independent reading.

453

Student Edition pp. 452–453

Retelling

Envision It!

Have students work in pairs to retell the selection, using the Envision It! Retelling Cards as prompts. Remind students that they should accurately describe the main topic and important ideas in a logical order and use key vocabulary as they retell. Monitor students' retellings.

Scoring rubric

> **Top-Score Response** A top-score response makes connections beyond the text, describes the main topic and important ideas using accurate information, evaluates facts and opinions, and draws conclusions from the text.

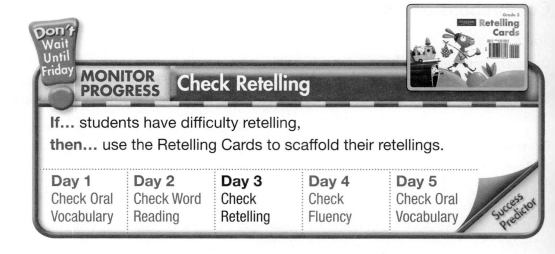

Don't Wait Until Friday

MONITOR PROGRESS Check Retelling

If... students have difficulty retelling,

then... use the Retelling Cards to scaffold their retellings.

Day 1	Day 2	Day 3	Day 4	Day 5
Check Oral Vocabulary	Check Word Reading	**Check Retelling**	Check Fluency	Check Oral Vocabulary

Success Predictor

Think Critically

Text to self

1. If I were a muralist, I would paint a mural of the sporting arena downtown. The mural would celebrate my hometown team playing in the World Series.

Think like an author

2. The author used the subtitle *Art for the People* because all of the murals are intended to share messages with people and to be enjoyed by people. The author writes about education, immigration, and hope because those things are important to her.

Graphic sources

3. The graphic sources are a photo and a chart. The photo conveys exactly what the mural looks like. The chart lists the artists, locations, and titles of some of the murals described in the selection.

Important ideas

4. The three most important ideas in the story are: Muralists paint many different kinds of murals; murals tell about people, history, celebrations, and freedom; muralists use artistic expression to share their ideas and speak through their artwork.

 **Writing on Demand**

5. **Look Back and Write** To build writing fluency, assign a 10–15 minute time limit.

Suggest that students use a prewriting strategy, such as brainstorming or using a graphic organizer, to organize their ideas. Remind them to establish a topic sentence and support it with facts, details, or explanations. As students finish, encourage them to reread their responses, revise for organization and support, and proofread for errors in grammar and conventions.

Scoring rubric

> **Top-Score Response** A top-score response uses details to tell about several of the murals and muralists in the story.
>
> **A top-score response should include:**
>
> • Some of the murals represent people in their neighborhoods and where they came from.
>
> • Some of the murals represent hopes for the future through education and hard work.
>
> • Some of the murals show symbols of American freedom.

Differentiated Instruction

SI **Strategic Intervention**
Have students work in pairs to brainstorm a list of what the murals in the story represent.

Meet the Author

Have students read about author Katacha Díaz on p. 453. Ask how she expresses her respect for artists in *Talking Walls: Art for the People.*

Independent Reading

After students enter their independent reading information into their Reading Logs or a journal, have them summarize what they have read. Remind students that a summary should be no more than a few sentences about the main idea of a text.

E L L

English Language Learners
Retelling Use the Retelling Cards to discuss the selection with students. Place the cards in an incorrect order and have students work together to organize the cards in order.

Check Retelling

Success Predictor

Model Fluency
Accuracy

Model fluent reading

Have students turn to p. 448 of *Talking Walls: Art for the People.* Have students follow along as you read this page. Tell them to listen to how you read each word, including the names of the artists with accuracy. Be sure to pronounce words clearly and pause at commas.

Guide practice

Have the students follow along as you read the page again. Then have them reread the page as a group without you until they read with no mistakes. Ask questions to be sure students comprehend the text. Continue on the same way on p. 449.

Reread for Fluency

Corrective feedback

If... students are having difficulty reading with accuracy, **then...** prompt:

- Where do you see periods, dashes, and commas?
- What should you do when you see these marks?
- Read the sentence again. Pause when you see these marks.

ROUTINE Oral Rereading

1. **Select a passage** For *Talking Walls: Art for the People,* use p. 447.
2. **Model** Have students listen as you read accurately with no errors.
3. **Guide practice** Have students read along with you.
4. **On their own** For optimal fluency, students should reread three or four times with accuracy.

Routines Flip Chart

Research and Study Skills
Alphabetical Order

Teach

Ask students what kind of information appears in alphabetical order. Students may mention dictionary or glossary entries, books in a library, and peoples' names in a telephone or address book. Tell students that being able to alphabetize will help them find information quickly. Have students look in the Glossary of their Student Edition and use it to review the following:

- **Alphabetical order** means that information is arranged or listed in the order of the letters of the alphabet.

- In glossaries, words are listed alphabetically.

- To put words in alphabetical order, look at their first letters. If the first letters are the same, look at their second letters. If the second letters are the same, look at their third letters.

Have students read some of the entries in the Glossary, noticing that all of the words are listed in alphabetical order.

Guide practice

Discuss these questions:

Which word would come first in a glossary—plenty or plug? (plenty)

How did you determine which word came first? (Alphabetized by using the third letter in each word.)

Ask students to use alphabetical order to find specific words in the Glossary.

On their own

Have students review and complete p. 415 of the *Reader's and Writer's Notebook*.

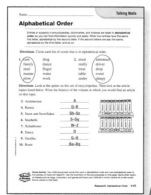

Reader's and Writer's
Notebook p. 415

Objectives
- Analyze data for usefulness.
- Combine sentences.
- Spell frequently misspelled words.

Research and Inquiry
Analyze

Teach

Tell students they will analyze the information they collected on Day 2. Based on the information gathered, they may need to refocus their original inquiry question and collect information from reference texts.

Model

Think Aloud When I began my research I thought that freedom of expression and freedom of speech were the same thing. Then I learned that freedom of expression is not only freedom of saying things but also includes sharing information or ideas in other ways. I will refocus my inquiry question to include this information. My revised question is *In what ways are people granted the freedom to express themselves verbally and non-verbally?*

Guide practice

Have students analyze their findings. They may need to refocus their inquiry question to better fit the information they found. Remind students that if they have difficulty improving their focus, they can ask a reference librarian or a local expert for guidance.

Remind students that keywords will be listed in alphabetical order in the back of most reference texts.

On their own

Have students work with a partner to summarize their research findings. Partners should comment on whether the research fully supports and answers the inquiry question.

Conventions
Combining Sentences

Review

Recall that sentences can be combined in the following instances:

- when two simple sentences can make a compound sentence
- when two sentences have the same subject
- when two sentences have the same predicate
- when two sentences repeat information

Daily Fix-It

Use Daily Fix-It numbers 5 and 6 in the right margin.

Connect to oral language

Have students identify repeated information in the pairs of simple sentences below. Then have them combine the sentences.

> **Stephanie lives in the city. She visits the country.** (Stephanie lives in the city, and she visits the country.)
>
> **I will find my lost shoes. I will buy new shoes.** (I will find my lost shoes or buy new shoes.)

On their own

For additional support, use *Let's Practice It!* page 386 on the *Teacher Resources DVD-ROM*.

Let's Practice It!
TR DVD•386

Spelling
Final Syllables *-ion* and *-ure*

Frequently misspelled words

The words *we're* and *were* can be confusing to spell. Think carefully before you write these words. Think of which word means *we are*. I'll read several sentences. Think about which word correctly completes each sentence, and then write the sentence.

1. **The movie _____ seeing starts at 7:00.** (we're)
2. **They _____ late for class.** (were)
3. **What _____ you saying?** (were)
4. **_____ leaving early in the morning.** (We're)

On their own

For more support, use the *Reader's and Writer's Notebook* p. 416.

Differentiated Instruction

 Strategic Intervention

Using graphic organizers Help students draw graphic organizers that show two boxes at the left of the page with arrows pointing to one box on the right of the page.

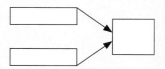

Provide two simple, related sentences for students to write in the boxes on the left. Guide them in combining the two sentences to make one sentence in the box on the right.

Daily Fix-It

5. The class's mural feachures a celebration, and is painted in bright colors. (*features; celebration and*)

6. The mural is the most biggest piece of art in the neighbor hood. (*the biggest; neighborhood*)

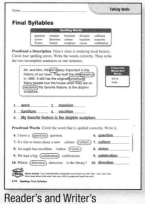

Reader's and Writer's Notebook p. 416

Objectives

• Understand the criteria for writing an effective description.

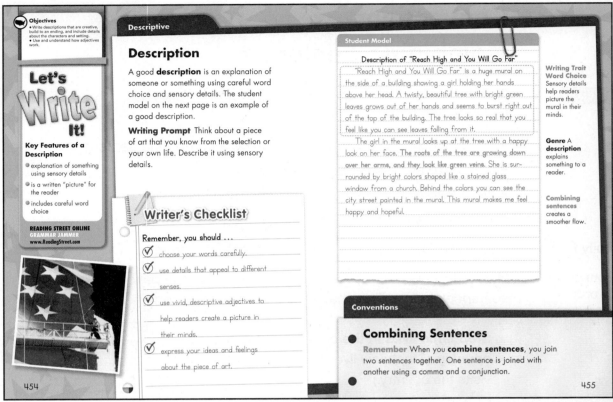

Student Edition pp. 454–455

Let's Write It!
Description

Teach

Use pp. 454–455 in the Student Edition. Direct students to read the key features of description, which appear on p. 454. Remind students that they can refer to the information in the Writer's Checklist as they write their own descriptions.

Read the student model on p. 455. Point out the sensory details and the careful word choice in the model that help the reader imagine what the mural looks like.

Connect to conventions

Remind students that combining sentences means joining two sentences that contain some of the same information. Point out how some of the sentences in the model may have started out as two simple sentences.

Writing—Description
Writing Trait: Word Choice

Display rubric

Display Scoring Rubric 28 from the *Teacher Resources DVD-ROM.* Review the criteria for each trait under each score, and then have students rate the model for a given trait. Require students to support their answers with specific examples from the model. If a student rates the model below 4 for a particular trait, ask other students to agree or disagree with the rating, and have them offer support for that response. Remind students that you will use this rubric to evaluate their descriptions.

Scoring Rubric: Description

	④	③	②	①
Focus/Ideas	Clear focus and description of a person, place, or thing	Fairly clear focus and description of a person, place, or thing	Little focus on a person, place, or thing	No focus or description of a person, place, or thing
Organization	Clear main idea; strong use of details	Unclear main idea; adequate use of details	No main idea; unclear use of details	No attempt at main idea; no organization of details
Voice	Writer is clearly interested in what is being described	Some evidence of interest in what is being described	Little evidence of interest in what is being described	No interest in what is being described
Word Choice	Strong use of vivid words that appeal to the senses	Some vivid words that appeal to the senses	Little attempt to use vivid words; descriptions do not appeal to the senses	Incorrect or limited word choice; no detailed descriptions
Sentences	Clear sentences of various lengths and types	Sentences of a few lengths and types	Little attempt at various lengths and types of sentences	No attempt at various lengths and types of sentences
Conventions	Few errors; all short sentences combined; correct use of commas	Several minor errors; most short sentences are combined; fair use of commas	Many errors; few short sentences combined; weak use of commas	Numerous errors; no short sentences combined; no use of commas

Main idea web

Explain that students will use the main idea webs they worked on yesterday to help draft their descriptions. If they have not completed their webs, have them work in groups or with partners to brainstorm sensory details or other descriptive language to complete their webs.

Write

You will use your main idea web to help you write the draft of your description. Remember that your draft is only the beginning of your composition. Drafting is the time to get your ideas down on paper. You will have time to revise your description tomorrow.

Objectives
• Write descriptive words.

Writing, continued
Writing Trait: Word Choice

MINI-LESSON

Choosing Descriptive Words

■ **Introduce** Explain to students that writing a good description means choosing words that help the reader imagine what something is like. Words that appeal to the senses—taste, touch, smell, hearing, and sight—are descriptive words. Adjectives and active verbs are descriptive words. With descriptive words, a noun like *pencil* becomes *the sharp red pencil.* Display the Drafting Tips for students. Remind them that the focus of drafting is to get their ideas down in an organized way. Then display Writing Transparency 28A.

Description of Ori's Cat collage

My friend Ori made a collage of a cat. it hangs on the wall at her apartment. It hangs over the sofa. The cats fur is made of swirls of bumpy yarn. The yarn is bright greene, like grass in spring. A thin line of sky blue yarn outline the cat's plump body. The cat's silver bottle cap eyes shine out at you. They sparkle with a coating of Silver glitter. The cat's front paws are made of white yarn, and its whiskers is made of stiff white pipe cleaners that stuck out from the picture.

The cat's bright green fur and white paws stand out against the black cardboard background. Crouching there with its tail wrapped around its body, it looks like it might leap right out at you. Looking at the collage makes me feel happy and energetic.

Unit 6. Talking Walls: Art for the People   Writing Model **28A**

Writing Transparency 28A, TR DVD

Drafting Tips

✔ Use your main idea web to help organize your paragraphs. Write one paragraph for each supporting idea.

✔ Choose words that appeal to the senses, adjectives, and active verbs to describe the piece of art.

✔ Remember that you will have a chance to check spelling, grammar, and mechanics later in the writing process.

Think Aloud I'm going to write the first paragraph of my description. My title will be "Description of Ori's Cat Collage." My first sentence will be my main idea: *My friend Ori made a collage of a cat.* When I draft, I think more about my topic and expand on the ideas I wrote in my web during the planning stage. I think of ways I can best describe the collage so that readers can imagine what it is like. I'll compare the green yarn to grass so readers can see it.

Read the draft on the transparency aloud, emphasizing your choice of descriptive words and phrases over more ordinary words and phrases. For example, you might consider the word *fat* before choosing the word *plump.* Direct students to use the drafting tips to guide them as they write their drafts.

ROUTINE Quick Write for Fluency Team Talk

1 **Talk** Pairs of students discuss the descriptive words they've chosen to include in their compositions.

2 **Write** Students write a sentence describing something, using some of the words they chose and correct comma use.

3 **Share** Students read their partner's paragraph and check for correct use of commas.

Routines Flip Chart

Wrap Up Your Day

✔ **Build Concepts** Have students discuss the themes of the mural "A Shared Hope."

✔ **Graphic Sources** How do the captions help you understand the selection?

✔ **Important Ideas** What important idea does the mural "Dreams of Flight" represent?

Differentiated Instruction

 Advanced

Have students choose three sentences from their drafts and use a thesaurus to write as many different versions of that sentence as they can. The sentence variations should retain the same meaning while at the same time displaying different descriptive words and sentence structures.

Preview DAY 4

Tell students that tomorrow they will read about a playful use of language that was created long ago.

Objectives
- Expand the weekly concept.
- Develop oral vocabulary.

Today at a Glance

Oral Vocabulary
view, lyrics

Phonics/Word Analysis
Schwa

Genre
Palindromes

Reading
"The History of Palindromes"

Let's Learn It!
Fluency: Accuracy
Vocabulary: ⊙ Unknown words
Media literacy: Talk show

Research and Inquiry
Synthesize

Conventions
Combining sentences

Spelling
Final syllables *-ion* and *-ure*

Writing
Description

Concept Talk

Question of the Week
⒬ Why is freedom of expression important?

Expand the concept

Remind students that this week they have read about how muralists display their freedom of expression through significant works of art that make us pause and think. Tell students that today they will read about the history of a playful use of language called palindromes.

Anchored Talk

Develop oral vocabulary

Use graphic sources—photographs and captions—to review pp. 446–451 of *Talking Walls: Art for the People*. Then discuss the Amazing Words *significant* and *pause*. Add these and other concept-related words to the concept map. Use the following questions to develop students' understanding of the concept. Encourage students to ask their own relevant questions, make pertinent comments, and use appropriate details in their answers.

- Think about all of the different murals. What *significant* messages did the artists express through their art?

- What mural makes you *pause* the most to think about what freedom means to you?

Strategy Response Log

INTERACT with TEXT

Have students review the characteristics of a photo essay on p. 34 of the *Reader's and Writer's Notebook.* Then have them compare *Talking Walls: Art for the People* to another example of a photo essay that they have read or know about.

Oral Vocabulary
Amazing Words

Amazing Words

creative	lecture
expressive	significant
emotion	pause
artistic	view
exquisite	lyrics

Teach Amazing Words

Amazing Words **Oral Vocabulary Routine**

1. **Introduce** Write the word *view* on the board. Have students say it aloud with you. We read about David Botello's *view* of the world. How did he want children to *view* the world? (Dreams can come true if you work hard.) Have students determine the definition of *view*. (A view is a way of looking at or thinking about something.)

2. **Demonstrate** Have students answer questions to demonstrate understanding. What is Paul Botello's *view* of education? (He thinks that people can have a better life through education.)

3. **Apply** Have students apply their understanding. How would your *view* of education affect how much you studied?

See p. OV•3 to teach *lyrics*.

Routines Flip Chart

Apply Amazing Words

As students read "The History of Palindromes" on pp. 456–457, have them think about how people might *view* palindromes and how a palindrome phrase might be used as *lyrics* of a song.

Connect to reading

Help students establish a purpose for reading. As students read today's selection about the history of palindromes, have them think about how the Question of the Week and the Amazing Words *view* and *lyrics* apply to palindromes.

ELL **Produce Oral Language** Use the Day 4 instruction on ELL Poster 28 to extend and enrich language.

ELL Poster 28

Talking Walls: Art for the People **456b**

Objectives
- Identify and read words with the schwa sound.
- Read words fluently independent of context.

Word Analysis Review
Schwa

Review schwa

To review unaccented syllables with the schwa sound, write *cardinal, robin, commit, method, cabin, letter, pretzel, circus, holiday,* and *ablaze.* You learned that unaccented syllables with schwa can be spelled with any vowel. Let's review the schwa sound by looking at these words. In what words is the schwa sound spelled *a? (cardinal, ablaze).* Continue in the same way for words with schwa spelled *e (letter, pretzel), i (robin, cabin, holiday), o (commit, method),* and *u (circus).* Remind students that they can divide words into syllables and then try the schwa sounds for each vowel in a word until they recognize the word.

Corrective feedback

If students are unable to answer the questions about the schwa sound, refer them to Sound-Spelling Card 144.

Guide practice

Draw a two-column chart with the heads *Schwa* and *No schwa.* Write the following words on the board: *sister, Sunday, ago, popcorn, famous, family, rabbit, marble, walking, seesaw.* Let's read the words. Listen for the unaccented syllable to determine if you hear the schwa sound. Write each word in the appropriate column. Then have students read the words. Ask volunteers to underline the vowel that stands for the schwa sound in words in the first column.

Schwa	No schwa
sister	Sunday
ago	popcorn
famous	rabbit
family	walking
marble	seesaw

On their own

For additional practice, use *Let's Practice It!* page 387 on the *Teacher Resources DVD-ROM.*

Let's Practice It!
TR DVD•387

Fluent Word Reading
Spiral Review

Read words independent of context

Display these words. Tell students that they can already decode some words on this list. Explain that they should know other words because they appear often in reading.

Have students read the list three or four times until they can read at the rate of two to three seconds per word.

Word Reading

ceiling	true	livelihood	payment	put
brownish	neighbor	one	the	sure
of	full	book	any	new
look	everything	school	suit	messy

Corrective feedback

If... students have difficulty reading whole words,
then... have them use sound-by-sound blending for decodable words or chunking for words that have word parts, or have them say and spell high-frequency words.

If... students cannot read fluently at a rate of two to three seconds per word,
then... have pairs practice the list until they can read it fluently.

Differentiated Instruction

 Strategic Intervention

Schwa To assist students having difficulty with the schwa sound, have them write the vowels *a, e, i, o, u,* and *y* on separate cards. Under each vowel, have students write a cue word in which the schwa sound is represented by that vowel. For example: *a (about), e (cover), i (decimal), o (harmony), u (medium), y (oxygen).* Encourage students to refer to these cue cards as they attempt to decode other words with the schwa sound.

Spiral Review

These activities review:
- previously taught high-frequency words *of, everything, one, the, any, sure.*
- vowel patterns *ei, eigh;* suffixes *-y, -ish, -hood, -ment;* spellings of /ü/, /u̇/.

English Language Learners
Fluent word reading Have students listen to a more fluent reader say the words. Then have them repeat the words.

Objectives
- Read words fluently in context.
- Apply knowledge of sound-spellings to decode unknown words when reading.
- Practice fluency with oral rereading.

Read words in context

Display these sentences. Call on individuals to read a sentence. Then randomly point to review words and have students read them. To help you monitor word reading, high-frequency words are underlined and decodable words are italicized.

MONITOR PROGRESS | Sentence Reading

Are you <u>sure</u> I need a *new suit* for *school*?
Look up at <u>the</u> *brownish* spot on the *ceiling.*
My *neighbor* did not receive *payment* for <u>one</u> *book.*
Is it *true* that Dad's *livelihood* depends on selling <u>everything</u>?
Do not *put* <u>any</u> cans *full* <u>of</u> *messy* paint on the table.

If... students are unable to read an underlined high-frequency word,

then... read the word for them and spell it, having them echo you.

If... students have difficulty reading an italicized decodable word,

then... guide them in using sound-by-sound blending or chunking.

Reread for Fluency

Have students reread the sentences to develop automaticity decoding words.

 ROUTINE **Oral Rereading**

1. **Read** Have students read all the sentences orally.
2. **Reread** To achieve optimal fluency, students should reread the sentences three or four times.
3. **Corrective Feedback** Listen as students read. Provide corrective feedback regarding their fluency and decoding.

Routines Flip Chart

Blend and Read

Read words independent of context

Have students turn to p. 155 in *Decodable Practice Readers 3.2* and find the first list of words. Each word in this list has the final syllable *-tion, -ion, -ture, -ive,* or *-ize.* Let's read these words. Be sure that students pronounce each final syllable correctly.

Next, have students read the high-frequency words.

Preview Decodable Practice Passage

Have students read the title and preview the story. Tell them that they will read words with final syllables *-tion, -ion, -ture, -ive,* and *-ize.*

Read words in context

Chorally read the story along with the students. Have students identify words in the story with final syllables *-tion, -ion, -ture, -ive,* and *-ize.* Make sure that students are monitoring their accuracy when they decode words.

Team Talk Pair students and have them take turns reading the story aloud to each other. Monitor students as they read to check for proper pronunciation and appropriate pacing.

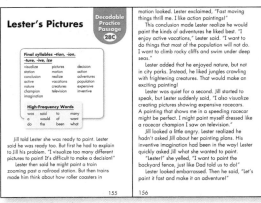

Decodable Practice
Passage 28C

Differentiated Instruction

A Advanced

Decodable and high-frequency words Have students write a letter to a neighbor using some of the decodable and high-frequency words found in the sentences on p. 456e.

Let's Think About Genre
Palindromes

Introduce palindromes

Explain to students that what we read is structured differently depending on the author's reasons for writing and what kind of information he or she wishes to convey. Different types of text are called genres. Tell students that palindromes is one type of genre.

Discuss the genre

Discuss with students what is special about a palindrome. For example, ask: What do you notice about palindromes? (Possible response: The word or phrase reads the same forward or backward.) Why do you think people invented palindromes so long ago and still use them today? (Possible response: People invented them to have fun with language.)

On the board, draw a concept map like the one below. Write the word *Palindromes* in the middle circle. Brainstorm with students palindromes they are familiar with. In addition to words and phrases, numbers can also be palindromes. Add students' suggestions to the concept map.

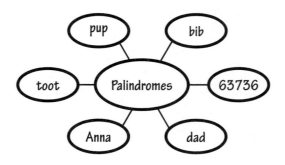

Guide practice

Then have students work in pairs to list other palindromes. They may conduct an online search to find other examples. Ask them to share their lists with the class.

Connect to reading

Tell students that they will now read about the history of palindromes. Ask students to find additional examples of palindromes in the text.

Small Group Time

DAY 4

Break into small groups before reading or revisiting "The History of Palindromes."

Teacher Led

SI Strategic Intervention

Teacher Led p. DI•55
- Practice retelling
- Genre focus
- **Read/Revisit** "The History of Palindromes"

OL On-Level

Teacher Led p. DI•60
- Practice retelling
- Genre focus
- **Read/Revisit** "The History of Palindromes"

A Advanced

Teacher Led p. DI•65
- Genre focus
- **Read/Revisit** "The History of Palindromes"

ELL

Place English language learners in the groups that correspond to their reading abilities in English.

Practice Stations
- Read for Meaning
- Get Fluent
- Words to Know

Independent Activities
- AudioText: "The History of Palindromes"
- *Reader's and Writer's Notebook*
- Research and Inquiry

Academic Vocabulary

palindromes words or phrases that are spelled the same backward and forward

Objectives

• Identify and write palindromes.

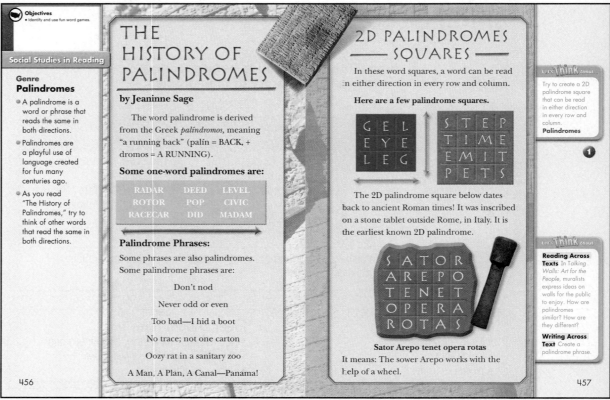

Student Edition pp. 456-457

Guide Comprehension

Teach the genre

Genre: Palindromes Explain that there are different types of palindromes. Ask: What do you think a 2D palindrome square is?

Corrective feedback

If... students are unable to explain a 2D palindrome square,
then... use the model to guide students in explaining this type of palindrome.

Model the genre

 Think Aloud 2D palindrome squares are a set of squares in which a word can be read in either direction in every row and column. 2D palindromes date back to ancient Roman times.

On their own

Have partners show each other how the words in the 2D palindrome square can be read in either direction.

Extend Thinking
Think Critically

Higher-order thinking skills

Compare and Contrast • Analysis Compare the palindrome phrases in "The History of Palindromes." Which phrase do you think is the most clever? Why? Responses will vary.

Draw Conclusions • Synthesize Palindromes are playful uses of language. What other playful uses of language are similar to palindromes? Possible responses: onomatopoeia, alliteration, rhyme

Let's Think About...

❶ Students should create a 2D palindrome square that can be read in either direction in every row and column. Have students start from the top left corner of the square. You may want to provide them with a bank of short words to try using.

Reading Across Texts

Possible responses: They are different because some murals do not contain any words at all and palindromes are all words. They are the same because murals and palindromes both require a lot of planning and creativity.

Writing Across Texts

Once students have written their palindromes, have them create illustrations to go with them. Have students work together to combine their work and publish a book of palindromes that can be read by the class.

Differentiated Instruction

 Strategic Intervention

Graphic sources Have students work with a partner to read each word in every row and column on the 2D palindrome squares. Have partners write each word they read and then compare all of the words on their list.

 Advanced

Learn about ancient palindromes Have students use the library or Internet to learn about other ancient palindromes. Have them share their findings with the class and discuss the words and messages the palindromes contain.

English Language Learners
Cognates The Spanish word *historia* may be familiar to Spanish speakers as the cognate for *history*.

Objectives
- Read grade-level text with accuracy.
- Use a dictionary or glossary to find words' meanings.
- Conduct an interview.

Check Fluency WCPM
SUCCESS PREDICTOR

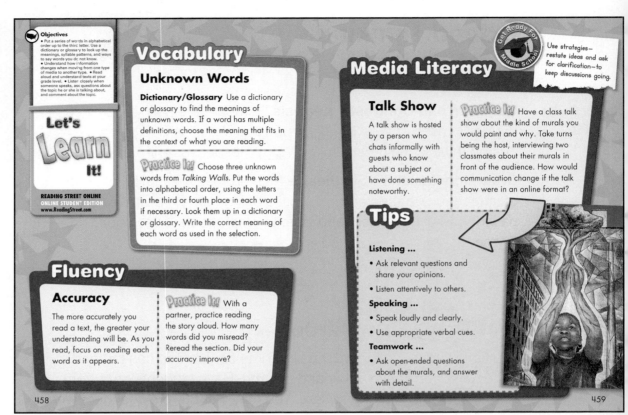

Student Edition pp. 458–459

Fluency
Accuracy

Guide practice

Use the Student Edition activity as an assessment tool. Make sure the reading passage is at least 200 words in length. As students read aloud with partners, walk around to make sure they are reading the text accurately to enhance comprehension.

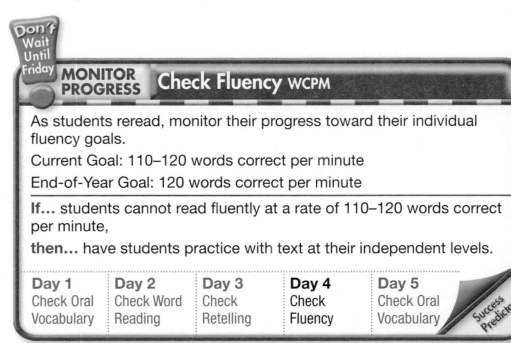

Don't Wait Until Friday

MONITOR PROGRESS Check Fluency WCPM

As students reread, monitor their progress toward their individual fluency goals.

Current Goal: 110–120 words correct per minute

End-of-Year Goal: 120 words correct per minute

If... students cannot read fluently at a rate of 110–120 words correct per minute,

then... have students practice with text at their independent levels.

Day 1	Day 2	Day 3	**Day 4**	Day 5
Check Oral Vocabulary	Check Word Reading	Check Retelling	Check Fluency	Check Oral Vocabulary

Success Predictor

Vocabulary
Unknown Words

Teach

Dictionary/Glossary Write these words on the board: *success, symbolize,* and *depict.* Remind students that the words in a dictionary or glossary appear in alphabetical order. To alphabetize, use the first letter in each word. If the first letters are the same, use the second letters, and so on.

Guide practice

- Have children alphabetize the words *success, symbolize,* and *depict.* Then have them look up each word in a dictionary or glossary and write a definition.

On their own

- Walk around the room as students work. Make sure they have correctly alphabetized the words. Check to see that students can quickly and accurately locate the words using a dictionary or glossary. Ask students to point out how each word is divided into syllables and make sure they pronounce each word correctly.

Media Literacy
Talk Show

Teach

Have students work in groups of three to stage talk shows using the Look Back and Write on page 452. One student from each group will act as the host of the talk show and should prepare interview questions to ask during the show. The other two students will portray artists, while the rest of the class will pose as the audience. The artists will explain why they painted their murals and what their murals represent, or stand for. Remind students to monitor their speaking rate and volume, speak coherently, employ eye contact, and enunciate clearly to communicate their ideas effectively. Students should rehearse their roles together.

Guide practice

Be sure students follow the oral instructions above to prepare for their talk shows. Have students restate the instructions to classmates. Remind the students posing as the audience to listen attentively to each speaker.

On their own

Have students conduct the talk show interviews. After each talk show, have students discuss how communication would change if the talk show were in an online format.

Talk Show

Tell students that each talk show host should prepare questions ahead of time and share them with the artists. The questions should be about things the host thinks would interest the audience, as well as about the artist's reason for painting each mural and what each mural stands for. Encourage the artists to reread the *Talking Walls: Art for the People* text to find answers to the questions before the interview. As each mural is discussed, have the artists display that picture in the text.

Objectives

- Present information in the form of a review or definition.
- Combine sentences.
- Spell words with common final syllables *-ion* and *-ure*.

Research and Inquiry
Synthesize

Teach

Have students synthesize their research findings and results. Remind students that when they synthesize, they combine relevant ideas and information from different sources to develop answers to their inquiry questions. Have students explain how using alphabetical order helped them organize their research.

Guide practice

Students can use a word processing program to create a short review of the First Amendment or write a definition of freedom of expression. Have students revise their review or definition so that it is clear and gramatically correct.

On their own

Have students write a brief explanation of their research findings. Then have them organize and combine information for their presentation. Have students create a works-cited page from their notes including the web addresses, authors and the dates the web sites were last updated for each search.

Daily Fix-It

7. Carlos begun a sculpchure to go with the mural. *(began; sculpture)*

8. He is making it out of clay and he will finish it next tuesday. *(clay, and; Tuesday)*

Conventions
Combining Sentences

Test practice

Remind students that grammar skills, such as combining sentences, are often assessed on important tests. Remind students that they can combine sentences in the following ways:

- combine subjects
- combine predicates
- join two simple sentences with a comma and a conjunction
- join sentences that provide information about the same topic

Daily Fix-It

Use Daily Fix-It numbers 7 and 8 in the right margin.

On their own

For additional practice, use the *Reader's and Writer's Notebook* p. 417.

Reader's and Writer's Notebook p. 417

Spelling
Final Syllables *-ion* and *-ure*

Practice spelling strategy

Supply pairs of students with index cards on which the spelling words have been written. Have one student read a word while the other writes it. Then have students switch roles. Have them use the cards to check their spelling and correct any mis-spelled words.

On their own

For additional practice, use *Let's Practice It!* page 388 on the *Teacher Resources DVD-ROM.*

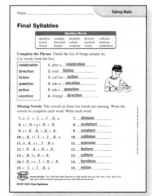

Let's Practice It!
TR DVD•388

Writing—Description
Revising Strategy

MINI-LESSON

Writing Transparency 28B,
TR DVD

Revising Strategy: Consolidating

Yesterday we wrote a description about a piece of art. Today we will revise our drafts. The goal is to make your writing clearer, more interesting, and more informative.

Display Writing Transparency 28B. Remind students that revising does not include corrections of grammar and mechanics. Tell them that this will be done later, when they proofread their work. Then introduce the revising strategy of consolidating.

When you revise, you look for places where you have repeated words or ideas. In those places, you can consolidate, or combine, information. Look for sentences that contain the same words or information and combine them.

Remind students that as they revise, they should look for additional ways to make their writing clearer and more interesting, including adding sensory details that support the main idea.

Revising Tips

✔ Make sure all your supporting details refer to the main idea.

✔ Look for even more places to use strong adjectives, verbs, and words that appeal to the senses.

✔ Consolidate information that is repeated in your description by combining sentences.

Peer conferencing

Peer Revision Have pairs of students exchange papers for peer revision. Students should write 1) the strongest part of the description; 2) the weakest part of the description; and 3) one idea about how to improve the composition. Direct students to pass their written comments to the writer. Refer to the *Teacher Resources DVD-ROM* for more information about peer conferencing.

Have students revise using the comments they collected during Peer Revision as well as the key features of description and the revising tips. Check to make sure students are using the revising strategy of consolidating.

Corrective feedback

Circulate around the room to monitor and confer with students as they revise. Remind students correcting errors that they will have time to edit tomorrow. They should be working on content and organization today.

ROUTINE **Quick Write for Fluency** **Team Talk**

① **Talk** Pairs of students discuss what it might be like to live in a country where there is no freedom of expression.

② **Write** Students write briefly about what it might be like to live in a country where there is no freedom of expression.

③ **Share** Students read their writings aloud to their partners. Partners then check each other's writing for descriptive words.

Routines Flip Chart

Wrap Up Your Day

✔ **Build Concepts** What did you learn about palindromes?

✔ **Oral Vocabulary** Monitor students' use of oral vocabulary as they respond: Do you need to be an artistic and creative person to create palindromes?

✔ **Text Features** Discuss how the palindrome squares help students understand text.

Write Guy
Jeff Anderson

Focus Your Editing

In the editing process, students can easily get bogged down by everything that needs to be fixed. Editing one aspect at a time helps students focus their efforts and concentrate on one task, while making it easier for you as a teacher to fully explain and reteach the concept, moving students toward correctness. Sometimes less really is more.

English Language Learners
Support revision Have students listen for choppy sentences while they or a partner reads their story aloud. Once students have made their revisions, have them read their stories aloud again.

Preview DAY 5

Remind students to think about why freedom of expression is important.

Objectives
- Review the weekly concept.
- Review oral vocabulary.

Today at a Glance

Oral Vocabulary

Comprehension
◉ Graphic sources

Lesson Vocabulary
◉ Unknown words

Phonics/Word Analysis
◉ Final syllables

Literary Terms
Personification

Assessment
Fluency
Comprehension

Research and Inquiry
Communicate

Spelling
Final syllables -ion, -ure

Conventions
Combining sentences

Writing
Description

Check Oral Vocabulary
SUCCESS PREDICTOR

Concept Wrap Up

Question of the Week
Why is freedom of expression important?

Review the concept

Have students look back at the reading selections to find examples that best demonstrate why freedom of expression is important.

Review Amazing Words

Display and review this week's concept map. Remind students that this week they have learned ten Amazing Words related to freedom of expression. Have students use the Amazing Words and the concept map to answer the question *Why is freedom of expression important?* Encourage students to make pertinent comments during the discussion.

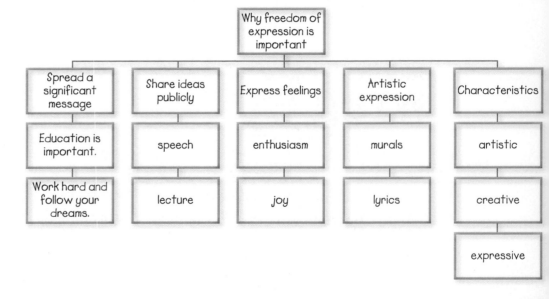

ELL **Check Concepts and Language** Use the Day 5 instruction on ELL Poster 28 to monitor students' understanding of the lesson concept.

ELL Poster 28

Amazing Ideas

Connect to the Big Question

Have pairs of students discuss how the Question of the Week connects to the Big Question: *What does freedom mean?* Encourage students to ask relevant questions about things they don't understand. Tell students to use the concept map and what they have learned from this week's Anchored Talks and reading selections to form an Amazing Idea—a realization or "big idea" about Freedom. Then ask each pair to share its Amazing Idea with the class.

Amazing Ideas might include these key concepts:

- Freedom enables people to speak and act freely.
- People express themselves in many different ways.
- Freedom of expression is not something you should take for granted.

Write about it

Have students write a few sentences about their Amazing Idea, beginning with "This week I learned…" Tell students to include supporting sentences with details.

Amazing Words

creative	lecture
expressive	significant
emotion	pause
artistic	view
exquisite	lyrics

It's Friday

MONITOR PROGRESS **Check Oral Vocabulary**

Have individuals use this week's Amazing Words to describe freedom of expression. Monitor students' abilities to use the Amazing Words and note which words you need to reteach.

If… students have difficulty using the Amazing Words,

then… reteach using the Oral Vocabulary Routine, pp. 431a, 436b, 446b, 456b, OV•3.

Day 1	Day 2	Day 3	Day 4	**Day 5**
Check Oral Vocabulary	Check Word Reading	Check Retelling	Check Fluency	Check Oral Vocabulary

Success Predictor

ELL

English Language Learners
Concept map Work with students to add new words to the concept map.

Check Oral Vocabulary Success Predictor

Objectives
- ◎ Review graphic sources.
- ◎ Review unknown words.
- ◎ Review final syllables (*-tion, -ion, -ture, -ive, -ize*).
- • Review personification.

Comprehension Review

⟳ Graphic Sources

Teach graphic sources

Review the definition of graphic sources on p. 434. Remind students that graphic sources are ways of showing information visually. They provide additional information about the text and help readers better understand what they are reading. For additional support have students review pp. EI•10–EI•11 on graphic sources.

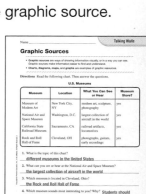

Student Edition pp. EI•10–EI•11

Guide practice

Have student pairs find an example of a graphic source in *Talking Walls: Art for the People.* Then have pairs tell what information they learned from the graphic source.

On their own

For additional practice with graphic sources, use *Let's Practice It!* page 389 on the *Teacher Resources DVD-ROM.*

Let's Practice It!
TR DVD•389

Vocabulary Review

⟳ Unknown Words

Teach unknown words

Remind students to use a dictionary or a glossary to help them understand the meanings, syllabication, and pronunciation of unknown words.

Guide practice

Review with students how to find the correct meaning, syllabication, and pronunciation of *support* using a dictionary. Tell students that some words have more than one definition listed.

On their own

Have students use a dictionary or glossary to look up the meaning of a lesson vocabulary word. Then ask students to write a sentence that demonstrates the correct meaning of the word. Have partners read their sentences to verify that they can pronounce the word correctly.

Word Analysis Review
Final Syllables

Teach final syllables

Write the following sentences on the board. Have students read each one, first quietly to themselves and then aloud as you track the print.

1. They began construction on the massive mansion.
2. Did you bring your permission slip for our outdoor adventure night?
3. We will learn about the culture and celebrations of Native Americans.
4. The oversized invention wouldn't fit in the convention hall.
5. Which direction is the furniture store from here?

Team Talk Have partners identify and underline the final syllables *-tion, -ion, -ture, -ive,* and *-ize* in the words in the sentences. Then point to underlined words at random and have the group read them together.

Literary Terms Review
Personification

Teach personification

Have students reread pp. 446–451 of *Talking Walls: Art for the People.* Remind students that when an animal or object is personified, it is given human traits. Students should look for verbs that describe actions normally done by people.

Guide practice

Point out the last sentence in the second paragraph of the "A Shared Hope" section of *Talking Walls: Art for the People.* Discuss with students how the author personifies the mural. (The mural *tells* children that education is the key to success.) Have students find another example of personification in the "Dreams of Flight" section and discuss.

On their own

Point out the example of personification in the title *Talking Walls: Art for the People.* Have students put *talking walls* in the center of a word web and complete the web by adding circles that tell what the talking walls "say" to people.

English Language Learners
Graphic sources Provide practice by having students find examples of graphic sources in other selections in their Student Edition. Discuss how each graphic source helps students better understand what they are reading.

Objectives
- Read grade-level text with fluency.

Plan to Assess Fluency

☑ **Week 1** Assess Advanced students.

☑ **Week 2** Assess Strategic Intervention students.

☑ **This week assess On-Level students.**

☐ **Week 4** Assess Strategic Intervention students.

☐ **Week 5** Assess any students you have not yet checked during this unit.

Set individual goals for students to enable them to reach the year-end goal.

- Current Goal: 110–120 WCPM
- Year-End Goal: 120 WCPM

Assessment

Check words correct per minute

Fluency Make two copies of the fluency passage on p. 459k. As the student reads the text aloud, mark mistakes on your copy. Also mark where the student is at the end of one minute. To check the student's comprehension of the passage, have him or her retell you what was read. To figure words correct per minute (WCPM), subtract the number of mistakes from the total number of words read in one minute.

WCPM

Corrective feedback

If… students cannot read fluently at a rate of 110–120 WCPM,
then… make sure they practice with text at their independent reading level. Provide additional fluency practice by pairing nonfluent readers with fluent readers.

If… students already read at 120 WCPM,
then… have them read a book of their choice independently.

Small Group Time

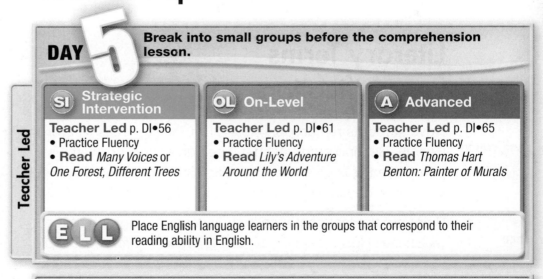

DAY 5 Break into small groups before the comprehension lesson.

Teacher Led

SI Strategic Intervention	OL On-Level	A Advanced
Teacher Led p. DI•56 • Practice Fluency • **Read** *Many Voices* or *One Forest, Different Trees*	**Teacher Led** p. DI•61 • Practice Fluency • **Read** *Lily's Adventure Around the World*	**Teacher Led** p. DI•65 • Practice Fluency • **Read** *Thomas Hart Benton: Painter of Murals*

ELL Place English language learners in the groups that correspond to their reading ability in English.

Practice Stations
- Words to Know
- Get Fluent
- Read For Meaning

Independent Activities
- Grammar Jammer
- Concept Talk Video
- Vocabulary Activities

Name _____

Tips for Taking Great Travel Pictures

One of our freedoms is the freedom to travel, and it is fun to take   15
pictures when you do. They will help you remember your trips. For   27
your next trip, you can take great pictures too. Just follow these easy   40
directions.   41

At times, a close-up shot is best. Let's say you are taking a picture   55
of a sculpture. Use the zoom feature on your camera. That will let you   69
capture small details. The zoom also works well for taking shots of   81
nature. Use it to snap a picture of a native plant or a single tree.   96

Sometimes you may want to take a picture of something in motion.   108
You must be fast to take an action picture. Frame your picture first. Make   122
sure you are very still. Then use a fast shutter speed. If you do this, you   138
can take good shots of nature or people in motion.   148

You might want to take shots of the people you meet. Let's say you   162
are at a local celebration. Always ask before taking your shot. You may   175
think you are just being social. However, others might think you are   187
rude. Even if a person encourages you to take pictures, still ask. Then   200
you will not make anyone angry.   206

Follow these rules. If you do, you will take great pictures. You will   219
be able to look at them and remember your trip.   229

MONITOR PROGRESS • Check Fluency

Objectives
- Read grade-level text with comprehension.

Assessment

Check graphic sources

◉ **Graphic Sources** Use "A Small Town Votes" on p. 459m to check students' understanding of graphic sources.

1. Why was there an election in Smithson? (to determine whether or not a new highway would be built)

2. Based on the chart, did the majority of people vote for or against the highway being built? (The majority of people voted for the highway to be built.)

3. Based on the map, would the new highway be more on the east or west side of the town? (more on the west side of town)

Corrective feedback

If... students are unable to answer the comprehension questions, **then...** use the Reteach lesson in the *First Stop* book.

Name _____

A Small Town Votes

There was an election in the town of Smithson. Voters had to decide whether or not to approve a new highway that would go through town.

Some citizens wanted the highway because it would make travel around Smithson easier. Many also thought the highway would aid the town's businesses.

Other citizens did not want the highway because they were afraid it would mean too much traffic in their local neighborhood. Many of these citizens were also concerned about the expense of building a new highway.

The voting took place on a Tuesday in April. The chart and map show how people voted and where the new highway would go.

	East Smithson	West Smithson
Number of citizens	345	388
Number of yes votes	250	156
Number of no votes	95	232

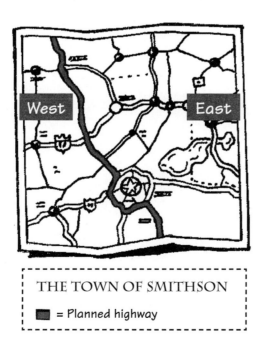

THE TOWN OF SMITHSON

■ = Planned highway

MONITOR PROGRESS

• Graphic sources

Objectives
- Communicate inquiry results.
- Administer spelling test.
- Review combining sentences.

Research and Inquiry
Communicate

Present ideas Have students share their inquiry results by presenting their information and giving a brief talk on their research. Have students display their review or definition that they created on Day 3.

Listening and speaking Remind students how to be good speakers and how to communicate effectively with their audience.

- Respond to relevant questions with appropriate details.
- Speak coherently about the topic.
- Speak clearly and loudly.
- Make eye contact with audience members.

Remind students of these tips for being a good listener.

- Listen attentively and wait until the speaker has finished before raising your hand to ask a relevant question.
- Be polite, even if you disagree.

Spelling Test
Final Syllables *-ion, -ure*

Spelling test To administer the spelling test, refer to the directions, words, and sentences on p. 435c.

Conventions
Extra Practice

Teach Remind students that combining sentences improves choppy or repetitive writing.

Guide practice Have students write two simple sentences describing a favorite art project.

> **I painted a picture of a turtle. I used green and blue paint.**

Have students exchange papers with a partner and combine the sentences. (*I painted a picture of a blue and green turtle.*)

Daily Fix-It Use Daily Fix-It numbers 9 and 10 in the right margin.

On their own Write the pairs of simple sentences below. Direct students to look back in *Talking Walls: Art for the People* to find the sentences combined. Discuss with students which sentence from the selection is a compound sentence. Students should complete *Let's Practice It!* page 390 on the *Teacher Resources DVD-ROM.*

1. **Muralists are asked by a town to create a work of art on a wall. They are asked by a school or business.** (*Muralists are asked by a town, school, or business to create a work of art on a wall.* p. 440)

2. **He interprets their stories by making sketches. He makes plans for the painting of the mural.** (*He interprets their stories by making sketches, and then he makes plans for the painting of the mural.* p. 444)

3. **Paul loved painting murals. Paul was inspired to become an artist like his brother.** (*Paul loved painting murals and was inspired to become an artist like his brother.* p. 446)

Daily Fix-It

9. The mural was a success and the class will paint unother soon. (*success, and; another*)

10. What subjeck will they choose for the next mural. (*subject; mural?*)

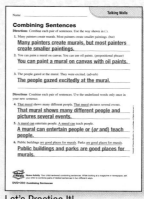

Let's Practice It!
TR DVD•390

Writing—Description
Voice

Review revising Remind students that yesterday they revised their descriptions of artwork, paying particular attention to consolidating by combining sentences. Today they will edit and proofread their descriptions.

MINI-LESSON

Proofread for Voice

■ **Teach** When we proofread, we look closely at our work, searching for errors in mechanics, spelling, and grammar. Today we will also focus on voice, which communicates to the reader how the writer feels about the topic.

■ **Model** Let's look at the description of Ori's cat collage. What words and phrases tell you that I am interested in my topic? Point out that *grass in spring, shine,* and *sparkling* tell the reader that the writer is excited about the collage. In the second paragraph, the writer uses the words *happy* and *energetic* to describe the nature of that interest. I tried to use words that would show how much I like the cat collage. But the part that says, *it looks like it might leap right out at you,* doesn't fit with the voice in the rest of the description. I think I'll change it to something more positive, like *it looks like it might want to play.* I'll reread my description a few more times, looking for other errors. Explain to students that they should do the same, and encourage them to keep the voice consistent.

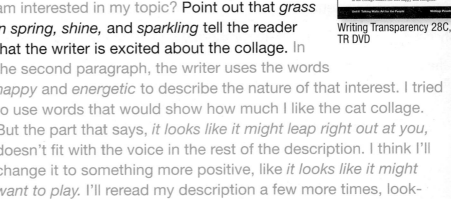

Writing Transparency 28C, TR DVD

Proofread Display the Proofreading Tips. Ask students to proofread their compositions, using the Proofreading Tips and paying particular attention to voice. Circulate around the room answering students' questions. When students have finished editing their own work, have pairs proofread one another's descriptions.

Proofreading Tips

✔ Use words and phrases that show you are interested in your topic.

✔ Check for correct spelling, punctuation, capitalization, and grammar.

✔ Be sure that compound sentences have a comma and a conjunction.

Present Have students incorporate revisions and proofreading edits into their descriptions to create a final draft.

Have students display their descriptions along with a photocopy or a student reproduction of the piece of art they are describing. Invite parents or other students to tour the display, while students act as gallery hosts. Then collect the images and descriptions in a class book.

ROUTINE   Quick Write for Fluency   Team Talk

1. **Talk** Pairs discuss the purpose of murals.

2. **Write** Students write for two or three minutes on the effects murals have on the public.

3. **Share** Students exchange writing with their partners, who read it aloud.

Routines Flip Chart

Teacher Note

Writing self-evaluation Make copies of the Writing Self-Evaluation Guide on p. 39 of the *Reader's and Writer's Notebook* and hand out to students.

English Language Learners

Support editing Remind students where to place commas in compound sentences. Provide several practice sentences, and guide students to punctuate them correctly.

Poster preview Prepare students for next week by using Week 4, ELL Poster 29. Read the Poster Talk-Through to introduce the concept and vocabulary. Ask students to identify and describe objects and actions in the art.

Selection summary Send home the summary of *Two Bad Ants,* in English and the students' home languages, if available. Students can read the summary with family members.

Preview NEXT WEEK

Why are rules and laws important to freedom? Next week you will be reading about two ants that make an unfortunate decision.

Weekly Assessment

Use pp. 199–206 of *Weekly Tests* to check:

✔ **Phonics** Final syllables *-tion, -ion, -ture, -ive, -ize*

✔ ◉ **Comprehension Skill** Graphic Sources

✔ **Lesson Vocabulary**

encourages	settled
expression	social
local	support
native	

✔ **Review Comprehension Skill**
Fact and Opinion

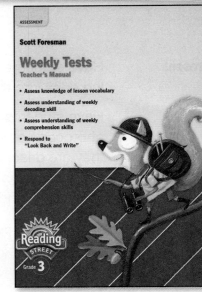

Weekly Tests

Advanced

On-Level

Differentiated Assessment

Use pp. 163–168 of *Fresh Reads for Fluency and Comprehension* to check:

✔ ◉ **Comprehension Skill** Graphic Sources

✔ **Review Comprehension Skill** Fact and Opinion

✔ **Fluency** Words Correct Per Minute

SI
Strategic Intervention

Fresh Reads for Fluency and Comprehension

Managing Assessment

Use *Assessment Handbook* for:

✔ **Weekly Assessment Blackline Masters for Monitoring Progress**

✔ **Observation Checklists**

✔ **Record-Keeping Forms**

✔ **Portfolio Assessment**

Assessment Handbook

Teacher Notes

Small Group Time

Pacing Small Group Instruction

5-Day Plan

DAY 1
• Reinforce the concept
• Read Leveled Readers
   Concept Literacy
   Below Level

DAY 2
• ◉ Graphic Sources
• ◉ Important Ideas
• Revisit Student Edition
   pp. 438–445

DAY 3
• ◉ Unknown Words
• Revisit Student Edition
   pp. 446–451

DAY 4
• Practice Retelling
• Read/Revisit Student
   Edition pp. 456–457

DAY 5
• Reread for fluency
• Reread Leveled
   Readers

3- or 4-Day Plan

DAY 1
• Reinforce the concept
• Read Leveled Readers

DAY 2
• ◉ Graphic Sources
• ◉ Important Ideas
• Revisit Student Edition
   pp. 438–445

DAY 3
• ◉ Unknown Words
• Revisit Student Edition
   pp. 446–451

DAY 4
• Practice Retelling
• Read/Revisit Student
   Edition pp. 456–457
• Reread for fluency
• Reread Leveled
   Readers

3-Day Plan: Eliminate the shaded box.

SI *Strategic Intervention* **DAY 1**

Build Background

■ **Reinforce the Concept** Reinforce the weekly question *Why is freedom of expression important?* This week's concept is freedom of expression. When you express yourself, you say or write or show what you think or feel. What are some ways that you express yourself? *(Students may say that they express themselves by talking, writing, singing, drawing, painting, or dancing.)* What is the opposite of expressing yourself? *(Some students may say keeping silent.)* Add new words to the concept map. This week we are going to read about murals, which are large paintings on walls or ceilings. In what way is painting a mural a good way to express yourself? *(A mural is a large painting, so it is easy to see.)* Explain that painters create murals to express feelings about a community, a time in history, or other subjects.

Preview Decodable Practice Reader 28A

■ **Before Reading** Review the words on p. 145 of *Decodable Practice Readers 3.2.* Then have students blend these words from the text: *inventor, surrounded, creaked, alarmed, invisible, reverse, spoonful,* and *gasped.* Be sure students understand the meaning of such words as *alarmed* and *reverse.* Guide students through the text by doing a picture walk.

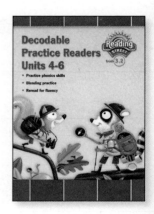

Decodable Practice Readers Units 4-6
• Practice phonics skills
• Blending practice
• Reread for fluency

Objectives
• Participate in teacher-led discussions by answering questions with appropriate detail.

For a complete literacy instructional plan and additional practice with this week's target skills and strategies, see the **Leveled Reader Teaching Guide.**

Concept Literacy Reader

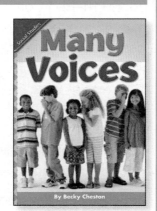

- **Read** *Many Voices*

- **Before Reading** Preview the book with students, focusing on key concepts and vocabulary. Then help students set a purpose for reading.

- **During Reading** Read the first two pages aloud while students track along with the print. Then have students finish reading the book with a partner.

- **After Reading** After students finish reading, ask: In what ways do the children express their feelings? *(with rhyme in poems; with songs; with colors in art; with words in letters to others; with dance)*

Below-Level Reader

- **Read** *One Forest, Different Trees*

- **Before Reading** Help students use the illustrations to preview the book. Then help students set a purpose for reading.

- **During Reading** Read pp. 3–5 aloud. Then do a choral reading of pp. 6–9. If students are able, have them read and discuss the remainder of the book with a partner. Ask: What kinds of trees does Sue draw? *(She draws many kinds of trees. Some look like real trees, one looks like an octopus, and one looks like a monkey.)*

- **After Reading** Ask students to look at and discuss the concept map. Connect the Below-Level Reader to the weekly question *Why is freedom of expression important?* We can express ourselves in many different ways. How do the students' tree drawings support this idea? *(The drawings are all different. Some look like real trees, and some don't.)*

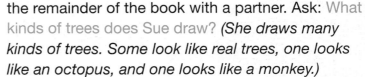

MONITOR PROGRESS

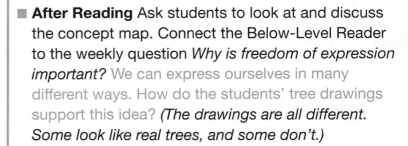

If... students have difficulty reading the selection with a partner,

then... have them follow along as they listen to the Leveled Readers DVD-ROM.

If... students have trouble understanding Sue's problem,

then... reread p. 3 and discuss the children's project.

Objectives
- Participate in teacher-led discussions by answering questions with appropriate detail.

Student Edition pp. EI•10–11

More Reading

Use additional Leveled Readers or other texts at students' instructional levels to reinforce this week's skills and strategies. For text suggestions, see the Leveled Reader Database or the Leveled Readers Skills Chart on pp. CL24–CL29.

SI *Strategic Intervention*   DAY **2**

Reinforce Comprehension

Skill Graphic Sources Review with students the *Envision It!* pp. EI•10–EI•11 on graphic sources. Then use p. 434 to review the definition of graphic sources. Graphic sources present information visually, which means in ways you can see. Charts, tables, graphs, diagrams, and maps are all examples of graphic sources. In which of your textbooks have you seen graphic sources? *(Students might mention math, science, and social studies textbooks.)*

Strategy Important Ideas Review the meaning of important ideas on p. 434. Point out to students that graphic sources often organize, summarize, or extend important information in a selection. For additional support, refer students to *Envision It!* p. EI•19.

Revisit *Talking Walls: Art for the People* on pp. 438–445. As partners read aloud, have them apply the comprehension skill and the comprehension strategy to the photo essay.

- What area does the map on p. 444 show? *(the United States)*

- How are important locations marked on the map? *(with pushpins)*

- What is the title of Hector Ponce's mural? *("Immigrant")*

- Where is his mural located? *(Los Angeles, California)*

- What important idea does the mural "Immigrant" express? *(Immigrants helped to create the neighborhood in which the mural is located.)*

Use the During Reading Differentiated Instruction for additional support for struggling readers.

MONITOR PROGRESS

If... students have difficulty reading along with the group,
then... have them follow along as they listen to the AudioText.

Objectives
- Locate specific information in graphic features of text.
- Locate facts about other texts.

 **SI** Strategic Intervention

DAY 3

Reinforce Vocabulary

■ **Reread for Fluency** Use Decodable Practice Reader 28A.

■ **Decoding Multisyllabic Words** Write *festivals* on the board and model how to look for meaningful parts in the word. I see a chunk at the beginning of the word: *fes.* I see a part in the middle: *ti.* I see a chunk at the end of the word: *vals.* I say each chunk slowly: *fes ti vals.* I say the chunks fast to make a whole word: *festivals.* Is it a real word? Yes, I've heard the word *festivals* before.

Use the Multisyllabic Words routine on the *Routines Flip Chart* to help students read these other words from the photo essay: *artistic, muralists, depict, democracy, seamstress, interprets, fashioned, extending, graduated, accomplished,* and *residents.*

◉ **Unknown Words/Dictionary or Glossary** Write the word *native* on the board. I have never seen the word *native* before, and I don't see any word parts that I can use to figure out its meaning. Perhaps I can find the definition in a dictionary or a glossary. I see that the definition of *native* in the glossary is "belonging to someone because of that person's birth." That definition makes sense in the context for *native* on p. 440.

■ **Revisit** *Talking Walls: Art for the People* on pp. 446–451. Review *Words!* on p. W•14. Encourage students to use a dictionary to figure out the meaning of any unknown words. Explain that students can find dictionaries online as well as in book form.

Use the During Reading Differentiated Instruction for additional support for struggling readers.

Student Edition p. W•14

More Reading

Use additional Leveled Readers or other texts at students' instructional levels to reinforce this week's skills and strategies. For text suggestions, see the Leveled Reader Database or the Leveled Readers Skills Chart on pp. CL24–CL29.

MONITOR PROGRESS

If... students need more practice with the lesson vocabulary,

then... use *Envision It! Pictured Vocabulary Cards*.

Objectives
• Use a dictionary or glossary to determine meanings of unknown words.

Small Group Time

Practice Retelling

- **Retell** Guide students in using the Retelling Cards to summarize the information.

  - What do all of the murals have in common? *(They are all large and colorful.)*

  - Why does the author call murals "talking walls"? *(The murals tell what the artists feel. For the artists, painting the images is like talking about their feelings. The artists "speak" to viewers through their murals.)*

  - The author calls murals "art for the people." What does that mean? *(Instead of being in museums, most of these paintings are on the sides of buildings. That means that many people can see them.)*

If students struggle, model a fluent retelling.

Genre Focus

- **Before Reading or Revisiting** "The History of Palindromes" on pp. 456–457, read aloud the genre information about palindromes on p. 456. Which of the following words is a palindrome—*live, solos,* or *wallow? (solos)*

- **During Reading or Revisiting** Have students locate and read the boldfaced headings.

  - What are some examples of one-word palindromes on the first page? (radar, deed, level)

  - What are some examples of palindrome phrases on the first page? *("Don't nod"; "Never odd or even")*

  - What three words appear in the palindrome square at the top left of the second page? *(gel, leg, eye)*

- **After Reading or Revisiting** Guide students through the Reading Across Texts and Writing Across Texts activities, prompting if necessary.

MONITOR PROGRESS

If... students have difficulty retelling the selection,

then... have them review the selection using the photos and text features.

Objectives
- Identify playful uses of language.

For a complete literacy instructional plan and additional practice with this week's target skills and strategies, see the **Leveled Reader Teaching Guide.**

Concept Literacy Reader

■ **Model** Model the fluency skill of accuracy for students. Ask students to listen carefully as you read aloud the first two pages of *Many Voices.* Have students note that you read the words exactly as they are written and do not leave out words or make any substitutions. Explain to students that, if you had read the wrong words or left out words, it would be difficult to understand the story.

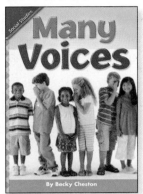
Many Voices

■ **Fluency Routine**

1. Have students reread passages from *Many Voices* with a partner.

2. For optimal fluency, students should reread three to four times.

3. As students read, monitor fluency and provide corrective feedback. Have students note that you read every word exactly as written.

See *Routines Flip Chart* for more help with fluency.

■ **Retell** Have students retell *Many Voices.* Prompt as necessary.

Below-Level Reader

■ **Model** Ask students to listen carefully as you read aloud the first two pages of *One Forest, Different Trees,* emphasizing accuracy.

One Forest, Different Trees

■ **Fluency Routine**

1. Have students reread passages from *One Forest, Different Trees* with a partner or individually.

2. For optimal fluency, students should reread three to four times.

3. As students read, monitor fluency and provide corrective feedback.

See *Routines Flip Chart* for more help with fluency.

■ **Retell** For additional practice, have students retell *One Forest, Different Trees* page by page using the illustrations. Prompt students as necessary.

● Why are the children drawing pictures of trees? *(to make a picture of a forest for the wall)*

● What kind of tree does Sue draw at first? *(a real-looking tree)*

● What does Nat say the tree pictures should look like? *(green lollipops)*

MONITOR PROGRESS

If... students have difficulty reading fluently,

then... provide additional fluency practice by pairing nonfluent readers with fluent ones.

Objectives
● Read aloud grade-level appropriate text with fluency.

Small Group Time

Pacing Small Group Instruction

15–20 min

5-Day Plan

DAY 1	• Expand the concept • Read On-Level Reader
DAY 2	• Graphic Sources • Important Ideas • Revisit Student Edition pp. 438–445
DAY 3	• Unknown Words • Revisit Student Edition pp. 446–451
DAY 4	• Practice Retelling • Read/Revisit Student Edition pp. 456–457
DAY 5	• Reread for fluency • Reread On-Level Reader

3- or 4-Day Plan

DAY 1	• Expand the concept • Read On-Level Reader
DAY 2	• Graphic Sources • Important Ideas • Revisit Student Edition pp. 438–445
DAY 3	• Unknown Words • Revisit Student Edition pp. 446–451
DAY 4	• Practice Retelling • Read/Revisit Student Edition pp. 456–457 • Reread for fluency • Reread On-Level Reader

3-Day Plan: Eliminate the shaded box.

OL On-Level — DAY 1

Build Background

■ **Expand the Concept** Discuss the weekly question *Why is freedom of expression important?* Then expand the concept. People are free to express themselves in many ways. People show their ideas, feelings, opinions, hopes, experiences, or cultures through art, food, music, or other activities. Discuss the meaning of the words on the concept map on p. 431.

On-Level Reader

For a complete literacy instructional plan and additional practice with this week's target skills and strategies, see the **Leveled Reader Teaching Guide.**

■ **Before Reading** *Lily's Adventure Around the World,* help students preview the book by looking at the title, cover, and pictures. What is this book about? Is it about a real person, or is it a story with made-up characters and events? *(Help students understand that is a fictional story that includes some actual places.)*

Lily's Adventure Around the World

Have students create a three-column chart titled *Chicago Neighborhoods* with the headings *Mexican, Polish,* and *Chinese.* Explain that students will complete their three-column charts as they read.

■ **During Reading** Read aloud the first three pages as students follow along. Then have them finish reading on their own. Remind students to add details to their three-column charts as they read. What foods do Lily and her family buy in each neighborhood? *(enchiladas, helados, and chayote cactus in Pilsen; sausages and gooseberry compote in Archer Park; ginger tea and fresh crabs in Chinatown)*

■ **After Reading** Have partners compare their three-column charts.

• Which neighborhood would you most like to visit? Why? *(Have students support their choices with evidence from the text.)*

• How does the topic relate to the weekly question *Why is freedom of expression important? (People in the different neighborhoods express their cultures in different ways.)*

Objectives
• Participate in teacher-led discussions by answering questions with appropriate detail.

 **OL** On-Level — DAY **2**

Expand Comprehension

Skill Graphic Sources Use p. 434 to review the definition of *graphic sources*. For additional review, see Graphic Sources on *Envision It!* pp. EI•10–EI•11. Graphic sources present information visually, which means in ways you can see. Charts and tables are examples of graphic sources. What are some others? *(Students may mention graphs, diagrams, maps, and cutaway illustrations.)*

Strategy Important Ideas Review the definition of important ideas. As students read, encourage them to think about the important ideas in the text. Point out that graphic sources often reinforce important ideas. How do the map and the table reinforce the idea that murals exist across America? *(The map and the table both indicate a variety of locations for murals.)* For additional support, use the Extend Thinking questions during reading or refer students to p. EI•19 of *Envision It!*

Revisit *Talking Walls: Art for the People* on pp. 438–445. As students read, have them apply the comprehension skill and strategy to the photo essay.

- What type of graphic source is shown on p. 444? *(map)*

- What important information does the graphic source present? *(information about places, such as the boundaries of countries and states and the locations of cities and towns)*

- Why is this type of graphic source included in the photo essay? *(The essay describes murals in different places, and the map helps the reader locate those places.)*

- Look ahead to p. 448. What type of graphic source is shown? *(a chart, also called a table)*

- How is the information organized? *(in rows and columns)*

- Why is this type of graphic source included in the photo essay? *(to summarize important information about the murals)*

Student Edition pp. EI•10–EI•11

More Reading

Use additional Leveled Readers or other texts at students' instructional levels to reinforce this week's skills and strategies. For text suggestions, see the Leveled Reader Database or the Leveled Readers Skills Chart on pp. CL24–CL29.

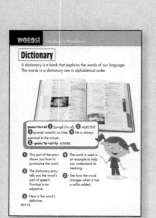

Student Edition p. W•14

More Reading

Use additional Leveled Readers or other texts at students' instructional levels to reinforce this week's skills and strategies. For text suggestions, see the Leveled Reader Database or the Leveled Readers Skills Chart on pp. CL24–CL29.

Expand Vocabulary

Unknown Words/Dictionary or Glossary
Write the word *seamstress* on the board as you say it aloud. Early in the essay, the author asks you to find a seamstress in the mural "Immigrant." If this word is unknown to you and you can't get the meaning from word parts or context, you can look the word up in a dictionary or glossary.

- What definition does the dictionary give for *seamstress*? *("a woman who sews")*

- How can you figure out whether this meaning makes sense in the selection? *(The mural includes a picture of a woman using a sewing machine. She must be the seamstress.)*

Revisit *Talking Walls: Art for the People* on pp. 446–451. Write the word *instrumental* as you say it aloud. At the end of the essay, the author says that muralists "are instrumental in reminding Americans everywhere of the freedoms that help our democracy work." What does *instrumental* mean? If this word is unknown to you and you can't get the meaning from word parts or context, you can look up the word in a dictionary or glossary.

- What definition does the dictionary give for *instrumental*? *("useful or helpful")*

- How can you figure out whether this meaning makes sense in the selection? *(Substituting the word* useful *or the word* helpful *for the word* instrumental *in the phrase, which results in a phrase that makes sense.)*

- Is it easier to figure out the meaning of *instrumental* by using a dictionary and context clues or by breaking the word into parts? *(The base word is* instrument, *so using word parts as clues might lead one to think the word had to do with musical instruments. Using a dictionary is probably easier.)*

Objectives

- Use a dictionary or glossary to determine meanings of unknown words.

Practice Retelling

■ **Retell** To assess students' comprehension, use the Retelling Cards. Monitor retelling and prompt students as needed.

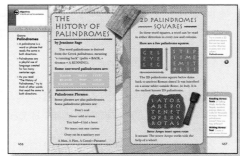

Genre Focus

■ **Before Reading or Revisiting** "The History of Palindromes" on pp. 456–457, read aloud the genre information about palindromes on p. 456. Remind students of the weekly question *Why is freedom of expression important?* Ask: How might a palindrome be a form of self-expression? *(It is a use of language through which a person might playfully express an idea.)* Help students preview "The History of Palindromes" and set a purpose for reading.

■ **During Reading or Revisiting** Have students read with you while tracking along with the print. Ask:

- How is this selection organized? *(The author describes several types of palindromes and gives examples.)*

- How is this selection different from the photo essay *Talking Walls: Art for the People?* *(It has no photographs. It doesn't give as much information. It has a more formal style.)*

- How do the arrows help you understand the text? *(They show that the palindrome squares can be read from left to right and from top to bottom.)*

- The author explains that the ancient palindrome square "was inscribed on a stone tablet." How can you use context clues to guess at the meaning of the word *inscribed? (The word* written *would make sense substituted for* inscribed, *so those two words may have the same meaning.)*

- How can you find out whether your guess is correct? *(Check a dictionary.)*

■ **After Reading or Revisiting** Have students share their reaction to "The History of Palindromes." Then have them search classroom books or the Internet for palindromes or palindrome phrases. Tell them to list the examples they find, and then display their lists in the class.

Objectives
- Identify playful uses of language.

Small Group Time

On-Level Reader

■ **Model** Read aloud p. 3 of the On-Level Reader *Lily's Adventure Around the World,* emphasizing accuracy.

■ **Fluency Routine**

Lily's Adventure Around the World

1. Have students reread passages from *Lily's Adventure Around the World* with a partner.

2. For optimal fluency, students should reread passages three to four times.

3. As students read, monitor fluency and provide corrective feedback. Have students note that each word should be read exactly as written. Then discuss why it is important to identify words correctly without leaving any out and without making substitutions.

See *Routines Flip Chart* if students need more help with fluency.

■ **Retell** For additional practice, have students use illustrations as a guide to retell *Lily's Adventure Around the World.* Prompt as necessary.

• What is this story mostly about? *(Lily's adventures in several ethnic neighborhoods in Chicago)*

• What neighborhoods does Lily visit? *(a Mexican neighborhood called Pilsen, a Polish neighborhood called Archer Park, and Chinatown)*

• How are the neighborhoods similar and different? *(They are all within the city limits of Chicago, but the people in the neighborhoods eat different foods, have different hobbies, and speak different languages.)*

• What did you learn from reading this story? *(A new home can lead to fun discoveries.)*

Objectives
• Read aloud grade-level appropriate text with fluency.

A Advanced   **DAY 1**

Build Background

■ **Extend the Concept** Discuss with students the weekly question *Why is freedom of expression important?* Why is freedom of expression so valuable? *(It's important to be allowed to express thoughts, feelings, opinions, goals, and hopes. If people didn't have freedom of expression, they wouldn't be able to share ideas and beliefs.)* Why might people try to take away freedom of expression from others? *(when they don't like the message that is being expressed)*

Advanced Reader

For a complete literacy instructional plan and additional practice with this week's target skills and strategies, see the **Leveled Reader Teaching Guide**.

■ **Before Reading** *Thomas Hart Benton: Painter of Murals*, have students use the images to predict what they will read about and set a purpose for reading.

■ **During Reading** Have students read the Advanced Reader independently.

- Why did Thomas choose not to paint using abstract styles and unusual colors? *(He didn't feel these styles were for everyday people.)*

- How does seeing the murals help you understand the text? *(The murals make it easier to understand what the artist painted and what his style of painting was.)*

Thomas Hart Benton: Painter of Murals

- How is the photograph on pp. 20–21 helpful? *(It shows the artist's detailed and realistic style—his self-portrait looks exactly like him.)*

■ **After Reading** Have students review the concept map and explain how the book helps students answer the weekly question *Why is freedom of expression important?*

- What did Thomas Hart Benton express through his paintings? *(his view of American history and culture)*

- Why do you think freedom of expression was important to him? *(It allowed him to paint as he wanted.)*

■ **Now Try This** Assign "Now Try This" at the end of the Advanced Reader.

Objectives
- Practice in teacher-led discussions by answering questions with appropriate detail.

Pacing Small Group Instruction
15–20 min

5-Day Plan

DAY 1	• Extend the concept • Read Advanced Reader
DAY 2	• ⦿ Graphic Sources • ⦿ Important Ideas • Revisit Student Edition pp. 438–445
DAY 3	• ⦿ Unknown Words • Revisit Student Edition pp. 446–451
DAY 4	• Palindromes • Read/Revisit Student Edition pp. 456–457
DAY 5	• Reread for fluency • Reread Advanced Reader

3- or 4-Day Plan

DAY 1	• Extend the concept • Read Advanced Reader
DAY 2	• ⦿ Graphic Sources • ⦿ Important Ideas • Revisit Student Edition pp. 438–445
DAY 3	• ⦿ Unknown Words • Revisit Student Edition pp. 446–451
DAY 4	• Palindromes • Read/Revisit Student Edition pp. 456–457 • Reread for fluency • Reread Advanced Reader

3-Day Plan: Eliminate the shaded box.

DAY 2

More Reading

Use additional Leveled Readers or other texts at students' instructional levels to reinforce this week's skills and strategies. For text suggestions, see the Leveled Reader Database or the Leveled Readers Skills Chart on pp. CL24–CL29.

A *Advanced*

Extend Comprehension

Skill Graphic Sources Explain that graphic sources are ways of showing information visually. Remind students that graphic sources summarize, organize, reinforce, or extend the ideas in a selection.

Strategy Important Ideas Review the definition of the strategy. As they read the rest of the selection, encourage students to think about important ideas. Sometimes graphic sources explain important ideas that are also stated in the main selection text; sometimes graphics add different ideas that are also important. During reading, use the Extend Thinking questions and the During Reading Differentiated Instruction for additional support.

■ **Revisit** *Talking Walls: Art for the People* on pp. 438–445. Then have students look at the graphic sources throughout the selection.

• How do the photographs of the murals help you understand the text? *(They show how large and colorful the murals are.)*

• How do the captions help you? *(They identify mural titles and locations.)*

• What other graphic sources did the author include, and how are these helpful? *(The map and chart provide a great deal of information in a small space.)*

• What important ideas are the artists expressing in these murals? *(patriotism, working hard to achieve dreams, celebrating the people who live in a particular neighborhood of Los Angeles)*

■ **Critical Thinking/Creative Thinking** Challenge students to evaluate and reflect on what they have read.

• Compare and contrast the work of the different artists. *(Some show realistic images, while others create pictures that include impossible things, such as a tree growing out of a girl's arms.)*

• If you could paint a mural anywhere, what would you paint and why? Give reasons for your answer.

Objectives
• Locate specific information in graphic features of text.
• Locate facts about other texts.

 **A** Advanced

DAY 3

Extend Vocabulary

Unknown Words/Dictionary or Glossary
Point out the glossary at the back of the textbook. Explain that students can check the glossary or a dictionary if they have trouble determining the meanings of words.

Revisit *Talking Walls: Art for the People* on pp. 446–451. Then read the following sentences from *Talking Walls: Art for the People* that contain words that may be unknown to students.

- "Do you know that some painters use walls as their canvas?" Where can you find the meaning of the word *canvas*? *(in a dictionary)* What does *canvas* mean? *(It is a sturdy cloth on which artists paint.)*

- "The mural encourages children to reach for the future through education." What meaning does the dictionary give for *encourage*? *("to give confidence")* What kind of picture or cartoon could you draw to show the meaning of *encourage*? *(possible answer: a cartoon of someone smiling and saying "You can do it!")*

- "Students are standing at the bottom of the painting holding objects that symbolize their future." What meaning does the dictionary give for *symbolize*? *(represent)* How can you test whether the meaning you found is correct? *(by substituting represent for symbolize to see if it also makes sense in the sentence)*

- "Some murals inspire or amuse us, while others stir our hearts." What does *amuse* mean? *("entertain, cause to laugh")* What do you think the author means by "stir our hearts"? *(make our hearts beat faster, make us feel strong emotions)*

- "Community murals tell stories of personal, political, and social beliefs of the local residents." What meaning does the dictionary give for *residents*? *("people who live in a particular place")*

More Reading
Use additional Leveled Readers or other texts at students' instructional levels to reinforce this week's skills and strategies. For text suggestions, see the Leveled Reader Database or the Leveled Readers Skills Chart on pp. CL24–CL29.

Objectives
- Use a dictionary or glossary to determine meanings of unknown words.

Small Group Time

Genre Focus

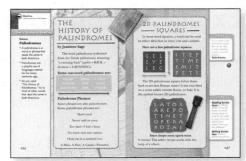

The History of Palindromes

- **Before Reading or Revisiting** "The History of Palindromes" on pp. 456–457, review the panel information on palindromes. Then have students use the text features to set a purpose for reading. Next have students read "The History of Palindromes" on their own.

- **During Reading or Revisiting** Encourage students to think creatively. For example, ask: Which of the palindrome phrases might serve as a headline for a newspaper story about a health problem? *("Oozy rat in a sanitary zoo")* A warehouse robbery? *("No trace; not one carton")*

- **After Reading or Revisiting** Have students discuss Reading Across Texts. Then have them do Writing Across Texts independently. Palindromes were popular in ancient Roman times and are popular today. Why do you think that is? *(They are fun, they make people think, and they sometimes make people laugh.)* If you wish, have students create and share their own palindromes.

Objectives
- Identify playful uses of language.

Thomas Hart Benton: Painter of Murals

- **Reread for Fluency** Have students silently reread passages from the Advanced Reader. Then have them reread aloud with a partner or individually. As students read, monitor fluency and provide corrective feedback. If students read fluently on the first reading, they do not need to reread three to four times. Assess the fluency of students in this group using p. 459j.

- **Retell** Have students summarize the main idea and key details from the Advanced Reader *Thomas Hart Benton: Painter of Murals.*

- **Now Try This** Have students complete their charts and mini-murals.

Objectives
- Read aloud grade-level appropriate text with fluency.

 **English Language Learners**

The ELL lessons are organized by strands. Use them to scaffold the weekly curriculum of lessons or during small group time instruction.

Academic Language

Students will hear or read the following academic language in this week's core instruction. As students encounter the vocabulary, provide a simple definition or concrete example. Then ask students to suggest an example or synonym of the word and identify available cognates.

Skill Words	graphic sources	syllables *(sílabas)*
	sensory details	schwa
	combining sentences	
Concept Words	scaffold	mural *(mural)*
	immigrants	musician *(músico)*
	(immigrantes)	

*Spanish cognates in parentheses

Concept Development

 Why is freedom of expression important?

■ **Preteach Concept**

• **Prior Knowledge** Have students turn to pp. 430–431 in the Student Edition. Call attention to the pictures of all the children and tap into students' knowledge of expressing yourself. How do these children express themselves? Did you ever speak in front of the class? Did you sing or play music for someone? How did it feel? How do you express yourself?

• **Discuss Concept** Elicit students' knowledge and experience of freedom of expression. How is the boy reading his paper in front of the class expressing himself? What would it be like if we could not say what we want? Supply background information as needed.

• **Poster Talk-Through** Read the Poster Talk-Through on ELL Poster 28 aloud and work through the Day 1 activities.

■ **Daily Concept and Vocabulary Development** Use the daily activities on ELL Poster 28 to build concept and vocabulary knowledge.

Objectives
• Learn new language structures, expressions, and basic and academic vocabulary heard during classroom instruction.

Content Objectives
• Use concept vocabulary related to the idea of freedom of expression.

Language Objectives
• Understand meaning and express ideas about art and familiar topics.

Daily Planner

DAY 1	• **Frontload Concept** • **Preteach** Comprehension Skill, Vocabulary, Phonics/Spelling, Conventions • **Writing**
DAY 2	• **Review** Concept, Vocabulary, Comprehension Skill • **Frontload Main Selection** • **Practice** Phonics/Spelling, Conventions/Writing
DAY 3	• **Review** Concept, Comprehension Skill, Vocabulary, Conventions/Writing • **Reread Main Selection** • **Practice** Phonics/Spelling
DAY 4	• **Review Concept** • **Read ELL/ELD Readers** • **Practice** Phonics/Spelling, Conventions/Writing
DAY 5	• **Review** Concept, Vocabulary, Comprehension Skill, Phonics/Spelling, Conventions • **Reread ELL/ELD Readers** • **Writing**

*See the ELL Handbook for ELL Workshops with targeted instruction.

Concept Talk Video

Use Concept Talk Video Routine (*ELL Handbook,* p. 477) to build background knowledge about expressing freedom. For listening practice, see Use Classroom Resources (*ELL Handbook,* pp. 406–407).

Support for English Language Learners

Language Objectives

- Understand and use basic vocabulary.

- Learn meanings of grade-level vocabulary.

Cognates

For Spanish learners, point out that the word for *social* is spelled the same as the Spanish word *sociál.* Reinforce the concept that these languages share many words that are the same or similar.

ELL Workshop

Use Classroom Resources (*ELL Handbook*, pp. 406–407) provides practice with basic sight vocabulary used in written materials.

Basic Vocabulary

■ **High-Frequency Words** Use the vocabulary routines and the high-frequency word list on p. 471 of the *ELL Handbook* to systematically teach newcomers the first 300 sight words in English. Students who began learning ten words per week at the beginning of the year are now learning words 271–280. The *ELL Handbook* (p. 456) contains a bank of strategies that you can use to ensure students' mastery of high-frequency words.

Lesson Vocabulary

■ **Preteach** Introduce the Lesson Vocabulary using this routine:

1. Distribute copies of this week's Word Cards (*ELL Handbook,* p. 191).

2. Display ELL Poster 28 and reread the Poster Talk-Through.

3. Using the poster illustrations, model how a word's meaning can be expressed with other similar words: The sculpture of the girl has a happy look, or *expression,* on her face.

4. Use these sentences to reveal the meaning of the other words.

   - The teacher *encourages* her students to do their best (gives hope or courage)

   - The class made her a card as an *expression* of their gratitude. (an act of showing feelings)

   - My family enjoys going to the *local* swimming pool. (nearby)

   - Tiffany is a *native* of Texas. (born in a particular place)

   - Her family *settled* in the countryside long ago. (went to live)

   - The block party was a fun *social* occasion. (gathering of people)

   - We made posters to show our *support* of the team. (encouragement)

Objectives

- Use strategic learning techniques such as concept mapping, drawing, memorizing, comparing, contrasting, and reviewing to acquire basic and grade-level vocabulary.
- Use accessible language and learn new and essential language in the process.

 English Language Learners

■ **Reteach**

- Use the ELL Poster 28 for a vocabulary activity. Help students use the Lesson Vocabulary to discuss images in the poster art. Have them discuss the various *expressions* on the children's faces, point to the *native* clothing on the sculptures that the artist is creating for a *local social* gathering. If you were the artist, would you *support* the project? Discuss the reasons that the artist would be *encouraged* to make the figures in the poster.

■ **Writing** Allow students to use the Word Cards to write answers that complete the following sentence frames.

- Doing the right thing _____ others to do the same. **(encourages)**

- The artist painted the mural as an _____ of hope for his community. **(expression)**

- A _____ school used the money to buy books. **(local)**

- The famous sculptor is a _____ of my hometown. **(native)**

- They _____ in California after leaving New York. **(settled)**

- The community enjoyed gathering for _____ occasions. **(social)**

- The students picked up trash in the park to show their _____. **(support)**

 Leveled Support

Beginning Have students work in pairs. Provide the first letter of the word as a clue for the answer.

Intermediate Have students rewrite the complete sentence on their paper.

Advanced/Advanced High Have students generate their own sentences using the Lesson Vocabulary words.

Language Objectives
- Produce drawings, phrases, or short sentences to show understanding of Lesson Vocabulary.

ELL Teacher Tip
Research shows that children acquire language most readily when they are actively involved in learning activities. Classroom activities should integrate reading, writing, listening, and speaking, as these language skills develop interdependently. Have students write, speak, read, and listen to the vocabulary words as they study the lesson throughout the week.

Objectives
- Write using newly acquired basic vocabulary and content-based grade-level vocabulary.

Support for English Language Learners

Content Objectives
- Monitor and adjust oral comprehension.

Language Objectives
- Discuss oral passages.
- Use a graphic organizer to take notes.

ELL Teacher Tip
As you read, you may wish to write the names of the artists and their nicknames on the board. Encourage students to refer to the list as they fill out the Main Idea graphic organizer.

ELL Workshop
Encourage students to demonstrate listening comprehension of the Read Aloud and other spoken messages. Provide Retell or Summarize (*ELL Handbook*, pp. 408–409) for practice.

ELL · English Language Learners

Listening Comprehension

Read Aloud

Not All Artists Are the Same

Some artists paint pictures. Others artists work with clay. But some artists work with objects that you might never expect to be in a piece of art.

Wayne Kusy is one of these artists. Kusy builds model ships out of toothpicks. He has been building ships since he was ten years old. Each ship had tiny details. One time Kusy built a 10-foot model of the *Titanic*.

Tressa Prisbrey is called "Grandma." She is also an artist. She has spent 25 years building Bottle Village. Prisbrey collected old bottles. Then she put them together with concrete. She builds walls and buildings. She uses many objects from the junkyard for her village. Many people visit Bottle Village because it is an amazing piece of artwork.

Charlie Lucas also uses scrap metal from the dump for his art. He is called the "Tin Man." Lucas has built dinosaurs, birds, and even an airplane from the metal he pulls from the dump. He says they are his toys.

All of these artists use everyday objects to make artistic creations that amaze us all.

Prepare for the Read Aloud The modified Read Aloud above prepares students for listening to the oral reading "Toothpicks, Bottles, Tin, and Rocks" on p. 431b.

■ **First Listening: Listen to Understand** Write the title of the Read Aloud on the board. This is about three artists who use unusual objects to create amazing art. Listen to find out what they make. What do they use to make it? Afterward, ask the question again and have students share their answers.

■ **Second Listening: Listen to Check Understanding** Using a Main Idea graphic organizer (*ELL Handbook*, p. 487), work with students to find the main idea of the selection and record it in the top box of the graphic organizer. Then work with students to name the three examples of unusual artists in the three details boxes of the chart.

Objectives
- Demonstrate listening comprehension of increasingly complex spoken English by following directions, retelling or summarizing spoken messages, responding to questions and requests, collaborating with peers, and taking notes commensurate with content and grade-level needs.

Phonics and Spelling

■ **Final Syllables *-tion, -ture, -ive, -ize*** Some words in English end with the common syllables *-tion, -ture, -ive,* and *-ize.* Write *mixture, decision, competitive,* and *magnetize* on the board. Repeat the words as I say them.

■ **Teach** Circle the syllable pattern in each word. Identify the root of each word. Have students pronounce each word accurately. Each word has a base word that can stand alone. Explain this spelling rule. Sometimes the spelling changes a little when the final syllable is added.

■ **Practice** Write the words *selection, departure, creative,* and *capitalize* on the board and read them aloud. Guide students as they say the words and identify the syllable pattern. Underline the syllable pattern in each word and discuss each word's meaning. Provide practice for students at their language proficiency level.

Vocabulary Skill: Unknown Words

■ **Preteach and Model** Write *seamstress* on the board. Look at p. 442 in the Student Edition. Point to the word seamstress. We know it is in the mural. We don't know what it is. Let's use a dictionary to find the meaning. Demonstrate using a dictionary to look up this word. Copy the dictionary page onto a transparency so all students can see what an entry looks like.

■ **Practice** Write these words on the board: *democracy, sketches, billboard, dinosaur, project.* Provide practice for students at their proficiency level.

Beginning/Intermediate Read the words aloud to Beginning learners. Help students find the definitions in a dictionary and explain the meaning of each word. Have Intermediate students read the words aloud.

Advanced/Advanced High Ask students to work with a partner to look up the definition for each word. Have students share their definitions with the class.

Content Objectives

• Identify final syllables *-tion, -ture, -ive, -ize.*

• Determine meanings of unknown in text.

Language Objectives

• Apply spelling rules with final syllables *-tion, -ture, -ive, -ize.*

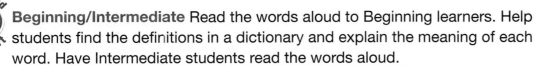 **Transfer Skills**

Syllables The suffix *-tion* has similar forms in other languages including French (*-tion*), Spanish (*-ción, -sión*), and Portuguese (*çäo*). For example, the English word *direction* is *direction* in French, *dirección* in Spanish, and *direçäo* in Portuguese.

Objectives
• Learn relationships between sounds and letters of the English language to represent sounds when writing in English.
• Spell familiar English words with increasing accuracy, and employ English spelling patterns and rules with increasing accuracy as more English.

Talking Walls: Art for the People **DI•70**

Support for English Language Learners

Content Objectives
- Distinguish information presented in graphic sources.
- Gather information from graphic sources.

Language Objectives
- Discuss information in a graphic source.
- Explain the content of a graphic source.

ELL Workshop
Encourage students to ask questions to monitor their understanding of instruction of comprehension skills. Use Ask Clarifying Questions (*ELL Handbook,* pp. 406–407) for practice.

ELL English Language Learners

Comprehension
Graphic Sources

■ **Preteach** A graphic source is a map, a caption, or a graph in a book. These graphic sources can help you find information. Have students turn to p. EI•11 in the Student Edition. Read the text aloud together. Have students name the graphic sources in the examples. Have them tell what information they can gather about Spider monkeys from the graphics (live in South America, have prehensile tails, and eat fruit).

■ **Reteach** Distribute copies of Picture It! (*ELL Handbook,* p. 192). Have students look at the map. Tell the students to listen for the names and locations of the artists as you choral read the passage. Then, ask students to look at the outline map. What do you notice? (José Clemente Orozco-Dartmouth, NH; Diego Rivera-Detroit, MI; David Alfaro Siqueiros-Los Angeles, CA. Possible response: There are Mexican artists across the United States.)

Beginning Choral read the passage with the students. Have them circle the artists' names and underline the locations of their work. Ask: *How could you use the map to show this information?*

Intermediate/Advanced/Advanced High Have students read the passage with a partner. Ask the partners to discuss: "How are the text and map the same? How are the two sources different? How do they work together?"

MINI-LESSON

Social Language

Tell students that there are several kinds of graphic sources and their names help describe how they look. Have students turn to pp. EI•10–EI•11. A bar graph has bars. A circle graph is in a circle. A line graph has a line to show change. Show examples of each type of graph and write the name beneath each one.

Objectives
- Use visual and contextual support and support from peers and teachers to read grade-appropriate content area text, enhance and confirm understanding, and develop vocabulary, grasp of language structures, and background knowledge needed to comprehend increasingly challenging language.

 ELL English Language Learners

Talking Walls
Art for the People
by Katacha Díaz

Student Edition pp. 438–439

Reading Comprehension
Talking Walls: Art for the People

■ **Frontloading** Have students look through *Talking Walls: Art for the People,* pp. 438–451 in the Student Edition, and tell what they think makes it look like nonfiction, a selection about real things. Have students talk to each other about what they know about marals. Distribute copies of the English summary of *Talking Walls* (*ELL Handbook,* p. 193). Have students read the summary aloud with you. Encourage them to ask questions about any ideas or unfamiliar words. If you have sent copies of the summary home, have students read it again with family members.

Preview the selection by having students look at the pictures.

Sheltered Reading Ask questions such as the following to guide students' comprehension:

- **pp. 442–443** What does the mural "Immigrant" show in Los Angeles, CA? (the immigrant experience)

- **pp. 444–445** What did Joshua Sarantitis do before he painted "Reach High and You Will Go Far"? (He spoke to people in the community.)

- **p. 446** What is the message of "A Shared Hope" mural at Esperanza School? (Education is the key to success.)

- **p. 449** Why did David Botello change a boy to a girl in his mural, "Dreams of Flight"? (He wanted all children to know that girls can dream of flying model airplanes too.)

■ **Fluency: Accuracy** Remind students that reading with accuracy means that they pronounce each letter and word part clearly. Read the last paragraph of the selection on p. 451, pronouncing each word with accuracy. Point out the words with suffixes, such as instrumental, reminding, freedoms. Have pairs of students choose a paragraph on pp. 438–439. Have students read with accuracy as their partners listen and offer feedback. For more practice, use the Fluency: Paired Reading Routine (*ELL Handbook,* p. 474).

After Reading Use the Retelling strip on p. 452 to have students summarize the selection so that the content becomes familiar. Make a 3-column chart that names three of the artists from the selection and the name of their murals.

Content Objectives
- Monitor and adjust comprehension.
- Derive meaning from media.

Language Objectives
- Read with accuracy.
- Summarize text using visual support.

Audio Support
Have students listen to the main selection using the eSelection or the AudioText CD to build and reinforce language attainment. Have students tell what they learned after listening.

ELL Teaching Routine
For more practice summarizing, use the Retelling/ Summarizing Nonfiction Routine (*ELL Handbook,* pp. 408–409).

Objectives
- Understand the general meaning, main points, and important details of spoken language ranging from situations n which topics, language, and contexts are familiar to unfamiliar.

Support for English Language Learners

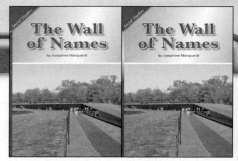

ELD Reader   ELL Reader

ELL — English Language Learners

For additional leveled instruction, see the **ELL/ELD Teaching Guide.**

Comprehension
The Wall of Names

- **Before Reading** Distribute copies of the ELL and ELD Readers, *The Wall of Names,* to students at their reading level.

  - **Preview** Read the title aloud with students: This is a nonfiction text about a special place in Washington, D.C. Invite students to look at the pictures in the book and name what they see. Have them predict what kind of wall the text will discuss.

  - **Set a Purpose for Reading** Let's read to find out what a wall of names is.

- **During Reading** Follow the Reading Routine for both reading groups.

  1. Read the entire Reader aloud slowly.

  2. Reread pp. 2–4, pausing to build background or guide comprehension. Have Beginning students finger-point as you read. Use the questions in the chart to check students' comprehension.

  3. Have students read pp. 2–4 independently.

  4. Repeat steps 2–3 above for pp. 5–8 of the Reader.

- **After Reading** Use the exercises on the inside back cover of each Reader and invite students to share their writing. In a whole-group discussion, Why do you think people wanted to see the wall? Record their answers on the board and invite them to point to pictures in the book to support their answers.

ELD Reader Beginning/Intermediate

- **p. 2** How did veterans raise money to build the memorial? (they collected money)

- **p. 3** What law did President Jimmy Carter sign in 1980? (a law that supported the creation of the memorial)

- **p. 4** Why were the designs displayed with numbers instead of names? (so the judges couldn't tell who created each design)

Writing How did people react to the wall when it was completed? Find the sentence in the book that tells what happens after the ceremony. Copy the sentence. Then read it aloud to your partner.

ELL Reader Advanced/Advanced High

- **pp. 2–4** Why did leaders decide to build the wall of names? (They wanted to remember the American soldiers who died in the Vietnam War.)

- **pp. 4–5** Who won the contest to design the memorial? (Maya Lin) Read aloud the sentence that gives you the answer. (She was a 21-year-old architecture student named Maya Lin.)

Study Guide Distribute copies of the ELL Reader Study Guide (*ELL Handbook,* p. 196). Scaffold comprehension of identifying details by helping students look back through the Reader in order to fill in the graphic organizer. Review their responses together. (See *ELL Handbook,* pp. 209–212.)

Objectives
- Demonstrate listening comprehension of increasingly complex spoken English by following directions, retelling or summarizing spoken messages, responding to questions and requests, collaborating with peers, and taking notes commensurate with content and grade-level needs.

 English Language Learners

Conventions
Combining Sentences

- **Preteach** Display these sentences: _We woke up. We ate our breakfast._ What is the subject of both sentences? (We) You can combine two sentences that have the same subject: _We woke up and ate our breakfast._ Display these sentences: _Maria came to school. I came to school._ What is the predicate of both sentences? (came to school) You can combine two sentences that have the same predicate: _Maria and I came to school._

- **Teach/Model** Present the concept and provide examples of sentences with the same subject and the same predicate.

Same Subject	<u>Ben</u> ate a sandwich. <u>Ben</u> ate an apple. <u>Ben</u> ate a sandwich and an apple.
Same Predicate	Miguel <u>visited our home.</u> Jane <u>visited our home.</u> Miguel and Jane <u>visited our home.</u>

- **Oral Language** Make a set of sentence cards: _Wendy plays the guitar. Ed took a test. Joe ate lunch._ Make a second set and distribute: _Benito plays the guitar. Ed finished his class. Rita ate lunch._ Read a sentence from the first set. The student holding a sentence with the same subject or predicate reads it. Have a volunteer form a combined sentence.

  To provide students additional instruction and practice in singular possessive nouns, use the lesson in the _ELL Handbook_ (p. 317).

Beginning/Intermediate Have students review the examples replacing subjects with names from the class. Have them read the combined sentences aloud.

Advanced/Advanced High Have pairs of students generate sentences using the Lesson Vocabulary words.

Content Objectives
- Combine sentences accurately.

Language Objectives
- Speak in complete sentences.
- Write sentences with a plural subject or predicate.

 Transfer Skills

Arabic, Hebrew, and some Asian languages use a right-to-left or up-to-down directionality in reading. Students who speak these languages need more opportunities to develop their print awareness of left-to-right reading. Reinforce this concept through activities such as oral reading of books and classroom print.

Support for English Language Learners

Content Objectives

- Identify sensory details in reading materials.

Language Objectives

- Write descriptive paragraphs using sensory details.
- Share feedback for editing and revising.

ELL *English Language Learners*

Sensory Details

■ **Introduce** Have students turn to p. 445 in the Student Edition. Have students describe aloud what the see in the mural. Then, display the Writing Model and read it aloud. Review that sensory details are those that appeal to the senses of seeing, touching, tasting, hearing, and smelling. What senses does the description appeal to? (seeing, touching, hearing) Give examples of the sensory details. (silently, green vines, brightly colored, warm yellow) Underline the sensory details and explain that these words make the writing come alive.

Writing Model

Silently, the mural shares the hope of a community. It shows a young girl with her arms stretched high. Green vines climb her arms and end in a proud green tree at the tips of her fingers. The mural is brightly colored on the edges. The light behind the girl is warm yellow.

■ **Practice** Write this incomplete paragraph on the board. Work together to add sensory details to help the writing come alive.

The mural on page 433 looks like _____. The rocks make the painting feel ____. The musical instruments are _____.

■ **Write** Have students write a paragraph with sensory details about one of the murals in the selection *Talking Walls.* Encourage them to use specific and detailed language to tell how the mural appeals to their senses.

Beginning Have students draw a picture of a mural that appeals to the senses, using bright colors, interesting textures, and other sensory items, such as food or musical instruments.

Intermediate Have students work with a partner to develop the sentence frame in the Practice activity above. Have partners develop a paragraph that carefully describes the mural on p. 433.

Advanced/Advanced High Have students work independently to write a paragraph. Then have them exchange their work with a partner for feedback.

Objectives

- Narrate, describe, and explain with increasing specificity and detail to fulfill content area writing needs as more English is acquired.

Customize Your Writing

Weekly Writing Focus
Writing Forms and Patterns

- Instruction focuses on a different **product** each week.
- Mini-lessons and models help students learn key features and **organizational patterns**.

Grade 3 Products fable, friendly letter, news article, autobiography, summary, realistic fiction, and so on

Grade 3 Organization Patterns poetic forms, compare and contrast, main idea and details, narrative, letter, and so on

Daily Writing Focus
Quick Writes for Fluency

- **Writing on Demand** Use the Quick Write routine for **writing on demand**.

- The Quick Write **prompt and routine** extend skills and strategies from daily writing lessons.

Unit Writing Focus
Writing Process ①②③④⑤

- Six **writing process** lessons provide structure to move students through the steps of the writing process.
- One-week and two-week pacing allows lessons to be used in **Writing Workshop**.

Steps of the Writing Process Plan and Prewrite, Draft, Revise, Edit, Publish and Present

Grade 3 Writing Process Products personal narrative, how-to report, cause-and-effect essay, problem-solution essay, persuasive essay, research report

Writing on Reading STREET

MINI-LESSON

- Daily 10-minute mini-lessons focus instruction on the **traits** and **craft** of good writing.

- Instruction focuses on one writing trait and one writer's craft skill every week.

Traits focus, ideas, organization, voice, word choice, sentences, conventions

Craft drafting strategies, revising strategies, editing strategies

Read Like a Writer

- Use **mentor text** every week as a model to exemplify the traits of good writing.

- **Interact with text** every week to learn the key features of good writing.

Mentor Text Examine literature in the Student Edition.

 Underline, circle, and highlight model text in the *Reader's and Writer's Notebook.*

Write Guy
Jeff Anderson

Need Writing Advice?

Writing instruction is all about creating effective writers. We don't want to crush the inner writer in a child by over-correcting and over-editing. What makes effective writing instruction? Children need to write, write, write! But is that enough? Probably not. All kinds of instruction and guidance go into making an effective writer.

The Write Guy offers advice on teacher and peer conferencing, focusing on writing traits, revising strategies, editing strategies, and much, much more.

Customize Your Writing

Sometimes you want to spend more time on writing—perhaps you do a **Writing Workshop**. This one- or two-week plan for the unit level writing projects can help.

1 Week Plan

1 Week Plan	Day 1	Day 2	Day 3	Day 4	Day 5
1 Plan and Prewrite	■	■			
2 Draft			■		
3 Revise				■	
4 Edit					■
5 Publish					■

2 Week Plan

2 Week Plan	Day 1	Day 2	Day 3	Day 4	Day 5	Day 6	Day 7	Day 8	Day 9	Day 10
1 Plan and Prewrite	■	■	■	■						
2 Draft					■	■	■			
3 Revise								■		
4 Edit									■	
5 Publish										■

Grade 3 Unit Writing Projects

Internet Guy
Don Leu

Unit Writing Project 1–21st Century Project

Unit 1 E-Pen Pals

Unit 2 Story Exchange

Unit 3 Photo Writing

Unit 4 Classroom Profile

Unit 5 E-Newsletter

Unit 6 Discussion Forum

Unit Writing Project 2–Writing Process

Unit 1 Personal Narrative

Unit 2 How-to Report

Unit 3 Cause-and-Effect Essay

Unit 4 Problem-Solution Essay

Unit 5 Persuasive Essay

Unit 6 Research Report

21st Century Writing

Discussion Forum

Writing Project Create a question and response on an aspect of freedom to promote discussion among students.

Purpose Enhance skills in using Internet wiki Web sites as well as using applications for word processing.

Audience Student, peers, teacher

In this workshop, we will write some questions about freedom and write responses to these questions to promote discussion and comments by other students. We will use the Internet to post our questions and responses, read ones posted by other students, and make appropriate comments and responses to their postings.

Key Features of a Discussion Forum

- proposes questions relating to the same topic or theme
- includes responses to the questions that may include the writers' opinions
- is written to encourage comments and opinions from readers
- is written to appeal to a specific audience
- is written, designed, or published electronically

Academic Vocabulary

Discussion Forum A Web site that allows students to post discussion topics and make comments and responses.

Teacher Tip

Explore Online Do an online search for "education + wiki" to find Web sites that host discussion forums for students. Using one of the sites, show students appropriate discussion questions and responses, as well as comments on the responses.

Differentiated Instruction

 Strategic Intervention

Introduce Terms Introduce and discuss terminology related to a discussion forum, such as *A forum is an Internet program that allows people to discuss topics and exchange ideas.*

Objectives

• Understand and identify the features of a discussion forum.
• Organize ideas to prepare for writing.

 **Plan and Prewrite**

Read Like a Writer

▪ **Examine Model Text** Display several sample questions and responses from a discussion forum. Students get involved in discussion forums that discuss topics in which they are interested. They express their ideas and opinions on the topic and read the responses of others. Discuss the purpose and audience of the questions and responses you show students. You are going to write a response to a question on freedom to promote discussion and comments by other students.

▪ **Explore Model Text** Let's look at an example of a question about freedom and a response to that question. This is the kind of question and response that you will write. Display and read aloud to students 21st Century Transparency TC7. Ask them to identify key features of a discussion forum in the student model.

Question: Which after-school activity should I choose?

There are so many fun things to do after school. How do you choose which is the best one for you? This is a choice students should have fun making. Think about your interests. Think about what you would like to learn. Think about how much time it takes. I like soccer. We practice two days a week. I am learning to be part of a team, and I get a great work out!

Unit 6 Discussion Forum   21st Century Writing **TC7**

21st Century Transparency TC
TR DVD

Determine discussion questions

We will write questions and responses about freedom to promote discussion and comments by other students. In each response, we will express our ideas and opinion about the question. First, we need to think of some questions about freedom that we would like to discuss. Encourage students to brainstorm a list of questions on different aspect of freedom. Write questions on the board.

Responding to the question

Now that we have a list of possible questions to choose from, you can start thinking about a response you would write to one of these questions. Organize students into small groups, and have each group choose one of the questions to discuss. Encourage students to discuss what they know about the topic and their ideas and opinions on the topic. Give each student a copy of a web, or have students draw a web to use. Have them write the topic of their discussion in the center and their ideas about the topic in the outer ovals.

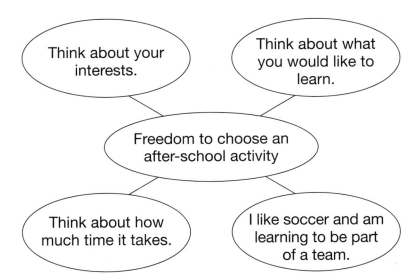

Corrective feedback

If... students have trouble deciding which question to discuss,

then... suggest that they answer these questions: *Do I know anything about this topic? Do I have ideas and opinions to share about it?* Two *yes* answers indicate a possible topic.

 Plan and Prewrite

MINI-LESSON

Understanding a Wiki Web Site

Think Aloud A wiki is a Web site or similar online reference that allows users to add information and edit content. When you use a wiki Web site, you need to remember that users most likely have added information that expresses their opinions. If you are writing a report and need facts, a wiki Web site is not the best place to go, but if you want to share ideas and opinions about a topic with others, a wiki Web site is a good place to go.

◼ Display a page from a wiki discussion forum on a projector. Read through several of the questions, responses, and comments. Discuss how the writers introduce discussion topics with questions and responses and how readers add their comments to these.

Plan and Prewrite

Using a wiki

You need to be registered to use many wiki Web sites. I have given each of you a registration name. Whenever you use the Web site, you should use this registration name only. You should not use your real name. It is fun to share information and ideas on the Internet, but you should not share any personal information. Display the home page of the wiki educational Web site on which you have registered and show children where to click to access the appropriate discussion forum for students. Read through the list of questions and discussion topics that other students have already posted to give students an idea of the variety of topics they could respond to. Remind students that the class is going to add their questions about freedom and post their responses to the questions.

Expressing opinions

When you participate in a discussion forum, it is good to share your ideas and experience with a topic being discussed. You can give your opinion in a polite and courteous manner. Remember everyone has the freedom to express ideas. You should never be critical of another person's ideas and opinions. If you disagree, you should say, "Here's another idea to consider ...." Help students write statements of opinion in a straightforward, polite manner. Have them consider the following questions when expressing opinions:

- Do I have experience that supports my opinion?

- Do I know facts that support my opinion?

- How can I express my opinion without telling someone else what to do?

- How can I express my opinion in a simple, straightforward manner?

Differentiated Instruction

 Strategic Intervention

Fact versus Opinion Remind students that statements of fact can be proved using reference sources, but statements of opinion are beliefs or feelings that cannot be proved. Sometimes people write their opinions as if they are facts. Encourage students to question whether a statement is a fact or an opinion.

Teacher Tip

Internet Safety Be aware of and follow your school and district guidelines for registering students to an educational wiki Web site.

Technology Tip

Using a Wiki Although wikis can be a fun way to share ideas, students should not use them as reference sources.

Objectives
- Write a first draft of a discussion forum response.
- Revise a draft of a discussion forum response.

 Draft

Organize ideas

Have students use the web they made earlier to review their ideas and opinions. Tell them to write the question they are responding to next to the center oval if they have not already done so.

Getting started

Have students begin their drafts by writing the question. Then they can write sentences about each of the ideas and opinions they have noted in the outer ovals. Encourage them to continue to refer to their webs as they write.

Examine model text

Display 21st Century Transparency TC7 and review with students.

 This student has written the question first. Next, the student responds to the question with ideas that the questioner should consider. Then the student gives his or her opinion and supports the opinion with comments.

21st Century Transparency TC
TR DVD

Develop draft

Remind students that the purpose of writing a draft is to record their ideas in an organized way. Display or read to students Agreeing and Disagreeing (below). Although a response on a discussion forum is a less formal kind of writing than a classroom profile or newsletter, the response should still be written clearly with support for ideas and opinions.

Agreeing and Disagreeing

✔ Part of the fun of a discussion forum is seeing how many people respond. If you are reviewing responses from others and you find one with which you agree, you can respond by simply saying, "I like these ideas and agree with you."

✔ If you disagree with a response, you can say, "I disagree. Here are other ideas to consider" and list your ideas.

③ Revise

MINI-LESSON

Varying Sentence Types

■ One way to make writing more interesting is to vary the kinds of sentences you use. Instead of always writing statements, include some questions or exclamations. Read these examples with students:

All statements	There are so many fun things to do after school. Choosing what to do can be hard. Think about your interests. Think about what you would like to learn. I like soccer. We practice two days a week. I am learning to be part of a team.
Variety of sentences	There are so many fun things to do after school. How do you choose which is the best one for you? Think about your interests. Think about what you would like to learn. I like soccer. We practice two days a week. I am learning to be part of a team, and I get a great work out!

Discuss with students how the paragraph was improved by varying the types of sentences.

Peer conferencing

Have students exchange their drafts for peer revision. Ask them to write at least two revision suggestions, paying particular attention to where different kinds of sentences could be used. Have students consider these suggestions as they revise their responses.

Revise drafts

Earlier we wrote drafts of our discussion forum responses. Now we will revise our drafts. When we revise, we incorporate comments from peer conferencing and try to make our writing clearer and more interesting. We can look for places where we can use different kinds of sentences.

Corrective feedback

If... students have difficulty identifying which sentences could be written as questions or exclamations,
then... have them read their response and circle a sentence that could be rewritten with strong feeling as an exclamation, and circle a sentence that could be rewritten as a question. Work with them to rewrite the sentences.

④ Edit

MINI-LESSON

Using the Computer to Edit

■ The grammar and spelling checker is a useful tool to identify errors in your writing. Carefully read each suggestion that the checker makes before you accept it to be sure that the correction is needed. **Have students use the grammar and spelling checker in the word processing program that they used to write their discussion forum response.**

■ Making edits with a computer is easy. Combining two sentences, inserting sentences, deleting sentences, and rearranging sentences can be done easily and quickly. **Type the following sentences in a word processing program and display them on a projector:**

I like soccer. I am learning to be part of a team, and I get a great work out! Think about your interests. Think about what you would like to learn. Think about how much time it takes.

Read the sentences aloud. The writer wrote his or her opinion first, and then his or her ideas. When revising, he or she might decide to switch the order. **Demonstrate how to highlight the first and second sentences and cut and paste them at the end.** You can use the *cut* and *paste* commands in a word processor to move parts of sentences or entire sentences so that your response reads better.

■ Have students practice moving and rearranging the following sentences using the word processing commands *cut* and *paste*.

I am learning to speak Spanish and about the culture of Mexico. It helps me understand others. I am in a Spanish club after school. Do you speak more than one language?

Edit drafts   Ask students to edit their own drafts. After they use the word processing program to make most of the changes, have them print out their article and read it sentence by sentence to make further edits. Ask them to check their drafts for spelling, grammar, punctuation, and capitalization.

5 Publish and Present

MINI-LESSON

Posting the Discussion Forum

▪ Display the discussion forum page of the wiki Web site to which you have registered the students. Model how to post a question and response on the discussion forum. Sometimes you may type your response in a discussion forum without preparing it first, but since we have written our responses already we can copy them into the Web site, or copy and paste them into the Web site.

▪ Model how to sign onto the discussion forum. Remind students to use the registered names you have given each of them. Show them where to click to make a posting. Model how to find the folder where students have saved their responses and copy and paste the final response into the message box on the Web site.

English Language Learners
English Conventions Assist students in editing spelling and grammatical errors. Discuss how to correct each error and the reason for the change. Use the appropriate lessons in the *ELL Handbook* to support teaching English conventions.

Objectives
- Post discussion forum questions and responses to the Internet.
- Present discussion forum questions and responses.

5 Publish and Present

Options for presenting

Offer students two options for presenting their work:

Print a hard copy of their newsletter to take home to their families and to display in the classroom.	Convert the file to Portable Document Format (PDF) and make it available for download on a class or school Web site or educational file-sharing site.

Posting to the forum

Now that we have written and revised our question and responses regarding an aspect of freedom, it is time to post these to a discussion forum. We will use the Web site you are registered to and make our postings.

Help students log on and post their questions and responses. Every few days have a group of students log on and review the responses and comments other students have made to the class's postings. Make sure you have read the comments first to check for any inappropriate material.

Give each student an opportunity to respond to comments made by other students to his or her original question and response. Remind students to use only their registered names and to be courteous to all comments.

Customize Literacy in Your Classroom

Table of Contents
for Customize Literacy

Customize Literacy is organized into different sections, each one designed to help you organize and carry out an effective literacy program. Each section contains strategies and support for teaching comprehension skills and strategies. *Customize Literacy* also shows how to use weekly text sets of readers in your literacy program.

Weekly Text Sets
to Customize Literacy

The following readers can be used to enhance your literacy instruction.

	Decodable Readers	Concept Literacy Reader	Below-Level Reader	On-Level Reader	Advanced Reader	ELD Reader	ELL Reader
Unit 6 WEEK 1	At the Zoo; Kat's Kite; Balloons!	The Statue of Liberty	The Statue of Liberty: A Gift from France	Symbols, Signs, and Songs of America	The French Connection	The Eagle: A Symbol of Freedom	The Eagle: A Symbol of Freedom
Unit 6 WEEK 2	A Circus Life for Ben; Sylvester's Notes; Picnic Poster	The Eagle Is Free	New York's Chinatown	A Pet Bird	China's Special Gifts to the World	Gina Becomes a Citizen	Gina Becomes a Citizen
Unit 6 WEEK 3	Chase Takes a Vacation; Talkative Millie; Lester's Pictures	Many Voices	One Forest, Different Trees	Lily's Adventure Around the World	Thomas Hart Benton: Painter of Murals	The Wall of Names	The Wall of Names

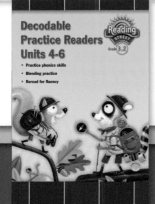

Customize Literacy in Your Classroom

Instruction in comprehension skills and strategies provides readers with avenues to understanding a text. Through teacher modeling and guided, collaborative, and independent practice, students become independent thinkers who employ a variety of skills and strategies to help them make meaning as they read.

Envision It!
A Comprehension Handbook

Mini-Lessons for Comprehension Skills and Strategies

Unit 1	Literary Elements, Sequence, Compare and Contrast, Author's Purpose, Background Knowledge, Summarize, Story Structure
Unit 2	Main Ideas and Details, Compare and Contrast, Draw Conclusions, Author's Purpose, Monitor and Clarify, Predict and Set Purpose
Unit 3	Draw Conclusions, Literary Elements, Graphic Sources, Generalize, Cause and Effect, Important Ideas, Text Structure
Unit 4	Generalize, Graphic Sources, Fact and Opinion, Cause and Effect, Inferring, Questioning
Unit 5	Draw Conclusions, Main Ideas and Details, Sequence, Compare and Contrast, Author's Purpose, Visualize, Summarize
Unit 6	Fact and Opinion, Cause and Effect, Graphic Sources, Literary Elements, Generalize, Questioning, Inferring

Envision It! Visual Skills Handbook

Author's Purpose
Categorize and Classify
Cause and Effect
Compare and Contrast
Draw Conclusions
Fact and Opinion
Generalize
Graphic Sources
Literary Elements
Main Idea and Details
Sequence

Envision It! Visual Strategies Handbook

Background Knowledge
Important Ideas
Inferring
Monitor and Clarify
Predict and Set Purpose
Questioning
Story Structure
Summarize
Text Structure
Visualize

Anchor Chart Anchor charts are provided with each strategy lesson. These charts incorporate the language of strategic thinkers. They help students make their thinking visible and permanent and provide students with a means to clarify their thinking about how and when to use each strategy. As students gain more experience with a strategy, the chart may undergo revision.

See pages 107–134 in the *First Stop on Reading Street* Teacher's Edition for additional support as you customize literacy in your classroom.

Good Readers DRA2 users will find additional resources in the *First Stop on Reading Street* Teacher's Edition on pages 110–112.

Contents

Section 1 Planning

Pacing Guide

This chart shows the instructional sequence from *Scott Foresman Reading Street* for Grade 3. You can use this pacing guide as is to ensure you are following a comprehensive scope and sequence. Or, you can adjust the sequence to match your calendar, curriculum map, or testing schedule.

Grade 3

REVIEW WEEK

READING	UNIT 1 Week 1	Week 2	Week 3	Week 4	Week 5	UNIT 2 Week 1	Week 2
Comprehension Skill	Character, Setting, and Theme	Sequence	Sequence	Compare and Contrast	Author's Purpose	Main Idea and Details	Compare and Contrast
Comprehension Strategy	Background Knowledge	Summarize	Visualize	Background Knowledge	Story Structure	Monitor and Clarify	Visualize
Vocabulary Strategy/Skill	Context Clues/ Homonyms	Word Structure/ Compound Words	Dictionary/ Glossary/ Unknown Words	Context Clues/ Multiple-Meaning Words	Word Structure/ Prefixes and Suffixes	Context Clues/ Synonyms	Context Clues/ Unfamiliar Words
Fluency	Accuracy	Rate	Expression	Accuracy	Appropriate Phrasing	Accuracy	Expression
Phonics and Spelling	Short Vowels; Syllables VC/CV	Plurals -s, -es, -ies	Base Words and Endings	Vowel Digraphs	Vowel Diphthongs	Syllable Patterns V/CV, VC/V	Final Syllable -le

REVIEW WEEK

	UNIT 4 Week 1	Week 2	Week 3	Week 4	Week 5	UNIT 5 Week 1	Week 2
Comprehension Skill	Generalize	Graphic Sources	Fact and Opinion	Fact and Opinion	Cause and Effect	Compare and Contrast	Main Idea and Details
Comprehension Strategy	Summarize	Important Ideas	Inferring	Questioning	Monitor and Clarify	Visualize	Inferring
Vocabulary Strategy/Skill	Context Clues/ Unfamiliar Words	Dictionary/ Glossary/ Unknown Words	Context Clues/ Multiple-Meaning Words	Context Clues/ Multiple-Meaning Words	Dictionary/ Glossary/ Unknown Words	Context Clues/ Synonyms	Context Clues/ Homophones
Fluency	Accuracy	Appropriate Phrasing	Expression	Appropriate Phrasing	Rate	Rate	Accuracy
Phonics and Spelling	Irregular Plurals	Vowels: r- Controlled	Prefixes pre-, mid-, over-, out-, bi-, de-	Suffixes -er, -or, -ess, -ist	Syllable Pattern VCCCV	Syllable Pattern CV/VC	Homophones

Are you the adventurous type? Want to use some of your own ideas and materials in your teaching? But you worry you might be leaving out some critical instruction kids need? Customize Literacy can help. "

REVIEW WEEK

REVIEW WEEK

UNIT 3

Week 3	Week 4	Week 5	Week 1	Week 2	Week 3	Week 4	Week 5
Draw Conclusions	Author's Purpose	Main Idea and Details	Draw Conclusions	Character, Setting, Plot	Graphic Sources	Generalize	Cause and Effect
Questioning	Predict and Set Purpose	Text Structure	Important Ideas	Inferring	Text Structure	Story Structure	Predict and Set Purpose
Word Structure/ Compound Words	Context Clues/ Antonyms	Context Clues/ Unfamiliar Words	Context Clues/ Homophones	Dictionary/ Glossary/ Unknown Words	Dictionary/ Glossary/ Unknown Words	Context Clues/ Unfamiliar Words	Word Structure/ Prefixes and Suffixes
Rate	Appropriate Phrasing	Rate	Expression	Accuracy	Appropriate Phrasing	Rate	Expression
Compound Words	Consonant Blends	Consonant Digraphs	Contractions	Prefixes	Consonant Sounds /j/, /s/ and /k/	Suffixes *-ly, -ful, -ness, -less, -able, -ible*	Consonant Patterns *wr, kn, mb, gn, st*

REVIEW WEEK

REVIEW WEEK

UNIT 6

Week 3	Week 4	Week 5	Week 1	Week 2	Week 3	Week 4	Week 5
Sequence	Draw Conclusions	Author's Purpose	Fact and Opinion	Cause and Effect	Graphic Sources	Plot and Theme	Generalize
Monitor and Clarify	Summarize	Background Knowledge	Questioning	Inferring	Important Ideas	Story Structure	Inferring
Word Structure/ Compound Words	Context Clues/ Unfamiliar Words	Context Clues/ Homonyms	Word Structure/ Prefix *un-*	Context Clues/ Antonyms	Dictionary/ Glossary/ Unknown Words	Word Structure/ Prefixes and Suffixes	Context Clues/ Homographs
Expression and Punctuation Cues	Accuracy	Appropriate Phrasing	Rate	Appropriate Phrasing	Accuracy	Rate	Expression
Vowel Patterns for /ò/	Vowel patterns *ei, eigh*	Suffixes *-y, -ish, -hood, -ment*	Vowel Sounds /ü/ and /ú/ as in *moon* and *foot*	Schwa	Final Syllables	Prefixes; Prefixes, Suffixes, Endings	Related Words

Pacing Guide

Grade 3 LANGUAGE ARTS

UNIT 1 / REVIEW WEEK / UNIT 2

	Week 1	Week 2	Week 3	Week 4	Week 5	Week 1	Week 2
Speaking and Listening	News Report	Description	Tell a Story	Panel Discussion	Book Report	Speech	Persuasive Speech
Grammar	Sentences	Subjects and Predicates	Types of Sentences	Types of Sentences	Compound Sentences	Common and Proper Nouns	Singular and Plural Nouns
Weekly Writing	Narrative Poem	Fable	Thank-You Note	Description	Realistic Fiction	Poem	Fairy Tale
Trait of the Week	Word Choice	Conventions	Organization	Voice	Sentences	Word Choice	Word Choice
Writing	E-Pen Pals/Personal Narrative						

UNIT 4 / REVIEW WEEK / UNIT 5

	Week 1	Week 2	Week 3	Week 4	Week 5	Week 1	Week 2
Speaking and Listening	Presentation	Weather Forecast	Interview	Sportscast	Book Review	Introduction	Drama
Grammar	Singular and Plural Pronouns	Subject and Object Pronouns	Possessive Pronouns	Contractions	Prepositions	Adjectives and Articles	Adjectives That Compare
Weekly Writing	Persuasive Text	Story	Biography	Autobiography	Summary	Letter to the Editor	Personal Narrative
Trait of the Week	Conventions	Conventions	Sentences	Organization	Word Choice	Organization	Conventions
Writing	Classroom Profile/Problem-Solution Essay						

UNIT 3 (continued) — REVIEW WEEK

Week 3	Week 4	Week 5
Presentation	Interview	Description
Irregular Plural Nouns	Singular Possessive Nouns	Plural Possessive Nouns
Persuasive Ad	Friendly Letter	Directions
Focus/Ideas	Conventions	Organization

Story Exchange/How-to Report

UNIT 3 — REVIEW WEEK

Week 1	Week 2	Week 3	Week 4	Week 5
Commercial	Drama	Voicemail	Description	Oral Report
Action and Linking Verbs	Main and Helping Verbs	Subject-Verb Agreement	Past, Present, and Future Tense	Irregular Verbs
Fiction	Drama: Play	Formal Letter	News Article	Compare/Contrast Composition
Voice	Sentences	Conventions	Sentences	Focus/Ideas

Photo Writing/Cause-and-Effect Essay

(continued) — REVIEW WEEK

Week 3	Week 4	Week 5
Song or Poem	Radio Ad	Retelling
Adverbs	Adverbs That Compare	Conjunctions
Poem	Invitation	Book Review
Word Choice	Focus/Ideas	Conventions

E-Newsletter/Persuasive Essay

UNIT 6 — REVIEW WEEK

Week 1	Week 2	Week 3	Week 4	Week 5
Announcement	Express an Opinion	Talk Show	Description	Song
Capital Letters	Abbreviations	Combining Sentences	Commas	Quotations and Parentheses
Notes	Poem	Description	Comic Book	Historical Fiction
Focus/Ideas	Organization	Word Choice	Conventions	Word Choice

Discussion Forum/Research Report

Teaching Record Chart

This chart shows the critical comprehension skills and strategies you need to cover. Check off each one as you provide instruction.

Reading/Comprehension	DATES OF INSTRUCTION		
Use ideas (e.g., illustrations, titles, topic sentences, key words, and foreshadowing clues) to make and confirm predictions.			
Ask relevant questions, seek clarification, and locate facts and details about stories and other text and support answers with evidence from text.			
Establish purpose for reading selected texts and monitor comprehension, making corrections and adjustments when that understanding breaks down (e.g., identifying clues, using background knowledge, generating questions, re-reading a portion aloud).			
Paraphrase the themes and supporting details of fables, legends, myths, or stories.			
Compare and contrast the settings in myths and traditional folktales.			
Describe the characteristics of various forms of poetry and how they create imagery (e.g., narrative poetry, lyrical poetry, humorous poetry, free verse).			
Explain the elements of plot and character as presented through dialogue in scripts that are read, viewed, written, or performed.			
Sequence and summarize the plot's main events and explain their influence on future events.			
Describe the interactions of characters including their relationships and the changes they undergo.			
Identify whether the narrator or speaker of a story is first or third person.			

❝ Tired of using slips of paper or stickies to make sure you teach everything you need to? Need an easier way to keep track of what you have taught, and what you still need to cover? Customize Literacy can help. **❞**

Reading/Comprehension	DATES OF INSTRUCTION		
Explain the difference in point of view between a biography and an autobiography.			
Identify language that creates a graphic visual experience and appeals to the senses.			
Read independently for a sustained period of time and paraphrase what the reading was about, maintaining meaning and logical order (e.g., generate a reading log or journal; participate in book talks).			
Identify the topic and locate the author's stated purposes in writing the text.			
Identify the details or facts that support the main idea.			
Draw conclusions from the facts presented in text and support those assertions with textual evidence.			
Identify explicit cause and effect relationships among ideas in texts.			
Use text features (e.g., bold print, captions, key words, italics) to locate information and make and verify predictions about contents of text.			
Identify what the author is trying to persuade the reader to think or do.			
Follow and explain a set of written multi-step directions.			
Locate and use specific information in graphic features of text.			
Establish purposes for reading selected texts based upon own or others' desired outcome to enhance comprehension.			
Ask literal, interpretive, and evaluative questions of a text.			
Monitor and adjust comprehension using a variety of strategies.			
Make inferences about a text and use evidence from the text to support understanding.			
Summarize information in a text, maintaining meaning and logical order.			
Make connections between literary and informational texts with similar ideas and provide evidence from the text.			

Section 2 Instruction

Fact and Opinion

Fact and Opinion
A statement of fact can be proven true or false.
A statement of opinion tells someone's ideas or feelings.

Objectives:
- Students define *fact* and *opinion*.
- Students use clue words to identify statements as fact or opinion.
- Students name ways to check statements of fact.

What is it? **A statement of fact** tells something that can be proved true or false. A **statement of opinion** tells a person's ideas or feelings and cannot be proved true or false. At Grade 3, students are identifying statements of fact and opinion and are naming ways to check statements of fact.

How Good Readers Use the Skill Students meet statements of facts and opinions throughout their day. We want to teach them how to distinguish the two and understand ways to check the veracity of factual statements and be able to judge statements of opinion thoughtfully. Evaluating statements of fact and statements of opinion boosts students' comprehension and helps them avoid being misled.

Texts for Teaching

Student Edition
- *Rocks in His Head,* 3.2, pages 94–104
- *America's Champion Swimmer: Gertrude Ederle,* 3.2, pages 124–139
- *The Story of the Statue of Liberty,* 3.2, pages 374–385

Leveled Readers
- See pages 24–29 for a list of Leveled Readers.

Mini-Lesson 1

Teach the Skill

Use the **Envision It!** lesson on page EI•7 to visually review facts and opinions with students.

Remind students that:
- a statement of **fact** tells something that can be proved true or false.
- a statement of **opinion** tells a person's ideas or feelings and cannot be proved true or false.

Practice

Write the following on the board and read them with students.
The Story of Ferdinand was *written by Munro Leaf.*
Everybody should read The Story of Ferdinand.
The Story of Ferdinand *was first published in 1936.*
Ask: Which statements are fact? How can you tell? Which is a statement of opinion?

Talk with students about how the facts (statements 1 and 3) could be proved to be true. (They could look at an actual book or they could check the internet or ask a librarian.) Point out the word *should* and explain that opinions often contain judgment words such as *should, I think,* and *best.*
If... students have difficulty distinguishing statements of fact, **then...** ask: *Could you check this information out? How?*

Apply

As students read, have them be alert for statements of fact and opinion.

Writing

Students can write a sentence with a statement of fact and one with a statement of opinion.

Mini-Lesson 2

Teach the Skill

Use the **Envision It!** lesson on page EI•7 to visually review fact and opinion with students.

Remind students that:

- a statement of **fact** tells something that can be proved true or false.
- a statement of **opinion** tells a person's ideas or feelings and cannot be proved true or false.
- clue words and phrases such as *I think, I believe, cute, best,* and so on can signal an opinion.

Practice

Give students a familiar nonfiction selection and have partners read it together to identify statements of fact and opinion. Have them complete a chart, listing the statements they identify. Help students suggest how statements of fact can be checked.

Statement	Fact?	Opinion?
Mount Rushmore has the faces of four Presidents	Yes. We could look in an encyclopedia	

If... students have difficulty distinguishing opinions,
then... ask: *Can you prove this is the* [cutest] *or is that just what someone thinks?*

Apply

As students read, have them look for statements of fact and opinion.

Writing

Students can look at a photograph and write a caption that includes a statement of fact and a statement of opinion.

Mini-Lesson 3

Teach the Skill

Use the **Envision It!** lesson on page EI•7 to visually review fact and opinion with students.

Remind students that:

- a statement of **fact** tells something that can be proved true or false.
- a statement of **opinion** tells a person's ideas or feelings and cannot be proved true or false.
- clue words and phrases such as *best, in my opinion, I believe, I think,* and so on can signal an opinion.

Practice

Remind students that statements of opinion often have judgment words, such as *should, must,* or *best,* or phrases, such as *I think* and *in my opinion.* Let partners work together to write a paragraph that includes both statements of fact and opinion. Give pairs a topic or let them choose one of their own. Have students complete a chart like the one for Mini-Lesson 2 to show their facts and opinions. Then have students share their paragraphs.
If... students have difficulty writing statements of fact and opinion,
then... give them a topic and sentence starters to complete, such as *The weather today is... I think this kind of weather is...*

Apply

As students read, have them look for statements of fact and think about how they would check them out.

Writing

Students can write a few sentences that are statements of fact and then add a statement of opinion, underlining it.

Section 2 Instruction

Cause and Effect

Student Edition p. EI•3

What is It? A **cause** is why something happens. An **effect** is the result of the cause. Not all causal relationships are stated directly or signaled by clue words, such as *because, so,* and *since*. In these cases, students must infer either cause or effect, using information in the text and their prior knowledge. At Grade 3, readers use the terms *cause* and *effect* in their analysis of text.

How Good Readers Use the Skill Students experience cause-and-effect relationships every day. To be successful, they need to recognize these relationships in fiction as well as in all content areas. The ability to do so will help them increase their understanding when dealing with longer, more difficult texts. Readers begin their understanding of causal relationships by thinking about *What happened? Why did it happen?* Students then learn that a cause may have multiple effects and one effect can have many causes and that sometimes clue words signal causal relationships.

Texts for Teaching

Student Edition
- *Around One Cactus,* 3.1, pages 510–527
- *Fly, Eagle, Fly!* 3.2, pages 158–171
- *Happy Birthday Mr. Kang,* 3.2, pages 402–419

Leveled Readers
- See pages 24–29 for a list of Leveled Readers.

Objectives:
- Students define cause and effect.
- Students identify cause-and-effect relationships.
- Students understand that some, but not all, cause-and-effect relationships are signaled by clue words.

 Mini-Lesson 1

Teach the Skill
Use the **Envision It!** lesson on page EI•3 to visually review cause and effect.

Remind students that:
- an **effect** is *what* happens, and a **cause** is *why* it happens.
- **clue words** such as *because, so,* and *since* can help readers figure out cause-and-effect relationships.

Practice
Write the following sentences on the board. Have students identify the cause and effect within each sentence.
The power went out at Joseph's house so he had to use a flashlight to see. (Cause: The power went out. Effect: Joseph had to use a flashlight.)
Because I played soccer on one of the hottest days of the year, I was very sweaty. (Cause: I played soccer on a hot day. Effect: I was sweaty.)
Circle the clue word. Discuss how these words help determine the cause-effect relationship in each sentence.
If... students have difficulty identifying cause and effect,
then... provide additional example sentences and ask *What happened?* and *Why did that happen?*

Apply
As students read the assigned text, have them complete a cause and effect graphic organizer to help students identify cause-and-effect relationships.

Writing
Students can write sentences that include a cause-and-effect relationship using appropriate clue words.

Go Digital!   Leveled Reader Database   Envision It! Animations

Customize Literacy

Mini-Lesson 2

Teach the Skill

Use the **Envision It!** lesson on page EI•3 to visually review cause and effect.

Remind students that:

- an **effect** is *what* happens, and a **cause** is *why* it happens.
- **clue words** such as *because, so,* and *since* can help readers figure out cause-and-effect relationships.
- a passage can have multiple causes or multiple effects.

Practice

Read aloud the following and have students listen for cause-effect relationships.

Last week we went on a field trip to a nature preserve. My friend Steve got lost because he ran ahead of the class. Our teacher, Ms. Olsen noticed he was missing when she took attendance at lunch. She ran back down the trail looking for Steve. She found him in the parking lot by the school bus. Ms. Olsen got really mad, so she made Steve stay by her side the rest of the trip

Ask students: What event set off several other things? (Steve running ahead resulted in him getting lost, Ms. Olsen getting mad, and so on.) Have students retell the events using the words *cause* and *effect*.

If... students have difficulty identifying the cause and effects, **then...** have students find clue words and use them to answer what happened and why.

Apply

As students read the assigned text, have them complete a cause-and-effect graphic organizer to help them chart the cause-and-effect relationships.

Writing

Give students a topic, such as a football game, and have them write about it using cause-and-effect relationships.

Mini-Lesson 3

Teach the Skill

Use the **Envision It!** lesson on page EI•3 to visually review cause and effect.

Remind students that:

- an **effect** is *what* happens, and a **cause** is *why* it happens.
- **clue words** such as *because, reason, so,* and *since* can help readers figure out cause-and-effect relationships.
- a passage can have multiple causes or multiple effects.
- cause-and-effect relationships are not always explicitly stated within a text.

Practice

Read aloud and have students identify the causes and effects.

Allie is the star pitcher on our team. She broke her arm, so she could not play on Saturday. I was asked to pitch instead, so I practiced throwing all week. When Saturday came, the game was cancelled because it was thundering and lightening. Since I didn't have to pitch, I didn't find out if I was as good as Allie. Maybe I will next week

If... students have difficulty identifying the causal relationships, **then...** have them read two sentences at a time and identify what happened and why it happened.

Apply

As students read the assigned text, have them complete the graphic organizer to help students find cause-and-effect relationships in the selection.

Writing

Students can write a passage with several cause-and-effect relationships.

Graphic Sources

Objectives:
- Students interpret information in simple graphics.
- Students use graphics as a prereading tool.

What is it? **Graphics sources**, including charts, maps, diagrams, graphs, and time lines, provide information visually using few words, symbols, and/or numbers. Graphic sources accompany science, math, and social studies texts, as well as some fiction. At Grade 3, students use graphics to preview; they put information from reading or research into simple graphic forms.

Student Edition pp. EI•10–EI•11

How Good Readers Use the Skill Students see different kinds of graphics—maps, charts, diagrams, and so on—in many situations. In their reading, graphics provide lots of information in a visual way. Students first use graphics such as maps and diagrams to preview and make predictions about what a text will be about. They then understand that graphic sources aid in their comprehension of text. Students also learn to create graphics from their reading. Older readers interpret and create more sophisticated graphic aids, matching them to text. They learn to compare and evaluate how well different graphic sources communicate and synthesize information.

Texts for Teaching

Student Edition
- *Seeing Stars,* 3.1, pages 446–457
- *Hottest, Coldest, Highest, Deepest,* 3.2, pages 62–75
- *Talking Walls: Art for the People,* 3.2, pages 438–451

Leveled Readers
- See pages 24–29 for a list of Leveled Readers.

Teach the Skill
Use the **Envision It!** lesson on pages EI•10–EI•11 to visually review graphic sources.

Remind students that:
- **graphic sources** show information visually.
- **graphic sources** include maps, charts, diagrams, pictures with captions, and graphs.

Practice
Preview a text that has graphics, pausing at each one. Model reading the title and all other words on the graphic. Decide what any symbols stand for. Ask: What kind of information does this give us? Why do you think the author included a graphic instead of describing it using words? Point out that a graphic can help readers get a lot of information quickly, for example, a map can show the route across a big area. Bar and line graphs can let readers compare information. Diagrams help readers visualize a complex process, such as the water cycle.
If... students have difficulty reading a graphic source,
then... have them put what the graphic shows in their own words.

Apply
As students read, have them match each graphic with the text it goes with.

Writing
Students can make a mini-glossary of graphic sources, defining each one and including a sketch of it.

 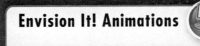

Mini-Lesson 2

Teach the Skill

Use the **Envision It!** lesson on pages EI•10–EI•11 to visually review graphic sources with students.

Remind students that:

- **graphic sources** show information visually.
- **graphic sources** include maps, charts, diagrams, pictures with captions, and graphs.

Practice

Provide a few selections, fiction and informational, that include graphics. Include a map, photos with captions, and a chart or graph. Show the selections to students and have them make predictions about what the selection will be about. Be sure students can name each graphic and explain what it shows. To help them, ask questions: What kind of graphics are included? What kind of information do they provide? Would you expect this graphic to tell more about a story? Or would you expect it to tell more about a topic? After students preview and make predictions, read portions of the article aloud to check their predictions.

If... students have difficulty predicting from graphics,

then... read the part of the text that the graphic explains or illustrates to help them see a connection.

Apply

As students read the assigned text, have them pay attention to the graphics and think about why the author included them.

Writing

Students can draw and label a simple map of the classroom or school.

Mini-Lesson 3

Teach the Skill

Use the **Envision It!** lesson on pages EI•10–EI•11 to visually review graphic sources with students.

Remind students that:

- **graphic sources** show information visually.
- **graphic sources** include maps, charts, diagrams, pictures with captions, and graphs.
- writers add graphics to illustrate their writing or tell more about their topic.

Practice

Provide a passage or two from a selection that students have read with the graphics removed. Or let students choose a piece of their own writing. Tell them to add two graphics to the passage. They can add a picture with a caption and one other graphic, such as a map, a chart, a diagram, and so on. These graphics should have a title and a few words tell what the graphic shows. Encourage students to add graphics that either tell more about the selection or illustrate some aspect of it. Let volunteers explain their graphics and tell why they included them with the passage.

If... students have difficulty matching a graphic source with text,

then... give them a choice of two, one that fits much better than the other, and have the student choose.

Apply

As students read the assigned text, have them pay attention to the graphics and think about why the author used them.

Writing

Students can cut out pictures from magazines and write captions for them.

Instruction

Questioning

Mini-Lesson

Questioning

Questioning is asking good questions about important text information. Questioning takes place before, during, and after reading.

To question
• read with a question in mind
• stop, think, and record your questions as you read
• make notes when you find information
• check your understanding and ask questions to clarify

Let's think About Reading!

When I question, I ask myself
• Have I asked a good question with a question word?
• What questions help me make sense of my reading?
• What does the author mean?

EI•23

Student Edition p. EI•23

Objectives:

- Students identify relevant questions to ask before, during, and after reading that relate to important information in the text.
- Students use question words in their questions.
- Students answer different kinds of questions.

Texts for Teaching

Student Edition

- *Prudy's Problem and How She Solved It,* 3.1, pages 274–289
- *America's Champion Swimmer: Gertrude Ederle,* 3.2, pages 124–139
- *The Story of the Statue of Liberty,* 3.2, pages 374–385

Leveled Readers

- See pages 24–29 for a list of Leveled Readers.

Understand the Strategy

Questioning is asking good questions about important text information. Good readers ask and answer questions to preview, set purposes, construct meaning, clarify text, locate specific information, interpret text, and evaluate text.

Teach

Use the **Envision It!** lesson on page EI•23 to visually review questioning.

Remind students that we ask questions to help us get ready to read and to make sense of what we read. Show a picture and have students use question words (*who, what, when, where, why*) to ask about it. Then model using these question words as you preview an unfamiliar piece of text. Think aloud and write your questions on the board. Emphasize that questions should be ones that try to get at important information.

Asking Good Questions

Questions	Answers
Who are the people in the canoe?	
What kind of dog is that?	
Where are they all going?	
When did this trip take place?	
Why are some men wearing uniforms?	

After students read, help them look for answers to their questions. Help them understand that different kinds of questions require different actions on their part to answer.

- **In the Book:** The answers to these kinds of questions are right in the text, although they might be in two places. You might have to search.
- **In My Head:** These questions are answered by using information from the text along with your own ideas. Sometimes the author leaves clues in the text that can help answer these questions.

Practice

Provide a selection for students to read and practice questioning. Have students try to answer their questions during and after reading.

If... students have difficulty asking questions,

then... model asking questions using question words.

Apply

Always have students preview and then write a few questions to guide their reading.

Anchor Chart

Anchor charts help students make their thinking visible. With an anchor chart, the group can clarify their thinking about how to use a strategy. Display anchor charts so readers can refer to them as they read. Here is a sample chart for questioning.

Questioning

1. Look over the story before you start to read. Write down questions. Use the question words: *Who? What? When? Where? Why? How?*

2. Try to find answers to your questions as you read. Write these down next to your questions. Do you have other questions? Write these down too.

3. Keep asking questions to make sure you understand what you are reading.
Do I get this? Does this make sense?
Is this an important part? What can I do to remember it?
Can I connect this to something else I have heard or read about? How is it the same or different?

4. Talk about the story with your group. Share your questions and answers.

5. When you have questions to answer, remember the answer-question tips:

In the Book—find the answers in the text
In My Head—use information from the text, including clues from the author, and your own ideas

Anchor Chart

Instruction

Using Multiple Strategies

Good readers use multiple strategies as they read. You can encourage students to read strategically through good classroom questioning. Use questions such as these to help students apply strategies during reading.

Answer Questions

- Who or what is this question about?
- Where can you look to find the answer to this question?

Ask Questions

- What do you want to know about _____?
- What questions to do you have about the _____ in this selection? Use the words *who, what, when, where, why,* and *how* to ask your questions.
- Do you have any questions after reading?

Graphic Organizers

- What kind of graphic organizer could you use to help you keep track of the information in this selection?

Monitor and Clarify

- Does the story or article make sense?
- What don't you understand about what you read?
- Do you need to reread, review, read on, or check a reference source?
- Do you need to read more slowly or more quickly?
- What is a _____? Where could you look to find out?

Predict/Confirm Predictions

- What do you think this story or article will be about? Why do you think as you do?
- What do you think you will learn from this selection?
- Do the text features help you predict what will happen?
- Based on what has happened so far, what do you think will happen next?
- Is this what you thought would happen?
- How does _____ change what you thought would happen?

Preview

- What do the photographs, illustrations, or graphic sources tell about the selection?
- What do you want to find out? What do you want to learn?

Background Knowledge

- What do you already know about _____?
- Have you read stories or articles by this author before?
- How is this selection like others that you have read?
- What does this remind you of?
- How does your background knowledge help you understand _____?
- Did the text match what you already knew? What new information did you learn?

Story Structure

- Who are the characters in this story? the setting?
- What is the problem in this story? How does the problem get solved?
- What is the point of this story?

Summarize

- What two or three important ideas have you read so far?
- How do the text features relate to the important ideas?
- Is there a graphic organizer that can help you organize the information before you summarize?

Text Structure

- How has the author organized the writing?
- What clues tell you that the text is structured _____?

Visualize

- When you read this, what do you picture in your mind?
- What do you hear, see, or smell?
- What do you think _____ looks like? Why do you think as you do?

" You know explicit strategy instruction is a must! But you also want students to use strategies every time they read. **Customize Literacy** shows you how to help them do this. "

Glossary of Literacy Terms

This glossary lists academic language terms that are related to literacy.
They are provided for your information and professional use.

A

alliteration	the repetition of a consonant sound in a group of words, especially in poetry
allusion	a word or phrase that refers to something else the reader already knows from history, experience, or reading
animal fantasy	a story about animals that talk and act like people
answer questions	a reading strategy in which readers use the text and prior knowledge to answer questions about what they are reading
antonym	a word that means the opposite of another word
ask questions	a reading strategy in which readers ask themselves questions about the text to help make sense of what they read
author's point of view	the author's opinion on the subject he or she is writing about
author's purpose	the reason the author wrote the text
autobiography	the story of a real person's life written by that person

B

background knowledge	the information and experience that a reader brings to a text
biography	the story of a real person's life written by another person

C

cause	why something happens
character	a person, an animal, or a personified object in a story
chronological order	events in a selection, presented in the order in which they occurred
classify and categorize	put things, such as pictures or words, into groups
climax	the point in a story at which conflict is confronted
compare	tell how things are the same
comprehension	understanding of text being read—the ultimate goal of reading
comprehension strategy	a conscious plan used by a reader to gain understanding of text. Comprehension strategies may be used before, during, or after reading.
conclusion	a decision or opinion arrived at after thinking about facts and details and using prior knowledge
conflict	the problem or struggle in a story
context clue	the words, phrases, or sentences near an unknown word that give the reader clues to the word's meaning
contrast	tell how things are different

details	small pieces of information
dialect	form of a language spoken in a certain region or by a certain group of people that differs from the standard form of that language
dialogue	written conversation
diary	a day-to-day record of one's activities and thoughts
draw conclusions	arrive at decisions or opinions after thinking about facts and details and using prior knowledge

D

effect	what happens as the result of a cause
etymology	an explanation of the origin and history of a word and its meaning
exaggeration	a statement that makes something seem larger or greater than it actually is
expository text	text that contains facts and information. Also called *informational text.*

E

fable	a story, usually with animal characters, that is written to teach a moral, or lesson
fact	piece of information that can be proved to be true
fairy tale	a folk story with magical characters and events
fantasy	a story that could not really happen
fiction	writing that tells about imaginary people, things, and events
figurative language	the use of language that gives words a meaning beyond their usual definitions in order to add beauty or force
flashback	an interruption in the sequence of events of a narrative to include an event that happened earlier
folk tale	a story that has been passed down by word of mouth
foreshadowing	the use of hints or clues about what will happen later in a story

F

generalize	make a broad statement or rule after examining particular facts
graphic organizer	a drawing, chart, or web that illustrates concepts or shows how ideas relate to each other. Readers use graphic organizers to help them keep track of and understand important information and ideas as they read. Story maps, word webs, Venn diagrams, and KWL charts are graphic organizers.
graphic source	a chart, diagram, or map within a text that adds to readers' understanding of the text

G

Instruction

H

historical fiction	realistic fiction that takes place in the past. It is an imaginary story based on historical events and characters.
humor	writing or speech that has a funny or amusing quality
hyperbole	an exaggerated statement not meant to be taken literally, such as *I'm so hungry I could eat a horse.*

I

idiom	a phrase whose meaning differs from the ordinary meaning of the words. *A stone's throw* is an idiom meaning "a short distance."
imagery	the use of language to create beautiful or forceful pictures in the reader's mind
inference	conclusion reached on the basis of evidence and reasoning
inform	give knowledge, facts, or news to someone
informational text	writing that contains facts and information. Also called *expository text*.
interview	a face-to-face conversation in which someone responds to questions
irony	a way of speaking or writing in which the ordinary meaning of the words is the opposite of what the speaker or writer is thinking; a contrast between what is expected and what actually happens

J

jargon	the language of a special group or profession

L

legend	a story coming down from the past about the great deeds of a hero. Although a legend may be based on historical people and events, it is not regarded as historically true.
literary elements	the characters, setting, plot, and theme of a narrative text

M

main idea	the big idea that tells what a paragraph or a selection is mainly about; the most important idea of a text
metacognition	an awareness of one's own thinking processes and the ability to monitor and direct them to a desired goal. Good readers use metacognition to monitor their reading and adjust their reading strategies.
metaphor	a comparison that does not use *like* or *as*, such as *a heart of stone*
meter	the pattern of beats or accents in poetry

monitor and clarify	a comprehension strategy by which readers actively think about understanding their reading and know when they understand and when they do not. Readers use appropriate strategies to make sense of difficult words, ideas, or passages.
mood	the atmosphere or feeling of a written work
moral	the lesson or teaching of a fable or story
motive	the reason a character in a narrative does or says something
mystery	a story about mysterious events that are not explained until the end, so as to keep the reader in suspense
myth	a story that attempts to explain something in nature

M

narrative	a story, made up or true, that someone tells or narrates
narrator	the character in a selection who tells the story
nonfiction	writing that tells about real things, real people, and real events

N

onomatopoeia	the use of words that sound like their meanings, such as *buzz* and *hum*
opinion	someone's judgment, belief, or way of thinking
oral vocabulary	the words needed for speaking and listening
outcome	the resolution of the conflict in a story

O

paraphrase	retell the meaning of a passage in one's own words
personification	a figure of speech in which human traits or actions are given to animals or inanimate objects, as in *The sunbeam danced on the waves.*
persuade	convince someone to do or to believe something
photo essay	a collection of photographs on one theme, accompanied by text
play	a story that is written to be acted out for an audience
plot	a series of related events at the beginning, middle, and end of a story; the action of a story
poem	an expressive, imaginative piece of writing often arranged in lines having rhythm and rhyme. In a poem, the patterns made by the sounds of the words have special importance.
pourquoi tale	a type of folk story that explains why things in nature came to be. *Pourquoi* is a French word meaning "why."

P

Instruction

predict tell what a selection might be about or what might happen in a text. Readers use text features and information to predict. They confirm or revise their predictions as they read.

preview look over a text before reading it

prior knowledge the information and experience that a reader brings to a text. Readers use prior knowledge to help them understand what they read.

prop an item, such as an object, picture, or chart, used in a performance or presentation

reading vocabulary the words we recognize or use in print

realistic fiction a story about imaginary people and events that could happen in real life

repetition the repeated use of some aspect of language

resolution the point in a story where the conflict is resolved

rhyme to end in the same sound(s)

rhythm a pattern of strong beats in speech or writing, especially poetry

rising action the buildup of conflicts and complications in a story

science fiction a story based on science that often tells what life in the future might be like

semantic map a graphic organizer, often a web, used to display words or concepts that are meaningfully related

sensory language the use of words that help the reader understand how things look, sound, smell, taste, or feel

sequence the order of events in a selection or the order of the steps in which something is completed

sequence words clue words such as *first*, *next*, *then*, and *finally* that signal the order of events in a selection

setting where and when a story takes place

simile a comparison that uses *like* or *as*, as in *as busy as a bee*

speech a public talk to a group of people made for a specific purpose

stanza a group of lines in a poem

steps in a process the order of the steps in which something is completed

story map a graphic organizer used to record the literary elements and the sequence of events in a narrative text

story structure how the characters, setting, and events of a story are organized into a plot

summarize give the most important ideas of what was read. Readers summarize important information in the selection to keep track of what they are reading.

supporting detail piece of information that tells about the main idea

symbolism the use of one thing to suggest something else; often the use of something concrete to stand for an abstract idea

S

tall tale a humorous story that uses exaggeration to describe impossible happenings

text structure the organization of a piece of nonfiction writing. Text structures of informational text include cause-effect, chronological, compare/contrast, description, problem/solution, proposition/support, and ask/answer questions.

theme the big idea or author's message in a story

think aloud an instructional strategy in which a teacher verbalizes his or her thinking to model the process of comprehension or the application of a skill

tone author's attitude toward the subject or toward the reader

topic the subject of a discussion, conversation, or piece of text

T

visualize picture in one's mind what is happening in the text. Visualizing helps readers imagine the things they read about.

V

Instruction

Section 3 Matching Books and Readers

Leveled Readers Skills Chart

Scott Foresman Reading Street provides more than six hundred leveled readers. Each one is designed to:

- Practice critical skills and strategies
- Build vocabulary and concepts
- Build fluency
- Develop a lifelong love of reading

Grade 3

Title	Level*	DRA Level	Genre	Comprehension Strategy
The Opposite Cousins	F	10	Realistic Fiction	Background Knowledge
It's a Fair Swap!	F	10	Expository Nonfiction	Summarize
Life in the Arctic	F	10	Nonfiction	Visualize
Let's Surprise Mom	F	10	Realistic Fiction	Background Knowledge
E-mail Friends	F	10	Realistic Fiction	Story Structure
The Frozen Continent: Antarctica	F	10	Expository Nonfiction	Monitor and Clarify
Buddy Goes to School	G	12	Realistic Fiction	Visualize
The Metal Detective	G	12	Realistic Fiction	Questioning
Growing Vegetables	G	12	Narrative Nonfiction	Predict and Set Purpose
All About Birds	G	12	Nonfiction	Text Structure
Raisins	G	12	Nonfiction	Important Ideas
The Hunters and the Elk	G	12	Fiction	Inferring
Pictures in the Sky	H	14	Expository Nonfiction	Text Structure
Rescuing Whales	H	14	Expository Nonfiction	Story Structure
The Field Trip	H	14	Expository Nonfiction	Predict and Set Purpose
The Winning Point	H	14	Realistic Fiction	Summarize
How to Measure the Weather	H	14	Expository Nonfiction	Important Ideas
Grandpa's Rock Kit	H	14	Narrative Nonfiction	Inferring
Across the English Channel	H	14	Expository Nonfiction	Questioning
Swimming Like Buck	I	16	Animal Fantasy	Monitor and Clarify
A Tea Party with Obâchan	I	16	Realistic Fiction	Visualize
Independence Day/El Día de la Independencia	I	16	Nonfiction	Inferring
A Child's Life in Korea	I	16	Expository Nonfiction	Monitor and Clarify
The World of Bread!	I	16	Expository Nonfiction	Summarize
A Walk Around the City	I	16	Expository Nonfiction	Background Knowledge
The Statue of Liberty: A Gift From France	I	16	Expository Nonfiction	Questioning
Camping with Aunt Julie	J	18	Realistic Fiction	Background Knowledge
Let's Make a Trade!	J	18	Expository Nonfiction	Summarize
Ice Fishing in the Arctic	J	18	Nonfiction	Visualize
The Shopping Trip	J	18	Fiction	Background Knowledge

* Suggested Guided Reading Level. Use your knowledge of students' abilities to adjust levels as needed.

The chart here and on the next few pages lists titles of leveled readers appropriate for students in Grade 3. Use the chart to find titles that meet your students' interest and instructional needs. The books in this list were leveled using the criteria suggested in *Matching Books to Readers* and *Leveled Books for Readers, Grades 3–6* by Irene C. Fountas and Gay Su Pinnell. For more on leveling, see the *Reading Street Leveled Readers Leveling Guide.*

Target Comprehension Skill	Additional Comprehension Instruction	Vocabulary
Character, Setting, and Theme	Draw Conclusions	Context Clues/Homonyms
Sequence	Fact and Opinion	Word Structure/Compound Words
Sequence	Generalize	Dictionary/Glossary/Unfamiliar Words
Compare and Contrast	Main Idea	Context Clues/Multiple Meanings
Author's Purpose	Compare and Contrast	Word Structure/Prefixes and Suffixes
Main Idea and Details	Generalize	Context Clues/Synonyms
Compare and Contrast	Sequence	Context Clues/Unfamiliar Words
Draw Conclusions	Realism and Fantasy	Compound Words/Word Structure
Author's Purpose	Generalize	Context Clues/Antonyms
Main Idea and Details	Compare and Contrast	Context Clues/Unfamiliar Words
Draw Conclusions	Generalize	Homophones/Context Clues
Character, Setting, and Plot	Theme	Unknown Words/Dictionary/Glossary
Graphic Sources	Author's Purpose	Unknown Words/Dictionary/Glossary
Generalize	Sequence	Context Clues/Unfamiliar Words
Cause and Effect	Draw Conclusions	Prefixes/Suffixes/Word Structure
Generalize	Plot	Unfamiliar Words/Context Clues
Graphic Sources	Main Idea	Unknown Words/Dictionary/Glossary
Fact and Opinion	Fact and Opinion	Context Clues/Multiple Meanings
Fact and Opinion	Generalize	Context Clues/Multiple Meanings
Cause and Effect	Character	Unknown Words/Dictionary/Glossary
Compare and Contrast	Generalize	Context Clues/Synonyms
Main Idea and Details	Draw Conclusions	Context Clues/Antonyms
Sequence	Author's Purpose	Word Structure/Compound Words
Draw Conclusions	Main Idea	Context Clues/Unfamiliar Words
Author's Purpose	Generalize	Context Clues/Homonyms
Fact and Opinion	Fact and Opinion	Word Structure/Prefixes
Character and Setting	Theme	Context Clues/Homonyms
Sequence	Draw Conclusions	Word Structure/Compound Words
Sequence	Author's Purpose	Dictionary/Glossary/Unfamiliar Words
Compare and Contrast	Character	Context Clues/Multiple Meanings

Leveled Readers Skills Chart Continued

Grade 3

Title	Level*	DRA Level	Genre	Comprehension Strategy
New York's Chinatown	J	18	Expository Nonfiction	Inferring
One Forest, Different Trees	J	18	Realistic Fiction	Important Ideas
Swimming in a School	J	18	Animal Fantasy	Story Structure
Greek Myths	J	18	Nonfiction	Inferring
The Market Adventure	K	20	Realistic Fiction	Story Structure
These Birds Can't Fly!	K	20	Expository Nonfiction	Monitor and Clarify
Iguana Takes a Ride	K	20	Animal Fantasy	Visualize
The Last Minute	K	20	Realistic Fiction	Questioning
Our Garden	K	20	Realistic Fiction	Predict and Set Purpose
Bills and Beaks	L	24	Historical Fiction	Text Structure
In the Fields	L	24	Historical Fiction	Important Ideas
The Thunder and Lightning Men	L	24	Folktale	Inferring
Meet the Stars	L	24	Realistic Fiction	Text Structure
What a Day!	L	24	Realistic Fiction	Story Structure
Desert Life	L	24	Expository Nonfiction	Predict and Set Purpose
A Trip	M	28	Realistic Fiction	Summarize
Measuring the Earth	M	28	Expository Nonfiction	Important Ideas
Fun with Hobbies and Science!	M	28	Expository Nonfiction	Inferring
Great Women in U.S. History	M	28	Biography	Questioning
Buddy Ran Away	M	28	Realistic Fiction	Monitor and Clarify
Cowboy Slim's Dude Ranch	M	28	Realistic Fiction	Visualize
Celebrate Around the World	N	30	Nonfiction	Inferring
Joanie's House Becomes a Home	N	30	Realistic Fiction	Monitor and Clarify
Kapuapua's Magic Shell	N	30	Folktale	Summarize
Bobby's New Apartment	N	30	Realistic Fiction	Background Knowledge
Symbols, Signs, and Songs of America	N	30	Narrative Nonfiction	Text Structure
A Pet Bird	O	34	Expository Nonfiction	Inferring
Lily's Adventure Around the World	O	34	Realistic Fiction	Important Ideas
The Three Bears and Goldilocks	O	34	Animal Fantasy	Story Structure
Sweet Freedom!	O	34	Nonfiction	Inferring

* Suggested Guided Reading Level. Use your knowledge of students' abilities to adjust levels as needed.

You know the theory behind leveled books: they let you match books with the interest and instructional levels of your students. You can find the right reader for every student with this chart.

Target Comprehension Skill	Additional Comprehension Instruction	Vocabulary
Cause and Effect	Generalize	Context Clues/Antonyms
Graphic Sources	Generalize	Dictionary/Glossary/Unknown Words
Plot and Theme	Realism and Fantasy	Word Structure/Prefixes and Suffixes
Generalize	Compare and Contrast	Homographs/Context Clues
Author's Purpose	Generalize	Word Structure/Prefixes and Suffixes
Main Idea and Details	Compare and Contrast	Context Clues/Synonyms
Compare and Contrast	Draw Conclusions	Context Clues/Unfamiliar Words
Draw Conclusions	Sequence	Compound Words/Word Structure
Author's Purpose	Plot	Context Clues/Antonyms
Main Idea and Details	Setting	Context Clues/Unfamiliar Words
Draw Conclusions	Author's Purpose	Homophones/Context Clues
Character, Setting, and Plot	Main Idea	Unknown Words/Dictionary/Glossary
Graphic Sources	Plot	Unknown Words/Dictionary/Glossary
Generalize	Character	Context Clues/Unfamiliar Words
Cause and Effect	Generalize	Dictionary/Glossary/Unfamiliar Words
Generalize	Author's Purpose	Unfamiliar Words/Context Clues
Graphic Sources	Fact and Opinion	Unknown Words/Dictionary/Glossary
Fact and Opinion	Draw Conclusions	Context Clues/Multiple Meanings
Fact and Opinion	Main Idea and Details	Context Clues/Multiple Meanings
Cause and Effect	Sequence	Unknown Words/Dictionary/Glossary
Compare and Contrast	Main Idea	Context Clues/Synonyms
Main Idea and Details	Compare and Contrast	Homophones/Context Clues
Sequence	Draw Conclusions	Word Structure/Compound Words
Draw Conclusions	Theme	Context Clues/Unfamiliar Words
Author's Purpose	Realism and Fantasy	Context Clues/Homonyms
Main Idea	Fact and Opinion	Word Structure/Prefixes
Cause and Effect	Main Idea	Context Clues/Antonyms
Graphic Sources	Compare and Contrast	Unknown Words/Dictionary/Glossary
Plot and Theme	Character	Word Structure/Prefixes and Suffixes
Generalize	Author's Purpose	Homographs/Context Clues

Matching Books & Readers

Leveled Readers Skills Chart *Continued*

Grade 3

Title	Level*	DRA Level	Genre	Comprehension Strategy
Mr. Post's Project	P	38	Realistic Fiction	Background Knowledge
What's Money All About?	P	38	Expository Nonfiction	Summarize
Journey Across the Arctic	P	38	Fiction	Visualize
The Road to New York	P	38	Realistic Fiction	Background Knowledge
With a Twist	P	38	Fantasy	Story Structure
All About Penguins	P	38	Expository Nonfiction	Monitor and Clarify
Puppy Problems	Q	40	Realistic Fiction	Visualize
A Family of Collectors	Q	40	Realistic Fiction	Important Ideas
The Magic of Coyote	Q	40	Realistic Fiction	Predict and Set Purpose
Animals of the Concrete Jungle	Q	40	Expository Nonfiction	Text Structure
Grape Season	Q	40	Realistic Fiction	Important Ideas
Grandmother Spider Steals the Sun	Q	40	Folktale	Inferring
Animal Tracking: Learn More About Animals	Q	40	Expository Nonfiction	Text Structure
Whales and Other Amazing Animals	R	40	Expository Nonfiction	Story Structure
Coral Reefs	R	40	Expository Nonfiction	Predict and Set Purpose
Extraordinary Athletes	R	40	Biography	Summarize
Largest, Fastest, Lightest, Longest	R	40	Expository Nonfiction	Questioning
Gemstones Around the World	R	40	Expository Nonfiction	Inferring
Changing Times	R	40	Expository Nonfiction	Questioning
Toby the Smart Dog	R	40	Humorous Fiction	Monitor and Clarify
His Favorite Sweatshirt	S	40	Realistic Nonfiction	Visualize
Life Overseas	S	40	Expository Nonfiction	Inferring
It's a World of Time Zones	S	40	Expository Nonfiction	Monitor and Clarify
Mixing, Kneading, and Baking: The Baker's Art	S	40	Narrative Nonfiction	Summarize
Let's Go Have Fun!	S	40	Expository Nonfiction	Background Knowledge
The French Connection	S	40	Narrative Nonfiction	Questioning
China's Special Gifts to the World	T	50	Expository Nonfiction	Graphic Organizers
Thomas Hart Benton: Painter of Murals	T	50	Biography	Important Ideas
The Best Field Trip Ever!	T	50	Expository Fiction	Story Structure
Free in the Sea	T	50	Expository Nonfiction	Predict and Set Purpose

* Suggested Guided Reading Level. Use your knowledge of students' abilities to adjust levels as needed.

You know the theory behind leveled books: they let you match books with the interest and instructional levels of your students. You can find the right reader for every student with this chart. 99

Target Comprehension Skill	Additional Comprehension Instruction	Vocabulary
Character and Setting	Theme	Context Clues/Homonyms
Sequence	Draw Conclusions	Word Structure/Compound Words
Sequence	Setting	Dictionary/Glossary/Unfamiliar Words
Compare and Contrast	Character	Context Clues/Multiple Meanings
Author's Purpose	Sequence	Word Structure/Prefixes and Suffixes
Main Idea and Details	Compare and Contrast	Context Clues/Synonyms
Compare and Contrast	Cause and Effect	Context Clues/Unfamiliar Words
Graphic Sources	Realism and Fantasy	Compound Words/Word Structure
Author's Purpose	Sequence	Context Clues/Antonyms
Main Idea and Details	Fact and Opinion	Context Clues/Unfamiliar Words
Draw Conclusions	Main Idea	Homophones/Context Clues
Character, Setting, and Plot	Fact and Opinion	Dictionary/Glossary/Unfamiliar Words
Graphic Sources	Compare and Contrast	Unknown Words/Dictionary/Glossary
Generalize	Author's Purpose	Context Clues/Unfamiliar Words
Cause and Effect	Draw Conclusions	Prefixes and Suffixes/Word Structure
Generalize	Draw Conclusions	Unfamiliar Words/Context Clues
Compare and Contrast	Author's Purpose	Word Structure/Compound Words
Fact and Opinion	Cause and Effect	Context Clues/Multiple Meanings
Fact and Opinion	Generalize	Context Clues/Multiple Meanings
Cause and Effect	Character and Setting	Unknown Words/Dictionary/Glossary
Compare and Contrast	Draw Conclusions	Context Clues/Synonyms
Main Idea and Details	Cause and Effect	Homophones/Context Clues
Sequence	Draw Conclusions	Word Structure/Compound Words
Draw Conclusions	Main Idea	Context Clues/Unfamiliar Words
Author's Purpose	Compare and Contrast	Context Clues/Homonyms
Fact and Opinion	Generalize	Word Structure/Prefixes
Cause and Effect	Generalize	Context Clues/Antonyms
Graphic Sources	Author's Purpose	Unknown Words/Dictionary/Glossary
Plot and Theme	Realism and Fantasy	Word Structure/Prefixes and Suffixes
Generalize	Compare and Contrast	Context Clues/Synonyms

Matching Books & Readers

What Good Readers Do

You can use the characteristics and behaviors of good readers to help all your students read better. But what are these characteristics and behaviors? And how can you use them to foster good reading behaviors for all your students? Here are some helpful tips.

Good Readers enjoy reading! They have favorite books, authors, and genres. Good readers often have a preference about where and when they read. They talk about books and recommend their favorites.

Develop this behavior by giving students opportunities to respond in different ways to what they read. Get them talking about what they read, and why they like or dislike it.

This behavior is important because book sharing alerts you to students who are somewhat passive about reading or have limited literacy experiences. Book sharing also helps you when you select books for the class.

Good Readers select books they can read.

Develop this behavior by providing a range of three or four texts appropriate for the student and then letting the student choose.

This behavior is important because students gain control over reading when they can choose from books they can read. This helps them become more independent in the classroom.

 Good Readers read independently for longer periods of time.

Develop this behavior by taking note of the level of support students need during guided reading. Use this information to gauge independent reading time accordingly.

This behavior is important because students become better readers when they spend time reading many texts at their independent level.

Good Readers use text features to help them preview and set purposes.

Develop this behavior by having students use the title and illustrations in fiction texts or the title, contents, headings, and other graphic features in nonfiction texts to make predictions about what they will be reading.

This behavior is important because previewing actually makes reading easier! Looking at features and sampling the text enables readers to predict and set expectations for reading.

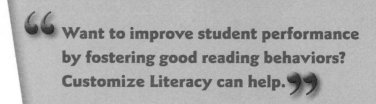

> **Want to improve student performance by fostering good reading behaviors? Customize Literacy can help.**

Good Readers predict and ask questions before and while they read.

Develop this behavior by asking questions. After reading a passage, ask students what they think will happen next in a fiction text. Have them ask a question they think will be answered in a nonfiction text and read on to see if it is.

This behavior is important because when students predict and ask questions as they read, they are engaged. They have a purpose for reading and a basis for monitoring their comprehension.

Good Readers read meaningful phrases aloud with appropriate expression.

Develop this behavior by giving students lots of opportunities to read orally. As they read, note students' phrasing, intonation, and attention to punctuation and give help as needed.

This behavior is important because reading fluently in longer, meaningful phrases supports comprehension and ease in reading longer, more complex texts.

Good Readers read aloud at an appropriate reading rate with a high percent of accuracy.

Develop this behavior by timing students' oral reading to calculate their reading rates. You can also record students' miscues to determine a percent of accuracy. This will help identify problems.

This behavior is important because when students read fluently texts that are "just right," they find reading more enjoyable. A fluent reader is able to focus more on constructing meaning and is more likely to develop a positive attitude toward reading.

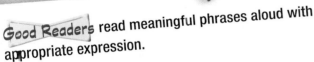

Matching Books & Readers

Good Readers use effective strategies and sources of information to figure out unknown words.

Develop this behavior by teaching specific strategies for figuring out unknown words, such as sounding out clusters of letters, using context, reading on, and using references.

This behavior is important because when readers have a variety of strategies to use, they are more able to decode and self-correct quickly. Readers who do these things view themselves as good readers.

CH- QU- ST-

Good Readers construct meaning as they read and then share or demonstrate their understanding.

Develop this behavior by having students retell what they read or write a summary of what they read in their own words.

This behavior is important because the ability to retell or write a summary is essential for success in reading. It shows how well a student has constructed meaning.

Good Readers locate and use what is explicitly stated in a text.

Develop this behavior by asking questions that require students to go back into the text to find explicitly stated information.

This behavior is important because the ability to recall, locate, and use specific information stated in a text enables readers to respond to literal questions as well as to support opinions and justify their responses.

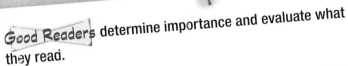 make connections.

Develop this behavior by asking questions to help students make connections: *What does this remind you of? Have you ever read or experienced anything like this?*

This behavior is important because making connections helps readers understand and appreciate a text. Making connections to self, the world, and other texts supports higher-level thinking.

Good Readers interpret what they read by making inferences.

Develop this behavior by asking questions to help students tell or write about what they think was implied in the text: *Why do you think that happened? What helped you come to that conclusion?*

This behavior is important because the ability to go beyond the literal meaning of a text enables readers to gain a deeper understanding. When students make inferences, they use background knowledge, their personal knowledge, and the text to grasp the meaning of what is implied by the author.

Good Readers determine importance and evaluate what they read.

Develop this behavior by always having students identify what they think is the most important message, event, or information in a text.

This behavior is important because readers must be able to sort out important from interesting information. The ability to establish and/or use criteria and provide support when making judgments is an important critical-thinking skill.

Good Readers support their responses using information from a text and/or their own background knowledge.

Develop this behavior by always asking students to give the reason(s) they identified an event, message, or idea as most important.

This behavior is important because the ability to justify one's response is important for all learners. It enables others to know the basis for a decision and provides an opening for further discussion.

Conversation Starters

Asking Good Questions When students read interesting and thought-provoking books, they want to share! You can encourage students to think critically about what they read. Use questions such as the following to assess comprehension as well as evoke good class/group discussions.

Author's Purpose

- Why did the author write this piece?

- How does figuring out the author's purpose help you decide how to read the text?

Cause and Effect

- Why did these events happen? How might they have been different if the causes had been different?

- Are there several causes that result in a single effect?

- Is there a single cause that has several effects?

Compare and Contrast

- What clue words show the author is comparing and/or contrasting in this article?

- How are the fictional characters and events in this story like and/or different from real people and events you know of?

Draw Conclusions

- Based on what you have read, seen, or experienced, what can you conclude about this event in the selection?

- This story seems to be a fantasy. Why might you conclude this?

- What words help you draw conclusions about the relationship between the characters?

Fact and Opinion

- What clue word or words signal that this is a statement of opinion?

- How could this statement of fact be proved true or false?

Generalize

- What generalization can you make about the story or the characters in it? What examples lead to that generalization?

- What details, facts, and logic does the author use to support this generalization?

Graphic Sources

- How does the author use graphic sources (chart, maps, illustrations, time lines, and so on) to support ideas and opinions?

- This selection has many graphic sources. Which one or ones best help you understand the events or ideas in the selection? Why?

Literary Elements: Character, Setting, Plot, Theme

- Describe the main character at the beginning of the story and at the end of the story. How and why does he or she change?

- How is the setting important to the story? How might the story be different if its time or its place were different?

- What does the main character want at the beginning of the story? How does the main character go about trying to achieve this?

- In a few sentences, what is the plot of the story?

- What is the theme of the story? Use details from the story to support your statement.

Main Idea and Details

- What is the main idea of this paragraph or article? What are some details?

- The author makes this particular statement in the article. What details does the author provide to support that statement?

Sequence

- How is the sequence of events important in the text?

- Is the order of events important in this story? Why or why not?

- Based on what has already happened, what will most likely happen next?

Connecting Science and Social Studies

Scott Foresman Reading Street Leveled Readers are perfect for covering, supporting, or enriching science and social studies content. Using these books ensures that all students can access important concepts.

Grade 3 Leveled Readers

Science

Earth and Space Science

Nonfiction Books
- *The Frozen Continent: Antarctica*
- *Fun with Hobbies and Science!*
- *Gemstones Around the World*
- *Grandpa's Rock Kit*
- *How to Measure the Weather*
- *Measuring the Earth*
- *Meet the Stars*
- *Pictures in the Sky*

Fiction Books
- *What a Day!*
- *Journey Across the Arctic*

Life Science

Nonfiction Books
- *A Pet Bird*
- *All About Birds*
- *All About Penguins*
- *Animal Tracking: Learn More About It*
- *Animals of the Concrete Jungle*
- *Coral Reefs*
- *Desert Life*
- *The Field Trip*
- *Free in the Sea*
- *Growing Vegetables*
- *Ice Fishing in the Arctic*
- *Largest, Fastest, Lightest, Longest*
- *Life in the Arctic*
- *Raisins*
- *Rescuing Whales*
- *These Birds Can't Fly!*
- *Whales and Other Amazing Animals*

Life Science

Fiction Books
- *The Best Field Trip Ever!*
- *Bills and Beaks*
- *Buddy Ran Away*
- *Grape Season*
- *The Hunters and the Elk*
- *In the Fields*
- *Swimming in a School*
- *Swimming Like Buck*
- *Toby the Smart Dog*

Grade 3 Leveled Readers

Social Studies

Citizenship

Nonfiction Books
- Sweet Freedom!
- Symbols, Signs, and Songs of America

Fiction Books
- Buddy Goes to School
- Camping with Aunt Julie
- The Opposite Cousins
- Our Garden
- Puppy Problems

Culture

Nonfiction Books
- A Child's Life in Korea
- A Walk Around the City
- Celebrate Around the World
- China's Special Gifts to the World
- His Favorite Sweatshirt
- Let's Go Have Fun!
- Life Overseas
- Mixing, Kneading, and Baking
- New York's Chinatown
- The French Connection
- The World of Bread!

Fiction Books
- A Tea Party with Obâchan
- Bobby's New Apartment
- Cowboy Slim's Dude Ranch
- E-mail Friends

Culture

- Grandmother Spider Steals the Sun
- Iguana Takes a Ride
- Kapuapua's Magic Shell
- The Last Minute
- Lily's Adventure Around the World
- The Magic of Coyote
- One Forest, Different Trees
- The Road to New York
- The Three Bears and Goldilocks
- The Thunder and Lightning Men

Economics

Nonfiction Books
- It's a Fair Swap!
- It's a World of Time Zones
- Let's Make a Trade
- What's Money All About?

Fiction Books
- A Family of Collectors
- Joanie's House Becomes a Home
- Let's Surprise Mom
- The Market Adventure
- The Metal Detective
- Mr. Post's Project
- The Shopping Trip

History

Nonfiction Books
- Across the English Channel
- Celebrate Independence Day/Celebra El Día de la Independencia
- Changing Times: Women in the Early Twentieth Century
- Greek Myths
- The Statue of Liberty: A Gift From France

Fiction Books
- A Trip
- The Winning Point
- With a Twist

More Great Titles

Biography
- Extraordinary Athletes
- Great Women in U. S. History
- Thomas Hart Benton: Painter of Murals

Connecting Science and Social Studies

Need more choices? Look back to Grade 2.

Grade 2 Leveled Readers

Science

Earth and Space Science

Nonfiction Books

- All About Astronauts
- An Astronaut Spacewalk
- Desert Animals
- Deserts
- Hurricane!
- Look at Our Galaxy

Fiction Books

- Blizzard!
- Maggie's New Sidekick
- Rainbow Crow Brings Fire to Earth
- A Slice of Mud Pie

Life Science

Nonfiction Books

- Arachnid or Insect?
- Compost: Recycled Waste
- Farming Families
- How a Seed Grows
- How Can Animals Help?
- How Do Plants Grow?
- How to Grow Tomatoes
- Plants Grow Everywhere
- A Vet for All Animals

Fiction Books

- Annie Makes a Big Change
- Camping at Crescent Lake
- Growing Up
- Too Many Rabbit Holes
- Where Is Fish?

Physical Science

Nonfiction Books

- Many Types of Energy
- Sink or Float?

Fiction Books

- The Hummingbird
- Our School Science Fair

Grade 2 Leveled Readers

Social Studies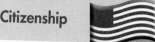

Citizenship

Nonfiction Books

- *America's Birthday*
- *The Barn Raising*
- *Be Ready for an Emergency*
- *Everyone Can Make a Difference!*
- *Join an Adventure Club!*
- *Keeping Our Community Safe*
- *Protect the Earth*
- *The Rescue Dogs*
- *Service Workers*
- *Special Animal Helpers*
- *Using a Net*
- *What Can You Do?*
- *Working Dogs*

Fiction Books

- *Andrew's Mistake*
- *Camping with Pup*
- *Freda the Signmaker*
- *Hubert and Frankie*
- *Let's Work Together!*
- *Marty's Summer Job*
- *Sally and the Wild Puppy*
- *Stripes and Silver*
- *Too Many Frogs!*
- *Training Peanut*

Culture

Nonfiction Books

- *Celebrations and Family Traditions*
- *Living in Seoul*
- *Showing Good Manners*
- *Special Chinese Birthdays*
- *A World of Birthdays*

Fiction Books

- *Ana Is Shy*
- *The Camping Trip*
- *Country Friends, City Friends*
- *Dotty's Art*
- *The First People to Fly*
- *Glooskap and the First Summer: An Algonquin Tale*
- *Happy New Year!*
- *The International Food Fair*
- *Just Like Grandpa*
- *Living on a Ranch*
- *The New Kid in Bali*
- *Voting Day*

Economics

Nonfiction Books

- *Services and Goods*

Fiction Books

- *Country Mouse and City Mouse*
- *A Quiet Place*
- *Snakeskin Canyon*

History

Nonfiction Books

- *A Few Nifty Inventions*
- *The Hoover Dam*
- *Living in a Democracy*
- *Making Travel Fun*
- *Saint Bernards and Other Working Dogs*
- *Starting a New Life*
- *Women Play Baseball*

Fiction Books

- *At Home in the Wilderness*
- *A Class Play*
- *A Cowboy's Life*
- *Down on the Ranch*
- *Hank's Tortilla Factory*

Government

Nonfiction Books

- *Communicating Then and Now*
- *Let's Send a Letter!*

More Great Titles

Biography

- *American Revolution Heroes*
- *Baseball Heroes Make History*
- *Thomas Adams: Chewing Gum Inventor*
- *Three Great Ballplayers*

Connecting Science and Social Studies

Need more choices? Look ahead to Grade 4.

Grade 4 Leveled Readers

Science

Earth and Space Science

Nonfiction Books

- *Danger: The World Is Getting Hot!*
- *Darkness Into Light*
- *Day for Night*
- *Earth's Closest Neighbor*
- *Let's Explore Antarctica!*
- *Looking For Changes*
- *The Mysteries of Space*
- *One Giant Leap*
- *Orbiting the Sun*
- *Putting a Stop to Wildfires*
- *Severe Weather: Storms*
- *Storm Chasers*
- *Wondrously Wild Weather*

Fiction Books

- *Exploring the Moon*
- *Flash Flood*
- *Life on Mars: The Real Story*
- *Stuart's Moon Suit*
- *Surviving Hurricane Andrew*
- *To the Moon!*

Life Science

Nonfiction Books

- *Birds Take Flight*
- *Come Learn About Dolphins*
- *Dolphins: Mammals of the Sea*
- *Florida Everglades: Its Plants and Animals*
- *The Gray Whale*
- *How Does Echolocation Work?*
- *Migration Relocation*
- *Mini Microbes*
- *Mysterious Monsters*
- *Plants and Animals in Antarctica*
- *Saving Trees Using Science*
- *Sharing Our Planet*
- *What in the World Is That?*

Life Science

Fiction Books

- *The Missing Iguana Mystery*
- *Protecting Wild Animals*
- *The Salamander Stumper*
- *Top Hat Tompkins, the Detective*

Grade 4 Leveled Readers

Social Studies

Citizenship

Nonfiction Books
- *Equality in American Schools*
- *Danger! Children at Work*
- *Dogs on the Job*

Fiction Books
- *Mountain Rescue*
- *The Super Secret Surprise Society*

Culture

Nonfiction Books
- *The Black Ensemble Theater*
- *The Diné*
- *From Spain to America*
- *What It Takes to Stage a Play*

Fiction Books
- *A Book of Their Own*
- *A New Home*
- *Birthday Surprise*
- *Cheers for the Cheetahs*
- *The Grizzly Bear Hotshots*
- *Living with Grandpa Joseph*
- *The Show Must Go On!*
- *Something to Do*
- *To Be a Star*

Economics

Nonfiction Books
- *The Alaskan Pipeline*
- *Ranches in the Southwest*
- *Ranching in the Great American Desert*
- *Two Powerful Rivers*

Fiction Books
- *The Seahaven Squids Host a Pet Wash*

History

Nonfiction Books
- *Becoming a Melting Pot*
- *The Civil Rights Movement*
- *Code Breakers: Uncovering German Messages*
- *Let's Get to Know the Incas*
- *The Long Journey West*
- *Meet the Maya*
- *The Navajo Code Talkers*
- *Pompeii, the Lost City*
- *The Rosetta Stone: The Key to Ancient Writing*
- *The Sauk and Fox Native Americans*
- *Speaking in Code*
- *The Story of Libraries*
- *Thor Heyerdahl's Incredible Raft*
- *We Shall Overcome*
- *The Women's Movement*

History

Fiction Books
- *Bessie Coleman*
- *The Incredible Alexander Graham Bell*

Geography

Nonfiction Books
- *America's National Parks*
- *Maine, Now and Then*
- *A Trip to Capital Hill*
- *The Wonders of Western Geography*

Fiction Books
- *From Sea to Shining Sea*

Government

Nonfiction Books
- *The Power of the People*
- *The United States Government*

More Great Titles

Biography
- *Amazing Female Athletes*
- *Jim Thorpe*
- *John Muir*
- *The Legacy of César Chávez*
- *Lewis and Clark and the Corps of Discovery*

Planning Teacher Study Groups

Adventurous teachers often have good ideas for lessons. A teacher study group is a great way to share ideas and get feedback on the best way to connect content and students. Working with other teachers can provide you with the support and motivation you need to implement new teaching strategies. A teacher study group offers many opportunities to collaborate, support each other's work, share insights, and get feedback.

Think About It

A weekly or monthly teacher study group can help support you in developing your expertise in the classroom. You and a group of like-minded teachers can form your own study group. What can this group accomplish?

- Read and discuss professional articles by researchers in the field of education.

- Meet to share teaching tips, collaborate on multi-grade lessons, and share resources.

- Develop lessons to try out new teaching strategies. Meet to share experiences and discuss how to further improve your teaching approach.

Let's Meet!

Forming a study group is easy. Just follow these four steps:

1. **Decide on the size of the group.** A small group has the advantage of making each member feel accountable, but make sure that all people can make the same commitment!

2. **Choose teachers to invite to join your group.** Think about who you want to invite. Should they all teach the same grade? Can you invite teachers from other schools? Remember that the more diverse the group, the more it benefits from new perspectives.

3. **Set goals for the group.** In order to succeed, know what you want the group to do. Meet to set goals. Rank goals in order of importance and refer often to the goals to keep the group on track.

4. **Make logistical decisions.** This is often the most difficult. Decide where and when you will meet. Consider an online meeting place where group members can post discussion questions and replies if people are not able to meet.

What Will We Study? Use the goals to help determine what your group will study. Consider what materials are needed to reach your goals, and how long you think is necessary to prepare for each meeting.

How Will It Work? Think about how you structure groups in your classroom. Then use some of the same strategies.

- **Assign a group facilitator.** This person is responsible for guiding the meeting. This person comes prepared with discussion questions and leads the meeting. This could be a rotating responsibility dependent on experience with various topics. This person might be responsible for providing the materials.

- **Assign a recorder.** Have someone take notes during the meeting and record group decisions.

- **Use the jigsaw method.** Not everyone has time to be a facilitator. In this case, divide the text and assign each portion to a different person. Each person is responsible for leading the discussion on that particular part.

Meet Again Make a commitment to meet for a minimum number of times. After that, the group can reevaluate and decide whether or not to continue.

66 Have some great teaching tips to share? Want to exchange ideas with your colleagues? Build your own professional community of teachers. **Customize Literacy** gets you started. 99

Building Community

Trial Lessons

Use your colleagues experience to help as you think about new ways to connect content and students. Use the following plan to create a mini-lesson. It should last twenty minutes. Get the support of your colleagues as you try something new and reflect on what happened.

Be Creative!

As you develop a plan for a mini-lesson, use these four words to guide planning: *purpose, text, resources,* and *routine.*

- **Purpose:** Decide on a skill or strategy to teach. Define your purpose for teaching the lesson.

- **Text:** Develop a list of the texts you could use. Ask your colleagues for suggestions.

- **Resources:** Make a list of the available resources, and consider how to use those resources most effectively. Consider using the leveled readers listed on pages CL24–CL29 and CL36–CL41 of Customize Literacy.

- **Routine:** Choose an instructional routine to structure your mini-lesson. See the mini-lessons in Customize Literacy for suggestions.

Try It!

Try out your lesson! Consider audio- or videotaping the lesson for later review. You may wish to invite a colleague to sit in as you teach. Make notes on how the lesson went.

How Did It Go?

Use the self-evaluation checklist on page CL45 as you reflect on your trial lesson. This provides a framework for later discussion.

Discuss, Reflect, Repeat

Solicit feedback from your teacher study group. Explain the lesson and share your reflections. Ask for suggestions on ways to improve the lesson. Take some time to reflect on the feedback. Modify your lesson to reflect what you have learned. Then try teaching the lesson again.

Checklist for Teacher Self-Evaluation

How Well Did I ...	Very Well	Satisfactory	Not Very Well
Plan the lesson?			
Select the appropriate level of text?			
Introduce the lesson and explain its objectives?			
Review previously taught skills?			
Directly explain the new skills being taught?			
Model the new skills?			
Break the material down into small steps?			
Integrate guided practice into the lesson?			
Monitor guided practice for student understanding?			
Provide feedback on independent practice?			
Maintain an appropriate pace?			
Assess student understanding of the material?			
Stress the importance of applying the skill as they read?			
Maintain students' interest?			
Ask questions?			
Handle student questions and responses?			
Respond to the range of abilities?			

Building Community

Books for Teachers

Students aren't the only ones who need to read to grow. Here is a brief list of books that you may find useful to fill your reading basket and learn new things.

A Professional Bibliography

Afflerbach, P. "Teaching Reading Self-Assessment Strategies." *Comprehension Instruction: Research-Based Best Practices.* The Guilford Press, 2002.

Bear, D. R., M. Invernizzi, S. Templeton, and F. Johnston. *Words Their Way.* Merrill Prentice Hall, 2004.

Beck, I. L., M. G. McKeown. *Improving Comprehension with Questioning the Author: A Fresh and Expanded View of a Powerful Approach.* Scholastic, 2006.

Beck, I., M. G. McKeown, and L. Kucan. *Bringing Words to Life: Robust Vocabulary Instruction.* The Guilford Press, 2002.

Blachowicz, C. and P. Fisher. "Vocabulary Instruction." *Handbook of Reading Research,* vol. III. Lawrence Erlbaum Associates, 2000.

Blachowicz, C. and D. Ogle. *Reading Comprehension: Strategies for Independent Learners.* The Guilford Press, 2008.

Block, C. C. and M. Pressley "Best Practices in Comprehension Instruction." *Best Practices in Literacy Instruction.* The Guilford Press, 2003.

Daniels, H. *Literature Circles.* 2nd ed. Stenhouse Publishers, 2002.

Dickson, S. V., D. C. Simmons, and E. J. Kame'enui. "Text Organization: Instructional and Curricular Basics and Implications." *What Reading Research Tells Us About Children with Diverse Learning Needs: Bases and Basics.* Lawrence Erlbaum Associates, 1998.

Diller, D. *Making the Most of Small Groups: Differentiation for All.* Stenhouse Publishers, 2007.

Duke, N. and P. D. Pearson. "Effective Practices for Developing Reading Comprehension." *What Research Has to Say About Reading Instruction,* 3rd ed. Newark, DE: International Reading Association, 2002.

Fillmore, L. W. and C. E. Snow. *What Teachers Need to Know About Language.* Office of Educational Research and Improvement, U.S. Department of Education, 2000.

Fountas, I. C. and G. S. Pinnell. *Guiding Readers and Writers Grades 3–6: Teaching Comprehension, Genre, and Content Literacy.* Heinemann, 2001.

Guthrie, J. and E. Anderson. "Engagement in Reading: Processes of Motivated Strategic, Knowledgeable, Social Readers." *Engaged Reading: Processes, Practices, and Policy Implications.* Teachers College Press, 1999.

Harvey, S. and A. Goudvis. *Strategies That Work: Teaching Comprehension to Enhance Understanding.* 2nd ed. Stenhouse Publishers, 2007.

Keene, E. O. and S. Zimmerman. *Mosaic of Thought.* 2nd ed. Heinemann, 2007.

Leu Jr., D. J. "The New Literacies: Research on Reading Instruction with the Internet and Other Digital Technologies." *What Research Has to Say About Reading Instruction,* 3rd ed. International Reading Association, 2002.

McKeown, M. G. and I. L. Beck. "Direct and Rich Vocabulary Instruction." *Vocabulary Instruction: Research to Practice.* The Guilford Press, 2004.

McTighe, J. and K. O'Connor. "Seven Practices for Effective Learning." *Educational Leadership,* vol. 63, no. 3 (November 2005).

Nagy, W. E. *Teaching Vocabulary to Improve Reading Comprehension.* International Reading Association, 1998.

National Reading Panel. *Teaching Children to Read.* National Institute of Child Health and Human Development, 1999.

Ogle, D. and C. Blachowicz. "Beyond Literature Circles: Helping Students Comprehend Information Texts." *Comprehension Instruction: Research-Based Practices.* The Guilford Press, 2001.

Pressley, M. *Reading Instruction That Works: The Case for Balanced Teaching,* 3rd ed. The Guilford Press, 2005.

Stahl, S. A. "What Do We Know About Fluency?" *The Voice of Evidence in Reading Research.* Paul H. Brookes, 2004.

Taylor, B. M., P. D. Pearson, D. S. Peterson, and M. C. Rodriguez. "The CIERA School Change Framework: An Evidence-Based Approach to Professional Development and School Reading Improvement." *Reading Research Quarterly,* vol. 40, no. 1 (January/February/March 2005).

Valencia, S. W. and M. Y. Lipson. "Thematic Instruction: A Quest for Challenging Ideas and Meaningful Learning." *Literature-Based Instruction: Reshaping the Curriculum.* Christopher-Gordon Publishers, 1998.

Building Community

The Story of the Statue of Liberty

Amazing Words Oral Vocabulary Routine

DAY 1

tribute

1. **Introduce** A *tribute* is something done to show thanks or respect.
2. **Demonstrate** The statue is a *tribute* to the soldiers who died in the war.
3. **Apply** Have students name someone or something that they think deserves a *tribute*.

enlighten

1. **Introduce** To *enlighten* means "to give knowledge or wisdom to."
2. **Demonstrate** The boy asked the older man to *enlighten* him about the past.
3. **Apply** Discuss the idiom "to see the light" and help students make the connection to the word *enlighten*.

contribution

1. **Introduce** A *contribution* is money, help, or advice that is given as a gift.
2. **Demonstrate** Nate's *contribution* to Earth Day was helping to plant trees in the local park.
3. **Apply** Discuss different kinds of *contributions* that people make every day.

DAY 2

competition

1. **Introduce** A *competition* is a contest.
2. **Demonstrate** Tom entered his science project in a state-wide *competition*.
3. **Apply** Have students describe a *competition* they've heard of, seen, or been involved in.

DAY 3

disgrace

1. **Introduce** A *disgrace* is a shame or a loss of honor or respect.
2. **Demonstrate** It is a *disgrace* to treat other people rudely.
3. **Apply** Discuss situations or conditions that students feel are a *disgrace*.

DAY 4

fund

1. **Introduce** A *fund* is a sum of money set aside for a special purpose.
2. **Demonstrate** The school has a *fund* of $4000 to buy new books.
3. **Apply** Have students think of things at school for which they could raise *funds*.

Happy Birthday Mr. Kang

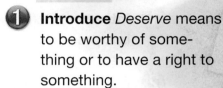 **Amazing Words** **Oral Vocabulary Routine**

DAY **1**

release

1. **Introduce** To *release* means to let someone or something go, to set it free.
2. **Demonstrate** Prisoners were *released* after the war. Callie *released* the dog from it's kennel and let it run around the yard.
3. **Apply** Work with students to make a list of synonyms for *release.*

loyal

1. **Introduce** To be *loyal* means "to show lasting affection and support for someone or something."
2. **Demonstrate** Maggie and Andy had been *loyal* friends for years. The soldiers served their country *loyally.*
3. **Apply** Have students discuss how they can show *loyalty* to a friend.

deserve

1. **Introduce** *Deserve* means to be worthy of something or to have a right to something.
2. **Demonstrate** The students *deserve* praise for their hard work. The dancers *deserved* applause for their wonderful performance.
3. **Apply** Have students discuss how they might show thanks to someone who *deserves* it.

DAY **2**

affectionate

1. **Introduce** *Affectionate* means loving or showing tenderness.
2. **Demonstrate** My dad is *affectionate* towards his mother.
3. **Apply** Ask students to tell with whom they are *affectionate.*

DAY **3**

nag

1. **Introduce** *Nag* means to annoy someone by complaining about something that needs to be done.
2. **Demonstrate** I will clean up my room if you won't *nag* me about it any longer!
3. **Apply** Have students come up with additional sentences that use the word *nag.* Point out that an old, worn out horse is also call a *nag.*

DAY **4**

wandering

1. **Introduce** *Wandering* is moving from place to place without any real purpose.
2. **Demonstrate** We spent the rainy afternoon *wandering* through the museum. Jan likes to *wander* through the woods.
3. **Apply** Have students describe times when they like to *wander.*

Talking Walls: Art for People

Amazing Words Oral Vocabulary Routine

DAY 1

expressive

1. **Introduce** Something that is *expressive* is full of meaning or feeling.

2. **Demonstrate** Bill's *expressive* voice was perfect for reading the Gettysburg Address at the school assembly.

3. **Apply** Have students read or recite something using an *expressive* voice.

emotion

1. **Introduce** An *emotion* is a strong feeling of any kind. Joy, grief, fear, hate, love, anger, and excitement are *emotions*.

2. **Demonstrate** Eric couldn't hide his *emotions* when he walked into the surprise birthday party.

3. **Apply** Discuss with students how people show various *emotions* such as joy, fear, anger, and excitement.

artistic

1. **Introduce** Someone who is *artistic* shows talent in music, dance, painting, writing, or the other arts.

2. **Demonstrate** Steve has many *artistic* skills and can draw, paint, and write.

3. **Apply** Have students talk about what they think it means to be *artistic*.

DAY 2

lecture

1. **Introduce** A *lecture* is a talk on a certain subject given to an audience.
2. **Demonstrate** Dr. Haines gave a *lecture* to the historical society on the history of our area.
3. **Apply** Ask students to name a topic that they think would make an interesting *lecture*.

DAY 3

pause

1. **Introduce** To *pause* means to stop somewhere for a short time.
2. **Demonstrate** Paul *paused* for a moment to look in the store window.
3. **Apply** Have students list synonyms for *pause*.

DAY 4

lyrics

1. **Introduce** *Lyrics* are the words of a song.
2. **Demonstrate** Tammy memorized the *lyrics* to all of the songs in *The Lion King*. Vic is going to write new *lyrics* for an old song.
3. **Apply** Have students name songs for which they know the *lyrics*.

UNIT 6

Acknowledgments

Acknowledgments

Text

Grateful acknowledgment is made to the following for copyrighted material:

28: From *The Man Who Invented Basketball: James Naismith and His Amazing Game* by Edwin Brit Wyckoff. Copyright © 2008 by Enslow Publishers, Inc. From Enslow Publishers, Inc.

46: From *My Turn At Bat: The Story of My Life* by Ted Williams and John Underwood. Copyright © 1969, 1988 by Ted Williams and John Underwood. From Simon & Schuster, Inc.

49: "Ted Williams Timeline" from www.sportingnews.com/archives/williams/timeline.html. From *The Sporting News.*

51: "Baseball Hall of Fame Information and Baseball Card Statistics for Ted Williams" from http://www.baseballhalloffame.org/hofers/detail.jsp?playerId=121341. From National Baseball Hall of Fame (NBHOF)

62: From *Hottest, Coldest, Highest, Deepest* by Steve Jenkins. Copyright © 1998 by Steve Jenkins. Reprinted by permission of Houghton Mifflin Company. All rights reserved.

94: *Rocks in His Head* by Carol Otis Hurst. Text copyright © 2001 by Carol Otis Hurst. Illustrations © 2001 by James Stevenson. Used by permission of HarperCollins Publishers.

124: *America's Champion Swimmer: Gertrude Ederle,* text copyright © 2000 by David A. Adler, illustrations copyright © 2000 by Terry Widener, reprinted by permission of Harcourt, Inc.

126: From "Women in History: Wilma Rudolph biography." Lakewood Public Library. http://www.lkwdpl.org/wihohio/rudo-wil.htm. Reprinted by permission of Women in History, Lakewood, Ohio.

158: From *Fly, Eagle, Fly!* by Christopher Gregorowski, illustrated by Niki Daly. Text copyright © 2000 by Christopher Gregorowski, illustrations copyright © 2000 by Niki Daly. Reprinted with permission of Margaret K. McElderry Books, an imprint of Simon & Schuster Children's Publishing Division. All rights reserved.

176: *Purple Coyote* by Cornette, illustrated by Rochette. Copyright © 1997 by L'Ecole des Loisirs, Paris. First American edition 1999—Originally published in France by Pastel, 1997. English translation copyright © 1999 by Random House, Inc. Published by arrangement with Random House Children's Books, a division of Random House, Inc., New York, New York. All rights reserved.

185: "Written at the Po-Shan Monastery" by Hsin Ch'i-chi, translated by Irving Yucheng Lo, from *Sunflower Splendor: Three Thousand Years of Chinese Poetry* by Wu-Chi Liu (Author), Irving Yucheng Lo (Editor), published by Indiana University Press, 1990. Reprinted by permission of Indiana University Press.

186: "Me with apologies to Joyce Kilmer ("Trees")" from *Because I Could Not Stop My Bike* by Karen Jo Shapiro. Text copyright © 2003 Karen Jo Shapiro. Illustrations copyright © 2003 by Matt Faulkner. Used with permission by Charlesbridge Publishing, Inc. All rights reserved.

187: "By Myself" from *Honey, I Love* by Eloise Greenfield. Text copyright © 1978 by Eloise Greenfield. Used by permission of HarperCollins Publishers.

198: *Suki's Kimono,* written by Chieri Uegaki and illustrated by Stéphane Jorisch is used with the permission of Kids Can Press Ltd., Toronto. Text © 2003 Chieri Uegaki. Illustrations © 2003 Stéphane Jorisch.

230: From *I Love Saturdays y domingos* by Alma Flor Ada. Text copyright © 2002 by Alma Flor Ada. Reprinted with permission of Atheneum Books for Young Readers, an Imprint of Simon & Schuster Children's Publishing Division. All rights reserved.

250: From *Scott Foresman Social Studies Communities,* 2003. Copyright © 2003 Pearson Education, Inc. Reprinted by permission of Pearson Education, Inc.

262: Reprinted with permission of the National Geographic Society from *Good-Bye, 382 Shin Dang Dong* by Frances Park and Ginger Park. Copyright © 2002 Frances Park and Ginger Park. Illustrations © 2002 Yangsook Choi.

284: The Lois Lenski Covey Foundation, Inc., for "Sing a Song of People' from *The Life I Live* by Lois Lenski. Copyright © 1965 by The Lois Lenski Covey Foundation, Inc. Reprinted by Permission of Licensor. Copyright © Renewed 1993, no. RE 615-252.

296: From *Jalapeño Bagels* by Natasha Wing. Text copyright © 1996 by Natasha Wing. Reprinted with permission of Atheneum Books For Young Readers, an imprint of Simon &

Schuster Children's Publishing Division. All rights reserved.

314: Excerpts from *Viva Mexico! The Foods* by George Ancona (Benchmark Books). Copyright © 2002 by George Ancona. Reprinted with permission of Marshall Cavendish Corporation.

328: From *Me and Uncle Romie: A Story Inspired by the Life and Art of Romare Bearden* by Claire Hartfield, illustrated by Jerome Lagarrigue, copyright © 2002 by Claire Hartfield, text. Copyright © 2002 by Jerome Lagarrigue, illustrations. Used by permission of Dial Books for Young Readers, A Division of Penguin Young Readers Group, A Member of Penguin Group (USA) Inc., 345 Hudson Street, New York, NY 10014. All rights reserved.

360: "My Friend in School" from *Deshawn Days.* Text copyright © 2001 by Tony Medina. Permission arranged with Lee & Low Books, Inc., New York, NY 10016.

362: "Lunch Survey," from *Swimming Upstream: Middle Grade Poems* by Kristine O'Connell George. Text copyright © 2002 by Kristine O'Connell George. Reprinted by permission of Clarion Books, an imprint of Houghton Mifflin Company. All rights reserved.

363: "Saying Yes" by Diana Chang is reprinted by permission of the author.

374: *The Story of the Statue of Liberty* by Betsy C. Maestro, illustrations by Giulio Maestro. Text copyright © 1986 by Betsy Maestro. Illustrations copyright © 1986 by Giulio Maestro. Used by permission of HarperCollins Publishers.

390: From *Scott Foresman Social Studies:* Communities, 2003. Copyright © 2003 Pearson Education, Inc. Reprinted by permission of Pearson Education, Inc.

402: From *Happy Birthday Mr. Kang* by Susan L. Roth. Copyright © 2001 Susan L. Roth. Reprinted with permission of the National Geographic Society.

468: *Two Bad Ants* by Chris Van Allsburg. Copyright © 1988 by Chris Van Allsburg. Reprinted by permission of Houghton Mifflin Company. All rights reserved.

502: "Atlantis: The Legend of a Lost City" by Christina Balit. Atlantis copyright © 1999 by Frances Lincoln Limited. Text and illustrations copyright © 1999 by Christina Balit.

532: "Words Free as Confetti" from *Confetti: Poems for Children.* Text copyright © 1996 by Pat Mora. Permission arranged with Lee and Low Books, Inc., New York, NY.

535: "I Watched an Eagle Soar" from *Dancing Teepees: Poems of the North American Indian Youth* by Virginia Driving Hawk Sneve. Copyright © 1989 by Virginia Driving Hawk Sneve. Reprinted from *Dancing Teepees* by permission of Holiday House, Inc.

Every effort has been made to locate the copyright owner of material reproduced in this component. Omissions brought to our attention will be corrected in subsequent editions.

Illustrations

Cover: Leo Timmers
EI•1–EI•15 Mike Lester
80–82 James Madsen
113 Larry Jones
230–244 Claudia Degliuomini
284 Remy Simard
296–309 Antonio Castro
332–344 Jerome Lagarrigue
362 Laurie Keller
532 Stephen Daigle
W•2–W•15 Nomar Perez.

Photographs

Every effort has been made to secure permission and provide appropriate credit for photographic material. The publisher deeply regrets any omission and pledges to correct errors called to its attention in subsequent editions.

Unless otherwise acknowledged, all photographs are the property of Pearson Education, Inc.

Photo locators denoted as follows: Top (T), Center (C), Bottom (B), Left (L), Right (R), Background (Bkgd)

18 (C) ©Joel Sartore/Getty Images, (B) ©Rebecca Emery/Getty Images
20 (BR) ©Hans Neleman/zefa/Corbis, (BL) ©Yellow Dog Productions/Getty Images
26 (B) ©Roy Dabner/epa/Corbis, (C) ©Dennis Macdonald/PhotoLibrary Group, Ltd., (TL) Jupiter Images

Acknowledgments

27 (C) ©Stephen Wilkes/The Image Bank/Getty Images
30 (TC) ©Shironina Lidiya Alexandrovna/Shutterstock
46 (CL) ©Bettmann/Corbis, (B) ©Stockxpert
47 (TR) ©Bettmann/Corbis, (BR) Jupiter Images
48 (CC) Corbis
49 (BR) ©William McKellar /Jupiter Images
50 (TL) ©AP Photo, (CR) ©DK Images
54 (CR) ©Frans Lanting/Minden Pictures, (B) ©Robert Harding Picture Library Ltd/Alamy Images
55 (CC) ©Bill Draker/Rolfnp/Alamy Images
60 (C) Alamy Images, (T) ©Greg Vaughn/Alamy Images, (B) ©Nik Keevil/Alamy
86 (B,) ©Ariel Skelley/Corbis
87 (CR) ©Don Smetzer/PhotoEdit
92 (B) ©Marko Dolopikos/Alamy, (C) ©Paul Doyle/Alamy Images, (T) ©SW Productions/Getty Images
110 (T, BC) ©ZZ/Alamy, (B) Jupiter Images
111 (BR) ©ZZ/Alamy
112 (CR) ©ZZ/Alamy
113 (TR, BR, BL) ©ZZ/Alamy
116 (B) ©Pete Saloutos/Corbis
117 (BR) ©Bequest of Mrs. Benjamin Ogle Tayloe/Collection of The Corcoran Gallery of Art/Corbis, (TR) GRIN/NASA
122 (T) ©Anne Griffiths Belt/Getty Images, (C) ©David Madison/Jupiter Images, (B) ©Peter Adams/Corbis
144 (BC) ©George Silk/Time Life Pictures/Getty Images, (TR) ©Underwood & Underwood/Corbis
146 (CR) ©George Silk/Time Life Pictures/Getty Images
147 (CL) ©George Silk/Time Life Pictures/Getty Images, (CR) Bettmann/Corbis
150 (BL) ©David Shale/Nature Picture Library, (B) ©Joe McDonald/Corbis
151 (BR) ©Rick & Nora Bowers/Alamy Images
156 (C) ©Yann Arthus-Bertrand/Corbis, (B) ©Anne-Marie Weber/Getty Images, (T) ©Mireille Vautier/Alamy Images
188 (C) ©Jeremy Horner/Getty Images
190 (BC) ©Brian A. Vikander/Corbis, (B) ©Kayle M. Deioma/PhotoEdit
191 (BR) ©E&Y Photography/Alamy Images
196 (B) ©Goolia Photography/Alamy, (T) Philip Duff, (C) PhotoLibrary
216 (BC) ©Christie's Images/Peter Harholdt/Corbis, (BR) Art Resource, NY
217 (CR) ©Lynn Goldsmith/Corbis, (TR) Art Resource, NY
218 (TR) ©Historical Picture Archive/Corbis, (CR) ©Werner Forman/Corbis, (BR) Getty Images
219 (BR) ©Pavlovsky Jacques/Corbis, (TR) Corbis, (CR) Getty Images
222 (C) ©D. Hurst/Alamy Images, (BL) ©David-Young-Wolff/Alamy Images, (BC) ©Kevin Dodge/Corbis
228 (B) ©Demin Tony/PhotoLibrary Group, Ltd., (C) ©Richard Cooke/Alamy Images, (T) ©Stefan Sollfors/Alamy Images
250 (TR) Getty Images, (BR) ©Morton Beebe/Corbis
251 (BR) ©Steve Vidler/SuperStock, (TR) Getty Images
254 (BL) ©Tibor Bogner/Corbis, (B) ©Vince Streano/Corbis
255 (BR) ©Robert W. Ginn/PhotoEdit
260 (C) Corbis, (T) ©Elmari Joubert/Alamy, (B) ©Stephen Oliver/Alamy Images
288 (BC, B) Jupiter Images
289 (BR) ©foodfolio/Alamy Images
294 (B) Corbis, (T) ©Massimo Borchi/Corbis, (C) ©Vario Images GmbH & Co. KG/Alamy Images
314 (CR) George Ancona
315 (BC) George Ancona
316 (BR, B) George Ancona
317 (TR) George Ancona
320 (B) ©George Doyle/Getty Images, (TL) ©Rhoda Sidney/PhotoEdit
321 (BR) Getty Images
326 (C) ©Randy Faris/Corbis, (B) ©travelstock44/Alamy
354 (BR) ©David Zimmerman/Corbis, (TR) ©Terry W. Eggers/Corbis
355 (BR) AP/Wide World Photos
356 (BR) ©Duomo/Corbis
357 (CR) ©David Thomas/PictureArts/Corbis, (BR) ©Royalty-Free/Corbis
364 (C) ©Kevin Dodge/Corbis
366 ©Randy Faris/Corbis
372 (C) ©David Noble/Alamy Images, (B)

©Kai Wiechmann/Getty Images, (T) ©Taurus Taurus/PhotoLibrary Group, Ltd.
390 (CC) ©Jim Erickson/Erickson Productions, (TR) Corbis
391 (CR) ©Robert Holmes/Corbis
394 ©Canopy Photography/Veer, Inc.
400 (C) ©Foodcollection/Alamy, (T) Getty Images, (B) ©VStock/Alamy
424 (C) ©Joseph Sohm/ChromoSohm Inc./Corbis, (BC) Jupiter Images
425 (CR) ©Sandra Baker/Alamy Images
426 (BC) The Granger Collection, NY
427 (TR) ©Bill Howe/Alamy Images
430 ©David Young-Wolff/PhotoEdit, (BL) Getty Images
431 (B) ©David Young-Wolff/PhotoEdit, (BR) Jupiter Images
435 (TR) ©JM Labat/Photo Researchers, Inc.
436 (C) ©Don B. Stevenson/Alamy Images, (T) ©Ed Bock/Corbis, (BC) Getty Images, (B) ©Jim West/Alamy Images
438 (C) Meg Saligman
440 (CC) ©Ben Valenzuela
441 (B) ©Hector Ponce/Rich Puchalsky
442 (T) ©Hector Ponce/Rich Puchalsky
444 (C) *Reach High and You Will Go Far* ©2000 by Joshua Sarantitis. All Rights Reserved. Sponsored by the Philadelphia Mural Arts Program. Photograph ©2000 by Joshua Sarantitis. All rights reserved.
445 (CC) ©Paul Botello
447 (B) Getty Images
448 (B) ©Gianni Tortoli/Photo Researchers, Inc., (B) David Botello
449 (T) ©Gianni Tortoli/Photo Researchers, Inc., (BR) ©The British Museum/©DK Images, (BC) Courtesy of the U.S. Capitol Historical Society
450 (TL, B) Meg Saligman
460 (B) ©Purestock/Getty Images
461 (BR) ©Blend Images/Jupiter Images
466 (B) Alamy, (C) ©Matt Cardy/Alamy Images, (T) ©PhotosIndia LLC/Alamy
494 (B) ©David R, Frazier Photolibrary, Inc./Alamy Images
495 (TR) AP Images, (CC) Jupiter Images
499 (TR) ©Richard T. Nowitz/Corbis
500 (T) ©Franz Waldhaeusl/Alamy, (B) ©American Images Inc/Getty Images, (C) ©Pictor/Alamy
524 (T) Jupiter Images
525 (BR) Jupiter Images
527 (T) Jupiter Images
528 (CR) ©Stockxpert
529 (CR) ©Matt Carr /Jupiter Images.

Teacher's Edition

Text

KWL Strategy: The KWL Interactive Reading Strategy was developed and is used by permission of Donna Ogle, National-Louis University, Skokie, Illinois, co-author of *Reading Today and Tomorrow,* Holt, Rinehart & Winston Publishers, 1988. (See also the *Reading Teacher,* February 1986, pp. 564–570.)

Understanding by Design quotes: Wiggins, G. & McTighe, J. (2005). *Understanding by Design.* Alexandria, VA: Association for Supervision and Curriculum Development.

Illustrations

Cover Leo Timmers

Running Head Linda Bronson

Photographs

Every effort has been made to secure permission and provide appropriate credit for photographic material. The publisher deeply regrets any omission and pledges to correct errors called to its attention in subsequent editions.

Unless otherwise acknowledged, all photographs are the property of Pearson Education, Inc.

Teacher Notes

Teacher Notes